I am convinced that to maintain one's self on this earth is not a hardship, but a pastime, if we will live simply and wisely.

THOREAU

To my distress and perhaps to my delight, I order things in accordance with my passions. . . . I put in my pictures everything I like. So much the worse for the things—they have to get along with one another.

PICASSO

I have been in love with painting ever since I became conscious of it at the age of six. I drew some pictures I thought fairly good when I was fifty, but really nothing I did before the age of seventy was of any value at all. At seventy-three I have at last caught every aspect of nature—birds, fish, animals, insects, trees, grasses, all. When I am eighty I shall have developed still further, and I will really master the secrets of art at ninety. When I reach a hundred my work will be truly sublime, and my final goal will be attained around the age of one hundred and ten, when every line and dot I draw will be imbued with life.

HOKUSAI
"The Art-Crazy Old Man"

T0268667

HENRY MILLER

BIG SUR
and the Oranges of
Hieronymus Bosch

A NEW DIRECTIONS PAPERBOOK

For permission to reprint quotations from other works the author and publisher are grateful to the following: The Antioch Press for M. J. Chatterjee's OUT OF CONFUSION; Dodd, Mead and Co. and William Heinemann Ltd. (London) for Robert Payne's FOREVER CHINA (Eng. title: CHUNGKING DIARY); University of Chicago and Faber & Faber Ltd. (London) for Wilhelm Fränger's THE MILLENNIUM OF HIERONYMUS BOSCH; Joseph Delteil for his JESUS II and DE JEAN JACQUES ROUSSEAU A MISTRAL; Dodd, Mead and Co., Methuen and Co. Ltd. (London) and Miss D. E. Collins for G. K. Chesterton's CHARLES DICKENS; Harcourt, Brace and Co. Inc. and Jonathan Cape Ltd. (London) for Count Keyserling's THE TRAVEL DIARY OF A PHILOSOPHER (vol. II); Olivier Perrin Editeur (Paris) for Genevieve-Irene Zidonis' O. V. DE L. MILOSZ: SA VIE, SON OEUVRE, SON RAYONNEMENT; Philosophical Library Inc. for Mikhail Naimy's KAHLIL GIBRAN: A BIOGRAPHY; Poetry-London for Elizabeth Smart's BY GRAND CENTRAL STATION I SAT DOWN AND WEPT; D. Rajagopal for J. Krishnamurti's THE POOL OF WISDOM; The Vedanta Society for THE GOSPEL OF RAMAKRISHNA; Librairie Briffaut (Paris) for RESTIF DE LA BRETONNE: TEMOIGNAGES ET JUGEMENTS: BIBLIOGRAPHIE; Dr. Leo L. Spears for his "Reasons Why Longer Life Is Possible" and *Manas,* (Los Angeles) for "Socrates for Europe" and a review of LIVING THE GOOD LIFE.

Library of Congress Catalog Card Number: 57-5542
ISBN 978-0-8112-0107-0

Book designed by Stefan Salter
Manufactured in the United States of America

New Directions Books are published for James Laughlin
by New Directions Publishing Corporation,
80 Eighth Avenue, New York 10011.

40 39 38 37

TABLE OF CONTENTS

PREFACE

This book consists of three parts and an epilogue originally intended
to be issued as a pamphlet under the title—*This Is My Answer!*
Written in 1946, while living at Anderson Creek, this epilogue has
since been shortened and revised. It now constitutes a sort of
vermiform appendix which can be read first or last, as the reader
chooses.

I had intended to give a bibliography of my published works,
including foreign language as well as American and English
editions, in an Appendix, but as this has already been done in a
book recently published, I refer those seeking this data to the publi-
cations named below.*

The only work in progress now is *Nexus*, the final volume of
the trilogy called *The Rosy Crucifixion*. *The World of Lawrence*,
fragments of which have appeared in some of the New Directions
anthologies, has long been abandoned. *Draco and the Ecliptic* is still
in the egg.

The following titles, all but one of which were originally published in English, in Paris, and most of which have now been translated into French, German, Danish, Swedish and Japanese, are
still banned in this country: *Tropic of Cancer, Aller Retour New
York, Black Spring, Tropic of Capricorn, The World of Sex, The
Rosy Crucifixion (Sexus* and *Plexus)*. *Sexus* is at present forbidden
to be published—in any language!—in France. In Japan the Japanese version of this work has been suppressed but not the English,

---

* *My Friend, Henry Miller*, by Alfred Perlès; published by Neville Spear-
man, Ltd., London, 1955, and also by the John Day Co., New York, 1956.

at least not yet. *Quiet Days in Clichy,* which has just gone to press (Paris), will probably also be banned—here and elsewhere.

As to how and where to get the banned books, the simplest way would be to make a raid on the customs house in any of our ports of entry.

My warmest thanks go to Charles Haldeman, who came all the way from Winter Park, Florida, to put Wilhelm Fränger's book on Hieronymus Bosch in my hands. May he forgive me for being such a poor host that day!

BIG SUR

and the Oranges of
Hieronymus Bosch

CHRONOLOGICAL

Early in 1930 I left New York with the intention of going to Spain. I never got there. Instead, I remained in France until June 1939, when I left for Greece to take a much needed vacation. Forced out of Greece early in 1940 because of the war, I returned to New York. Before becoming a resident of California I made the "air-conditioned nightmare" trip around America, which consumed a full year. During this period of almost two and a half years I wrote *The Colossus of Maroussi, The World of Sex, Quiet Days in Clichy,* parts of *The Air-conditioned Nightmare,* and the first book of *The Rosy Crucifixion (Sexus).*

In June 1942 I arrived in California to stay. For over a year I lived in Beverly Glen, just outside Hollywood. There I met Jean Varda, who induced me to come to Monterey on a visit. This was in February 1944. I stayed with Varda, in his Red Barn, for several weeks and then, at his suggestion, made a trip to Big Sur to meet Lynda Sargent. Lynda was then living in the log cabin around which the celebrated "Nepenthe" has since been built. I stayed on as a house guest for about two months, at which time Keith Evans, who was then in the service, offered me the use of his cabin on Partington Ridge. (Thanks to Lynda Sargent's efforts.) Here I remained from May 1944 until January 1946, during which time I made a brief trip to New York, remarried in Denver, and became the father of a daughter, Valentine. Upon Keith Evans' return to civil life we were obliged to seek other quarters. In January 1946 we moved to Anderson Creek, three miles down the road, where we rented one of the old convicts' shacks situated at the edge of a cliff. In February 1947 we returned to Partington Ridge, to occupy the house which Jean Wharton had originally built for herself. It was towards the very end of this year that Conrad Moricand arrived, to last only about three months. In 1948 a son, Tony, was born.

Partington Ridge is about fourteen miles south of the Big Sur Post Office and some forty odd miles from Monterey. Except for a pleasure trip to Europe in 1953, when I married again, I have been living on the Ridge ever since February 1947.

TOPOGRAPHICAL

It was twelve years ago on a day in February that I arrived in Big Sur—in the midst of a violent downpour. Toward dusk that same day, after a rejuvenating bath outdoors at the hot sulphur springs (Slade's Springs), I had dinner with the Rosses in the quaint old cottage they then occupied at Livermore Edge. It was the beginning of something more than a friendship. It would be more just, perhaps, to call it an initiation into a new way of life.

It was a few weeks after this meeting that I read Lillian Bos Ross' book, *The Stranger*. Till then I had been only a visitor. The reading of this "little classic," as it is called, made me more than ever determined to take root here. "For the first time in my life," to quote Zande Allen's words, "I felt to home in the world I was borned in."

Years ago our great American poet Robinson Jeffers began singing of this region in his narrative poems. Jack London and his friend George Stirling made frequent visits to Big Sur in the old days; they came on horseback, all the way from the Valley of the Moon. The general public, however, knew almost nothing of this region until 1937 when the Carmel-San Simeon highway, which skirts the Pacific for a distance of sixty miles or more, was opened up. In fact, until then it was probably one of the least known regions in all America.

The first settlers, mountain men mostly, of hardy pioneer stock, came around 1870. They were, as Lillian Ross puts it, men who had followed the buffalo trails and knew how to live on meat without salt. They came afoot and on horseback; they touched ground which no white men had ever set foot on before, not even the intrepid Spaniards.

So far as is known, the only human beings who had been here before were the Esselen Indians, a tribe of low culture which had subsisted in nomadic fashion. They spoke a language having no connection with that of other tribes in California or elsewhere in America. When the padres came to Monterey, around 1770, these Indians spoke of an ancient city called Excelen which was theirs but of which no vestiges have ever been found.

But perhaps I should first explain where the Big Sur region is located. It begins not far north of the Little Sur River (Malpaso Creek) and extends southward as far as Lucia, which, like Big Sur, is just a pin point on the map. Eastward from the coast it stretches to the Salinas Valley. Roughly, the Big Sur country comprises an area two to three times the size of Andorra.

Now and then a visitor will remark that there is a resemblance between this coast, the South Coast, and certain sections of the Mediterranean littoral; others liken it to the coast of Scotland. But comparisons are vain. Big Sur has a climate of its own and a character all its own. It is a region where extremes meet, a region where one is always conscious of weather, of space, of grandeur, and of eloquent silence. Among other things, it is the meeting place of migratory birds coming from north and south. It is said, in fact, that there is a greater variety of birds to be found in this region than in any other part of the United States. It is also the home of the redwoods; one encounters them on entering from the north and one leaves them on passing southward. At night one can still hear the coyote howling, and if one ventures beyond the first ridge of mountains one can meet up with mountain lions and other beasts of the wild. The grizzly bear is no longer to be found here, but the rattlesnake is still to be reckoned with. On a clear, bright day, when the blue of the sea rivals the blue of the sky, one sees the hawk, the eagle, the buzzard soaring above the still, hushed canyons. In summer, when the fogs roll in, one can look down upon a sea of clouds floating listlessly above the ocean; they have the appearance, at times, of huge iridescent soap bubbles, over which, now and then, may be seen a double rainbow. In January and February the hills are greenest, almost as green as the Emerald Isle. From November to February are the best months, the air fresh and invigorating, the skies clear, the sun still warm enough to take a sun bath.

From our perch, which is about a thousand feet above the sea, one can look up and down the coast a distance of twenty miles in either direction. The highway zigzags like the Grande Corniche. Unlike the Riviera, however, here there are but few houses to be seen. The old-timers, those with huge landholdings, are not eager to see the country opened up. They are all for preserving its virginal aspect. How long will it hold out against the invader? That is the big question.

The stretch of scenic highway referred to earlier was cut through at enormous expense, literally blasted out of the mountain side. It now forms part of the great international highway which will one day extend from the northern part of Alaska to Tierra del Fuego. By the time it is finished the automobile, like the mastodon, may be extinct. But the Big Sur will be here forever, and perhaps in the year A.D. 2,000 the population may still number only a few hundred souls. Perhaps, like Andorra and Monaco, it will become a Republic all its own. Perhaps the dread invaders will not come from other parts of this continent but from across the ocean, as the American aborigines are said to have come. And if they do, it will not be in boats or in airplanes.

And who can say when this region will once again be covered by the waters of the deep? Geologically speaking, it is not so long ago that it rose from the sea. Its mountain slopes are almost as treacherous as the icy sea in which, by the way, one scarcely ever sees a sail boat or a hardy swimmer, though one does occasionally spot a seal, an otter or a sperm whale. The sea, which looks so near and so tempting, is often difficult to reach. We know that the Conquistadores were unable to make their way along the coast, neither could they cut through the brush which covers the mountain slopes. An inviting land, but hard to conquer. It seeks to remain unspoiled, uninhabited by man.

Often, when following the trail which meanders over the hills, I pull myself up in an effort to encompass the glory and the grandeur which envelops the whole horizon. Often, when the clouds pile up in the north and the sea is churned with white caps, I say to myself: "This is the California that men dreamed of years ago, this is the Pacific that Balboa looked out on from the Peak of Darien, this is the face of the earth as the Creator intended it to look."

IN THE BEGINNING

In other, olden times there were only phantoms. In the beginning, that is. If there ever was a beginning.

It was always a wild, rocky coast, desolate and forbidding to the man of the pavements, eloquent and enchanting to the Taliessins. The homesteader never failed to unearth fresh sorrows.

There were always birds: the pirates and scavengers of the blue as well as the migratory variety. (At intervals the condor passed, huge as an ocean liner.) Gay in plumage, their beaks were hard and cruel. They strung out across the horizon like arrows tied to an invisible string. In close they seemed content to dart, dip, swoop, careen. Some followed the cliffs and breakers, others sought the canyons, the gold-crested hills, the marble-topped peaks.

There were also the creeping, crawling creatures, some sluggish as the sloth, others full of venom, but all absurdly handsome. Men feared them more than the invisible ones who chattered like monkeys at fall of night.

To advance, whether on foot or on horseback, was to tangle with spikes, thorns, creepers, with all that pricks, clings, stabs and poisons.

Who lived here first? Troglodytes perhaps. The Indian came late. Very late.

Though young, geologically speaking, the land has a hoary look. From the ocean depths there issued strange formations, contours unique and seductive. As if the Titans of the deep had labored for aeons to shape and mold the earth. Even millennia ago the great land birds were startled by the abrupt aspect of these risen shapes.

There are no ruins or relics to speak of. No history worth recounting. What was not speaks more eloquently than what was.

Here the redwood made its last stand.

At dawn its majesty is almost painful to behold. That same prehistoric look. The look of always. Nature smiling at herself in the mirror of eternity.

Far below, the seals bask on the warm rocks, squirming like fat brown worms. Above the steady roar of the breakers their hoarse bark can be heard for miles.

Were there once two moons? Why not? There are mountains that have lost their scalps, streams that boil under the high snows. Now and then the earth rumbles, to level a city or open a new vein of gold.

At night the boulevard is studded with ruby eyes.

And what is there to match a faun as it leaps the void? Toward eventime, when nothing speaks, when the mysterious hush descends, envelops all, says all.

Hunter, put down your gun! It is not the slain which accuse you, but the silence, the emptiness. You blaspheme.

I see the one who dreamed it all as he rides beneath the stars. Silently he enters the forest. Each twig, each fallen leaf, a world beyond all knowing. Through the ragged foliage the splintered light scatters gems of fancy; huge heads emerge, the remains of stolen giants.

"*My* horse! *My* land! *My* kingdom!" The babble of idiots.

Moving with the night, horse and rider inhale deep draughts of pine, of camphor, of eucalyptus. Peace spreads its naked wings.

Was it ever meant to be otherwise?

Kindness, goodness, peace and mercy. Neither beginning nor end. The round. The eternal round.

And ever the sea recedes. Moon drag. To the west, new land, new figures of earth. Dreamers, outlaws, forerunners. Advancing toward the other world of long ago and far away, the world of yesterday and tomorrow. The world within the world.

From what realm of light were we shadows who darken the earth spawned?

PART ONE

THE ORANGES OF THE MILLENNIUM

The little community of one, begun by the fabulous "outlander," Jaime de Angulo, has multiplied into a dozen families. The hill (Partington Ridge) is now nearing the saturation point, as things go in this part of the world. The one big difference between the Big Sur I encountered eleven years ago and that of today is the advent of so many new children. The mothers here seem to be as fecund as the soil. The little country school, situated not far from the State Park, has almost reached its capacity. It is the sort of school which, most unfortunately for our children, is rapidly disappearing from the American scene.

In another ten years we know not what may happen. If uranium or some other metal vital to the warmongers is discovered in these parts, Big Sur will be nothing but a legend.

Today Big Sur is no longer an outpost. The number of sightseers and visitors increases yearly. Emil White's "Big Sur Guide" alone brings swarms of tourists to our front door. What was inaugurated with virginal modesty threatens to end as a bonanza. The early settlers are dying off. Should their huge tracts of land be broken up into small holdings, Big Sur may rapidly develop into a suburb (of Monterey), with bus service, barbecue stands, gas stations, chain stores and all the odious claptrap that makes Suburbia horrendous.

This is a bleak view. It may be that we will be spared the usual horrors which accompany the tides of progress. Perhaps the millennium will be ushered in before we are taken over!

I like to think back to my early days on Partington Ridge, when there was no electricity, no butane tanks, no refrigeration—and the mail came only three times a week. In those days, and even later

when I returned to the Ridge, I managed to get along without a
car. To be sure, I did have a little cart (such as children play with),
which Emil White had knocked together for me. Hitching myself
to it, like an old billy goat, I would patiently haul the mail and
groceries up the hill, a fairly steep climb of about a mile and a
half. On reaching the turn near the Roosevelts' driveway, I would
divest myself of everything but a jock-strap. What was to hinder?

The callers in those days were mostly youngsters just entering or
just leaving the service. (They're doing the same today, though the
war ended in '45.) The majority of these lads were artists or would-
be artists. Some stayed on, eking out the weirdest sort of existence;
some came back later to have a serious go at it. They were all
filled with a desire to escape the horrors of the present and willing
to live like rats if only they might be left alone and in peace. What
a strange lot they were, when I think on it! Judson Crews of
Waco, Texas, one of the first to muscle in, reminded one—because
of his shaggy beard and manner of speech—of a latter-day prophet.
He lived almost exclusively on peanut butter and wild mustard
greens, and neither smoked nor drank. Norman Mini, who had
already had an unusual career, starting as in Poe's case with his
dismissal from West Point, stayed on (with wife and child) long
enough to finish a first novel—the best first novel I have ever read
and, as yet, unpublished. Norman was "different" in that, though
poor as a church mouse, he clung to his cellar, which contained
some of the finest wines (native and foreign) anyone could wish
for. And then there was Walker Winslow, who was then writing
If a Man Be Mad, which turned out to be a best seller. Walker
wrote at top speed, and seemingly without interruption, in a tiny
shack by the roadside which Emil White had built to house the
steady stream of stragglers who were forever busting in on him
for a day, a week, a month or a year.

In all, almost a hundred painters, writers, dancers, sculptors and
musicians have come and gone since I first arrived. At least a
dozen possessed genuine talent and may leave their mark on the

world. The one who was an unquestionable genius and the most spectacular of all, aside from Varda, who belongs to an earlier period, was Gerhart Muench of Dresden. Gerhart belongs in a category all by himself. As a pianist he is phenomenal, if not incomparable. He is also a composer. And in addition, a scholar, erudite to the finger tips. If he had done no more for us than to interpret Scriabin—and he did vastly more, all without result, alas! —we of Big Sur ought be forever indebted to him.

Speaking of artists, the curious thing is that few of this stripe ever last it out here. Is something lacking? Or is there too much . . . too much sunshine, too much fog, too much peace and contentment?

Almost every art colony owes its inception to the longing of a mature artist who felt the need to break with the clique surrounding him. The location chosen was usually an ideal one, particularly to the discoverer who had spent the better years of his life in dingy holes and garrets. The would-be artists, for whom place and atmosphere are all important, always contrive to convert these havens of retreat into boisterous, merry-making colonies. Whether this will happen to Big Sur remains to be seen. Fortunately there are certain deterrents.

It is my belief that the immature artist seldom thrives in idyllic surroundings. What he seems to need, though I am the last to advocate it, is more first-hand experience of life—more bitter experience, in other words. In short, more struggle, more privation, more anguish, more disillusionment. These goads or stimulants he may not always hope to find here in Big Sur. Here, unless he is on his guard, unless he is ready to wrestle with phantoms as well as bitter realities, he is apt to go to sleep mentally and spiritually. If an art colony is established here it will go the way of all the others. Artists never thrive in colonies. Ants do. What the budding artist needs is the privilege of wrestling with his problems in solitude—and now and then a piece of red meat.

The chief problem for the man who endeavors to live apart is the idle visitor. One can never decide whether he is a curse or a blessing. With all the experience which these last few years have provided, I still do not know how, or whether, to protect myself against the unwarranted intrusion, the steady invasion, of that prying, curious-minded species of "homo fatuoso" endowed with the annoying faculty of dropping in at the wrong moment. To seek a hide-out more difficult of access is futile. The fan who wants to meet you, who is *determined* to meet you, if only to shake your hand, will not stop at climbing the Himalayas.

In America, I have long observed, one lives exposed to all comers. One is expected to live thus or be regarded as a crank. Only in Europe do writers live behind garden walls and locked doors.

In addition to all the other problems he has to cope with, the artist has to wage a perpetual struggle to fight free. I mean, find a way out of the senseless grind which daily threatens to annihilate all incentive. Even more than other mortals, he has need of harmonious surroundings. As writer or painter, he can do his work most anywhere. The rub is that wherever living is cheap, wherever nature is inviting, it is almost impossible to find the means of acquiring that bare modicum which is needed to keep body and soul together. A man with talent has to make his living on the side or do his creative work on the side. A difficult choice!

If he has the luck to find an ideal spot, or an ideal community, it does not follow that his work will there receive the encouragement he so desperately needs. On the contrary, he will probably find that no one is interested in what he is doing. He will generally be looked upon as strange or different. And he *will* be, of course, since what makes him tick is that mysterious element "X" which his fellow-man seems so well able to do without. He is almost certain to eat, talk, dress in a fashion eccentric to his neighbors. Which is quite enough to mark him out for ridicule, contempt and isolation. If, by taking a humble job, he demonstrates that he is as good as the next man, the situation may be somewhat ameliorated. But not for long. To prove that he is "as good as the next man" means little or nothing to one who is an artist. It was his "otherness" which made him an artist and, given the chance, he will make his fellow-man other too. Sooner or later, in one way or another, he is bound to rub his neighbors the wrong way. Unlike the ordinary fellow, he will throw everything to the winds when the urge seizes him. Moreover, if he *is* an artist, he will be compelled to make sacrifices which worldly people find absurd and unnecessary. In following the inner light he will inevitably choose for his boon companion poverty. And, if he has in him the makings of a great artist, he may renounce everything, even his art. This, to the average citizen, particularly the good citizen, is preposterous and unthinkable. Thus it happens now and then that, failing to recognize the genius in a man, a most worthy, a most respected, member of society may be heard to say: "Beware of that chap, he's up to no good!"

The world being what it is, I give it as my candid opinion that anyone who knows how to work with his two hands, anyone who is willing to give a fair day's work for a fair day's pay, would be better off to abandon his art and settle down to a humdrum life in an out of the way place like this. It may indeed be the highest wisdom to elect to be a nobody in a relative paradise such as this rather than a celebrity in a world which has lost all sense of values. But this is a problem which is rarely settled in advance.

There is one young man in this community who seems to have espoused the kind of wisdom I refer to. He is a man with an independent income, a man of keen intelligence, well educated, sensitive, of excellent character, and capable not only with his hands but with brain and heart. In making a life for himself he has apparently chosen to do nothing more than raise a family, provide its members with what he can, and enjoy the life of day to day. He does everything single-handed, from erecting buildings to raising crops, making wines, and so on. At intervals he hunts or fishes, or just takes off into the wilderness to commune with nature. To the average man he would appear to be just another good citizen, except that he is of better physique than most, enjoys better health, has no vices and no trace of the usual neuroses. His library is an excellent one, and he is at home in it; he enjoys good music and listens to it frequently. He can hold his own at any sport or game, can vie with the toughest when it comes to hard work, and in general is what might be called "a good fellow," that is, a man who knows how to mix with others, how to get along with the world. But what he also knows and does, and what the average citizen can not or will not do, is to enjoy solitude, to live simply, to crave nothing, and to share what he has when called upon. I refrain from mentioning his name for fear of doing him a disservice. Let us leave him where he is, Mr. X, a master of the anonymous life and a wonderful example to his fellow-man.

While in Vienne (France) two years ago I had the privilege of making the acquaintance of Fernand Rude, the *sous-préfet* of Vienne, who possesses a remarkable collection of Utopian literature. On leaving, he presented me with a copy of his book, *Voyage en Icarie,** which is the account of two workers from Vienne who came to America just a hundred years ago to join Étienne Cabet's experimental colony at Nauvoo, Illinois. The description given of American life, not only at Nauvoo but in the cities they passed through—they arrived at New Orleans and left by way of New York—is worth reading today, if only to observe how essentially unchanged is our American way of life. To be sure, Whitman was giving us about this same time (in his prose works) a similar picture of vulgarity, violence and corruption, in high and low places. One fact stands out, however, and that is the inborn urge of the American to experiment, to try out the most crack-brained schemes having to do with social, economic, religious and even sex relations. Where sex and religion were dominant, the most amaz-

---

* The title is taken from the book of the same name by Étienne Cabet wherein the latter describes his (imaginary) Utopia. A remarkable work in this, that though Communistic in the romantic sense, it is an accurate blueprint of the totalitarian governments we now have.

ing results were achieved. The Oneida Community (New York), for example, is destined to remain as memorable an experiment as Robert Owen's in New Harmony (Indiana). As for the Mormons, nothing comparable to their efforts has ever been undertaken on this continent, and probably never will again.

In all these idealistic ventures, particularly those initiated by religious communities, the participants seemed to possess a keen sense of reality, a practical wisdom, which in no way conflicted (as it does in the case of ordinary Christians) with their religious views. They were honest, law-abiding, industrious, self-sustaining, self-sufficient citizens with character, individuality and integrity, somewhat corroded (to our present way of thinking) by a Puritan sobriety and austerity, but never lacking in faith, courage and independence. Their influence on American thought, American behavior, has been most powerful.

Since living here in Big Sur I have become more and more aware of this tendency in my fellow-American to experiment. Today it is not communities or groups who seek to lead "the good life" but isolated individuals. The majority of these, at least from my observation, are young men who have already had a taste of professional life, who have already been married and divorced, who have already served in the armed forces and seen a bit of the world, as we say. Utterly disillusioned, this new breed of experimenter is resolutely turning his back on all that he once held true and viable, and is making a valiant effort to start anew. Starting anew, for this type, means leading a vagrant's life, tackling anything, clinging to nothing, reducing one's needs and one's desires, and eventually—out of a wisdom born of desperation—leading the life of an artist. Not, however, the type of artist we are familiar with. An artist, rather, whose sole interest is in creating, an artist who is indifferent to reward, fame, success. One, in short, who is reconciled from the outset to the fact that the better he is the less chance he has of being accepted at face value. These young men, usually in their late twenties or early thirties, are now roaming about in our midst like anonymous messengers from another planet. By force of example, by reason of their thoroughgoing nonconformity and, shall I say, "nonresistance," they are proving themselves a more potent, stimulating force than the most eloquent and vociferous of recognized artists.

The point to note is that these individuals are not concerned with undermining a vicious system but with leading their own lives—on the fringe of society. It is only natural to find them gravitating toward places like Big Sur, of which there are many replicas in this vast country. We are in the habit of speaking of "the last frontier," but wherever there are "individuals" there will always be new frontiers. For the man who wants to lead the good life, which is a way of saying *his own life,* there is always a spot where he can dig in and take root.

But what is it that these young men have discovered, and which, curiously enough, links them with their forebears who deserted Europe for America? That the American way of life is an illusory kind of existence, that the price demanded for the security and abundance it pretends to offer is too great. The presence of these "renegades," small in number though they be, is but another indication that the machine is breaking down. When the smashup comes, as now seems inevitable, they are more likely to survive the catastrophe than the rest of us. At least, they will know how to get along without cars, without refrigerators, without vacuum cleaners, electric razors and all the other "indispensables" . . . probably even without money. If ever we are to witness a new heaven and a new earth, it must surely be one in which money is absent, forgotten, wholly useless.

Here I should like to quote from a review of *Living the Good Life,* by Helen and Scott Nearing.* Says the editor: "What we are trying to suggest is that the solution for a cluttered, frustrated existence is not merely in moving to the country and attempting to

---

* From *Manas,* Los Angeles, March 23, 1955.

practise 'the simple life.' The solution is in an attitude towards human experience which makes simple physical and economic arrangements almost a moral and esthetic necessity. It is the larger purpose in life which gives to its lesser enterprises—the obtaining of food, shelter and clothing—their essential harmony and balance. So often people dream of an ideal life "in community," forgetting that a "community" is not an end in itself, but a frame for higher qualities—the qualities of the mind and the heart. Making a community is not a magic formula for happiness and good; making a community is the result of the happiness and the good which people already possess in principle, and the community, whether of one family or several, is the infinitely variable expression of the excellences of human beings, and not their cause. . . ."

Digging in at Big Sur eleven years ago, I must confess that I had not the least thought or concern about the life of the community. With a population of one hundred souls scattered over several hundred square miles, I was not even conscious of an existent "community." My community then comprised a dog, Pascal (so named because he had the sorrowful look of a thinker), a few trees, the buzzards, and a seeming jungle of poison oak. My only friend, Emil White, lived three miles down the road. The hot sulphur baths were three miles farther down the road. There the community ended, from my standpoint.

I soon found out how mistaken I was, of course. It was no time before neighbors began popping up from all sides—out of the brush, it seemed—and always laden with gifts, as well as the most discreet and sensible advice, for the "newcomer." Never have I known better neighbors! All of them were endowed with a tact and subtlety such as I never ceased to marvel at. They came only when they sensed you had need of them. As in France, it seemed to me that I was once again among people who knew how to let you be. And always there was a standing invitation to join them at table, should you have need of food or company.

Being one of those unfortunate "helpless" individuals who knew nothing but city ways, it wasn't long before I had to call upon my neighbors for aid of one kind or another. Something was always going amiss, something was always getting out of order. I hate to think what would have happened had I been left entirely to my own resources! Anyway, with the assistance that was always willingly and cheerfully extended, I received instruction in how to help myself, the most valuable gift that can be offered. I discovered all too quickly that my neighbors were not only extremely affable, helpful, generous in every way, but that they were far more intelligent, far wiser, far more self-sufficient than I had fatuously thought myself to be. The community, from being at first an invisible web, gradually became most tangible, most real. For the first time in my life I found myself surrounded by kind souls who were not thinking exclusively of their own welfare. A strange new sense of security began to develop in me, one I had never known before. In fact, I would boast to visitors that, once a resident of Big Sur, nothing evil could possibly happen to one. I would always add cautiously: "But one has first to prove himself a good neighbor!" Though they were addressed to my visitor, I meant these words for myself. And often, when the visitor had departed, I would repeat them to myself like a litany. It took time, you see, for one who had always lived the jungle life of the big city to realize that he too could be "a neighbor."

Here I must say flatly, and not without a bad conscience, that I am undoubtedly the worst neighbor any community could boast of. That I am still treated with more than mere tolerance is something which still surprises me.

Often I am so completely out of it all that the only way I can "get back" is to look at my world through the eyes of my children. I always begin by thinking back to the glorious childhood I enjoyed in that squalid section of Brooklyn known as Williamsburg. I try to relate those squalid streets and shabby houses to the vast expanse of sea and mountain of this region. I dwell on the birds I never saw except for the sparrow feasting on a fresh pile of manure, or a stray pigeon. Never a hawk, a buzzard, an eagle, never a robin or a hummingbird. I think of the sky which was always hacked to pieces by roof-tops and hideous smoking chimneys. I breathe again the air that filled the sky, an atmosphere without fragrance, often leaden and oppressive, saturated with the reek of burning chemicals. I think of the games we played in the street, ignorant of the lure of stream and forest. I think, and with tenderness, of my little companions, some of whom later went to the pentitentiary. Despite it all, it was a good life I led there. A wonderful life, I might say. It was the first "Paradise" I knew, there in that old neighborhood. And though forever gone, it is still accessible in memory.

But *now,* now when I watch the youngsters playing in our front yard, when I see them silhouetted against the blue white-capped Pacific, when I stare at the huge, frightening buzzards swirling lazily above, circling, dipping, forever circling, when I observe the willow gently swaying, its long fragile branches drooping ever lower, ever greener and tenderer, when I hear the frog croaking in the pool or a bird calling from the bush, when I suddenly turn and espy a lemon ripening on a dwarfish tree or notice that the camellia has just begun to bloom, I see my children set against an eternal background. They are not even *my* children any longer, but just children, children of the earth . . . and I know they will never forget, never forsake, the place where they were born and raised. In my mind I am with them as they return from some distant shore to gaze upon the old homestead. My eyes are moist with tears as I watch them moving tenderly and reverently amid a swarm of golden memories. Will they notice, I wonder, the tree they were going to help me plant but were too busy then having fun? Will they stand in the little wing we built for them and wonder how on earth they ever fitted into such a cubicle? Will they pause outside the tiny workroom where I passed my days and tap again at the windowpane to ask if I will join them at play—*or must I work some more?* Will they find the marbles I gathered from the garden and hid so that they would not swallow them? Will they stand in reverie at the forest glade, where the little stream prattles on, and search for the pots and pans with which we made our make-believe breakfast before diving into the woods? Will they take the goat path along the flank of the mountain and look up in wonder and awe at the old Trotter house teetering in the wind? Will they run down to the Rosses, if only in memory, to see if Harrydick can mend the broken sword or Shanagolden lend us a pot of jam?

For every wonderful event in my golden childhood they must possess a dozen incomparably more wonderful. For not only did they have their little playmates, their games, their mysterious adventures, as did I, they had also skies of pure azure and walls of fog moving in and out of the canyons with invisible feet, hills in winter of emerald green and in summer mountain upon mountain of pure gold. They had even more, for there was ever the unfathomable silence of the forest, the blazing immensity of the Pacific, days drenched with sun and nights spangled with stars and—"Oh, Daddy, come quick, see the moon, it's lying in the pool!" And besides the adoration of the neighbors, a dolt of a father who preferred wasting his time playing with them to cultivating his mind or making himself a good neighbor. Lucky the father who is merely a writer, who can drop his work and return to childhood at will! Lucky the father who is pestered from morn till sundown by two healthy, insatiable youngsters! Lucky the father who learns to see again through the eyes of his children, even though he become the biggest fool that ever was!

"The Brothers and Sisters of the Free Spirit called their devotional community-life 'Paradise' and interpreted the word as signifying the quintessence of love."*

* *The Millennium of Hieronymus Bosch,* by Wilhelm Fränger (Chicago: University of Chicago Press, 1951), page 104.

Looking at a fragment of "The Millennium" (by Hieronymus Bosch) the other day, I pointed out to our neighbor, Jack Morgenrath, (formerly of Williamsburg, Brooklyn) how hallucinatingly real were the oranges that diapered the trees. I asked him why it was that these oranges, so preternaturally real in appearance, possessed something more than would oranges painted, say, by Cézanne (better known for his apples) or even by Van Gogh. To Jack it was simple. (Everything is quite simple to Jack, by the way. It's part of his charm.) Said Jack: "It's because of the ambiance." And he is right, absolutely right. The animals in this same triptych are equally mysterious, equally hallucinating, in their super-reality. A camel is always a camel and a leopard a leopard, yet they are altogether unlike any other camels, any other leopards. They can hardly even be said to be the camels and leopards of Hieronymus Bosch, magician though he was. They belong to another age, an age when man was one with all creation . . . "when the lion lay down with the lamb."

Bosch is one of the very few painters—he was indeed more than a painter!—who acquired a magic vision. He saw through the phenomenal world, rendered it transparent, and thus revealed its pristine aspect.* Seeing the world through his eyes it appears to us once again as a world of indestructible order, beauty, harmony, which it is our privilege to accept as a paradise or convert into a purgatory.

The enchanting, and sometimes terrifying, thing is that the world can be so many things to so many different souls. That it can be, and is, all these at one and the same time.

---

* "The human mind has drawn a net of logical relationships and practical ingenuity over the phenomenal world with which it is confronted; and so, by this intellectual and material domination of the world, it has removed itself to an infinite distance from the created world in which it once had a purely natural share. It was this natural world in which the Brethren of the Free Spirit saw the meaning of life." (*The Millennium of Hieronymus Bosch*, page 152.)

I am led to speak of the "Millennium" because, receiving as many visitors as I do, and from all parts of the globe, I am constantly reminded that I am living in a virtual paradise. ("And how did you manage to find such a place?" is the usual exclamation. As if *I* had any part in it!) But what amazes me, and this is the point, is that so very few ever think on taking leave that they too might enjoy the fruits of paradise. Almost invariably the visitor will confess that he lacks the courage—imagination would be nearer the mark—to make the necessary break. "You're lucky," he will say— meaning, to be a writer—"you can do your work anywhere." He forgets what I have told him, and most pointedly, about the other members of the community—the ones who really support the show—who are not writers, painters or artists of any sort, except in spirit. "Too late," he probably murmurs to himself, as he takes a last wistful glance about.

How illustrative, this attitude, of the woeful resignation men and women succumb to! Surely every one realizes, at some point along the way, that he is capable of living a far better life than the one he has chosen. What stays him, usually, is the fear of the sacrifices involved. (Even to relinquish his chains seems like a sacrifice.) Yet everyone knows that nothing is accomplished without sacrifice.

The longing for paradise, whether here on earth or in the beyond, has almost ceased to be. Instead of an *idée-force* it has become an *idée fixe*. From a potent myth it has degenerated into a taboo. Men will sacrifice their lives to bring about a better world—whatever that may mean—but they will not budge an inch to attain paradise. Nor will they struggle to create a bit of paradise in the hell they find themselves. It is so much easier, and gorier, to make revolution, which means, to put it simply, establishing another, a different, status quo. If paradise were realizable—this is the classic retort!— it would no longer be paradise.

What is one to say to a man who insists on making his own prison?

There is a type of individual who, after finding what he considers a paradise, proceeds to pick flaws in it. Eventually this man's paradise becomes even worse than the hell from which he had escaped.

Certainly paradise, whatever, wherever it be, contains flaws. (Paradisiacal flaws, if you like.) If it did not, it would be incapable of drawing the hearts of men *or* angels.

The windows of the soul are infinite, we are told. And it is through the eyes of the soul that paradise is visioned. If there are flaws in your paradise, open more windows! Vision is entirely a creative faculty: it uses the body and the mind as the navigator uses his instruments. Open and alert, it matters little whether one finds a supposed short cut to the Indies—or discovers a new world. Everything is begging to be discovered, not accidentally, but intuitively. Seeking intuitively, one's destination is never in a beyond of time or space but always here and now. If we are always arriving and departing, it is also true that we are eternally anchored. One's destination is never a place but rather a new way of looking at things. Which is to say that there are no limits to vision. Similarly, there are no limits to paradise. Any paradise worth the name can sustain all the flaws in creation and remain undiminished, untarnished.

If I have entered upon a vein which I must confess is one not frequently discussed here, I am nevertheless certain that it is one which secretly engages the minds of many members of the community.

Everyone who has come here in search of a new way of life has made a complete change-about in his daily routine. Nearly every one has come from afar, usually from a big city. It meant abandoning a job and a mode of life which was detestable and insufferable. To what degree each one has found "new life" can be estimated only by the efforts he or she put forth. Some, I suspect, would have found "it" even had they remained where they were.

The most important thing I have witnessed, since coming here, is the transformation people have wrought in their own being. Nowhere have I seen individuals work so earnestly and assiduously on themselves. Nor so successfully. Yet nothing is taught or preached here, at least overtly. Some have made the effort and failed. Happily for the rest of us, I should say. But even these who failed gained something. For one thing, their outlook on life was altered, enlarged if not "improved." And what could be better than for the teacher to become his own pupil, or the preacher his own convert?

In a paradise you don't preach or teach. You practice the perfect life—or you relapse.

There seems to be an unwritten law here which insists that you accept what you find and like it, profit by it, or you are cast out. Nobody does the rejecting, please understand. Nobody, no group here, would crave such authority. No, the place itself, the elements which make it, do that. It's the law, as I say. And it is a just law which works harm to no one. To the cynical-minded it may sound like the same old triumph of our dear status quo. But the enthusiast knows that it is precisely the fact that there is no status quo here which makes for its paradisiacal quality.

No, the law operates because that which makes for paradise can not and will not assimilate that which makes for hell. How often it is said that we make our own heaven and our own hell. And how little it is taken to heart! Yet the truth prevails, whether we believe in it or not.

Paradise or no paradise, I have the very definite impression that the people of this vicinity are striving to live up to the grandeur and nobility which is such an integral part of the setting. They behave as if it were a privilege to live here, as if it were by an act of grace they found themselves here. The place itself is so overwhelmingly bigger, greater, than anyone could hope to make it that it engenders a humility and reverence not frequently met with in Americans. There being nothing to improve on in the surroundings, the tendency is to set about improving oneself.

It is of course true that individuals have undergone tremendous changes, broadened their vision, altered their natures, in hideous, thwarting surroundings—prisons, ghettos, concentration camps, and so on. Only a very rare individual elects to *remain* in such places. The man who has seen the light follows the light. And the light usually leads him to the place where he can function most effectively, that is, where he will be of most use to his fellow-men. In this sense, it matters little whether it be darkest Africa or the Himalayan heights. God's work can be done anywhere, so to say.

We have all met the soldier who has been overseas. And we all know that each one has a different story to relate. We are all like returned soldiers. We have all been somewhere, spiritually speaking, and we have either benefited by the experience or been worsted by it. One man says: "Never again!" Another says: "Let it come! I'm ready for anything!" Only the fool hopes to repeat an experience; the wise man knows that *every* experience is to be viewed as a blessing. Whatever we try to deny or reject is precisely what we have need of; it is our very need which often paralyzes us, prevents us from welcoming a (good or bad) experience.

I come back once again to those individuals who came here full of needs and who fled after a time because "it" was not what they hoped to find, or because "they" were not what they thought themselves to be. None of them, from what I have learned, has yet found it or himself. Some returned to their former masters in the manner of slaves unable to support the privileges and responsibilities of freedom. Some found their way into mental retreats. Some became derelicts. Others simply surrendered to the villainous status quo.

I speak as if they had been marked by the whip. I do not mean to be cruel or vindictive. What I wish to say quite simply is that none of them, in my humble opinion, is a whit happier, a whit better off, an inch advanced in any respect. They will all continue to talk about their Big Sur adventure for the rest of their lives—wistfully, regretfully, or elatedly, as occasion dictates. In the hearts of some, I know, is the profound hope that their children will display more courage, more perseverance, more integrity than they themselves did. But do they not overlook something? Are not their children, as the product of self-confessed failures, already condemned? Have they not been contaminated by the virus of "security"?

The most difficult thing to adjust to, apparently, is peace and contentment. As long as there is something to fight, people seem able to brave all manner of hardships. Remove the element of struggle, and they are like fish out of water. Those who no longer have anything to worry about will, in desperation, often take on the burdens of the world. This not through idealism but because they must have something to do, or at least something to talk about. Were these empty souls truly concerned about the plight of their fellow-men they would consume themselves in the flames of devotion. One need hardly go beyond his own doorstep to discover a realm large enough to exhaust the energies of a giant, or better, a saint.

Naturally, the more attention one gives to the deplorable conditions outside the less one is able to enjoy what peace and liberty he possesses. Even if it be heaven we find ourselves in, we can render it suspect and dubious.

Some will say they do not wish to *dream* their lives away. As if life itself were not a dream, a very real dream from which there is no awakening! We pass from one state of dream to another: from the dream of sleep to the dream of waking, from the dream of life to the dream of death. Whoever has enjoyed a good dream never complains of having wasted his time. On the contrary, he is delighted to have partaken of a reality which serves to heighten and enhance the reality of everyday.

The oranges of Bosch's "Millennium," as I said before, exhale this dreamlike reality which constantly eludes us and which is the very substance of life. They are far more delectable, far more potent, than the Sunkist oranges we daily consume in the naive belief that they are laden with wonder-working vitamins. The millennial oranges which Bosch created restore the soul; the ambiance in which he suspended them is the everlasting one of spirit become real.

Every creature, every object, every place has its own ambiance. Our world itself possesses an ambiance which is unique. But worlds, objects, creatures, places, all have this in common: they are ever in a state of transmutation. The supreme delight of dream lies in this transformative power. When the personality liquefies, so to speak, as it does so deliciously in dream, and the very nature of one's being is alchemized, when form and substance, time and space, become yielding and elastic, responsive and obedient to one's slightest wish, he who awakens from his dream knows beyond all doubt that the imperishable soul which he calls his own is but a vehicle of this eternal element of change.

In waking life, when all is well and cares fall away, when the intellect is silenced and we slip into reverie, do we not surrender blissfully to the eternal flux, float ecstatically on the still current of life? We have all experienced moments of utter forgetfulness when we knew ourselves as plant, animal, creature of the deep or denizen of the air. Some of us have even known moments when we were as the gods of old. Most every one has known *one* moment in his life when he felt so good, so thoroughly attuned, that he has been on the point of exclaiming: *"Ah, now is the time to die!"* What is it lurks here in the very heart of euphoria? The thought that it will not, can not last? The sense of an ultimate? Perhaps. But I think there is another, deeper aspect to it. I think that in such moments we are trying to tell ourselves what we have long known but ever refuse to accept—that living and dying are one, that all is one, and that it makes no difference whether we live a day or a thousand years.

Confucius put it this way: "If a man sees Truth in the morning, he may die in the evening without regret."

In the beginning Big Sur looked to me like an ideal place in which to work. Today, though I enjoy working when I can, I look upon it with other eyes. Whether I work or whether I don't has come to assume less and less importance. I have had here some of the most bitter experiences of my life; I have also known here some of the most exalted moments. Sweet or bitter, I am now convinced that all experience is enriching and rewarding. Above all, instructive.

In these past ten years I have talked to hundreds and hundreds of individuals from all walks of life. Most callers, it seems to me, come to unload their problems. Occasionally I succeed in handing a man back his problems—and saddling him with a few new ones, weightier, knottier ones than he brought.

Many who come to pay me a visit make me the recipient of gifts, all sorts of gifts, from money to books, food, drink, clothing, even postage stamps. In return I can only offer the gift of myself. But all this is of little moment. What intrigues me is that, living in a nominally isolated spot, the world is closer to my door than if I were in the thick of it. It is not necessary for me to read the daily paper nor listen in on the news broadcasts. Whatever I need to know about conditions "out there" is brought to me, combed and sifted, in person.

And how very much the same it all is! Why drag one's carcass around? *"Stay put and watch the world go round!"* That's what I frequently tell myself.

Here I feel compelled to touch on a matter which, though highly personal, may nevertheless be of interest to "all and sundry." As a writer of some repute—perhaps *dubious* repute—I naturally num-

ber among my callers many young or would-be writers. When I
learn of their aims and purpose, in choosing authorship, I am
obliged to put myself the most scathing questions. In what way,
I ask myself, do I really differ from these fledglings? What have
I gained, turning out one book after another, that they lack? And
why should I encourage them when all they do is augment my own
honest doubts?

To elucidate . . . all these young men (and women), as I once
did myself, desire nothing more, nothing better, than to write what
they wish to write and to be read by as many people as possible.
They want to express themselves, they say. Very good. ("And
what's to hinder?" say I to myself.) After they have expressed
themselves, they want to be recognized and commended for their
efforts. *Naturally*. ("Who's to prevent it?") And being recognized,
being accepted, they want to enjoy the fruits of their labor.
("Human, all-too-human.") *But*—and here is the question, the vital
one: Do you, my dear young enthusiasts, have any idea what it
means when you say "the fruits of one's labor"? Have you ever
heard of "bitter fruit"? Do you not know that with recognition,
or "success," if you want to call it that, come all the evils in creation? Do you realize that, in accomplishing your purpose, you will
never be permitted to reap the reward you dream of? No doubt
you picture to yourself a quiet home in the country, a loving wife
who understands you, and a bevy of happy, contented children. You
visualize yourself turning out masterpiece after masterpiece in a
setting where all runs like clockwork.

What a deception you are in for! What plagues and scourges
lie in wait for you! Give us your mightiest thoughts, shake the
world to its foundations—but do not hope to escape your Calvary!
Once you have launched your creations, be certain they will be
turned against you. You will be unique if you are not overwhelmed
and engulfed by monsters of your own breeding. The day is sure
to come when you will look upon the world as if it had never
received the impact of a single uplifting thought. You will be

terrified and bewildered to see how thoroughly awry everything has gone, how utterly you and those you emulated have been misunderstood. The world you unwittingly helped to make will claim you, not as master or arbiter, but as its victim.

No, these things I cannot tell you in advance because, to begin with, you would never believe me. And you shouldn't! Listening to you, observing the ardor which lights your countenance, I am almost ready to believe that I am wrong. And I *am* wrong in putting it to you this way, since one thing is true beyond all dispute, and that is—no matter what the game, it is worth playing to the end. But can you bring yourself to regard your high task as "a game"?

There is one other thing to know . . . when you have expressed yourself to the fullest, then and only then will it dawn upon you that everything has already been expressed, not in words alone but in deed, and that all you need really do is say *Amen!*

It was here at Big Sur that I first learned to say *Amen!* And here too that I came to dwell with more than a feeling of mystification on that edifying observation of Céline's: "I piss on you all from a considerable height!" It was here, in the backwoods, as it were, that I discovered—*mirabile dictu!*—that three of my neighbors had read *Arabia Deserta*. It was also here, in my own home, that I met and retained as a guest for several months a man who had given up the ministry in order to lead a Christ-like life. It is here, and nowhere else, that I have witnessed people recast their ideas and live them out. And here, more than anywhere else, that I have listened to the greatest nonsense as well as the greatest wisdom.

Stay put and watch the world go round!

I know there are some who complain that Big Sur does not offer enough stimulus. My feeling, on the contrary, is that there is too much stimulus here. To the man whose senses are alive and alert there is not even the need to stir from one's threshold. For such a one there is a world here as full and rich, as compelling and instructive, as Thoreau found at Walden.

As a man who is in love with the world—the alien world—I must confess that I am also in love with my home, the first real home I have known. Doubtless those who appreciate "home" most are the eternal vagabonds, the outlaws. If I am ever to venture forth into the world again I trust I can now offer something of root as well as flower. To offer simply what Big Sur has taught me would be no small thing. I say Big Sur, not America. For, however much a part of America Big Sur may be, and it is American through and through, what distinguishes it is something more than the word America conveys. If I were to single out one element in the American temperament which has been exalted here, it would be kindness. It has always been the custom here on the Coast, when raising one's glass, to say: "Here's kindness!" I have never heard the expression used elsewhere. And when Harrydick Ross, my nearest neighbor, says "Kindness!" it means just that.

Reading my quaint biographical romances, people often ask how on earth I managed to keep my head above water during the black years of famine and drought. I have explained, of course, and in these very books, that at the last ditch someone always came to my rescue. Anyone who has a steady purpose is bound to attract friends and supporters. What man ever accomplished anything alone? The impressive thing, however, is that aid, when it does come, never comes from the expected quarter—where it *should* come from, as we think.

No, we are never alone. But one has to live apart to know it for the truth.

The first time I knew what it was to be alone, and to like it, was on the island of Corfu. The second time it happened, despite all my talk about *not* being alone, was here at Big Sur.

To be alone, if only for a few minutes, and to realize it with all one's being, is a blessing we seldom think to implore. The man of the big city dreams of life in the country as a refuge from all that plagues him and renders life intolerable. What he fails to realize, however, is that he can be more alone, if he chooses, in the midst of ten million souls than in a tiny community. To experience the feeling of aloneness is a spiritual achievement. The man who runs away from the city in search of this experience may find to his chagrin, particularly if he has brought with him all the cravings which city life fosters, that he has succeeded only in becoming lonely. "Solitude is for wild beasts or the gods," said someone. And there is truth in it.

Only when we are truly alone does the fullness and richness of life reveal itself to us. In simplifying our lives, everything acquires a significance hitherto unknown. When we are one with ourselves the most insignificant blade of grass assumes its proper place in the universe. Or a piece of manure, for that matter. Properly attuned, it's all one come Christmas, as we say. One thing becomes just as important as another, one person as good as another. Lowest and highest become interchangeable. The own precious self gets swallowed up in the ocean of being. It is then that the carrion bird no longer seems hideous, nor merely to be tolerated because of his scavenger propensities. Nor do the stones in the field then seem inanimate, or to be regarded with an eye toward future walls and buttresses. Even if it last for only a few moments, the privilege of looking at the world as a spectacle of unending life and not as a repository of persons, creatures and objects to be impressed into our service, is something never to be forgotten. The ideal community, in a sense, would be the loose, fluid aggregation of individuals who elected to be alone and detached in order to be at one with themselves and all that lives and breathes. It would be a God-filled community, even if none of its members believed in (a) God. It would be a paradise, even though the word had long disappeared from our vocabulary.

In all the cities and countries I dream of visiting one day there are, of course, no such communities. Even in the holiest places man is prone to act the fool, the bigot, the idolater. As I said before, today we find only individuals dedicated to "the good life." Nevertheless, these isolated individuals are bringing about a community which will one day replace the dismembered warring communities which are a disgrace to the name. The world does tend to become one, however much its component elements may resist. Indeed, the stronger the resistance the more certain is the outcome. We resist only what is inevitable.

I have talked of Big Sur as if it were a place apart, having little or no connection with the world. Nothing could be less true. Nowhere else in my travels have I found individuals more alert to what is going on in the world, nor better informed. It is rare that a community as small as this can boast so many world travelers. I never cease to be amazed when I hear that this one has just left for Siam, that one for Japan, Turkey, or Greece, another for India or Peru, another for Guatemala, Yucatan, or the Polynesian Islands. Some of my neighbors have dwelt for extended periods in very remote parts of the globe. Some have lived with the Indians (of both continents), some with the primitive peoples of Africa, Japan, India, Melanesia.

Nearly every one seems to be a specialist in some field, be it art, archaeology, linguistics, symbolism, Dianetics, Zen Buddhism or Irish folklore. Men like Ross and Tolerton, to mention two near neighbors, have a range of practical knowledge, not to speak of earthly and heavenly wisdom, which would be hard to match in any community. Others, like the Trotter boys, as they are still called, perform feats of strength in the daily pursuance of their tasks which would put glorified "strong men" to shame. Nearly all the women are excellent cooks, and the men as well ofttimes. Every

other home possesses a connoisseur of wines. And every other
father has the makings of an excellent mother.

I cannot refrain from repeating—never have I known a community in which there was so much talent, so many capable men and
women, so many resourceful, self-sufficient souls. Even that scally-
wag up in the hills who pretends to be a good for nothing, "a real
son of a bitch," as he lovingly labels himself, knows how to live
with himself and can be, when he chooses, a most gentle, lovable,
charitable person, one of those happy "misfits" who has tasted everything and who, God bless him!, has therefore no more respect for
the inside of a temple than the inside of a jail, no more consideration
for a scholar than for a tramp, no higher opinion of a judge than
of the culprit who keeps the judge in food and raiment.

And where else in this beloved country is a neighbor apt to turn
up unexpectedly in order to inquire what he can do for you?
Meaning by that—what needs fixing, mending or repairing? In an
emergency there are always a half-dozen fullbodied spirits within
shouting distance who can be relied upon to drop everything and
come to one's assistance. I have never known a situation to arise,
and I must say we have had some bizarre ones, with which these
volunteers could not cope. The moral of all this is—the less organization the better!

When all is said and done, there remains the inescapable fact
that to keep a footing here taxes all one's resources. One may be
capable, practical, determined, persevering, full of vitality, yet never
quite equal to the challenge which is constantly imposed. It is all
thrown at you pell-mell: landscapes, seascapes, forests, streams, birds
of passage, weeds, pests, rattlesnakes, gophers, earwigs, misfits, vagabonds, sunsets, rainbows, yarrow, hollyhocks, and that leech of the
plant world called the morning-glory. Even the rocks are seductive
and hypnotic. And where else on this earth will you find a tower-
ing wall of fog advancing from the date line with a knife-blue crest
behind which a setting sun shoots out "squirrels and lightning"?

It is all so inviting, so spectacular, so complete in itself, that at first you are emotionally stymied. The preliminary bout of intoxication which inevitably follows is one the alcoholic never knows. Comes a settling down period, generally accompanied by a slight touch of boredom—the ransom one pays for flirting with perfection. Then follows the trouble period, when inner doubts pave the way for domestic squabbles, and the whole horizon grows dark with conflict. When at last you hit bottom, you say—every one has said it at least once!—"Big Sur? Why, it's just like every other place!" Speaking thus, you voice a profound truth, since a place is only what you make it, what you bring to it, just as with a friend, a lover, a wife, a pet or a pursuit.

Yes, Big Sur can be a dream come true—or a complete washout. If there's something wrong with the picture, have a look at yourself in the mirror. The one difference between Big Sur and other "ideal" spots is that here you get it quick and get it hard. Get it between the eyes, so to say. The result is that you either come to grips with yourself or else turn tail and seek some other spot in which to nourish your illusions. Which leaves a whole universe to roam—and who is to care should you *never* come face to face with yourself?

Big Sur is not a Mecca, a Lourdes, or even a Lhasa. Nor is it a Klondike for the incurable idealist. If you are an artist and think to muscle in here, it would be wise to first find a patron, because the artist cannot live off the artist, and here every other individual, seemingly, is an artist of one sort or another. Even the plumbers.

What could one bring that would be of value to the community? Just a normal, modest desire to do whatever needs to be done in whatever way it can be done. Briefly, two capable hands, a strong heart, and a certificate of vaccination against disillusionment. If you have an intellect, bring it with you, but not the rubbish that usually goes with it. There are too many intellects here already. And, if you bring nothing else, bring a sense of humor, for you will need it here if you haven't needed it elsewhere. If you believe in medicine, bring your own medicine chest, for there are no doctors here except learned ones. And don't bring any pets unless you are prepared to make frequent trips to the veterinary, because, for reasons as yet unknown, the pets here take on all the illnesses of human kind as well as those of the animal kingdom.

As for Partington Ridge, whence this message emanates, there is still no telegraph, no telephone, no sewage system, no garbage disposal plant. To get rid of your empty bottles, tin cans and other refuse, you must own a car and drive an appreciable distance to the allotted dumping ground, or else engage the professional services of Howard Welch, the man from Missouri.

Thus far Big Sur has crept along with what's to hand. What is probably needed to put it on the map are—a brothel, a jail, and a gold-plated electric chair. It would also be wonderful to have a Jewish delicatessen, but that's probably asking too much all at once.

In tailing off I would like to quote the words of another Henry Miller, better known in these parts than yours truly. I refer to Henry Miller the cattle baron, a man who once owned so much land that one could start from the Mexican border and walk to Canada without ever taking foot off his possessions. Anyway, here is what he once said: "If a man is so unfortunate as to beg for food, give it to him and win his gratitude. Never make him work for it and get his hatred."

PART TWO

PEACE AND SOLITUDE: A POTPOURRI

1.

I had gone to bed to nurse a cold when it started, the hemorrhage. Whenever I take to bed (in broad daylight), which is my way of curing colds, hemorrhoids, melancholia or any ailment real or imaginary, I always put beside the bed a little bench laden with cigarettes, ash tray and reading matter. Just in case. . . .

After I had whiled away an hour or two in delicious reverie, I reached for the issue of *La Nouvelle Revue Française* which my friend Gerald Robitaille had sent me. It was the issue dedicated to Charles-Albert Cingria, who had passed away a few months before. In his letter Gerald asked if I had ever heard of Cingria. I had indeed. It so happens that I met Cingria, for the first and only time, at the home of Bravig Imbs, in Paris. It was a whole afternoon and evening that I spent, most fortunately, in Cingria's company. These few short hours stand out as one of the events in my life.

What I had not known, until I picked up the *revue,* was that at the time of this meeting Cingria was traversing one of the worst periods in his life. Who would have suspected that this man who had the look of a clown, or a defrocked priest, this man who never ceased talking, joking, laughing, drinking—it was New Year's Eve and we were consuming pitchers of eggnog—who would have dreamed, as I say, that this man would leave us to return to a miserable hole in the hall, where crusts of bread were hidden away under bureaus and commodes and where he could plainly hear the noises made by everyone who went to the W.C.*

---

* See the passage from Cingria's diary quoted by Pierre Guéguen in the March 1, 1955 issue of the *N.R.F.* His text is called *"Le Dandy."*

As I read the tributes that were paid him, as I perceived what a remarkable personality his was, what a fantastic life he had led, what precious things he had written, my head began to whirl. Thrusting the *revue* aside—I couldn't possibly read another line—the hemorrhage suddenly broke loose. Like a drunken boat I tossed about, wallowing in the flood of memories which assailed me. After a time I rose, found a notebook, and began inditing cryptic cues. It went on for several hours. I forgot that I had a cold, forgot what time it was.

It was after midnight when I reluctantly laid down the pencil and switched off the lights. As I closed my eyes I said to myself: "Now is the time to tell about your life in Big Sur."

And so I shall tell it; in the same disorderly fashion that it came to me the other day as I lay abed. . . .

I suspect that many who read my books, or talk about my life, believe that I am living in an ivory tower. If I am, it is a tower without walls in which fabulous and often "anachronistic" things happen. In following this fantasia the reader should bear in mind that cause and event, chronology, order of any kind—except the illogical order of life itself—is absent.

Picture a day, for example, an excruciating one, in which I have been interrupted at least half a dozen times, and then . . . well, after an exciting talk with a writer who has just come from Paris (or Rome or Athens), after another talk with a bore who wants to know every detail about my life, past and present, and whom I discover (too late) has never read a single one of my books, after examining the cesspool to see why it doesn't work, after shooing away three students who stand at the door and apologetically explain that all they want of me is my opinion of Job—yes, Job, no less!—and they are not joking, only too serious, alas! after one thing and another, with intermittent attempts to resume where I left off (the middle of a sentence), comes the incomparable Varda with a bouquet of *"jeunes filles en fleur."* Observing that I am unusually quiet, and not realizing that it is a result of exhaustion, he exclaims: "And here I have been telling these girls what a wonderful *raconteur* you are! Come, do tell them something about your 'anecdotal life'!" (A phrase of Zadkine's.)

Strangely enough, at one in the morning, the table littered with empty glasses, bread crumbs and bits of rind, the guests departed at last, silence once again enveloping us, what is it that is singing in my head but a line from one of Cendrars' books, an enigmatic line, in his own inimitable French, which had me electrified a few nights before. There is no relation whatsoever between this line of Cendrars' and the multitudinous events of the day. We, Varda and I, had not even mentioned Cendrars' name, which is unusual because, with certain of my friends—Varda, Gerhart Muensch, Giles Healey, Ephraim Doner—we sound off with Cendrars and finish with Cendrars. So there I sit with that curious, tantalizing line of his, trying to recall what evoked it and wondering how I shall finish the sentence I left on the roller hours and hours ago. I ask myself—I've asked it over and over—how ever did this extraordinary man, Cendrars, turn out so many books in such a short time (I refer to the period right after the Occupation) with only one hand, his left hand, and no secretary to aid him, no heat, little food, his beloved sons killed in the war, his huge library destroyed by the Huns, and so on. I sit there reliving, or trying to relive, his life, his books, his thoughts, his emotions. My day, full as it was, only begins there in the ocean of his prodigious being. . . .

It was "one of those days" when a woman with whom I had exchanged some correspondence arrived from Holland. My wife had only reecntly left me and I was alone with my little girl. She was only in the room a few minutes when I sensed that an instantaneous and mutual antipathy had sprung up between the two. I apologized to my visitor for continuing with the chores—I had decided to wash the floor and wax it—and felt most grateful when she offered to do the dishes for me. Meanwhile Val, my daughter, was making things even more difficult than usual; she seemed to take a perverse delight in interrupting our conversation, erratic as it was with all the hopping about I was doing. Then she went to the toilet, only to announce a moment later that it wouldn't flush. At once I dropped the mop, dashed for the pickaxe, and began removing the dirt which covers the septic tank. I had hardly begun when it started to rain. I continued nevertheless, somewhat annoyed, I confess, by my visitor's frequent comings and goings, by her hysterical exhortations to abandon the task. Finally I managed to get my arm into the inlet which, as usual, was encrusted with snarled roots. As I pulled the blockage away, out came the water—and with it what had been dropped in the toilet bowl. I was a pretty sight when I came back to the house to clean up. The floor, of course, was a mess, and the furniture still piled on the table and the bed.

My visitor, who had built up a picture of me as a world-famous writer, a man living apart in that sublime place called Big Sur, began to berate me—or perhaps she thought she was consoling me— for trying to do so many things which had nothing to do with my work. Her talk sounded so absurd to me that, somewhat flabbergasted, I asked her curtly who she thought was to do the dirty work . . . *God?* She continued in her vague way to dwell on what I ought not to be doing, meaning cleaning, cooking, gardening, taking care of a child, fixing cesspools and so on. I was getting hot under the collar when suddenly I thought I heard a car pull up in the turn around. I stepped outside and, sure enough, there was Varda tripping down the steps, followed by his usual retinue of friends and admirers.

"Well, well! How are you? What a surprise!"

Handshakes, introductions all around. The usual exclamations. "What a marvelous place!" (Even in the rain.)

My visitor from Holland drew me aside. With an imploring look she whispered: "What do we do now?"

"Put a good face on it," I said, and turned my back on her.

A few minutes later she tugged at my sleeve again to inquire plaintively if *I* would have to prepare a meal for all these people.

I skip what followed during the next few hours to give you her parting words: "I never dreamed that Big Sur was like this!"

Under my breath I added: "Nor did I!"

And there stands Ralph! Though it's midsummer he's wearing a heavy overcoat and fur-lined gloves. He has a book in his hand and, like a Tibetan monk, he's leisurely pacing back and forth, back and forth. I had been so occupied pulling up weeds that I hadn't noticed him immediately. It was only when I lifted my head to go in search of a mattock, which I had left near the fence, that I was aware of his presence in the turn around. Realizing that he was a queer one, I thought I might snatch the implement and sneak away without being hooked. I would just pay no attention to him; he might be sensitive and move off in a huff. But as I started toward the fence this queer apparition approached and started speaking to me. He spoke in such a low tone that I was obliged to move in closer. That was the clincher.

"Are you Henry Miller?" he says.

I nodded, though my impulse was to say no.

"I came to see you because I want to have a talk with you."

("Christ, here it begins," I said to myself.)

"I was just driven away"—brutally or insultingly, I believe he added—"by a woman. Maybe it was your wife."

To this I simply grunted.

He continued by informing me that he too was a writer, that he had run away from it all (meaning job and home) to live his own life.

"I came to join the cult of sex and anarchy," he said, quietly and evenly, as if he were talking about toast and coffee.

I told him there was no such colony.

"But I read about it in the papers," he insisted. He started to pull a newspaper out of his pocket.

"That was all an invention," said I. "You musn't believe everything you see in the papers." I gave a forced laugh.

He seemed to doubt my words. Went on to tell me why he thought he would make an eligible member—even if there were no colony. *(sic)* I cut him short. Told him I had work to do. He would have to excuse me.

Now his feelings were hurt. There followed a brief exchange of question and answer—rather impertinent questions, rather caustic answers—which only seemed to increase his disturbance. Suddenly he opened the book he was holding and, turning the pages rapidly, he found the passage he was looking for. He then proceeded to read it aloud.

It was a passage from the *Hamlet* letters in which my friend and co-author, Michael Fraenkel, had raked me over the coals. Had excoriated me, in fact.

When he had finished reading he looked at me coldly and accusingly, to say: "I guess that fits, doesn't it?"

I opened the gate and said: "Ralph, what in hell's the matter with you? Come on down and talk it over!"

I ushered him into my little den, sat him down, handed him a cigarette and urged him to unbosom himself.

In a few minutes he was in tears. Just a poor, defenseless, broken-hearted boy.

That same evening I dispatched him, with a note, to Emil White at Anderson Creek. He had told me that he would head for Los Angeles, where he had an aunt, now that he knew there was no cult of sex and anarchy. I thought he would spend the night at Emil's and move on. But, after a good dinner and a good night's rest, he discovered that Emil owned a typewriter. In the morning, after a good breakfast, he sat down to the machine and, though he had never written a line before, he suddenly took it into his head to write a book. After a few days Emil gently informed him that he couldn't put him up indefinitely. This didn't floor Ralph. Not at all. He informed Emil that it was just the sort of place he had always wanted to live in and that, if Emil would help him, he would find a job and earn his keep.

To make it brief, Ralph stayed on at Big Sur about six months, doing odd jobs, floating from one ménage to another, always getting into trouble. In general, behaving like a spoiled child. In the interim I received a letter one day from Ralph's father, somewhere in the Midwest, telling me how grateful he was to all of us for looking after Ralph. He related the trials and ordeals they had been through at home trying to get Ralph to lead a normal, sensible life. It was the usual story of the problem child, one I was only too familiar with from the old days when I hired and fired for the Cosmodemonic Telegraph Company.

One of the strange things about Ralph's behavior was that he was always turning up minus some necessary part of his apparel. He had shown up on a summer's day in a heavy overcoat and gloves. Now that it was cold he would show up naked to the waist. What about his shirt and jacket? He had burned them! He didn't like them any more, or else he had taken a dislike to the person who had given them to him. (We had all supplemented his wardrobe at one time or another.)

On a cold, nasty day in winter, as I was driving along a side street in Monterey, whom should I spy but Ralph, half-naked, shivering, and looking altogether woebegone. Lilik Schatz was with me. We got out and dragged Ralph to a cafeteria. He hadn't eaten for two days—ever since they had let him out of the clink, it seems. What disturbed him more than the cold was the fear that his father might come to fetch him.

"Why can't you let me stay with you?" he repeated over and over. "I wouldn't give you any trouble. You understand me, the others don't. I want to be a writer—like you."

We had been over this ground a number of times before. I could only repeat what I had told him, that it was hopeless.

"But I'm different now," he said. "I know better." He kept boring in, determined, like a child, to have his way. Lilik tried to reason with him but got nowhere. "You don't understand me," he would say.

Finally I became exasperated. "Ralph," I said, "you're just a plain nuisance. Nobody can put up with you. You're a pest. I'm not taking you home with me and I'm not going to look after you. I'm going to let you starve and freeze—it's the only way you'll come to your senses."

With this I got up and walked to the door. Ralph followed us to the car and, with one foot on the running board, continued to plead his case. I took off my coat, put it around his shoulders, and told Lilik to start the motor.

"You're on your own, Ralph!" I shouted, as we waved good-bye.

He seemed rooted to the spot, his lips still moving.

A few days later I heard that he had been picked up for being a vagrant and shipped home to his parents. That was the last I heard of him.

There's a knock at the door. I open it to find a clump of visitors wreathed in smiles. The usual declarations—"Just passing through. Thought we would look you up."

I don't know them from Adam. However . . . "Come on in!"

The usual preliminaries . . . "Beautiful place you have . . . How did you find it? . . . I thought you had children . . . Not disturbing you, I hope?"

Out of a clear sky one of them, a woman, pipes up: "Do you have any water colors for sale? I've always thought I'd like to own a Henry Miller water color."

I jumped. "Are you serious?"

She was indeed. "Where are they? Where are they?" she cried, hopping about from one corner of the room to the other.

I trot out the few I have on hand and spread them on the couch. As she looks through the pile I busy myself fixing drinks and preparing the dogs' meals. (First the dogs, then the visitors.)

I can hear them moving about, examining the paintings on the walls, none of them mine. I give no heed.

Finally the woman who expressed a desire to buy takes me by the sleeve and leads me to a door where my wife's work is tacked up. It's a carnival scene, blazing with color, full of people and things. A really jolly picture, but not a water color.

"Haven't you any more like *this?*" she asks. "It's just enchanting. A fantasy, isn't it?"

"No," I reply, not bothering to explain, "but I have one with a rainbow, did you notice? How about *rocks?* I've just discovered how to make rocks . . . not easy, you know." And with this I go into a long discourse as to how each picture represents a theme, or to put it another way, a problem. "A pleasure problem," I add. "I'd be a fool to give myself torture problems, wouldn't I?"

Carried away by these glib remarks, I then endeavored to explain that my work was nothing but an attempt to paint my own evolution as a painter. A highly dubious explanation which I scotched by adding: "Most of the time I just make pictures." Which must have sounded equally foolish and sententious.

Since she showed no signs of wilting or crumpling, I went on to say that only a year or so ago I painted nothing but buildings, crowds of buildings . . . so many, indeed, that sometimes the paper wasn't large enough to hold them all.

"I always began with the Potala," I said.

"The *Potala?*"

"Yes, in Lhasa. You must have seen it in the movies. The edifice with a thousand rooms—where the Dalai Lama lives. Built long before the Commodore Hotel."

At this point I am aware that the other visitors are not altogether at ease. Another drink would do the trick, but I'm not getting off my horse yet. Even if I ruin the sale, which is what I usually do, I've got to carry on. I take another tack, just as a feeler. A long, utterly irrelevant disquisition on some little-known French painter whose jungle scenes have haunted me for years. (How he could intermingle, interweave, intertwine boughs, leaves, heads, limbs, spears, pieces of sky—even rain, if he chose to—all with perfect clarity. And why not geometric precision? "And with geometric precision," I throw in.) Once again I feel that everyone is growing restive. Harassed, I make a feeble joke about jungle scenes being so delicious because, if you lose your touch, you can just scramble things. (I meant, of course, that it has always been easier, more instinctive, for me to make scrambled eggs than clear-cut trunks, boughs, leaves, flowers, shrubs.) "In the old days"—making a frantic switch—"I did nothing but portraits. I called them self-portraits because they all turned out like *me*." (Nobody laughs.) "Yes, I must have made over a hundred. . . ."

"Excuse me, but could I look at that painting on the door again?" It's my buyer.

"Certainly, certainly."

"I like it *so* much!"

"It's not mine, you know. My wife did it."

"I thought so. I mean, I knew it wasn't yours." It was said simply, with no malicious overtone.

She takes a good, thirsty look, then walks over to the bed over which the water colors are strewn and, selecting my favorite, one I had hoped to keep, she asks: "Would you let me have *this*?"

"I'd rather not, to be frank. But if you insist. . . ."

"Is there something wrong with it?" She let it fall on the bed like a dead leaf.

"No, not exactly." I picked it up, almost tenderly. "It's merely that I hoped to keep it for myself. It's the one *I* like best."

I made the *I* prominent to give her a way out. I was convinced that by this time *my* views on art must have impressed her as being screwy. To make doubly sure, I added that my friend Emil, a painter down the road, didn't think very much of it. "Too subjective."

The effect this had, unfortunately, was to make her eager to examine the painting more thoroughly. She bent over it, studied it, as if she had a magnifying glass to her eye. She turned it around several times. Apparently it looked good to her upside down, for suddenly she said: "I'll take it. That is, if I can afford it."

I could have doubled my price and scared her off, but I didn't have the heart for it. My feeling was that she had earned it—by trial and ordeal. So I made an even lower price than I had originally thought to ask and we sealed the bargain. She would have liked a frame to go with it, but unfortunately I had none to offer.

As they were about to leave she asked if I thought my wife would care to sell the one she liked so much. "It's a possibility," I replied. Then, impulsively, she stepped inside the doorway, took a quick look around, and said: "Maybe I ought to take another one along. Do you mind if I look through them again?"

I didn't mind too much. All I thought was—*how long?*

Fumbling through the pile once again she paused—appreciatively, I thought—to look more closely at one which nobody in his right senses would look at twice.

"What on earth can *this* be?" she cried, holding the painting aloft and struggling to repress her laughter.

"El Alamein, I call it. Where Rommel tricked the British—wasn't that it?"

(I had previously given her a windy spiel about another title, "The Battle of Trafalgar," so named because it was full of battered, capsized boats. I had had trouble making waves, hence the battered, capsized boats.)

"Did you say Rommel?" she asked.

"Yes, Rommel. That's him there in the foreground." I indicated where with my index finger.

She smiled benignly. "I thought it was a scarecrow."

"Cancer—schmanser, what's the difference?" Might as well put a good face on it.

"And what are those dark spots, those blobs, up near the hills? They *are* hills, aren't they?"

"Tombstones. After the battle, you see . . . I'm going to put inscriptions on them. Yes, I thought to write the inscriptions in white. They'll be hard to decipher, of course. Besides, they'll be in Hebrew."

"In Hebrew?"

"Why not? Who reads inscriptions on tombstones anyway?"

By this time her friends were calling for her. They were hoping to find time to visit another celebrity, in Watsonville.

"I'd better run," she said. "Maybe I'll write and ask you to send me one by mail. One less ... less esoteric." She giggled.

As she flew up the steps she waved her hand. "Ta-ta!" she cried.

"Ta-ta!" I echoed. "If you don't like the one you bought, just mail it back. It'll have a good home here."

After dinner that evening, thinking to empty my mind of images, I took the lantern and, going to a spot in the garden where the poison oak was thick, I hung the lantern to the bough of a tree and fell to. What a pleasure, what a ferocious pleasure, to pull up long, vicious roots of poison oak! (With gloves on.) Better than making water colors, sometimes. Better than *selling* water colors, certainly. But, as with painting, you can never be sure of the outcome. You may think you have a Rommel, only to find out it is nothing but a scarecrow. And now and then, in your ferocious haste, you pull up pomegranates instead of camphor weed.

Down at Lucia, some time after Norman Mini decamped, a chap named Harvey took over—as chief cook and bottle-washer. He pitched a tent right in the midst of the brush, the poison oak, the rattlesnakes, the fog and the bottle-flies, and there he made his abode with a wife and two small children. In this tent he tried to paint, to practice the violin and to write. He wanted most of all to write.

If ever I spotted a born writer, this fellow Harvey was certainly it. When he talked, and he was a good talker, a wonderful story-teller, it sounded as if he were reading from a book. Everything he related had form, structure, clarity and meaning.

But Harvey wasn't satisfied with this gift. He wanted to write. Occasionally, on his day off, he would drop in on me. He was always apologetic about taking up my time—which didn't prevent him from lingering for hours—but his excuse was, and he meant it sincerely, that he had need of me. To be honest, he was one man I always enjoyed listening to. For one thing, he possessed a profound knowledge of English literature, beginning from the beginning. I believe he had once been a teacher of English literature. He had been many other things too. He had taken a job as cook and handy man at Lucia, a lonely spot, because he thought it would give him a chance to try his hand at writing. Why he thought so I don't know. The job afforded him little spare time and the overcrowded tent was hardly an ideal work place. Besides, with the violin exercises and the easel painting only a da Vinci could have hoped to write too. But that was Harvey's way of going about it.

"I *want* to write," he would say, "and I just can't. It won't come. I sit at the machine for hours at a stretch and all I can produce is a few lines. And even these few lines are no good."

Every time he took leave of me he would remark how good he felt, how buoyed up. "Tomorrow," he would say, "I feel that it will go like a breeze." And then he would thank me warmly.

It went on like this for weeks and weeks, with only a trickle coming out despite our peptonic talks.

One of the fascinating things about Harvey, whose case is by no means unique, is that despite all the blockage, the paralysis (before the machine), he could relate the contents of a long novel—one of Dostoevsky's, for instance—with uncanny accuracy of detail, emphasizing and underlining the most complicated passages in a manner such as one imagines only writers can. In a single session Harvey could cover analytically, didactically and ecstatically such a string of writers as Henry James, Melville, Fielding, Laurence Sterne, Stendhal, Jonathan Swift, Hart Crane. Listening to Harvey talking books and authors was far more absorbing (to me) than listening to a celebrated professor of literature. He had a way of identifying himself with each and every author, a way of insinuating his own agonies into what probably were once theirs. He knew how to select, evaluate and elucidate, no gainsaying it.

But this ability, as one can readily surmise, came all too easy for our friend Harvey. It was as nothing for him to discuss the fine points of an intricate Henry James story while cooking and recooking a penguin. (He did actually carry off a wounded penguin which he found one day on the highway, and after three days and nights of wrestling with it, he did serve up a delicious meal!)

One afternoon, in the midst of a lengthy disquisition on the merits and demerits of Walter Pater, I suddenly put up my hand. An intriguing idea had flashed through my mind. An idea, needless to say, not even remotely connected with Walter Pater.

"Hold it, Harvey!" I cried and, reaching for his glass, I filled it to the brim. "Harvey, my good man, I think I've got something for you."

Harvey hadn't the least idea of what was going through my head. He looked at me blankly.

"Look here," I began, almost trembling with inner excitement, "to begin with, forget Walter Pater—and Henry James and Stendhal and all the other birds you like to shoot at. Fuck them! You're finished with them . . . they're just dead ducks. Your trouble is that you know too much . . . too much for your own good, I mean. I want you to bury these guys, wipe them out of your consciousness. Don't open another book, nor a magazine. Not even the dictionary. At least, not until you've tried what I'm about to suggest."

Harvey stared at me in a puzzled way, patiently waiting for the clue.

"You're always saying that you can't write. You tell me that every time you come. I'm sick of hearing it. What's more, I don't believe it. Maybe you can't write as you would like to write, but write you can! Even an idiot can learn to write, if he sticks at it long enough. Now here's my thought . . . I want you to leave soon"—I said this because I knew that if he started inquiring into my scheme it would all evaporate in talk—"yes, I want you to go home, get a good night's rest, and tomorrow, before breakfast, if possible, sit down to the machine and explain to it why it is that you can't write. Nothing more, nothing else. Is that clear? Don't ask me why I urge it, just try it out!"

I was surprised that he made no attempt to interrupt me. He had a queer expression on his face, as if he had just been given a jolt.

"Harvey," I continued, "even though the two are not the same— I mean talking and writing—I've noticed that you can talk most eloquently about anything under the sun. And you can talk about yourself, your own problems, just as brilliantly as you can about the next fellow. In fact, you're even better when you're talking about yourself. And that's what you're doing all the time, anyway, even when you pretend to be talking about Henry James or Herman Melville or Leigh Hunt. A man who has the verbal gift—and you certainly have it—shouldn't be stymied by a piece of white paper. Forget that it's a piece of white paper . . . pretend that it's an ear. Talk to it! Talk into it! With your fingers, of course. . . . *Can't write!* What nonsense! Of course you can write. You're a Niagara. . . . Now go home and do as I say. Let's end it right here. And remember, you're to write only about why you can't write. See what happens. . . ."

It took some firmness on my part to make Harvey run off, just like that, and not "go into it," as he was dying to do. But he did ease himself out. In fact, he was almost on the trot by the time he reached the car.

A week or two passed, then three or four, but no sign of Harvey. I was beginning to think my idea was not such a brilliant one after all. Then one day he showed up.

"Well, well!" I exclaimed. "So you're still alive! Tell me, did it work?"

"It sure did," he said. "I've been writing steadily ever since you put the bug in my head that day." He went on to explain that he was throwing up the job at Lucia. He was going back East where he came from.

"When I leave I'll put that bundle of manuscript in your mailbox. Take a glance at it if you ever have the time, will you?"

I promised faithfully that I would. Some few days later Harvey picked up and moved. But there was no bundle of manuscript in my mailbox. After a few weeks I received a letter from him in which he explained that he hadn't left the manuscript in my mailbox because he didn't think it was worth bothering me about. It was much too long, for one thing. Besides, he had given up the idea of becoming a writer. He didn't say what he was going to do for a living but I had the impression that he was going back to the teaching profession. That's the usual way out. When everything else fails, teach!

I've never heard from Harvey since. I've no idea what he's doing today. I'm still convinced that he's a writer; still convinced that one day he'll go back to it and stick to it. Why I speak with such conviction I don't know.

The tragic thing today is that, in the case of men like Harvey, even when they do break through the "sound barrier" they are killed off almost immediately. Either they write too well or not bad enough. Because of their great knowledge and familiarity with good literature, because of their innate taste and discrimination, they have difficulty in finding the level on which to reach the reading public. They particularly lack that liberating instinct so well formulated by the Zen masters: *"Kill the Buddha!"* They want to become another Dostoevsky, another Gide, another Melville.

On sober thought, my advice to Harvey (and to all who find themselves in Harvey's boots) struck me as being sound and sensible. If you can't give the is-ness of a thing give the not-ness of it! The main thing is to hook up, get the wheels turning, sound off. When your brakes jam, try going in reverse. It often works.

Once traction is established, the most important thing—how to

reach the public, or better, how to create your own public!—still
remains to be faced. Without a public it's suicide. No matter how
small, there has to be an audience. I mean, an appreciative, enthusiastic audience, a selective audience.

What few young writers realize, it seems to me, is that they must
find—create, invent!—the way to reach their readers. It isn't enough
to write a good book, a beautiful book, or even a better book than
most. It isn't enough even to write an "original" book! One has
to establish, or re-establish, a unity which has been broken and
which is felt just as keenly by the reader, who is a potential artist,
as by the writer, who believes himself to be an artist. The theme of
separation and isolation—"atomization," it's now called—has as
many facets to it as there are unique individuals. And we are all
unique. The longing to be reunited, with a common purpose and
an all-embracing significance, is now universal. The writer who
wants to communicate with his fellow-man, and thereby establish
communion with him, has only to speak with sincerity and direct-
ness. He has not to think about literary standards—he will make
them as he goes along—he has not to think about trends, vogues,
markets, acceptable ideas or unacceptable ideas: he has only to
deliver himself, naked and vulnerable. All that constricts and re-
stricts him, to use the language of not-ness, his fellow-reader, even
though he may not be an artist, feels with equal despair and bewilderment. The world presses down on all alike. Men are not
suffering from the lack of good literature, good art, good theatre,
good music, but from that which has made it impossible for these
to become manifest. In short, they are suffering from the silent,
shameful conspiracy (the more shameful since it is unacknowl-
edged) which has bound them together as enemies of art and
artist. They are suffering from the fact that art is not the primary,
moving force in their lives. They are suffering from the act,
repeated daily, of keeping up the pretense that they can go their
way, lead their lives, without art. They never dream—or they
behave as if they never realize—that the reason why they feel

sterile, frustrated and joyless is because art (and with it the artist) has been ruled out of their lives. For every artist who has been assassinated thus (unwittingly?) thousands of ordinary citizens, who might have known a normal joyous life, are condemned to lead the purgatorial existence of neurotics, psychotics, schizophrenics. No, the man who is about to blow his top does not have to fix his eye on the *Iliad,* the *Divine Comedy* or any other great model; he has only to give us, in his own language, the saga of his woes and tribulations, the saga of his non-existentialism. In this mirror of not-ness everyone will recognize himself for what he is as well as what he is not. He will no longer be able to hold his head up either before his children or before his neighbors; he will have to admit that he—not the other fellow—is that terrible person who is contributing, wittingly or unwittingly, to the speedy downfall and disintegration of his own people. He will know, when he resumes work in the morning, that everything he does, everything he says, everything he touches, pertains to the invisible poisonous web which holds us all in its mesh and which is slowly but surely crushing the life out of us. It does not matter what high office the reader may hold—he is as much a villain and a victim as the outlaw and the outcast.

Who will print such books, who will publish and disseminate them?

No one!

You will have to do it yourself, dear man. Or, do as Homer did: travel the highways and byways with a white cane, singing your song as you go. You may have to pay people to listen to you, but that isn't an insuperable feat either. Carry a little "tea" with you and you'll soon have an audience.

2.

"The pain was unbearable, but I did not want it to end: it had operatic grandeur. It lit up Grand Central Station like a Judgment Day."

In 1945 Poetry-London brought out a slim book by Elizabeth Smart bearing the title: *By Grand Central Station I Sat Down and Wept.* It is a very unusual little book, "a love story," the jacket says. The romance which inspired the book took place at Anderson Creek in the days when Varda ruled the roost. It must have been written about the same time as *The Stranger,* by Lillian Bos Ross, which will probably go on selling as long as there is a Big Sur.

Says Elizabeth Smart: "The legends here are all of blood-feuds and suicide, uncanny foresight and supernatural knowledge." She was probably thinking of Robinson Jeffers' narative poems. By the time Emil White arrived at Anderson Creek (1944), via the Yukon, there wasn't an artist in sight and all the convict shacks were deserted, even by the rats. There were no feuds, no gun fights, no stabbings, no suicides: it was quiet along the Coast. The war was drawing to a close, the floaters were drifting in. Soon the long-haired artists would appear and broken romances begin all over again. At night, as the creek rushed to the sea, the rocks and boulders gave out garbled, hallucinating versions of the calamities which lend spice to the place. The "Colony," made up of transient artists, would rehearse in the space of a few short years all but the bloody aspects of the legends.

Emil White's shack—it was indeed a shack!—was on the highway, hidden by a tall, overgrown hedge invaded by roses and morning-glories. We sat down one noon in the shade of this hedge to have

59

a bite. I had been helping him clean out the joint, which was gloomy, mildewed, reeking with the smell of rat dirt, garbage and worse. The little table at which we were having coffee and sandwiches was only a foot or two from the road. A car pulled up, a man and his wife got out. Throwing a half-dollar on the table, the man ordered coffee and sandwiches; he took it for granted that we were running a roadside café.

In those days, when Emil managed on seven dollars a week, everything included, I used to urge him to make a few pennies by serving coffee and sandwiches. Cafés were few and far between; gas stations were fifty miles apart. Many a time Emil was routed out of bed at two or three in the morning by a tourist looking for gas or water.

Then, one after another, the artists happened along: poets, painters, dancers, musicians, sculptors, novelists . . . everything but slack-wire artists. All poor, all trying to live on nothing, all struggling to express themselves.

Up to this time the only writer I had met, aside from Lillian Ross, was Lynda Sargent. Lynda had everything that goes to make a writer except that one indispensable thing—belief in one's self. She also suffered from ergophobia, a disease common to writers. A novel which she had been working on for years, a formidable one, was unfortunately destroyed by fire (and the house with it) shortly after she completed it. During the time I was her guest she showed me stories and novelettes, some finished, some unfinished, which were altogether remarkable. They were largely about New England characters whom she had known as a girl. It was a New England more like the legendary Big Sur: full of violence, horror, incest, broken dreams, despair, loneliness, insanity and frustration of every sort. Lynda related these stories with a granite-like indifference to the reader's emotions. Her language was rich, heavily brocaded, tumultuous and torrential. She had command of the whole keyboard. In some ways she reminded me of that strange woman from East Africa who wrote under the name of Isak Dinesen. Only Lynda was more real, more earthy, more bloodcurdling. She is still writing, I should add. The last word I had from her, written from a lonely lookout station in the mountains, was that she was just finishing another book.

Norman Mini, whom I have already mentioned, was—and still is—"another writer of promise," as publishers love to say. He was much more, indeed. He had in him the makings of a von Moltke, a Big Bill Haywood, a Kafka—and a Brillat-Savarin. I first met him at the home of Kenneth Rexroth, in San Francisco. He impressed me immediately. I sensed that he had suffered deep humiliations. I did not look upon him then as a writer but as a strategist. A military strategist. A "failed" strategist, who had now made life his battleground. That was Norman to me—a fascinating Norman, whom I could listen to indefinitely, and do still.

A year or two after this meeting Norman arrived in Big Sur with a wife and child, determined to write a book which had been germinating in his crop for years. I no longer remember the title of this work, which he finally consummated at Lucia, but I do remember the flavor of it. It might well have been entitled— *The Unspeakable Horror of this Man-made Universe*. There wasn't a flaw in it, unless the work itself was a flaw. It moved on ruthlessly, relentlessly and inexorably, a chthonian drama mirroring the nightmare of our daytime world.

How we sweated over that book! I say "we" because, along about the middle, Norman began to visit me frequently for injections. Moral injections, of course. Now the strategist came to the fore sharply. Faced with a stalemate, his military cunning—that is the best I can describe it—came into play. His forces were beautifully aligned, his powers had not deserted him, victory was within his grasp, but he could not make, or rather bring about, the move which would unleash the decisive battle.

I had not yet read a line of the book, nor in fact had he bothered to give me a clear outline of its plot. He talked about it as if it were a mash. He wanted no help in making the brew: what he wanted was deeper insight into the processes of fermentation. I ought to say here that Norman was the type who writes from phrase to phrase, line to line, feeling his way cautiously, critically, painfully, laboriously. The pattern was clear to him, probably stamped in geometrical fashion in his brain cells, but the writing came only in short spurts, mostly in trickles. He could not understand why, surcharged as he was, the flow should be blocked. Perhaps he had the wrong approach to the craft. Perhaps he ought to close his (critical) eyes and just put down anything, whatever came to mind. How did I manage to write as fast and as freely as I did? Was he afraid of himself or of what he was saying? Was he really a writer or did he only imagine it? Everyone had talent, and with cultivation, could produce something. But was that enough? There should be fire, passion, an obsessive urge. One should not be concerned whether a book turn out good or bad. One should write, think of nothing else. Write, write, write. . . .

Had his abode been Europe I doubt that Norman would have had such a struggle to express himself. For one thing, there he would have been able to make himself understood. His humility was genuine and touching. One felt that he was cut out for bigger things, that he had taken to writing in desperation, after all other avenues had been closed off. He was too sincere, too earnest, too truthful, to ever be a worldly success. His integrity was such, in fact, that it inspired fear and suspicion.

After making a few lame efforts to place his book with a publisher he gave up. Soon the job at Lucia petered out and he was obliged to return to the city. The next thing I knew, he had taken a job as janitor in the University of California at Berkeley. It was a night job and it gave him the opportunity to write during the day. Now and then he sat in on a lecture. Ironic to think that our humble janitor was possibly better equipped to lecture on such subjects as mathematics, history, economics, sociology, literature, than the professors he dropped in to listen to occasionally. What wonderful lectures he could have given on the art of being a janitor, I often thought. For, whatever Norman tackled he made an art of. That was his greatest fault, in the eyes of the worldly, this insistence on making an art of everything.

To my mind it is utterly unimportant whether Norman Mini becomes a recognized writer or not. What is important is that such an American continues to be in our midst.

The man who could write like a breeze was Walker Winslow. Walker had written several books, under various names, before coming to Big Sur. He had also written heaps of poems. But it was not until he began his autobiographical novel, *If a Man Be Mad,** that he found his true vein. Every day he wrote fifteen, twenty or thirty pages. He was at the machine from early morn till sundown. He never touched a drop of liquor during the few months it took him to finish this book. He drank huge quantities of coffee and smoked several packs of cigarettes a day. He did a lot of rewriting too, mostly condensation. While writing the book he received commissions to do other books. At one time, I remember, he was trying to write three books at once.

But, just as with Norman, writing was a secondary affair. Walker's forte was people. Most of his life he had been a tramp, a bum, a hobo, a beachcomber. With the soul of a saint. When he was not getting into trouble he was helping others. There were no lengths to which he would not go to aid a man in distress: he was a natural crutch for the weak and the afflicted. Writing books could only be in the nature of an interlude for Walker. He was not a Gorky, though in another society, one more receptive, more tolerant, more "reverent" of misfits and outcasts, he might have become another Gorky. Certainly Walker knew and understood the bottom dog as well as any Gorky. He also knew and understood John Barleycorn as few writers ever have. His problem was, and still is, not to master the literary craft but to master his own abysmal hunger for limitless experience.

---

* *If a Man Be Mad,* by Harold Maine (pseudonym) (New York: Doubleday & Co., 1947).

Another writer with a great sense of humanity whom I feel impelled to say a word about is Jake Kenney. Jake is not a resident of Big Sur, but he is limitrophe to it. He is a Russian at heart—Dostoevskian, in a large sense. Like so many potentially great writers, Jake is unable to get a look-in with the publishers. I read the manuscript of his first novel several times. *The Falling Sleep* he calls it. A marvelous title, when one knows the book. The only title. In spite of its faults—minor faults—the book has qualities one does not often encounter in American literature: sensitivity, passion, brotherhood. Too warm-blooded, no doubt. Makes one laugh and weep in a way that Americans resent, because they are ashamed to laugh and weep unrestrainedly.

Unfortunately, Jake Kenney is a capable man with his hands. He is a carpenter and builder as well as writer. Most unfortunate. Because, failing to earn a living with the pen, he can always earn it with his bare hands. And "we" who care not much how a man makes his living will never know what we have lost. Besides, do we really want *The Falling Sleep*? Or do we not prefer the "Put Me to Sleep" kind of literature?

Paul Rink, a near neighbor, is a similar "unfortunate." Being a jack of all trades, he's even worse off. He too has written his novel, and it has gone a-begging—to over twenty-five publishers. "Too good," they say. "Too this, too that." Foolishly, in my opinion, he has rewritten his opus several times. One publisher will accept it if he will reduce the first section of the book; another will take it if he will change the ending; a third will "consider" it if he will develop this character, this incident, this that and this other. Paul, believing them to be well-meaning, struggles to fit into the straitjacket—without being untrue to himself. Hopeless task! One should never, never do as publishers request. Put your manuscripts aside, write another and another and another. When they finally accept you, throw the first one at them again. Then they will say: "Why didn't you ever show us *this* work? It's a masterpiece!" Editors frequently forget what they've read, or what they've rejected. Somebody else read it, not me, they will say. Or, "we had a different policy then." With publishers the climate is always changing. However, to tell a writer who has yet to get his first book accepted that editors and publishers are idiotic and as lacking in judgment as other mortals, that they are not interested in literature per se, that their standards of value are as shifting as the sands, is useless. *Some where, some how, some day,* reasons the author. Good! "Advance always!" as Rimbaud says.

Near the Little Sur River, in a windy cove—a bitch of a place!— Eric Barker, an English poet, works as caretaker for the owner of a large cattle ranch.* The pay is meager, the task light, the hours are his own. In the morning he takes a dip in the icy canyon stream, in the afternoon in the sea. Between times he wards off fishermen, hunters, drunks—and rustlers, presumably. Sounds divine, if only the wind didn't blow steadily twenty-four hours of the day nine months of the year.

Eric has been writing poetry, nothing but poetry, for twenty-five years. He is a good poet. A modest, humble one, who never pushes himself. Men like John Cowper Powys and Robinson Jeffers esteem his work. Not until a few months ago did Eric receive his first recognition, in the shape of an award. It may be another twenty-five years before he receives another award. Eric doesn't seem to mind. He knows how to live with himself and with his fellowman. When he gets an inspiration he puts it down on paper. If he doesn't feel inspired he doesn't worry. He is a poet and he lives like a poet. Few writers can do it.

Hugh O'Neill is another poet. He lived at Anderson Creek for several years. Lived on less than a shoestring, I might say. I never saw him other than serene. As a rule he was silent; sometimes it was a grim silence he gave off, but usually it was pleasant, not deadening. Until he came to Big Sur, Hugh O'Neill had never done a thing with his hands. He was the scholarly type. Sud-

---

* Since I wrote the above he's been fired. H. M.

denly, out of necessity no doubt, he discovered that he could do all manner of work. He even hired himself out as carpenter, plumber, mason. He made fireplaces for his neighbors; some worked, some didn't. But they were all beautiful and sturdy to behold. Then he took to gardening—maintained an enormous patch of vegetables, meant for a single family, but sufficient to feed the entire colony at Anderson Creek. He took to fishing and hunting. He made pottery. He painted pictures. He learned how to put patches in his pants, darn his own socks, iron his clothes. Never have I seen a poet blossom into such a useful creature as did Hugh O'Neill. And remain poor at the same time. Deliberately so. He would say that he hated work. Yet there was no more active worker, no more industrious being, than this same Hugh O'Neill. What he hated was the workaday world, work that was meaningless. He preferred to starve rather than join up. And he could starve just as beautifully as he could labor. He did it graciously, almost as if to prove that starving was a pastime. He seemed to live on air. His walk too was a sort of walking on air. He was swift and noiseless.

Like Harvey, he could expatiate on a book with all the charm, subtlety and penetration of a professional lecturer. Being Irish, he could also twist a subject to fantastic proportions. One had to go back and reread the novel he was describing to find out how much of it was Hugh O'Neill's and how much the author's. He did the same with his own stories—I mean stories out of his life. Each time he told them he gave them a new angle. The best ones were about the war, about his days as a German prisoner. They were very much in the tone and spirit of the man who wrote *Men in War*: Andreas Latzko. They stressed the ridiculous—and the sublime— aspects which men reveal even in the worst situations. Hugh O'Neill was always laughing at himself, at the predicaments he found himself in. As if they were happening to someone else. Even in Germany, as a prisoner of war, ragged, hungry, wounded, hardly able to see, he found life amusing, grotesque, ridiculous.

There was not an ounce of hatred in him. He told of his humiliations almost as if he were sorry for the Germans, sorry that they, being men and no more, were put in the position they were.

But Hugh O'Neill could never put these stories to paper. He had material enough to make (at least) another great war novel. He always promised to write this book but he never did. Instead he would write stories, essays, poems, none of them anything like the yarns which captivated us. The war had marked him; it made ordinary life seem drab and senseless. He was happy doing nothing of importance. He loved to idle his time away, and to me it was a pleasure to watch him do it. Why should he write, after all? Would it not entrain the same bedevilment which other pursuits land men in, the men who keep the wheels turning?

There was a period when he owned an Irish harp. It suited him perfectly. It would have suited him even better could he have picked up his harp and wandered over the earth, singing his chanties, telling his tales, repairing a fence here, building a walk there, and so on. He was so light on his feet, so airy, so blithe, so absolutely unconcerned about the work of the world! What a pity that ours is not a society which permits a man to squander his days and rewards him—with a crust of bread and a thimbleful of whisky—for keeping his tail clear of trouble and ennui.

Some take it easy and get there just the same, some belabor themselves and make life hell for wife and children, some sweat it out, some have only to turn on the faucet and let it pour out, some start and never finish, and some are finished before they start. In the long run it doesn't make much difference, I suppose. Certainly not to publishers, and even less to the great reading public. If we don't produce Gorkys, Pushkins and Dostoevskys we produce Hemingways, Steinbecks and Tennessee Williamses. Nobody suffers. Only literature suffers. Stendhal wrote his *Chartreuse de Parme* in less than sixty days; Goethe took a lifetime to finish *Faust*. The comics and the Bible sell better than either of these.

Now and then I hear from Georges Simenon, one of the most

prolific writers alive, and the best in his genre. When he gets ready to write another book—the task of a few weeks—he notifies his friends that he will be obliged to neglect his correspondence for a while. Often I think to myself how wonderful it would be to complete a book in just a few months. How wonderful to notify all and sundry that you will be "off the air" for a time!

But to get back to the slave coast. . . . One man who seemed to have no trouble whatever turning it out was Rog Rogaway. Rogaway lived in the abandoned schoolhouse near Krenkel Corners; he lived there by permission of Ben Bufano who, in turn, had received permission from the authorities to use the place as a studio.

Rogaway was a tall, easygoing, sailorman type, with bones of rubber. He suffered from a serious intestinal ailment which he had contracted as a result of being blown up, along with his ship, by a submarine. He was so happy to receive the absurd pension which gave him leisure to paint that I'm sure he wouldn't have complained had his legs been blown off. He was a fool about dancing and about painting. He cultivated a sort of "Shuffle off to Buffalo" swing which, when combined with just the right (dirty) leer, gave him the look of Priapus with a cannon cracker up his ass.

Rogaway turned out a finished canvas every day, sometimes two or three. None ever seemed to give him satisfaction. Nevertheless he continued to turn them out day after day, and faster and faster, convinced that one day he would strike oil. When he ran out of canvas he took the ones that were a month old and painted over them. There was a gay, musical quality to all his work. Perhaps his paintings were no more than exercises, but they were not Swedish exercises.

The impressive thing about these "exercises" was where he practiced them. He might have worked in the schoolhouse—it was large enough—but Rog had a wife and two children, one an infant, and children drove him crazy. Bright and early every morning he disappeared behind the schoolhouse to follow a hidden trail which led him, after a few hundred yards, to what looked like an outhouse. This contraption which Rog had hastily slapped together later served Bufano as a place of meditation. No one rambling through the hills would ever have suspected that hidden in the brush was this den austerely decorated with Chinese silk paintings, Tibetan scrolls, pre-Columbian figurines and so forth, which Bufano had collected in his travels. Nor would the straggler ever dream that a painter, particularly one the size of Rogaway, had fashioned such a cubicle to work in. Bufano, who is short, had to make an opening in the wall, through which he stuck his feet, before he could stretch out full length to take a nap.

Even now I can see Rogaway in the fever of excitement which always seized him when tackling a fresh canvas. To take a squint at his work he was obliged to back out the doorway. Stepping inside again, he could see nothing but black spots. Now and then, backing out too ecstatically, he would trip on a strip of greasewood and tumble ass backwards into the brambles and nettles. He never bothered to brush himself off: the sting and prickle helped speed up his tempo. Rogaway's one and only concern was to produce the maximum before the sun lost its strength.

Evenings he relaxed. If there was no one to share the wine and the music, he drank and danced by himself. Wine was bad for his complaint; he drank it because there was nothing better he could afford. It required only a cupful to put him in the mood. Sometimes he danced without moving from the spot, just shaking his rubbery members like a deboned sardine. At times he disarticulated so perfectly that he resembled an octopus in the throes of ecstasy.

Rogaway's obsession was to find a still warmer climate, an ocean you could bathe in, and a rate of exchange that would permit him to live even more cheaply than he did at Big Sur. He got off to Mexico one day, stayed a year or so, switched to Majorca, then to the south of France, then Portugal. Of late he has been living— and painting of course!—in Taos, which is certainly far from any ocean, has a mean climate in winter, and is overrun with tourists.

Perhaps Rog has persuaded the Indians to let him join them in their snake dances. That's the only reason I can think of for such a move.

In the shack at Anderson Creek, where we were lucky to have a toilet, we had to do without music for a spell since we had no radio or phonograph. This didn't prevent Gilbert Neiman, another writer and a bosom friend, from hearing music. Music from *our* place, I mean. In the beginning, everyone who goes to live at Anderson Creek hears things. Some hear Beethoven symphonies, some hear military bands, some hear voices, some hear wails and shrieks. Particularly those who live near the canyon creek, which is the source of these eerie, disturbing sounds. Gilbert and his wife and daughter occupied the big house which was once Varda's. (Varda had converted the living room into a ballroom. It would also have made a wonderful billiard parlor.) But, as I was saying, Gilbert insisted that the "music" came from *our* house, which was a good hundred yards away. It came mostly at night, which he resented, because he was a poor sleeper. He was also a bad drinker, but I won't go into that. When I would question him about the music, what kind of music, he would answer: "It's that Varèse record." Whether he meant "Ionization," "Density 21.5," "Octandre" or "Intégrales," I never knew. "You know," he would say, "it's the one with Chinese blocks, sleigh bells, tambourine, gongs, chains and all that crap." Gilbert had good taste in music, adored Mozart, and in moments of repose and serenity enjoyed listening to Varèse. In every place they lived, and they always seemed to choose a quaint dump to live it, there were albums of records galore. At Bunker Hill (Los Angeles), which is almost as weird a place as Milwaukee, they often had little to eat but they always had music. In the little green house in Beverly Glen (just outside Hollywood), Gilbert would rub himself down with olive oil and hide behind the bushes in back of the house to take a sun bath, the music going full blast—Shostakovich, *Gaspard de la Nuit,* Beethoven quartets, Vivaldi, flamenco, Cantor Rosenblatt, and so on. Often the neighbors begged him to turn it down a little. When he worked on his book—in the garage—the music was always playing. (He would begin at midnight and finish at dawn.)

The book he had written at Beverly Glen, called *There's a Tyrant in Every Country,** was accepted and published during his early days at Big Sur. It was a honey of a book, too, though the neighbors were much divided about its merits. Myself, I've never read a better novel about Mexico. At any rate, Gilbert was now on a second book, *The Underworld.* It was during this period, when he had begun to work days instead of nights, that the music—the phantom music—began to disturb him greatly. Of course he was also drinking. He would begin cold sober and finish quite otherwise. Returning to normal, he would become—I can think of no more apt word for it—*delicious.*

Sober, Gilbert walked like an Indian—noiselessly, tirelessly, and on the balls of his feet. Drunk, he fell into a weaving motion, like a man in a trance, or a sleepwalker who skirts precipices, stumbles, teeters, totters, yet never goes over. In this condition his talk matched his walk. He literally wove his way through a subject—Leopardi, for instance, or the Tantras, or Paul Valéry—taking the most dangerous detours, hurdling impossible barriers, retracing his steps with infallible accuracy, falling, picking himself up, resortto pantomime when out of breath or at a loss for the right words. . . . He could come back to the exact place where he had left off—at the beginning of what was meant to be a parenthesis—an hour, two hours, later. Come back, I mean, to the phrase which he had left dangling in mid-air, and complete it. Now and then, in these flights, he would pause and, forgetting that we were hanging on his words, do a spot of meditation. He had acquired the habit, in Colorado, of being on the alert for messages. The messages were always from "Mamma Kali," as he called her. Sometimes Mamma Kali appeared to him in person, just as he was about

---

* Published by Harcourt, Brace & Co., New York, 1947.

to take a forkful of peas, and then he would go into a trance, the fork halfway to his lips, and gaze at the beloved one adoringly.

This was the grotesque side of Gilbert—by no means his least charming side. Another side represented the eternal student. He had specialized in the Romance languages and was thoroughly at home in French, Spanish and Italian. His translations from the French—Valéry, Baudelaire, Verlaine, Rimbaud, Fernandez—were superb. He was the first to translate Lorca's plays in this country. With *Blood Wedding* he started the vogue for Lorca's plays. He also translated Ramon Sender, perhaps the greatest novelist of Lorca's generation. The thing about Gilbert's translations was that he not only revealed his deep knowledge of Spanish and French but, what is more important, his most excellent knowledge of English. Though I don't believe he made any published translations from the Italian, the writer he often talked to me about was Giacomo Leopardi. It was hard to say which one he talked about with more fervor—Leopardi or the Duse. He could also talk about Charlie Chaplin and John Gilbert—particularly the latter's performance in *Flesh and the Devil*—with touching eloquence.

I should remark here that Gilbert had begun his career as a juvenile actor, in Colorado, I believe. Or perhaps it was in Kansas. He hated Kansas like poison. One could never tell, when he referred to that state, whether he had been born and raised there in this incarnation or a previous one. The actor in him was strong, and even in the Anderson Creek days, there were traces of the showman in his deportment. They would appear when he was sobering up and his voice returning, when he donned his shepherd's plaid suit, pomaded his hair, faintly perfumed his breast-pocket handkerchief, polished his shoes, flexed his muscles and took to strutting the imaginary boards of the imaginary billiard parlor where he would while away an imaginary hour or two with Paderewski. Getting back into form, he would usually begin an unfinished discourse on the unique merits of Céline, Dostoevsky or Wassermann. If he felt slightly vitriolic, he would put André Gide through a bath of sulphur and ammonia. But I'm getting off the track. . . .

The music! One night, about two in the morning, the door of our shack was thrown open with a bang and, before I knew what was happening, I felt a hand gripping my throat, squeezing it viciously. I knew damned well I wasn't dreaming. Then a voice, a boozy voice which I recognized instantly, and which sounded maudlin and terrifying, shouted in my ear: "Where's that damned gadget?"

"What gadget?" I gurgled, struggling to release the grip around my throat.

"The radio! Where are you hiding it?"

With this he let go his grip and began dismantling the place. I sprang out of bed and tried to pacify him.

"You know I have no radio," I shouted. "What's the matter with you? What's eating you?"

He ignored me, went on pushing things aside, tearing at the walls with furious talons, upsetting chinaware and pots and pans. Finding nothing, he soon relented, though still furious, still cursing and swearing. I thought he had gone out of his mind.

"What is it, Gilbert? What's happened?" I was holding him by the arm.

"What is it?" he yelled, and I could feel his glare even through the darkness. *"What is it?* Come on out here!" He grabbed my arm and started dragging me.

After we had gone a few yards in the direction of his house he stopped suddenly, and gripping me like a demon, he shouted: *"Now!* Now do you hear?"

"Hear what?" I said innocently.

"The music! It's the same tune all the time. "Its driving me crazy."

"Maybe it's coming from *your* place," said I, though I knew damned well it was coming from inside him.

"So you know where it is," said Gilbert, accelerating his pace and dragging me along like a dead horse. Under his breath he mumbled something about my "cunning" ways.

When we got to his house he dropped to his knees and began

sniffing around, just like a dog, in the bushes and under the porch. To humor him, I also got down on all fours, to search for the concealed gadget that was giving out Beethoven's *Fifth*. After we had crawled around the house and under it as far as we could, we lay on our backs and looked up at the stars.

"It's stopped," said Gilbert. "Did you notice?"

"You're crazy," I said. "It never stops."

"Tell me honestly," he said, in a conciliating tone of voice, "where did you hide it?"

"I never hid anything," I said. "It's there . . . in the stream. Can't you hear it?"

He turned over on one side, cupped his ear, straining every nerve to hear.

"I don't hear a thing," he said.

"That's strange," said I. *"Listen!* It's Smetana now. You know the one . . . *Out of My Life*. It's as clear as can be, every note."

He turned over on the other side and again he cupped his ear. He held this position for a few moments then rolled over on his back, smiling the smile of an angel. He gave a little laugh, then said:

"I know now . . . I was dreaming. I was dreaming that I was the conductor of an orchestra. . . ."

I cut him short. "But how do you explain the other times?"

"Drink," he said. "I drink too much."

"No you don't," I replied, "I hear it just the same as you. Only I know where it comes from."

"Where?" said Gilbert.

"I told you . . . from the stream."

"You mean someone has hidden it in the creek?"

"Exactly," I said.

I allowed a due pause, then added: "Do you know who?"

"No," he said.

"God!"

He began to laugh like a madman.

"God!" he yelled *"God!"* Then louder and louder. "God, God, God, God, God! Can you beat that?"

He was now convulsed with laughter. I had to shake him to make him listen to me.

"Gilbert," I said, just as gently as could be, "if you don't mind, I'm going back to bed. You go down by the creek and look for it. It's under a mossy rock on the left hand side near the bridge. Don't tell anybody, will you?"

I stood up and shook hands with him.

"Remember," I said, "not a soul!"

He put his fingers to his lips and went·Shhhh! Shhhh!

Everything unusual, be it said, originates at Anderson Creek. Because of the "artists," most likely. If a stray cow is mysteriously killed and butchered, some one from Anderson Creek did the job. If a passing motorist kills a deer on the highway, he always brings it to some poor artist at Anderson Creek, never to Mr. Brown or Mr. Roosevelt. If an old shack is demolished overnight, for its doors and windowpanes, it must have been one of the Anderson Creek gang who did it. If there are moonlight bathing parties at the sulphur baths—*mixed* parties—it's that Anderson Creek bunch again. Anything that's borrowed, lost, stolen or used to better purpose can be traced to Anderson Creek. That's the legend, at least. As one of the natives remarked in my presence one day—"They're just a bunch of morphodites!"

Just the same, it was at Anderson Creek that the first flying saucer made its appearance in Big Sur. The chap who told me the story said it happened early one morning. In shape it was more like a dirigible than the lamp-shade variety. It hovered close to shore, plainly visible, took off and returned two more times. Shortly after this two more sightings, one at dawn, another at twilight, were made by people staying at the sulphur baths. Then one day my friend Walker Winslow woke me up out of a sound sleep to witness a strange phenomenon just above the horizon, looking seaward. We observed the strange activity of what seemed like twin stars gyrating about an invisible pivot for about twenty minutes, after which the light grew too strong and it faded out. But it was reported—as a saucer phenomenon—next day by the government station along the coast. Soon thereafter a number of friends reported saucers, lights that followed their cars, and so on. None of them were drunks or dope fiends. Some of them were, or had been, downright sceptics about "this saucer business." One of the most vivid accounts was given by Eric Barker, then living at the Hunt Ranch near the Little Sur. In broad daylight, about four in the afternoon, he saw six small disks flying above his head at a brisk but not phenomenal speed. They were going out to sea. Eric swore that they were not buzzards, balloons or meteorites. Moreover, he is definitely not the type that "sees things." A few weeks later a visitor from Carmel was witness to a similar phenomenon. She was so moved by the sight that she became almost hysterical. Tom Sawyer and Dorothy Weston reported lights dancing in front of their car on the way home from Monterey one night. The performance continued for over five minutes and was repeated subsequently. Ephraim Doner, whose two feet are definitely planted in the earth, was escorted for over five miles by mysterious brilliant-colored lights one evening on leaving our home. His wife and daughter were with him and corroborated his words.

It was also at Anderson Creek that Gerhart Muench used to practice—on an old upright that Emil White had borrowed from someone. Now and then Gerhart gave us a concert, on this same "distempered" clavichord. Motorists would occasionally pull up short in front of Emil's cabin to listen to Gerhart practise. When Gerhart was broke and discouraged, often in a suicidal mood, I would urge him (seriously) to move the piano out, put it alongside the road, and do his stuff. I had a notion that if he would do it often enough some impresario would happen along and offer him a concert tour. (Gerhart is known all over Europe for his piano concerts.) But Gerhart never fell for the idea. Certainly it would have been vulgar and showy, but Americans dote on that sort of thing. Think of the publicity he might have had, had some enterprising soul discovered him sitting by the roadside hammering his way through Scriabin's ten sonatas!

But what I want to say about Anderson Creek—aside from the house that Jack built, complete with shower and toilet for less than three hundred dollars—is this. . . . Not only writers and artists live there, but ping-pong and chess players. (It was at Anderson Creek, let me say, that I rediscovered that curious book by a Chinese on the relation between the strategy employed by the Japanese at the Battle of Port Arthur and the Chinese game of chess. A most curious book, and if not as singular as the *I Ching* or *Book of Changes,* which Keyserling described as the most unique book ever written, it is nevertheless worth having a look at.) To begin with, I want to say that I have been playing chess ever since I was eight years old. I must add immediately that my game has improved but little in the last fifty-five years. Now and again my interest in the game is rekindled, sometimes through conversations with an expert like Ephraim Doner or through conversations with a man like Norman Mini, when he is talking military strategy. The last time it happened was as a result of talking with Charley Levitsky—of Anderson Creek.

Charley is one of those amiable, flexible, lovable persons who can play any game well, a man who plays for the love of playing, not merely to win. He will play any game you like—and beat you at it. It isn't that he *tries* so hard to win, he just can't help winning. After I had played a few games with him he suggested one day that it might prove more interesting if he were to give me a Queen. "A Queen and anything else you wish," is the way he put it. He won hands down, of course, and in short order. The experience promptly discouraged me. The following day, recounting the affair to my friend Perlès, who was then staying with us, I almost fell off my chair when he said: "A Queen and a rook, that's nothing! I'll give you all my pawns—and beat you." And by God, he did! He did it

three times in succession. Thinking that perhaps there was an un-
suspected advantage in making this kind of sacrifice, I said: "The
next game we play I'll give *you* all my pawns." I did and lost in
ten moves.

The moral of this story is: "Don't be gay when you're full of
shit!"

3.

Inch Connecticut was the name of the leading character in a day-
by-day serial which Paul Rink cooked up for the kids on Partington
Ridge. It began of itself, the serial, one morning while he and the
kids were waiting for the school bus to appear. It was a fantastic
yarn, by all accounts, which Paul managed to drag out over a
period of a year or more.

When I heard the name—Inch Connecticut—I was full of envy.
So much better than Isaac Dust or Saul Delirium! I wondered if it
was really his own invention.

The Inch Connecticut business was somewhat of a spur to me
inasmuch as I had just begun a serial of my own by way of entertaining the kids at dinner every evening. Mine had to do with a
little girl called Chama. (Pronounced *Chah*-ma.) Chama was the
real name of a real girl, the daughter of Merle Armitage. Merle and
his family had been to visit us one day, and his little girl, Chama,
who was about Valentine's age, had cast a spell over everyone. She
was very beautiful, quite self-possessed, and had the air of an

Indian princess. From the time she left until weeks later I heard nothing but Chama, Chama, Chama.

One night at dinner Val asked me where Chama was. ("Right now.") We were having a delicious meal, the wine was of the best, and the usual friction was absent. I was in fine fettle.

"Where's Chama?" I repeated. "Why, in New York, I guess."

"Where in New York?"

"At the St. Regis, most likely. That's a hotel." (I gave the St. Regis because I thought the name was colorful.)

"What is she doing there? Is her mother with her?"

Suddenly I had an inspiration. Why not give them a spiel about this beautiful little girl all alone in a swanky hotel in the middle of New York? Nothing to it! And with that I began what, all unknowingly, turned out to be a serial for the next few weeks.

Naturally they wanted me to serve it up at *every* meal, not just at dinner. But I squelched that idea quickly. I said that *if they behaved themselves*—what a loathsome expression—I would continue the story every evening, at dinner.

"Every evening?" queried little Tony, strangely moved.

"Yes, *every evening,*" I repeated. That is, *if you behave yourselves!*

They didn't, of course. What kids do? And of course I didn't serve it up to them every evening, as I said I would, but that wasn't because they misbehaved.

We always resumed the yarn by having Chama ring for the elevator. For some reason that elevator—I suppose the St. Regis *has* elevators!—intrigued them more than any other detail in my graphic description of scenes and events. It used to irritate me sometimes, the elevator business, because in working up the story I took pride in inventing the craziest sort of situations. Just the same, we always had to start the session with Chama ringing for the elevator.

("Make her go up and down the elevator again, Daddy!")

The angle which never ceased to puzzle them was—how did

Chama, who was just a little girl, manage all by herself in a great big city like New York? To be sure, I had laid the ground for this by giving them a bird's-eye view of New York. (Tony had never been farther than Monterey and Val had been to San Francisco just once.)

"How many people are there in New York, Daddy?" Tony would ask over and over.

And I would say, over and over: "About ten million."

"That's a lot, ain't it?" he would say.

"You bet! A hell of a lot! More than you can count."

"I bet there's a hundred million people in New York, aren't there, Daddy? A thousand million million."

"That's right, Tony."

Then Val: "There are *not* a hundred million people in New York, are there, Daddy?"

"Of course not!"

To get them off the subject . . . "Listen, nobody knows how many people there are in New York. That's the truth. Where were we, anyway?"

Then one of them would pipe up: "She's in bed having her breakfast, don't you remember?"

"Yeah, she just rang for the bellhop to come so she could tell him what she wants for breakfast. He has to take the elevator from the bottom, don't he, Dad?"

Of course I had endowed Chama with the most elegant, sophisticated manners. Had she been anything like the girl I described, in real life, her father would have disowned her. But Val and Tony thought she was real smart. Real cute, if you know what I mean.

"What did she always say, Daddy, when the boy knocked at her door?"

"*Entrez, s'il vous plaît!*"

"That's French, ain't it, Daddy?"

"It sure is. But Chama could speak several languages, did you know that?"

"Like what?"

"Like Spanish, like Italian, like Polish, like Arabic. . . ."

"That's no language!"

"What ain't no language?"

"*Arabic.*"

"O.K., Tony, me lad, what is it then?"

"It's a bird . . . or somethin'."

"It is *not* a bird, is it, Daddy?" pipes Val.

"It's a language," I said, "but nobody speaks it except the Arabs." (Nothing like giving them correct information right from the cradle.)

"We don't really care what she spoke," said Val. "Go on! What did she do after breakfast?"

That was a good lead. I had been wondering myself what Chama was to do after breakfast. Now I had to think fast.

Maybe a bus ride wouldn't be so bad. Up Fifth Avenue to the Bronx Zoo. The Zoo ought to hold them for three nights in a row. . . .

Getting Chama showered and dressed, ringing for the maid to do her hair and that sort of thing, telephoning the manager to find out which bus to take and, above all, waiting for the elevator to climb to the 59th story, took considerable time and ingenuity. By the time Chama hit the sidewalk, dressed like a starlet and ready to do the sights, I was beginning to weaken. My desire was to transfer her to the Zoo as quickly as possible, but no, they insisted on learning what caught Chama's eye (she was on the top deck) as the bus slowly wended its way up Fifth Avenue.

I gave them as good a description as I could of the streets and the sights I loathe. I didn't start from Fifty-ninth Street either, but from the Flatiron Building at Twenty-third Street and Broadway. To be exact, I started from the Western Union office there, from the ground floor, where I once had my headquarters, my last headquarters. They weren't much impressed, I must say, by the news that a new life had begun for me the day I walked out of that office and strolled up Broadway feeling like an emancipated slave. They wanted to look at the stores and shops, the signs, the crowds; they wanted to know all about that fruit juice stand at Times Square where for a dime one could get the tallest glass of delicious ice-cold fresh fruit juice, any and all flavors. (California, the land of milk and honey, of nuts and fruit, has no such stands.)

Chama meanwhile, seated beside a garrulous old woman with a bag of peanuts, is all agog. The woman is pointing out the high spots and Chama is helping her get rid of the peanuts. "You must keep an eye on your purse," says the old lady. "New York is full of thieves."

"You were a thief once, weren't you, Dad?" says Tony.

I try to brush him off but he wants to go into it.

"You were in prison and you escaped by digging a hole in the wall," says Val. "That was in Africa, when you were in the Foreign Legion, wasn't it, Daddy?"

"That's right, Val."

"But you *were* a thief, weren't you, Dad?" says Tony.

"Well, yes and no. I was a horse thief. That's a little different. I never stole money from children."

"You see, Val!"

Fortunately, we were just passing Rockefeller Center. I pointed out the ice skaters.

"Why doesn't it ever freeze in California?" asked Tony.

"Because it never gets cold enough." (That was an easy one.)

Central Park impressed them. So big, so beautiful. I didn't say anything about the cops creeping around in the bushes at night, looking for hungry lovers. Instead I told them how I used to go horseback riding every morning before going to work.

"You promised us a horse, remember?"

"Yeah, when are we going to get it?"

Passing an old mansion on the right, I thought of the days when I used to deliver clothes for Isaac Walker & Sons along this forbidding stretch. I thought of old man Hendrix particularly and how he lived all alone with a retinue of liveried servants. What a testy bugger he was, even when his liver gave him no trouble! I thought also of the Roosevelt family, the father, Emlen, and his three tall sons, all bankers, walking four abreast every morning, winter or summer, rain or shine, down Fifth Avenue to Wall Street, and back again after "work." They wore canes but no overcoats, no gloves. Wonderful to take a promenade like that every day, if you can afford it. My "promenades" up and down Fifth Avenue were of quite another character. More of a prowl than an airing. And without a cane, of course.

I cut the narrative that evening at the entrance to the Zoo. I forgot, beginning the next instalment, that I had left Chama searching for the elephants. Absent-mindedly I had switched to the Aquarium, down at the Battery. (The Aquarium was quite a hangout of mine in the days of the Atlas Portland Cement Company. Lacking the money to eat lunch, I used to pass the time studying marine life.) Anyway, just as I had worked them up over the ink fish, Val suddenly remembered that Chama was at the Zoo. So, back to the Zoo, where we strolled about for seven nights, not three or four. In fact, I began to think we'd never be able to extricate ourselves from the fascinating haunts of the beasts.

Thus it went, from one scene to another, including a ferryboat ride to Staten Island (the home of the damned) and another to Bedloe's Island, where we climbed up the inside of the Statue of Liberty. (Here a digression on the little statue of liberty at the Pont de Grenelle, Paris.) Night after night it went on, with detours and switchbacks, and now and then a trip to Coney Island or Rockaway Beach. Sometimes it was summer and sometimes it was winter; they didn't seem to notice the sudden changes of season.

Occasionally they demanded to know where Chama got all the money she was spending day in and day out. I answered (expertly) by explaining that her father was a rich man and that he had entrusted a sum of money to the manager of the hotel to be doled out to Chama as the manager saw fit.

"Never more than two dollars at a time," I added.

"That's a lot of money, ain't it, Dad?" From Tony.

"It's a lot for a little girl, yes. But then New York is a very expensive place to live." I didn't dare tell him what some little girls get for spending money from their rich parents.

"You never give us more than a quarter," said Val pensively.

"That's because we live in the country," said I. "There's no way to spend money here, is there?"

"There is *too*," said Tony. "I spent a dollar once at the State Park."

"Yeah, and you got sick afterwards," said Val.

"I don't like quarters," said Tony. "I like pennies."

"That's fine," said I. "The next time you ask for a quarter I'm going to give you pennies."

"How many?"

"Twenty-five."

"That's more than a quarter, ain't it?"

"A lot more," said I. "Especially for little boys."

When I had about run out of material I decided to fly Chama home to her parents, who were then living in New Mexico. I thought it would give them a thrill to get a description of the wonders of our vast and glorious continent from the air. So I hustled Chama off on one of the cheap lines which make frequent stops and a lot of crazy detours in order to take on freight.

From the La Guardia airport Chama took off one fine morning in the spring, headed west. I explained that the West only begins when you cross the Great Divide. They didn't seem to catch on very well, so I said: "The real West is the Far West . . . where the cowboys live and Indians and rattlesnakes." That meant California to them, especially the rattlesnakes. Anyhow, as I explained it, Chama would have to change planes at Denver. "Denver is off the path," I said, "but the plane has to stop there to pick up a live corpse."

"*A live corpse?*" screamed Val. "What's *that?*"

"It's a corpse that isn't quite cold," I said. I could see immediately that that explained nothing.

"Oh well, let's skip it," said I, and I had the plane land right in the center of a band of Indians dressed in full regalia, war paint, feathers, bells, drums, and everything.

Why Indians? First, to eradicate the live corpse, which was an error on my part, and second, to give Chama a rousing welcome from the true sons of the Far West. I told them that her father, Merle, had once lived with the Indians, that he had brought Caruso, Tetrazzini, Melba, Titta Ruffo, Gigli and other celebrities to meet the Indians—at exactly this spot.

"Who are they?" said Val. "The Cazzinis and Ruffios?"

"Oh, I forgot to tell you that. They were all famous opera singers."

"Yeah, soap opera," said Tony.

"I don't get it," said Val.

"Neither do I, except that Chama's father, this man Merle . . . you remember him! . . . he was once an impresario, a very famous one, too."

"Is it something like emperor?"

"Almost, dear Val, but not quite. An impresario is a man who finds places for singers to sing in—like Carnegie Hall and the Metropolitan Opera House."

"You never took *us* there!" piped Tony.

"He's a man"—I ignored the interruption—"who makes a living taking famous singers around the world. He gets paid for finding them jobs, do you see?" (They didn't see, but they swallowed it.) "Look," I said, hoping to make it *very* clear, "supposing that you, Val, became a great singer one day. (I always told you you had a lovely voice, didn't I?) Well, you would have to find a hall to sing in, wouldn't you?"

"Why?"

"Why, so that people could listen to you."

She shook her head as if she agreed, but I could tell that she was still nonplused.

"Couldn't I just sing over the radio?" she asked.

"Sure you could, but first someone would have to get you the job. Not everybody can sing over the radio."

"Did they travel all together?" asked Tony.

"When?" said I.

"When they went around the world like you said."

"Of course! Sure they did! That's how Merle got to know the Zulus and the Pygmies. . . . "

"Did they sing for the Zulus too?" Tony was real excited now. He remembered the Zulus because one of my fans, a woman living in Pretoria, had sent him a Zulu gun—a wooden one—as well as some other curious gifts of Zulu make. I had done my utmost, at the time, to play up the Zulus. A wonderful people, the Zulus. It's not every day that you get a chance to put in a good word for them.

However. . . . By this time they had forgotten where the hell we were. So had I.

Well, there's always Africa. Why not Africa? ("Dr. Livingstone, I presume?") It was a wonderful buggy ride, with side trips to the gold mines and a vain search for the Queen of Sheba's lost kingdom. I took them as far as Timbuctoo, an adventure which entailed a number of wild escapes from the hands of the bloody, fearsome Touaregs. The desert impressed them most of all, probably because there was no end to it; also because we got terribly thirsty and there was not a drop of water in sight. Every now and then we saw cities hanging upside down in the sky. That was fascinating too. Very. And finally we came to the animal kingdom: the lions and tigers, the elephants, the zebras, the ostriches, the gazelles, the giraffes, the apes, the champanzees, the gorillas. . . . They were all moving together, silently, peacefully, as in a choir. There was plenty of room for all, even for the crickets and the grasshoppers.

We might have gone on with the story to this day had not Paul Rink begun that Inch Connecticut yarn. Paul, being a teller of tales, knew how to put more oomph in his serial than I. He knew better how to create suspense. Besides, Inch Connecticut was right out of "Superman." As for my narrative, it belonged in the archives, along with Conan Doyle, Rider Haggard and such like. The wilds of Africa are nothing where Superman is concerned. And Inch Connecticut, from all I was able to gather, was a cut above Superman. So there I was, out on a limb. But happy for the experience. I had learned something. I learned one little thing which holds good even for holding the attention of adults. It's this: you can't feed it to them all at once. Even a lion has to take it piecemeal. A writer ought to know this from the start, but writers are funny animals: they have to learn things backwards sometimes.

Another thing. . . . When, for example, my son Tony remonstrates because I am about to grab a horror story out of his hand, when he says, "But little boys like murder once in a while!" one must never take such a remark seriously. Of course he isn't able to *read* the texts, he gets it from the pictures, and the pictures, as we all know, are thoroughly realistic. But it's one thing to look at picture books (the comics and the horrors) and it's another thing to sit through a bloodthirsty movie with a five-year-old who says he likes murder once in a while. *Kids don't like murder.* At least, not the way our movie heroes dish it out. They adore figures like King Arthur and Sir Lancelot, as I discovered to my joy and amazement. These heroes give fair fight. They don't beat men's brains to a pulp with a rock or a hunk of iron. They don't kick a man in the teeth when he's down. They charge with long bright lances, and when they use the broad sword it is a battle of skill as well as of strength. Usually a knight hands his opponent back his broken sword, if in the heat of the fray it is wrenched from his grip. Knights, the knights of old anyway, didn't stoop to pick up a broken bottle and mutilate a man's face with it. They fought according to a code, and even five-year-olds are susceptible to the glamour which surrounds codes of honor.

Maybe I'm wrong. Maybe city kids, even at the tender age of five, enjoy gangster films and all that goes into the making of them. But not country kids. . . .

4.

Every now and then, especially if there are no visitors for a spell, the water color mania comes over me. The "mania," as I call it, began in 1929, just a year before I left for France. Over the years I must have made about two thousand, most of which I have given away.

I've mentioned it elsewhere, but it's worth repeating, that the desire to paint was born one night when walking the deserted back streets of Brooklyn. My pal, O'Regan, was with me. We hadn't a cent between us and we were as hungry as wolves. (We had gone for a walk in the hope of meeting a "friendly face.") Passing the rear show window of a department store, we were arrested by a display of Turner's water colors. Reproductions, of course. That started it. . . .

I had never displayed the least ability to draw; at school, in fact, I was so hopelessly untalented that they used to permit me to skip the drawing class. I'm still bad at it, but it doesn't bother me much any more. Whenever I sit down to paint I feel happy; as I feel my way along I whistle and hum and sing and shout. Sometimes I put down the brush and do a jig.

I talk to myself too, as I paint. Aloud. (To encourage myself, I suppose.) Yes, I talk a blue streak. Crazy talk, what I mean. Friends have often said to me: "I like to drop in on you when you're painting, you make me feel good." (It's the contrary when I write. Then I'm usually withdrawn, abstracted, silent—often glum—neither a good host nor a good friend, nor even an "object" to communicate with.)

I say it was Turner's water colors which started it. But George Grosz had much to do with it too. Just a month or two before we stood in front of that department-store window my wife, June, had brought back from Paris an album of George Grosz' work called *Ecce Homo*. It had a self-portrait on the cover. When we came home from our jaunt that night, O'Regan and I, I sat down to copy that self-portrait. The resemblance I succeeded in achieving excited me so much that then and there I lost all my fears and inhibitions about drawing. It was only a year later that I arrived in Paris, where I soon got to know Hilaire Hiler and Hans Reichel. (Both Hiler and Reichel tried to give me instruction with regard to water color technique; they failed, naturally, because I am incapable of "taking lessons.") A little later I got to know Abe Rattner; watching him work, I was inspired to continue my efforts. Returning to America, in 1940, I had a few shows, none of them of much importance except the one in Hollywood where I almost sold out! It was at Beverly Glen, in "the green house," with John Dudley observing and criticizing over my shoulder as I worked on into the wee hours of the morning, that I began—in my own estimation, at least—to make real headway.

But the man I owe most to, in this connection, is my old boyhood friend, Emil Schnellock, who began as a commercial artist and now teaches art in a Southern college for girls. Back in 1929, it was Emil who encouraged me, guided me, inspired me. Droll now to think that he used to say then: "I wish I had the courage to paint like you, Henry." Meaning "wild and loose." Meaning with utter disregard for anatomy, perspective, structural composition, dynamic symmetry, and so forth. Naturally it was fun to paint as one pleased. Much better than doing realistic cans of tomatoes, milk bottles, sliced bananas and cream, or even pineapples.

Even in those days Emil had a wonderful familiarity with the world of art. It gave him tremendous pleasure to bring with him, when he visited me for a session, precious albums of reproductions of the masters. Often we spent the whole evening studying an album. Sometimes it would be a single reproduction of a master which would engage us in conversation of an evening. Say a painter like Cimabue, or Piero della Francesca. At that time my taste was thoroughly eclectic. I liked them all, it seemed, the good and the bad. The walls were always covered with cheap reproductions—Hokusai, Hiroshige, Bakst, Memling, Cranach, Goya, El Greco, Matisse, Modigliani, Seurat, Rouault, Breughel, Bosch.

Even that far back I was violently drawn to the work of children and of the insane. Today, if I were to choose—if I could afford the choice!—I would rather be surrounded by the work of children and the insane than by such "masters" as Picasso, Rouault, Dali or Cézanne. At various times I have endeavored to copy the work of a child or of a maniac. Studying, with intent to imitate, one of Tasha Doner's "masterpieces"—she was then a child of seven!—I made one of the best bridges ever. At that, it was not nearly as good as the bridge which Tasha had dashed off in my presence. As for the work of the insane, it takes a master (in my humble opinion) to even approach their style and technique. On days when the zany in me gets the upper hand, I make the attempt—but it never comes off. One has to get really insane to do it!

Sometimes I feel as if I must be slightly cracked, if not insane, to painstakingly copy a picture postcard which happens to strike my fancy. These picture postcards are continually arriving from all quarters of the globe. (Now and then I get a real jolt, as the day, for instance, when I received one from Mecca showing the Kaaba.) Often these cards are signed by people I don't know, by fans living in outlandish parts. ("Just read the *Colossus*. Wish you were here.")

By now I've accumulated a rather amazing collection of scenes: holy places, skyscrapers, ports and harbors, medieval castles and cathedrals, Chinese pagodas, donjons, exotic animals, the great rivers of the world, famous tombs, ancient scripts, Hindu gods and goddesses, primitive costumes, Oriental types, ruins, codices, celebrated nudes, the apples of Cézanne, the sunflowers of Van Gogh, every Crucifixion imaginable, the beasts and jungles of Rousseau, the monsters ("great men") of the Renaissance, the women of Bali, the samurai of old Japan, the rocks and waterfalls of old China,

Persian miniatures, the suburbs of Utrillo, Leda and the Swan (in all variations), the Pissing Boy (of Brussels), the odalisques of Manet, Goya, Modigliani, and, perhaps more than the works of any other painter, the magical themes of Paul Klee.

I honestly believe I have learned more—if I have learned at all—from looking at the work of other painters than in any other way. As with a book, I can look at a painting with the eyes of an aesthete as well as with the eyes of a man who is still struggling with the medium. Even bad paintings, I have found—even commercial art—yield food for thought. Nothing is bad when you look at it hungrily. (The first step in the art of appreciation.) Riding the subway in New York, how attentively—in those early days—I studied the folds and wrinkles of those Arrow Collar men!

Whether studying Nature is a help I am not so sure. Everyone will tell you that it is. But I'm speaking for my own incorrigible self. Certainly I've spent considerable time doing just this, particularly since living here in Big Sur. I doubt, though, that anyone looking at my landscapes (or seascapes) would be aware of the time and thought I give Mother Nature. Some are bewildered, some clap their hands (whether in glee or affright, I never know) when studying these compositions from Nature. Usually there is something in them which does not belong, something horrendous and unnatural which sticks out like a sore thumb. Perhaps these "flaws" are the result of an unconscious effort to insert my "trade-mark." To be quite honest, I'm never satisfied with doing plain Nature. Not in a painting, that is. It's quite otherwise when I'm alone with Nature, when I'm taking a walk in the forest or over the hills, or just paddling about on a deserted beach. Then Nature is all, and I, what's left of me, but an infinitesimal part of what I'm looking at. There's never any end to what one can see—just looking, not trying to observe anything in particular. Always, in such moods, comes that sublime moment when you "suddenly see." And you laugh all over, as we so aptly say. Does not Douanier Rousseau give us this sensation every time we look at his work? I mean, sudden sight and brimming laughter? Nearly all the "primitives" give us this sense of joy and wonder. With these masters of reality, who are usually anything but primitive, we are less concerned with how they viewed the world than how they felt toward it. They make us leap forward to embrace what we see; they make things almost unbearably real.

Here at Big Sur, at a certain time of the year and a certain time of the day only, a pale blue-green hue pervades the distant hills; it is an old, nostalgic hue which one sees only in the works of the old Flemish and Italian masters. It is not only the tone and color of distance, abetted by the magic fall of light, it is a mystical phenomenon, or so I like to think, born of a certain way of looking at the world. It is observable in the works of the older Breughel, for one. Strikingly present in the painting called "The Fall of Icarus," in which the peasant with his plough dominates the foreground, his costume just as enchanting and obsessional as the enchanting and obsessive sea far below him.

There are two magic hours of the day which I have only really come to know and wait for, bathe in, I might say, since living here. One is dawn, the other sunset. In both we have what I like to think of as "the true light": the one cold, the other warm, but both creating an ambiance of super-reality, or the reality behind reality. At dawn I look out to sea, where the far horizon is painted with bands of rainbow tints, and then at the hills that range the coast, ever entranced by the way the reflected light of dawn licks and warms the "backs of the drugged rhinoceroses." If there is a ship in sight the sun's bent rays give it a gleam and sparkle which is utterly dazzling. One can't tell immediately that it *is* a ship: it seems more like the play of northern lights.

Toward sundown, when the hills in back of us are flushed with that other "true light," the trees and scrub in the canyons take on a wholly different aspect. Everything is brush and cones, umbrellas of light—the leaves, boughs, stalks, trunks standing out separate and defined, as if etched by the Creator Himself. It is then one notices rivers of trees catapulting down the slopes! Or are they columns of soldiers (hoplites) storming the walls of the canyon? At any rate, at this hour one experiences an indescribable thrill in observing the spatial depths between the trees, between the limbs, boughs and branches, between the leaves. It is no longer earth and air, but light and form—heavenly light, celestial form. When this intoxicating reality reaches its height the rocks speak out. They assume more eloquent shapes and forms than the fossils of prehistoric monsters. They clothe themselves in vibrant-colored raiment glittering with metallic residues.

Fall and winter are the best times to get the "revelation," for then the atmosphere is clear, the skies more full of excitement, and the light of the sun, because of the low arc it describes, more effective. It's at this hour, after a light rain, that the hills are ringed with fuzzy trails which undulate with the undulating folds of the hills. Turning a bend, the hill before you stands out like the coat of an Airedale seen through a magnifying glass. So hoary does it look that one scans the horizon in search of a shepherd leaning against his crook. Memories of olden times return, the leavings of childhood reading: illustrations from story books, first gleanings of mythology, faded calendars, the chromos on the kitchen wall, bucolic prints on the walls of the man who extracted your tonsils. . . .

If we don't always start from Nature we certainly come to her in our hour of need. How often, walking the barren hills, I've stopped to examine a twig, a dead leaf, a fragrant bit of sage, a rare flower that has lingered on despite the killing heat. Or stood in front of a tree studying the bark, as if I had never before noticed that trunks are covered with bark, and that the bark as well as the tree itself leads its own life.

It's when the lupin has run its course, as well as the bluebonnets and the wild flowers, when the foxtails are no longer a menace to the dogs, when there is no longer a riot and profusion assailing the senses, that one begins to observe the myriad elements which go to make up Nature. (Suddenly, as I put it down now, Nature seems like a strange new word to me. What a discovery man made when he found the word, just one, to embrace this indescribable thesaurus of all enveloping life!)

Sometimes I come home on the double-quick, my mind so saturated with ideas and impressions that I feel I must hasten to make a few notes—for the morrow. If I have been writing, these thoughts and sensations have to do with pure irrelevancies. Useful ones, however, since they are often completed thoughts which had made themselves known in embryonic form months, even years, ago. This experience, which happens over and over, only convinces me the more that "we" create nothing, that "it" is doing it for us and through us, and that if we could really tune in, as it were, we would do as Whitman said—make our own Bibles. Indeed, when that dread "mind-machine" is working, the problem is how to take all that's coming over the waves. The same riot and profusion which I mentioned in connection with Nature evinces itself in the brain. Suddenly, this part of one which had been in abeyance, which one hardly knew was there, begins to exfoliate in all directions. The mind becomes a steaming jungle of thoughts.

There are other times when I seem to be in what I can only call an autodidactic mood. At such times I am instructing myself in the art of seeing with new eyes. I may be in a painting phase or getting ready to enter one. (These phases come over me like a sickness.) I will sit on the Angulo trail, facing the gigantic ten gallon hat at Torre Canyon, with a dog on either side of me—they go to school too—and look and look and look at a blade of grass, a deep shadow in the fold of a hill, a deer standing motionless, no bigger than a speck, or turn my gaze upon the churning lace which the sea makes around a clump of rock, or at the white collar of foam which fastens itself to the flanks of the "diplodoci," as I sometimes call the half-submerged beast-like mountains that rise up out of the ocean bed to bask in the sun. It's quite true, as Lynda Sargent used to say, that the Santa Lucia range is hermaphroditic. In form and contour the hills and mountains are usually feminine, in strength and vitality masculine. They look so very ancient, especially in the early morning light, and yet they are, as we know, only newly risen. The animals have done more to them than man, fortunately. And the wind and rain, the sunlight and moonlight still more. Man has known them only a short while, which accounts perhaps for the pristine quality which they still preserve.

If it be shortly after sunup of a morning when the fog has obliterated the highway below, I am then rewarded with a spectacle rare to witness. Looking up the coast toward Nepenthe, where I first stayed (then only a log cabin), the sun rising behind me throws an enlarged shadow of me into the iridescent fog below. I lift my arms as in prayer, achieving a wing-span no god ever possessed, and there in the drifting fog a nimbus floats about my head, a radiant nimbus such as the Buddha himself might proudly wear. In the Himalayas, where the same phenomenon occurs, it is said that a devout follower of the Buddha will throw himself from a peak—"into the arms of Buddha."

But, like the dreamy, wispy fog, I too am drifting. And how good it is just to drift! All the observations so painstakingly noted and memorized evaporate as I leave my place of contemplation to amble homeward. They evaporate, yet they are not lost. The essence remains, stored away in one's intangible parts, and when they are needed they will appear, like well-trained servants. Even if I do not succeed in making a wave as I knew it in a moment of "sudden seeing," I at least will be able to capture the waviness of the wave, which is almost better. Even if I forget how certain leaves are shaped, I at least will remember to denticulate them.

What is maddening is not to be able to capture the light which permeates the world of Nature. Light is the one thing we cannot steal, imitate, or even counterfeit. Even a Van Eyck, a Vermeer, a Van Gogh can but give a feeble illusion of its mysterious splendor. I recall the pang of joy which I experienced on viewing for the first time, in the cathedral at Ghent, Van Eyck's "Mystic Lamb." That, it seemed to me, was the closest I would ever get to the divine

light of Nature. It was, of course, a light that came from within—
a holy light, a transcendent light. It had been achieved by artifice,
the most sublime, skillful artifice, which, if we understood it
properly, if we were receptive—and how is it we are not?—might
yield us intimations of that imperishable light which outshines all
the suns of the unspeakably vast multiverse in which we are
drowned.

I want to come back to Tasha Doner for a moment. Whenever
I get desperate over my inability to paint what I see or feel, I always
summon Tasha to mind. When it comes to horses, for example,
Tasha can start at the front or the rear end—it makes no difference—
and always turn out a horse. If she tackles a tree, same thing. She'll
begin either with the leaves and branches or with the trunk—but it
always makes a tree, not a whisk broom or a bouquet of tin foil.
If she happens to begin at the left-hand side of the paper, she moves
straight across until she reaches the right-hand margin. Or vice
versa. If she starts in the middle, with a house, let us say, she first
puts in all the doors, windows, chimney and roof, the steps too, and
then proceeds to landscape the grounds. The sky she usually puts
in last, if there's room for a sky. If not, what matter? We don't
always need a sky, do we? The point is that between her thoughts
and her very busy fingers there's never a gap. She goes straight
to the mark, filling every inch of space yet leaving air to breathe
and perfume to inhale. There are crayon compositions on her walls
which I prefer to any Picasso, as I said before, and even to a Paul
Klee, which is saying more. Every time I visit the Doners I walk
reverently up to her pictures and study them anew. And every time
I study them I find something new in them.

Sometimes I wake up of a morning and, almost before I'm out of
bed, I say to myself: "Today I'll do a Cézanne, by God!" Meaning
one of those fugitive water-color landscapes which at first glance
seem to be nothing but notes and suggestions. After a few heart-
breaking efforts I realize that what I've got in hand is not going
to be a Cézanne at all but just another Henry Miller what-you-

may-call-it. Feeling hopelessly inadequate, I think to myself how wonderful it would be if Jack were to drop in. Jack Morgenrath of Livermore Ledge. There are times when it would be a real boon to put a few pertinent questions to a skilled painter friend like Jack. (Let me say in passing that this Jack knows how to work in fresco, oil, tempera, water color, gouache, crayon, pastelles, ink, any damned medium; he can also build a house, lay sewers, fix a watch, dismantle a motor—and put it together again!—or build a mouse trap which won't kill or maim the mouse but merely hold it captive until he is ready to release it.)

In a sober mood I realize that Jack is not the person to ask questions of the sort I have in mind. To begin with, it would take all day to get an answer, assuming he didn't ignore the question altogether. When you put a question to Jack it's like putting a coin in the juke box. There's a pause, an eternity of a pause sometimes, during which you can hear your question being referred back to the prime question-and-answer contraption which lies hidden in the exact center of the universe. It takes an eternity to reach the source, as I say, and an eternity for the response to travel back to Jack's lips, which usually begin to flutter before he is able to articulate. This is an idiosyncrasy I like in Jack. At first I thought he was trying to be difficult, trying to make things more complex than they naturally are. But I soon discovered otherwise. The thing to know about Jack is that he gives everything the same, equally serious consideration. If you show him a door that's out of kilter, he looks at it, examines it from every possible angle, meditates a while, scratches his poll, then says: "Looks like a major operation." Which means you may have to tear the house down to set the door plumb. But to Jack, tearing a house down is nothing. He'd tear a mountain apart if it really stood in his way. All of which is to say that Jack is by nature what we would call a Fundamentalist. He's a Fundamentalist and an Absolutist. Yet smooth and flexible, tolerant and gracious. An anomaly, in other words.

He is also wise beyond his years. If he thinks and moves like eternity itself, it's because he's *living* in a state of eternity. Thus, whether he's asked to build a fence, lay a sewer, prune an orchard, dig a ditch, repair a busted chair, or lay bricks, Jack goes about it with that somnambulistic clairvoyance which drives "active" people crazy. But when Jack is finished with a task, it's done. It stays done. And if you ask him a question it's answered full and straight, answered for good, so to speak.

When first I came to know him I had the impression that he was a bit of a braggart. Particularly with regard to his artistic talents. He never said explicitly that he was a past master of this or that, whatever it might be, but he left the impression that he had gone into it so thoroughly that there was no need for anyone (let alone Jack!) to explore it further. Listening to him in this vein I was often tempted to put a pencil in his hand and say: "Draw me a hat, will you?" Of course, Jack's retort would be: "What kind of hat?" And—"Do you want a rolled brim or a straight brim?" Followed by—"Personally, I think a fedora is what you have in mind."

But what I'm leading up to (in the best Morgenrath manner) is this—Jack gave me answers to many unvoiced questions. He gave answers which settled some of my problems forever. I may have been thinking painting, but Jack was thinking, as he habitually does, of what makes painting painting. Or, to put it in a nutshell, of what makes anything anything. Thus, in dwelling on the technique employed in this or that medium, Jack would convey to me subtly, forcefully and incontrovertibly the necessity for right thinking, right breathing, right being. It was always a gratuitous lesson I received—and it always set me flat on my ass.

Whenever Jack takes leave of me I invariably get to thinking about the Chinese, the Japanese, the Javanese, the Hindus. About their way of life and the meaning which they have given to life. Principally about the ever present element of art which permeates all Oriental life. And about reverence, reverence not only for the Creator but for the created, reverence for one another, for the creature world and the plant world, for stones and minerals, and for skill and talent in whatever guise it may present itself.

How does Jack manage to reflect this aura of ancient wisdom, benevolence and bliss? Jack is not an Oriental, though perhaps the next thing to it, by blood. Jack issued from the Polish Corridor, as did Doner, Marc Chagall, and so many poets, painters and thinkers who were spared the knout, the hot iron, the horses' hooves, all the mutilations of body and soul which the Slavs in their sadistic intoxication practice *ad nauseam.* Transplanted to the Brooklyn ghetto, Jack somehow contrived to forsake the ways of his ancestors and the ways of his neighbors, the latter already poisoned by the American virus of comfort and success. He even forsook art in his determination to free himself, to make his life an art. Yes, Jack is one of those rare souls who has no ambition whatever—except to lead the good life. And he makes no fuss about leading the good life either. He just leads it.

And so, when I'm studying a postcard from Mecca, or one of Utrillo's suburban scenes, I say to myself, "one thing is as good as another." *Am I happy? Does it make fun?* I forget about the good life; I forget my duties and responsibilities. I even forget about the poison oak which is cropping out strong again. When I paint I feel good. And if it makes *me* feel so good, the chances are it will make the other fellow feel good too. If it doesn't, I should worry. . . . Now what were those pigments I meant to use when looking at the hills a while ago? Oh yes, yellow ochre, Indian yellow, brown-red, raw sienna and a dash of rose madder. Perhaps a touch of raw umber too. Good! It'll probably look like baby shit, but who cares? *Moi, je suis l'ange de cocasse.* Somewhere I've just got to introduce a blob of *laque gérance.* What beautiful names the pigments have! Sound even better in French than in English. And don't forget, I remind myself, when you mail that book to what's his name in Immensee—or is it Helsingfors?—don't forget to wrap it in a "failed" water color! Strange, how people suddenly develop an appreciation for that which is tossed away!

Were I to ask fifty cents for a misfire job it would be refused me, but when I wrap a book with it—as if it weren't worth a fart—the recipient behaves as if he had been made a priceless gift.

It's like when I meet Harrydick in the woods. He's always bending down to pluck something. Sometimes it's only a dead leaf. "Look at that! Isn't it gorgeous?" he'll say. *Gorgeous?* That's a big word. I look at whatever it may be—I've seen it a thousand times and never noticed it—and sure enough, it *is* gorgeous. In fact, lying there in Harrydick's capable, sensitive hand, it's more than gorgeous . . . it's phenomenal, unique. Walking along—he's still holding it in his hand, will examine it even more lovingly when he gets home—he begins a dithyramb about the things which lie in one's path, the things we tread on daily, never even aware that we have crushed them under our heels. He talks about form, structure, purpose, about the unthinkable, inconceivable collaboration that goes on under the ground and above the ground, about fossils and folklore, about patience and tenderness, about the worries of the little creatures, about their cunning, skill, fortitude, and so on and so on, until I feel that it's not a dead leaf he's holding in his hand but a dictionary, encyclopaedia, manual of art, philosophy of history all rolled into one.

Now and then, often in the middle of a problem, I wonder if the fellow who was here the day before riffling through my water colors, I wonder if when he paused to look twice at a certain "monstrosity" he had the faintest notion of the circumstances in which it was conceived and executed? Would he believe me, I wonder, if I told him that it was done one-two-three, just like that, and five more to boot, while Gerhart Muench was practicing on my broken-down piano? Would he have the least inkling that it was Ravel who inspired it? Ravel of *Gaspard de la nuit?* It was while Gerhart was going over and over the "Scarbo" that I suddenly lost all control of myself and began to paint music. It was like a thousand tractors going up and down my spine at high speed, the way Gerhart's playing affected me. The faster the rhythm, the more thunderous and ominous the music, the better my brushes flew over the paper. I had no time to pause or reflect. On! On! Good Garbo! Sweet Garbo! Good Launcelot Garbo, Scarbo, Barbo! Faster! Faster! Faster! The paper was dripping paint on all sides. I was dripping with perspiration. I wanted to scratch my ass, but there was no time for it. On with it, Scarbo! *Dance,* you gazabo! Gerhart's arms are moving like flails. Mine too. If he goes pianissimo, and he can go pianissimo just as beautifully as he can fortissimo, I go pianissimo too. Which means I spray the trees with insecticide, cross my *t*'s and dot my *i*'s. I don't know where I am or what I'm doing. Does it matter? In one hand I have two brushes, in the other three, all of them saturated with pigment. So it goes, from one painting to another, and all the while singing, dancing, rocking, weaving, tottering, mumbling, cursing, shouting. Just for good measure I slide one of them to the floor and grind my heels into it. (Slavic ecstasy.) By the time Gerhart has sandpapered his finger tips I've turned out a half-dozen water colors (complete with coda, cadenza and vermiform appendix) that would scare the daylight out of a buzzard, octaroon or tomtit.

So I say, always look twice if you happen to notice a water color signed with my name. It may have been inspired by Ravel, Nijinsky or one of the Nijni Novgorod boys. Don't toss it away because it looks like a failure. Look for the trade-mark: the iron heel or the well-tempered clavichord. It may have a history behind it. Another day I'll take you to Hollywood and show you the twenty-five water colors Leon Shamroy was crazy enough to pay money for. Then you'll see how even a misfire painting, if properly framed, can make your mouth water. Leon paid me a good price for those water colors, bless his heart! He paid an even better price for the frames in which they hang. Two of them he later returned to me, freight prepaid. Wouldn't stand the test, these two. The test imposed by the magnificent frames, is what I mean. With the paintings I got the frames too. Which was mighty white of Leon, I thought. I tore up the water colors and inserted blank paper in the frames. Imitating Balzac, I wrote on the blank face of the one: "This is a Kandinsky." And on the other: "This is a piece of paper white on which we write our word or two and then comes night."

Signing off now. Time to eat.

5.

"Now works the peace and quiet of Scheveningen like a anaesteatic," as my friend Jacobus Hendrik Dun wrote me, circa 1922 or '23.

I often think of this quaint line when I'm at the sulphur baths and not a soul around, just sea, sky and seals. A few hours of communion with the elements eliminates all the detritus accumulated at the base of the skull as a result of entertaining visitors, reading boring manuscripts, answering letters from poets, professors and imbeciles of all denominations. It's amazing how easily and naturally the inner springs resume their functioning once you surrender to sheer idleness.

At the baths I usually run into Oden Wharton, an octogenarian who had the good sense to quit a hundred-thousand-a-year job, as executive of a steel corporation, at the age of forty-five. And do absolutely nothing! Oden has been doing it perfectly for almost forty years now and his conscience doesn't trouble him in the least. You wonder, when you talk to Oden, would the world really go to pots if we chucked everything and lived like the lilies in the field. He hasn't a penny now, dear Oden, but God looks after him. Getting rid of the fortune he had accumulated as a man of affairs took him a number of years. Some of them, quite a few, he spent in the Maine woods with a guide, hunting and fishing. Idyllic days, to hear Oden talk about them.

Now that he's really retired, a couple named Ed and Betty Eames look after Oden. By "look after" I mean—wait patiently until he drops dead of heart failure.* Oden is never ill, neither does time hang heavy on his hands. His days pass much like the butterfly's. If there's someone to talk to, he'll talk; if not, he reads. Twice a day, regular as Immanuel Kant, he strolls over to the baths and back again, a walk of about a mile. That's just sufficient to keep his muscles from atrophying. The reading matter which is piled up beside his armchair is innocuous enough to put him to sleep by eight o'clock; if it doesn't, the radio will.

I always enjoy my talks with Oden. But I enjoy still more talking to "Butch." "Butch," as we call him, is the Eames' little boy. He's about the same age as my Tony and blessed with the disposition of an angel. Now and then I drop Tony off to play with Butch while I go take a bath. They are about as different in temperament as the two faces of a coin.

It's only a year or so since Butch has been able to walk properly. He was born clubfooted, cross-eyed, and with a growth or protuberance on his nose which threatened to make a Cyrano de Bergerac of him. After numerous operations, with long sieges in the hospital, all these defects have been eradicated. Perhaps I am wrong in attributing his unbelievable good nature to the privations, frustrations and suffering he endured as a child. But that is the impression I have, and whether right or wrong, the fact is that Butch is like no other child in these parts.

He always comes running to greet you, a little wobbly on his feet still, his eyes still threatening to capsize any minute. But what

* Which is what he did a few months after the above was written.

a warmth and sincerity, what a radiance emanates from his shining countenance! He makes you feel as if you were a divine emissary, as if he saw you through a vision.

"I've got new shoes, see!" He puts out a foot as if it were made of gold or alabaster. "I can run now. Want to see?" And he runs a few yards, turns abruptly, then fixes you with a heavenly beam.

What can be more wonderful for a boy of seven than to walk, run, skip, jump? When Butch does it, you realize that if we possessed nothing more than this animal endowment we would still be blessed. Butch makes physical exertion seem like divine play. Indeed, every gesture which animates him is like a prayer of thanksgiving, like the rejoicing of an angelic being.

Like every youngster, he appreciates gifts. But with Butch, if you were to hand him an ordinary stone from the field, telling him it was for *him,* he would accept it and thank you for it with the same grateful exuberance that another lad would display only if handed a gold-plated fire engine. The surgeon's knife, the long days and nights alone in bed, the absence of playmates, the waiting, the hoping, the yearning he must have known in the very depths of his soul, have all contributed to "tenderize" his nature. He seems utterly incapable of comprehending that anyone would want to do him ill, even a rowdy, insensitive playmate. In his innocence, sublime to witness, he expects of others only goodness and kindness. There isn't an ounce of malice or envy in him. Nor resentment, nor craving. Sure, he would love to have playmates his own size, his own age, and not too rough and not too nasty, but if he can't, and usually he can't, he will make do with the birds, the flowers, a few odd toys and an inexhaustible fund of good nature. When he bursts into talk it's like a bird that's suddenly begun to warble in your ear.

Butch never asks for anything, unless it be something you happened to promise him. Even then, he asks in such a way—supposing you had forgotten to keep your promise—that you feel as if he had forgiven you in advance. Butch couldn't possibly think of anyone as "a stinker." Nor as a "sucker." Should he stumble, and really hurt himself, he doesn't sit and whine until you pick him up. No sir! With tears in his eyes he picks himself up and throws you one of his golden smiles which, in his language, means: "It was those foolish old feet of mine!"

One day, shortly after the last operation on his eyes, Butch paid us a visit. Tony was away and the old tricycle he had abandoned was standing in the garden. Butch asked if he might ride it. He had never ridden a bike, and to make matters more complicated, he was still not seeing right. He was seeing double, as he told me. He said it, of course, as if it were a delightful sensation. I helped him a bit in learning to steer, to back up, and so on. It took him no time to catch on. His feet were still rather awkward; every time he made a sharp turn he tilted at a dangerous angle. Now and then he toppled off, but was up again in a jiffy, always beaming, always rejoicing.

When it came time to go I knew that Butch had to have that bike. It wasn't much of anything anymore but it would do to practice on. I explained to him that as soon as Tony came home I would ask him if he would surrender it. (I knew he would because that would mean a new one for *him*.) I told Butch I would be going to town next day, that I would buy Tony a new bike and bring him the old one.

"Will you be down tomorrow then?" were his last words.

When he had gone I could think of nothing but that look on his face when he heard that he was to inherit Tony's old bike. Naturally, I was up and off to town early the next day. Unfortunately I couldn't get a bike Tony's size immediately at the department store where I had a charge account. And I didn't have the cash to buy one elsewhere.

(Everything costs a forutne these days. I bought a racing wheel from a six-day bike rider at Madison Square Garden in the old days for the price they now ask for a kid's bike.)

I should have gone to see Butch that evening and explained the situation to him. But I didn't. I just hoped that he wouldn't be too feverish—and that he would forgive me, in his usual way, when I did show up. It was four or five days later when I turned up with the old bike which was concealed in the back of the car. As I drove up there was Butch waiting for me, as if it were the appointed time. I could see that he was on the *qui vive*. At the same time I couldn't help but observe that he was holding himself in in case of a disappointment.

"Well, Butch, how are you?" I cried, getting out and giving him a warm hug. As he embraced me he looked furtively over my shoulder, toward the interior of the car.

"I'm just fine," he said, his face alight, his hands dancing with glee.

Not to keep him in suspense a moment longer than was necessary, I opened the back of the car and yanked the bike out.

"OH!" he exclaimed, quite beside himself now, "So you brought it! I thought maybe you forgot." Then he told me how he had been looking for me every day, every time a car pulled into their driveway.

I felt wretched, first for having held him up so long, and second for handing him a bike in such condition. The seat was coming off, the handle-bars were twisted, and I think one of the pedals was missing. Butch didn't seem to mind. He said his grandfather would put it in shape for him.

On the way home I got to speculating on Butch's future. He had something, I felt, that few American boys possess. If the army didn't get him and use him for cannon fodder, he might go far. He was already a diminutive Ramakrishna. I mean, one of those rare products of the soil—in any age, any clime—an ecstatic being, a being filled to overflowing with love. A passage from a book came to mind—about the children of Chungking:

"There is so much goodness in these waifs of Chungking that I begin to believe again, as I used to believe many years ago, that it would be much better if the world were given over to children, and anyone reaching the age of twelve should be painlessly executed."*

Despite all the talk about living for one's children, despite all that we do for our children—usually too much—the American child is not happy with his parents nor, what is worse, is he happy with himself. He senses that he is in the way, that he is a problem, that he is being bought off. No American educationalist could possibly write about the harmonious relationship between parents and children as Keyserling has written about the Japanese, in his *Travel Diary*. But then no European, or Oriental, could possibly describe the American woman as Keyserling has the Japanese. Let me quote a paragraph:

"There can only be one opinion about Japanese women on the part of anyone who has a little feeling for style, that is to say, on the part of any man who does not demand the performances of a hippopotamus from a butterfly: the Japanese woman is one of the most perfect, one of the few absolutely accomplished products of this creation. . . . It is really too delightful to behold women who are nothing but gracefulness; who pretend nothing but what they really are, who do not want to show off anything but what they can really do, whose heart is cultivated to the extreme. At the bottom of their souls there are not too many European girls who want anything more and anything else than their sisters in the Far East— they want to please, they want to be femininely attractive, and everything else, including intellectual interests, is a means to an end for them. How many of those who apparently have only mental aspirations would not breathe a sigh of relief if they could disregard this circuitous means of charm, which it is difficult for them to dispense with in their world, and present themselves as the Japanese women do! But this is just what they would succeed in with difficulty, what those who attempt it fail in. The modern girl is already too conscious to be perfect in a naive form, too knowing for an existence of pure gracefulness, above all, she is too rich in her nature

* *Forever China,* by Robert Payne (New York: Dodd, Mead & Co., 1945).

to be easily perfected at all. In lovableness no modern Western beauty can match herself with a well-educated Japanese lady."*

I mentioned earlier in this book that the new aspect of Big Sur reveals itself through the children who have been added to the population since 1944, when I first arrived. No doubt children played an important role in pioneer days, when the Pfeiffers, the Harlans, the Posts and other early settlers opened up the region. Today most of these children are grandparents. Today there are no longer any families which, like the old Harlan family, was sufficient unto itself. (For several decades the Harlans got along without using money.) No, the old days are gone forever. The new day is for the children who are crowding the country school.

The striking thing, to me, about these youngsters is their individuality. Each one is a personality, with his own well-defined character, his own unique way of behaving. Some, like the Daytons' boy, whose father is a woodcutter, live quite removed from the community, and are taught at home. Some, too young to attend school, accompany their fathers to work daily, and seem no worse for wear than if they had remained at home with their overburdened mothers. Sometimes the mother, between phases of marriage and divorce, has to take a job; then the child fends for himself most of the day, and because of it, becomes most self-sufficient.

I think of one little playmate of Tony's whom I am particularly fond of—Mike Hougland, or "Little Mike," as everyone calls him. Little Mike was already a "character" at the age of four. Once he stayed with us for a week while his mother went on a trip. What a marvelous addition to the family he was! Never have I seen a child so gentle, so contained, and so silent. No matter what you asked him he always said Yes, but in such a wee winnie winkle of a voice as to be almost inaudible. Even when he was offered food which he didn't like, or wasn't used to, he would come up with a

<hr>

* *The Travel Diary of a Philosopher,* by Count Hermann Keyserling (New York: Harcourt, Brace & Co., 1925), Vol. II.

tiny little Yes. Sometimes, to tease him, to see if he *could* say No, I would ask him if he would like me to spank him. And he would reply: "Yes." Sometimes he varied it and said: "Yes, please."

(The first word Tony learned to say was No. He didn't say it, he boomed it. NO! It took a year before anyone could make him say Yes.)

Yes, Mike was adorable. And, like that Sparkie on the radio (the program kids love most!), more of an elf than a boy. Sparkie, as everyone knows, talks a blue streak. And his way of speaking is abominable, atrocious, though the kids seem to love it. It took me days to catch on to his "elfin" lingo.

Mike's charm lies in his silence. It is a most knowing, meaningful silence. There is in it something of the sage and something of the saint. A saint more on the order of Joseph di Cupertino. Those who have read Cendrars' wonderful pages on him may recall that he was farmed out to the monks because he was such an utterly incapable dullard. In the eyes of God he was one of the blessed ones. It was his ecstatic love which sustained him in his spectacular flights of levitation.

There is nothing of the dullard about Mike, however silent, loving and elflike he may be. On the contrary, he is a constant source of wonder and mystification. He knows just what he wants and he usually gets what he wants, but quietly, unobtrusively, almost selflessly. I once bought Tony an expensive fire engine with the last money I had in the bank; a week later it was in Mike's possession. They had made a dicker. It was a fair enough trade too, since Tony had had enough of the fire engine three days after he acquired it. (Sounds horrible, but it's the God's truth.)

Mike can take a broken toy, any discarded object, indeed, and find it of absorbing interest for months on end. When he wishes to have an airplane—one of those wooden ones that cost only ten cents—he asks for just one, not a dozen at a time. He has a genius for making them perform record flights. And if they break he knows how to mend them. Not Tony. Tony takes after his father, who prefers to abandon a car on the highway and walk to the nearest town rather than lift the hood and soil his fingers. It isn't even a matter of soiling the fingers, really . . . it's that his father knows in advance that he is incapable of fixing anything, particularly mechanical things.

The three Lopez boys, on the other hand, will know how to fix anything, right anything, adapt themselves to anything, long before they become adults. The Lopez family, I must say at once, is my idea of a model family. The father, of Mexican origin, is one of those underpaid workers that any man in his right senses would give his right hand to keep forever as an employee. The mother is a mother in the real sense of the term. From Mexico they brought with them those precious attributes which Americans tend to underestimate and even to exploit: patience, tenderness, respect, reverence, gentleness, humility, forbearance and abounding love. The Lopez children reflect these virtues of the parents. There are three boys, two of them identical twins, and a girl who is the eldest. They get along like one big family. Almost like a holy family, I should say. With them the word family means something. Nothing can threaten it from within and probably nothing from without either. They have had a hard life here in "the land of the free and the brave," as Mexicans always do. But they have won the love and respect of all who know them and have watched them struggle.

When one of the restless mothers in the community wishes to dump her child on someone for a day, or a day and a night, or a week, or even for a month, it is to the Lopez family she invariably turns. Rosa Lopez never says No. The word is not in her vocabulary. *"Si señora!"* she says, and she takes the child into the fold as she would her own. And there, in the immaculate, overcrowded hut which they call home, this American child may see for the first time a picture of the Madonna, a taper burning before a crucifix, a rosary hanging from a nail in the wall. Perhaps also for the first time this American child will see an adult joining hands in prayer, lowering his eyes, repeating the litany. I am not a Catholic; I have no use for all the mummery and flummery which goes with

Catholicism. But I have a profound respect for the Lopez family, which is an ardent and a devout Catholic family. When I visit them I feel as one ought to feel, but seldom does, after visiting a church. I feel as if God's presence had made itself manifest. And though I am against rosaries, crucifixes, ikons and chromos of the Madonna, I say it is good that there is *one* family in Big Sur where these appurtenances of the faith are in evidence and convey what they were meant to convey.

The boys are incurable rascals, incurably happy, active, and helpful at home. There is not a trace of spite, of meanness or vulgarity in them. As is so often the case in America, the children of foreign families, poor foreigners especially, seem born with taste, sensitivity and an inner resourcefulness which are usually lacking in the American child. The Lopez kids have something additional. A chivalrous nature, I would call it. If they are obliged to play with children younger than themselves, which is frequently the case, they sponsor them as no grownup could. What I particularly like about them is that they play hard and rough: they have a vitality and a sense of play which seems inborn. You will never find them whimpering and whining. They were little men at five and six. As for Rosita, the daughter, she has been a little mother ever since she began to walk.

As a hired man, a gardener, Señor Lopez was never able to afford expensive toys for his children. He was only too thankful that they had their health. He loved his children very much and he knew how to handle them—gently but firmly. His wife, Rosa, had scarcely enough time each day to finish the household tasks. They had none of the conveniences which even the poorest American family considers indispensable. (I am using the past tense only because I am referring to their life at Krenkel Corners, in the years when we, too, were guilty of abusing Rosa's generous nature.) No, the Lopez family had never anything in the way of luxury. They considered themselves fortunate in that Señor Lopez had a job—possibly for life.

Did the children suffer because of the parents' restricted means?

Hardly. Just as in Spain one finds the happiest children in all
Europe, ragged, barefoot, naked though they often are, and generally filthy and starved—often beggars at three or four—so in Big
Sur one has to go to the home of the poorest family to find that joy
and contentment, that spontaneity, that love of life, which the
Lopez children ever exhibit. In a book devoted to London street
games, Norman Douglas, author of *South Wind,* makes it painfully clear that the children who have the most fun, the children
who are the most inventive, are those who have absolutely nothing
to play with. By contrast, look at the recreation grounds attached
to the public schools in our big cities. Millions of dollars spent on
expensive apparatus, yet the poor urchins look like little convicts
who have been given permission to exercise—or else like pent-up
demons who have a half-hour in which to wreak havoc.

One day I happened on the Lopez kids just as they were at work
building an imaginary city. It was in the back of the vegetable
garden, among the brambles and thistles which they had hastily
cleared away. The project already covered quite an area, and they
were only at the beginning of their enterprise. What got me were
the "materials" they were using to create this miniature world. What
were they, these materials? Tin cans, milk cartons, old matting,
matchboxes, toothpicks, marbles, beads, shoelaces, dominoes, playing
cards, used tires, rusty curling irons, bent nails, discarded toys, pin-
cushions, safety pins, broken scissors, pebbles, rocks, hunks of wood
. . . any god-damned thing that came to hand.

Only a few days before I had called on a friend of ours, a physician, whose son Tony wanted to play with while I did the shopping.
The doctor seemed extremely grateful that his son would have a
playmate for a few hours and graciously offered to drive Tony to
the house himself.

I had never been to his home before. When I arrived, toward
sundown, I found the Japanese gardener watering the flowers and
shrubs, but the kids were nowhere in sight. I dallied awhile, studying the beautiful, well-kept grounds, inspecting the spacious patio

with its lounging chairs and tables, admiring the house tree hidden in a majestic oak, staring in amazement at the assortment of apparatus—scups and swings, ladders, a "labyrinth" (it probably has another name), the bikes and trikes, the wagons and pushmobiles, and so on. Christ only knows what this devoted father had not thought to buy for his children. He was fond of children, and he believed in doing his utmost to make them happy. His wife, who was turning them out as fast as could be, also loved children. Fortunately. The children owned the place; the parents merely lived there.

But where were the two boys? After I had explored a few wings of the house—nobody seemed to be home—I came upon a huge room, the sort I would love to annex as a living room, which was obviously intended for the exclusive use of the children. There on the floor were Tony and the doctor's son, playing with a piece of wood and a string. What they were playing I never discovered. What I did learn, though, was that they were overjoyed to have hit upon something of their own contraption, something which didn't cost fifty or a hundred dollars, something that wasn't rubberized, chromium plated, jet propelled, and of the very latest model.

There is another family I cannot pass over without a word or two, since here, once again, the children dominate the scene. I mean the Fassett family whose abode is "Nepenthe," one of the show places along the Coast. Lolly and Bill, the parents, are busy seven months of the year running the establishment, which specializes in food, drink and dancing. The kids—up until recently, at any rate—specialized in raising hell. All five of them.

The point about the Fassett youngsters is this—they give the impression of *playing* at being children. They revel in the fact that they are just kids, and that it's the business of kids to have a good time. For inventiveness they are hard to match. Entering their quarters, if it's an unexpected call, you have the feeling of being introduced to a simian world. It's not only the chatter, the monkeyshines, the acrobatic, hair-raising stunts they put on, it's the pandemonium they know so well how to create, and delight in creating—particularly when papa and mamma are not hitting it off so well. But who would think of raising the word discipline in their presence? Discipline would be the death of them. All they need is space, more and more space. As it is, they have a wonderful roller-skating rink in the dance floor, which adjoins the dining room and bar outdoors. Evenings, before the place gets too crowded, the whole gang of them entertain the guests doing folk dances. They have a repertoire which would do credit to a professional dancer. To watch Kim, the youngest, who is still only a bit of a tot, is a delight. She floats about as if she were in heaven. They need no supervision and they get none. When they're weary they retire, to listen in quiet to a Beethoven quartet, Sibelius or an album of Shankar.

The parents, of course, are sometimes puzzled by the various problems this brood presents. Particularly Bill, the provider, who, before he hit on the brilliant idea of opening "Nepenthe," used to sit up nights wondering how to feed and clothe such a tribe. But those days are past. His chief problem now is: should Griff, the oldest one, be sent to Europe to have his fling or should he be permitted to stay in Big Sur and become a Jack of all trades. The major problem is—where will they all go to live, what part of the world, when Bill has made his pile?

A rather pleasant problem, I should say. *Why not Capri?*

"Henry was always a good boy!" That's a phrase of my mother's which is relayed to me at odd moments. I'll tell you why in a moment.

Jack Morgenrath has a son, Helmut, who is about three years younger than Tony. Nobody calls him Helmut. "Pookie" is the moniker he's been saddled with. And it fits him, for some strange reason. The difference in age between Pookie and Tony has made for a strange and touching relationship between them. To begin with, they live about six miles apart and so only get to see one another at fairly long intervals. (Long for a child.) Tony, it appears, is a sort of little god to Pookie. All the latter thinks about is—when will we go see Tony again? And Tony, who is a rather rough playmate, invariably reveals his tender, solicitous side when Pookie shows up. Like a big dog playing with a puppy.

Now and then I catch Pookie looking up at Tony with an expression compounded of love, admiration and wonder. It may be that he has just opened wide his mouth to say something and, in the fraction of a second which it takes for thought to reach tongue, Pookie undergoes a transformation which, if I am fortunate enough to witness it, always moves me deeply. Ever since a tiny child, Pookie has manifested this state of rapture which we almost never see any more in the countenance of an adult. It explains—to me, at least—why there is always this peculiar pause or hesitancy when Pookie opens his mouth to make an exclamatory remark. Evidently, the emotion which fills him is much greater than his ability to verbalize it. He wells up, is ready to spill over, and then—for a moment or two, a long moment or two—he is blocked. (Fra Angelico has captured the phenomenon again and again.)

Fascinatedly, my gaze travels from his mouth to his eyes. Suddenly the eyes become two liquescent pools of light. Gazing into them, I find myself looking up at the boy I so idolized as a child: Eddie Carney. There was just about the same difference in age between Eddie Carney and myself as there is between Tony and Pookie. Eddie was a demigod for whom I would lie, steal or commit murder, if he had asked it of me.

I have written about all these companions of the street (the old 14th Ward, Brooklyn) in *Black Spring*. I have mentioned all these chivalrous comrades by name: Eddie Carney, Lester Reardon, Johnny Paul, Jimmy Short, Stanley Borowski, and others. Their images are just as alive in my memory as if it were yesterday or the day before that I left that grand old neighborhood.

Recently, hoping to get some photographs of the streets in this old neighborhood as they looked in the 1890's, I inserted a letter in

"The Old Timers" column of a Brooklyn daily. To my joy and astonishment, some of my playmates were still alive, I discovered. Most of them, of course, had gone to the Elysian fields. The relatives of some who had passed away were kind enough to write me and enclose photographs of "my little chums," all going on seventy now. ("Time is running out," wrote one of the boys. I suppose he meant clock time.)

One of these letters came from the elder sister of my idol, Eddie Carney. She had inserted several photographs of Eddie—one as a boy of sixteen (in which he seemed hardly changed from the lad of ten that I knew), another in uniform, as a corporal in World War I, and a third after he had been demobilized, his lungs contaminated by poison gas. It's the one in uniform which stands out vividly in my mind. Such sadness, such resignation, such a sense of utter forsakenness is registered in his face! How could "they" have done that to the shining hero of my boyhood? The whole cruel, senseless story of war was written into this unrecognizable visage.

Reading his sister's letter over again, I discovered that Eddie had died just a few months before my letter appeared in the paper. Then my eye suddenly leaped to this phrase: *"Eddie was always a good boy."* With it a great flood of emotion swept over me. I wondered, deeply wondered, if *I* had always been "a good boy," as my mother was fond of telling people. It was probably true, all things considered, for I had no great remembrance of scoldings, naggings, beatings, and so forth. Not as a boy! The image of another "good boy" came to mind: Jack Lawton. At least, everybody thought him that.

Jack Lawton was one of the first pals I made in the new neighborhood—"the street of early sorrows"—which I have always compared unfavorably with the old neighborhood. What I recall particularly about this chum is that he seemed so much wiser, so much more sophisticated than I. It was he who initiated me into "the secrets of life," though we were of the same age. It was he who pointed out to me the defects, the stupidities, the vices of our elders. The good boy, no less! Entering his home, which was always in a state of disorder and filthy to boot, I would receive a welcome reserved only for angelic beings. His mother, a charming slovenly Englishwoman, who always invited the minister, the school principal and such "dignitaries" to tea, doted on me almost as though I were her own son. There was only this difference, and it registered deep in me: when she looked at Jack, even if it were to reprimand him, it was with eyes of love. That look I never encountered in the eyes of other mothers. In the homes of my other little friends I was ever aware of the scolding, the nagging, the cuffing that went on. All these disciplinary measures, to be sure, had anything but the desired effect.

No, thought I to myself, you must have had it pretty easy, my lad. You were never obliged to get out and hustle, in order to swell the family budget. You did as you pleased and went where you pleased. *Until.* . . . Until you decided of your own volition to go to work. You could have continued your studies, you could have prepared yourself for a career, you could have married the right woman and all that. Instead. . . . Well, those who have read my books know my life. I haven't glossed over the ugly parts. Up all the wrong alleys, down all the wrong streets—yet how right I was!—until I came to the end of my tether.

If it was a mistake not to finish school (it wasn't!), it was an even worse mistake to go to work. ("Work! The word was so painful he couldn't bring himself to pronounce it," says a character in one of Cossery's books.) Until I was almost eighteen I had known freedom, a relative freedom, which is more than most people ever get to know. (It included "freedom of speech," which has hung over into my writing.) Then, like an idiot, I entered the lists. Overnight, as it were, the bit was put in my mouth, I was saddled, and the cruel rowels were dug into my tender flanks. It didn't take long to realize what a shithouse I had let myself into. Every new job I took was a step further in the direction of "murder, death and blight." I think of them still as prisons, whorehouses, lunatic asylums: the Atlas Portland Cement Co., the Federal Reserve Bank, the Bureau of Economic Research, the Charles Williams Mail Order House, the Western Union Telegraph Co., etc. To think that I wasted ten years of my life serving these anonymous lords and masters! That look of rapture in Pookie's eyes, that look of supreme admiration which I reserved for such as Eddie Carney, Lester Reardon, Johnny Paul: it was gone, lost, buried. It returned only when, much later, I reached the point where I was completely cut off, thoroughly destitute, utterly abandoned. When I became the nameless one, wandering as a mendicant through the streets of my own home town. Then I began to see again, to look with eyes of wonder, eyes of love, into the eyes of my fellow-man. Perhaps because all the pride, the vanity, the arrogance with which I had been puffed up fell away. Possibly my "lords and masters" had unwittingly done me a good turn. *Possibly*. . . .

Anyway, in the interim since I turned writer—a good thirty years—I have hobnobbed with all varieties of man, from the highest to the lowest. I have known intimately saints and seers as well as those whom we disdainfully refer to as "the dregs of humanity." I don't know to which group I am the more indebted. But I do know this—if we were suddenly faced with an overwhelming calamity, if I had to choose just one man with whom I would share the rest of my life in the midst of chaos and destruction, I would pick that unknown Mexican peon whom my friend Doner brought one day to clear the weeds in our garden. I no longer remember his name, for he was truly without name.

He, more than any saint, was the truly selfless individual. He was also the most handsome, in a spiritual sense. In behavior and appearance he was what the Christ would be like, I imagine, if He were to appear again on earth. (Has He ever left it?) There was that look in his eyes, and it never left him—not even in sleep, I would hazard—which Pookie displays on occasion. He was a gem, of the human realm, for which we have ceased to search. A gem we tread upon unthinkingly, as we would a weed or a stone, whilst hunting for uranium or some other currently "rare" mineral which will give us, idiots that we are, priority over the rest of the human race in the race toward annihilation.

I had no way of communicating with this Mexican—my Spanish is nil—except by looks and gestures. But that was no handicap. On the contrary, it was a boon. All that any man could wish to communicate with another this "peon" communicated with his eyes. Whenever Gilbert Neiman wished to tell me about "the goodness and the nobility of man," he would talk about the Mexicans. The Mexican Indians. He seemed to know them from way back. Indeed, his going to Mexico, where he had intended to stay forever, was in the nature of a fulfillment, fulfillment of some beautiful experience which had begun in a previous incarnation. I remember so well how Gilbert, eloquent as could be when it came to Mexico and things Mexican, would suddenly grow speechless, would stutter and stammer, then grow even more eloquently silent, in trying to describe "his friend"—the one and only—Eusebio Celón.

"You don't know," he would say, "you have no idea, you can't *possibly* imagine, what these people are like until you go there and live with them."

I believed him then, I believe him even more today. All the grace, all the dignity, all the tenderness and loving kindness of the people of these two continents seems to be epitomized in the despised "Indio."

And how did my good friend, who was a "wet-back," naturally, come off after three years of backbreaking labor and little pay in this glorious State of California? Did he accumulate a small fortune (the bait we hold out to them) to bring back to his family below the Rio Grande? Did he save enough, at least, to permit himself a month's holiday with his loved ones?

He returned as he came, with a torn shirt and a ragged coat, his pockets empty, his shoes busted, his skin tanned a little deeper from exposure to wind and sun, his spirit unquenchable but

bruised, grateful, let us proudly assume, for the poor food he had
been handed and for the lousy mattress he had been privileged to
sleep on. He had one treasure which he could produce as evidence
of the rewards of sweat and toil: a certificate for a cemetery plot
which some smart aleck had sold him. How he would return to
occupy this plot, at the appointed time, nobody had explained to
him. Nobody could. He will never occupy it, we who sold it to
him know. His place, gem that he is, is not in the Monterey
Cemetery but in the bed of a fevered river, in the ruins of an ancient
civilization, in the waste of a scorched earth.

6.

It was at Anderson Creek that I completed the essay on Rimbaud,*
which was born of an unsuccessful attempt to translate *A Season in
Hell*. It was the beginning of my own third or fourth "Season in
Hell," though at the time I wasn't fully aware of it. George Leite,
from whom I had inherited the shack we occupied at the edge of a
cliff, had just published a fragment of this essay in *Circle*. It was
the part dealing with "analogies, affinities, correspondences and
repercussions."

As every lover of Rimbaud's work knows, one of the minor
annoyances which afflicted him during his sojourn in Abyssinia was

---

* Originally published in two sections in the New Directions Annuals 9
and 11, it has now been reprinted in one volume under the title: *The Time
of the Assassins* (New York: New Directions, 1956).

the money which he carried in his belt. In one of his letters he writes: "I always carry over 40,000 gold francs about with me in my belt. They weigh about forty pounds, and I am beginning to get dysentery from the load."

Returning to America in 1940, with the war in full swing, I was cut off from my French royalties. Jack Kahane, my original publisher (the Obelisk Press), died the day war was declared, leaving an eighteen-year-old son, Maurice, who had absolutely no head for business—so his family and friends thought—to take over. I remember well the cablegram I received from Maurice while on the island of Corfu; it was to the effect that if I would continue to write for the Obelisk Press he would be happy to send me a thousand francs a month regularly. That was a decent sum in those days and I was only too happy to agree.

Of course I hadn't the slightest notion then of returning to America. I was planning to remain in Greece, which I already looked upon as home.

On the heels of this good news from Maurice came the fall of Paris, followed by a complete blackout. I never received the first thousand francs he had intended to send me. As the war dragged on I came to the conclusion that the Obelisk Press had folded up and that Maurice, who had now taken the surname of Girodias, had been killed or else taken prisoner by the Germans. That the G.I.'s were to buy my books as fast as they were thrown on the market was something I never even dreamed of.

It was during the year 1946 that we lived at Anderson Creek. Ever since my return from Europe I had waged a struggle to keep my head above water. Though we were paying only five dollars a month rent for the hovel we occupied, we were always in debt to the mailman who supplied us with food as well as other necessities. Sometimes we owed him as much as two or three hundred dollars. We never bought any clothes for ourselves; even the baby used castoff things. But we did enjoy good wines, thanks to Norman Mini whose cellar we almost drained. Even the purchase of a cheap second-hand car was out of the question. To go to town, forty-five miles distant, we were obliged to hitchhike. In short, my earnings were just about sufficient to keep a goat alive.

Anyway, it was a delightful hand-to-mouth situation, relieved only by the thoughtful generosity of fans who divined our need. We might have gone on living like paupers indefinitely. The war in Europe had ended, the one in the East was still flourishing, and the cold war was in the bag, as they say. We had managed to acquire two important items: a stove which didn't smoke from every crack and crevice and a decent mattress to lie on, the latter a gift from our neighbors, the Mac Collums. Valentine, our infant daughter, was still in her first year and therefore did not need much in the way of food or clothing. Nor did I need a car (as I now do) to dispose of the garbage and refuse which accumulated. The sea was right at our back door, at the foot of a steep precipice. One had to be alert-minded, in dumping the garbage, so as not to throw the baby over the cliff with the garbage. ("Change the water, not the goldfish!")

Then one fine foggy day, when all the green in Nature sang out in chlorophyllic glee, there came a letter from Maurice Girodias. The envelope bore the postmark Paris. I looked at the envelope some time before ripping it open.

The letter was a long one, and as I skimmed through it, rapidly, my eye fell on this—

FORTY THOUSAND DOLLARS

I threw the letter on the table and began to chuckle. I had read too hastily, I thought. An optical illusion . . . I lit a cigarette, picked the letter up again, slowly, cautiously, and read it carefully, word for word.

It was *not* an optical illusion. In the midst of a long explanation about the difficulties he had encountered in keeping the press alive during the Occupation, in a rapid account of the success my work was meeting with over there, was buried a sentence in which he explicitly stated that he, Maurice Girodias, was holding for me, in accumulated royalties, a sum equivalent to *forty thousand dollars*.

I turned the letter over to my wife to read. She nearly fainted. To increase our suspense and agitation, the letter made it all too clear that, under existing circumstances, it was impossible to transfer this fabulous sum to my bank account (I had none) in America. Would I not please come over and get it?

("Dear Government," Ahmed Safa began, "We wish to inform you by the enclosed letter that our house is about to fall down, and that Si Khalil, the repulsive owner, doesn't want to repair it. . . . We hope that you will come and take a look at the house so you can see for yourself, but if you can't, we'll bring the house to you. . . .")*

If I was not able to come, the letter stated, he, Girodias, would endeavor by one means or another to send me a thousand or two thousand dollars per month. He explained that there were always travelers who wanted dollars for francs and vice versa.

I distinctly recall the panic which seized me at the prospect of receiving a thousand or two thousand *dollars* per month. "No, not that!" I cried, "I'll be demoralized!"

"You could go to France, collect the money, invest it in a house and land, and live there again."

"You could buy a yacht and sail around the world."

"You could buy up an old castle in the provinces . . . there are plenty for sale, and dirt cheap."

These were some of the suggestions my friends promptly made. The one thing I could not do was to go to Paris, collect the money, and bring it home. That was taboo.

Now money is not one of the things which are conspicuous in my horoscope. When I study it soberly, my destiny, I realize that it is a good one. It decrees, in effect, that I shall always have what I

---

* *The House of Certain Death,* by Albert Cossery (New York: New Directions, 1949).

need, and no more. Where money is concerned, I am to dance for it. *Soit!*

Such were the thoughts running through my head during the exchange which went on between my wife and myself. However true and sincere the letter sounded, I had a growing suspicion that at bottom it was just a hoax. Cosmococcic flim-flam, in other words. The conviction grew in me that I would never see those forty thousand dollars, neither in specie, coin, bullion, nor script, nor even in zloty or piastres.

Impulsively I went to the doorway at the edge of the sunken kitchen and, looking out toward the Land of the Rising Sun, I burst out laughing. I laughted so long and so hard that my guts ached. And over and over I repeated: "It's not for *me!* It's not for *me!*" Then I'd laugh some more. I suppose it was my way of weeping. Between laughs I could hear my mother's words ringing in my ears. *"Why don't you write something that will sell?"*

"If only he would send me a hundred a month, that would be swell," I kept saying to myself. A hundred a month—*regularly*—would have solved our problems. (It would have *then*. Today no sum is large enough to solve anybody's problems. The bombs eat up everything.)

Since it weighed nothing, "my load," I didn't get dysentery. But I did suffer nightmares and illusions of grandeur. At times I felt like the deposed hotel porter in *The Last Laugh*, only instead of lavishing my fortune and my affections on a toilet attendant, I lavished them on my friend Emil or, at times, on Eugene, the poor Russian who had smiled at me from the top of the ladder one black day in the year 1930, when I was at the end of my wits, just having made a futile tour of the outskirts of Paris in search of a crust or a bone to stop the gnawing in my stomach.

Why I never did go to Paris in search of the fortune that awaited me is a story in itself. Instead, I wrote letters suggesting this, then that, all useless suggestions because, where money is involved, I have only the most impractical ideas. Before I had time to be bored dealing out imaginary checks, there came a devaluation of the franc, followed in short order by another devaluation, an even "healthier" one, if I may say, than the first. These cut my "fortune" to about one third of the original sum. Then Maurice, my publisher, began having trouble with his creditors. He was living high—who wouldn't?—had bought a house in the country, rented luxurious offices in the rue de la Paix, drank only the best wines, and invented situations, or so it seemed to me, which demanded that he make frequent trips from one end of the continent to the other. But all this was nothing compared to the fatal mistake he made when, at the height of his intoxication, he began "picking the wrong horses." What possessed him I don't know, but for some insane reason he proceeded to turn out one book after another which nobody wanted to read. In doing so, he was eating into my fortune—what was left of it. He didn't mean to, of course. But only pocket-book editors can keep dead horses alive!

At the lowest ebb there occurred one of those "miracles" which are constantly cropping up in my life and which I have almost grown to rely on when things get really tough. We were still at Anderson Creek, and that hundred a month which I had been willing to settle for was no more forthcoming than the thousand or two thousand a month which Girodias had offered to transmit "in one way or another." The whole business had taken on the flavor of a bad dream. Something to joke about occasionally. ("Remember when you almost became a millionaire?")

One day Jean Wharton, whom I had met during my first days in Big Sur and with whom we had become firm friends, came to visit us. She owned a cozy little house on Partington Ridge, where we had dined with her a number of times. This day, apropos of nothing at all, she calmly asked us if we wouldn't like to have her house, and the land with it. She thought that we had need of a place like hers, and that our need was greater than hers. After a few more words she went on to say that it seemed to her as if her home really belonged to *us*.

We were, of course, dumbfounded, delighted, overwhelmed. We would like nothing better, *but,* we sadly admitted, we hadn't a penny. Nor did we know, we hastened to add, when we *would* have any money worth speaking of. I made it quite clear that we had no resources and no tangible prospects. The best I could hope for, as a now "famous" writer, was to eke out a modest living.

Her answer to this, and I shall never forget it, was: "You don't need money. The place is yours, if you want it. You can move in any time. Pay me when your ship comes in." After a slight pause, she added: "I know the money *will* come to you—at the right time."

On that we sealed the bargain.

Here I must interrupt to relate what happened a few minutes ago when I was taking a nap. I say "taking a nap," but more truthfully I mean—when I was *trying* to take a nap. In lieu of sleep I got messages. This business has been going on ever since I got the happy thought about the oranges of Hieronymus Bosch. This noon it was bad, very bad. I could hardly taste the delicious lunch my wife, Eve, had prepared for me. As soon as I had finished lunch, I threw a few sticks of wood on the fire, rolled myself up in a blanket, and prepared to take my usual snooze before resuming work. (The more snoozes I take the more work I do. It pays off.) I closed my eyes, but the messages kept on coming. When they became too insistent, too clamorous, I would open my eyes and call out—"Eve, jot this down on the pad for me, will you? Just say—'abundance' . . . 'pilfering' . . . 'Sandy Hook.'" I thought that in tabbing a few key words I could turn off the current. But it didn't work. Whole sentences poured in on me. Then paragraphs. Then pages. . . . It's a phenomenon that always astounds me, no matter how often it happens. Try to bring it about and you fail miserably. Try to squelch it and you become more victimized.

Forgive me, but I must go into it further. . . . The last time it happened was while I was writing *Plexus.* During the year or so that I was occupied with this work—one of the worst periods, in other respects, that I have ever lived through—the inundation was almost continuous. Huge blocks—particularly the dream parts—came to me just as they appear in print and without any effort on my part, except that of equating my own rhythm with that of the mysterious dictator who had me in his thrall. In retrospect I wonder about this period, for the reason that every morning on entering my little studio I had first to quell the surge of anger, disgust and loathing which the daily drama inevitably aroused. Quieting myself as best I could, reproving and admonishing myself aloud, I would sit before the machine—and strike the tuning fork. Bang! Like a sack of coal it would spill out. I could keep it up for three or four hours at a stretch, interrupted only by the arrival of the mail-man. At lunch more wrangling. Just sufficient to bring me to the boil. Then back to my desk, where I would again tune in and race on until the next interruption.

When I had finished the book, a rather long one, I was so keyed up that I confidently expected to write two more books—*pronto*. However, nothing worked out as I had expected. The world went to smash about me. My own little world, I mean.

For three years thereafter I was unable to advance more than a page at a time, with long intervals between these spurts. The book which I was endeavoring to write—getting up the courage to write, would be better!—I had been thinking and dreaming about for over twenty-five years. My despair reached such a point that I was almost convinced my writing days were over. To make matters worse, my intimate friends seemed to take pleasure in insinuating that I could write only when things were bad for me. It was true that seemingly I had no longer anything to fight. I was only fighting myself, fighting the venom which I had unconsciously stored up.

To come back to the Voice. . . . There was *The World of Lawrence,* to take another instance. Begun at Clichy, continued in Passy, and abandoned after the writing of some seven to eight hundred pages. A misfire. A flop. Yet what a grand affair it was! Never had I been so possessed. In addition to the finished pages, I piled up a mountain of notes and a staggering heap of citations, taken not only from Lawrence's writings but from dozens of other writers, all of which I strove unsuccessfully to weave into the book. Then there were the charts and diagrams—the ground plan—with which I decorated the doors and walls of the studio (Villa Seurat), waiting for inspiration to continue the task and praying for a solution to the dilemma in which I found myself.

It was the "dictation" which got me down. It was like a fire which refused to be extinguished. For months it went on, without let up. I couldn't take a drink, even standing at a bar, without being forced to whip out pad and pencil. If I ate out, and I usually did, I would fill a small notebook during the course of a meal. If I climbed into bed and made the mistake of switching off the light, it would begin all over again, like the itch. I was that frazzled I could scarcely type a few coherent pages a day. The situation reached the height of the ludicrous when I suddenly realized one day that of everything I had written about the man I could just as well have said the opposite. I had indubitably reached that dead end which lies so artfully hidden in the phrase "the meaning of meaning."

That voice! It was while writing the *Tropic of Capricorn* (in the Villa Seurat) that the real shenanigans took place. My life being rather hectic then—I was living on six levels at once—there would come dry spells lasting for weeks some times. They didn't bother me, these lulls, because I had a firm grip on the book and an inner certainty that nothing could scotch it. One day, for no accountable reason, unless it was an overdose of riotous living, the dictation commenced. Overjoyed, and also more wary this time (especially about making notes), I would go straight to the black desk which a friend had made for me, and, plugging in all the wires, together with amplifier and callbox, I would yell: *"Je t'écoute . . . Vas-y!"* (I'm listening . . . go to it!) And how it would come! I didn't have to think up so much as a comma or a semicolon; it was all given, straight from the celestial recording room. Weary, I would beg for a break, an intermission, time enough, let's say, to go to the toilet or take a breath of fresh air on the balcony. Nothing doing! I had to take it in one fell swoop or risk the penalty: excommunication. The most that was permitted me was the time it took to swallow an aspirin. The john could wait, "it" seemed to think. So could lunch, dinner, or whatever it was I thought necessary or important.

I could almost *see* the Voice, so close, so impelling, so authoritative it was, and withal bearing such ecumenical import. At times it sounded like a lark, at other times like a nightingale, and sometimes—really eerie, this!—like that bird of Thoreau's fancy which sings with the same luscious tones night and day.

When I began the Interlude called "The Land of Fuck"—meaning "Cockaigne"—I couldn't believe my ears. *"What's that?"* I cried, never dreaming of what I was being led into. "Don't ask me to put *that* down, please. You're only creating more trouble for me." But my pleas were ignored. Sentence by sentence I wrote it down, having not the slightest idea what was to come next. Reading copy the following day—it came in instalments—I would shake my head and mutter like a lost one. Either it was sheer drivel and hogwash or it was sublime. In any case, I was the one who had to sign his name to it. How could I possibly imagine then that some few years later a judicial triumvirate, eager to prove me a sinner, would accuse me of having written such passages "for gain." Here I was begging the Muse *not* to get me into trouble with the powers that be, *not* to make me write out all those "filthy" words, all those scandalous, scabrous lines, pointing out in that deaf and dumb language which I employed when dealing with the Voice that soon, like Marco Polo, Cervantes, Bunyan *et alii,* I would have to write my books in jail or at the foot of the gallows . . . and these holy cows deep in clover, failing to recognize dross from gold, render a verdict of guilty, guilty of dreaming it up "to make money"!

It takes courage to put one's signature to a piece of pure ore which is handed you on a platter straight from the mint. . . .

And only yesterday—what a coincidence!—coming from a walk

in the hills, a thin, transparent fog touching everything with quicksilver fingers, only yesterday, I say, coming in view of our grounds, I suddenly recognized it to be "the wild park" which I had described myself to be in this same *Capricorn*. There it was, swimming in an underwater light, the trees spaced just right, the willow in front bowing to the willow in back, the roses in full bloom, the pampas grass just beginning to don its plumes of gold, the hollyhocks standing out like starved sentinels with big, bright buttons, the birds darting from tree to tree, calling to one another imperiously, and Eve standing barefoot in her Garden of Eden with a grub hoe in her hand, while Dante Alighieri, pale as alabaster and with only his head showing above the rim, was making to slake his awesome thirst in the bird bath under the elm.

7.

Where was I? Oh yes, Jean Wharton and the little house on Partington Ridge. . . . At last a home of my own, with almost three acres of land surrounding it. As predicted, the francs came through in the nick of time; enough to pay for house and land outright.

To begin with, Jean Wharton is the first and only person of my acquaintance who not only talked of "the abundance of the earth" but demonstrated it in her everyday life, in her relations with friends and neighbors.

Back in the days of the Villa Seurat, when I first began to correspond with Dane Rudhyar, I learned that the Aquarian Age which we have just entered, or are about to enter, may be justly called "The Age of Plenitude." Even at the threshold of this new era it has become evident to all that the resources of this planet are inexhaustible. I refer to physical resources. As for spiritual resources, has there ever been a deficiency? Only in man's mind.

The air is full of theories about the new order, the new dispensation. Marvelous pictures are painted of the period just around the bend, when we of this earth will see the end of making war, when atomic energy will be utilized for the benefit of all mankind. But no one *acts* as if this glorious age which is dawning were an imminent, wholly realizable, thoroughly practicable one, indeed the only viable one. It is a beautiful subject for discussion at cocktail hour, when all the current topics have been chewed to a frazzle. Usually a rider to the flying saucer business. Or to Swami So-and-So's latest book.

Jean Wharton, I repeat, is the only person I ever met who was in the new age with both feet. She was one of the first members of the community I met during my stay at Lynda Sargent's log cabin. I can still see her coming through the door of the little post office at Big Sur, clad in a huge raincoat, her face almost buried under a fisherman's hat. Her flashing eyes were tender, expressive and full of warm awareness. I felt at once the radiance which emanated from her and, on leaving the post office, questioned Lynda about her. I did not see her again for a number of weeks because, as I later learned, she was traveling back and forth over the continent in response to appeals from those who needed her aid.

When I moved into Keith Evans' cabin on Partington Ridge I often strolled about Jean Wharton's newly built home and gazed upon it longingly. Everything was still raw, including the grounds. Now and then I peered through the windows, and always I found the same book lying on view, or so it seemed, though it had been left there unintentionally. The book was *Science and Health*.

It was customary then for people to refer to Jean Wharton as a Christian Scientist, or "something of that sort," but always with an intonation which hinted that she was "different." I suspect that no one, at that time, had any inkling of the travail she was experiencing in her endeavor to clarify her position. What I mean to say is that, in developing and testing her own views of life, in following the path of Truth, she had made a breach with the past— and with those who thought they understood her—which sometimes placed her in an embarrassing light. I might put it another way and say that she no longer "belonged." Even her intimate friends could no longer classify her. She voiced ideas now and then which to them seemed contradictory, or worse still, "heretical." And sometimes absurd or utterly untenable. She had definitely moved on— that is the point. And if one moves fast enough the gap can become tremendous, painful too for those unable to follow. I doubt if anyone within her orbit quite understood what was going on. "Jean was changing." That was the best they could put it.

How I, with my background, ever got to share this woman's inmost thoughts is something of a mystery even today. However, as our acquaintance progressed, became transformed into a deep friendship, one which permitted the freest exchange of ideas and opinions, I perceived more and more clearly why she could unburden herself to me who had traveled such a different path. It was not the past which was important, it was the now. For me, just as for her, the present had become the all. For me, desperately so. In conversing with her this desperation vanished. She was in it, of it, one with it.

I must say here, at once, that Jean Wharton did not begin by airing her views. Not with me, at any rate. She began by being a kindly, helpful neighbor. Our dwellings were separated by only a few hundred yards, but we were hidden from one another's sight. It was only very gradually, and in a wholly natural way, that I began to receive any direct language about her "spiritual leanings." What I did get, right from the outset, was the beneficent effect of her clear, straight thinking. That she had very definite views about most everything I was quite aware of, and I found this refreshing; there was nothing insistent or combative in the way she presented her views.

Though I had no need of a healer, or thought I hadn't, I could not help but sense her possession of this power every time I found myself in her presence. And, perhaps for the first time in my life, I was discreet about prying into the origin and the nature of this gift. No matter how brief the conversation which passed between us, I always remarked to myself afterwards that I felt better, felt like a real human being, as we say. I am not referring to an improved physical condition, such as can be induced by an extra shot of vitamins, though that was noticeable too; I mean rather a state of spiritual well-being which, unlike the euphorias I had been subject to in the past, left me calm, poised, self-possessed, and, not only at one with the world but confirmed in my at-one-ness.

Still I made no special effort to get to know her better. It was only after we had taken possession of her house, only after she had passed through a few inner crises and reached a state of certitude which, for a less disciplined individual, would have been fraught with peril, that we began to have prolonged and involved exchanges of thought which were truly revelatory to me. As to the nature and substance of her views—her philosophy of life, if you like—I hesitate to attempt to expound them in a few words. She herself has performed this feat in a little book called *Blueprints for Living.** In this book she has condensed her thoughts to a crystalline substance, leaving nothing vague or obscure, yet permitting the reader to fill in for himself. The effect produced by this method has been to heighten the controversy which the mere mention of her name almost always entails. Perhaps I should amplify. Jean Wharton is one of those individuals who, however clear they make themselves, are always in danger of being misunderstood. She can be crystal clear, in talk or in print, yet awaken doubt, ridicule and anxiety in those who read or listen to her. Perhaps this is the price

---

* By J. P. Wharton; distributed by Wharton Publishers, Box 303, Los Gatos, California.

one pays for being utterly lucid. There is a good reason, however, for this paradoxical dilemma in which she sometimes finds herself. It is that her message can only be given through example. It is something to be lived, not discussed. And it is just this fact which utterly fails to convince some. Ramakrishna expressed it thus:

"Give thousands of lectures, you cannot do anything with worldly men. Can you drive a nail into a stone wall? The head will be broken without making any impression on the wall. Strike the back of an alligator with a sword, it will receive no impression. The mendicant's bowl (of gourd-shell) may have been to the four great holy places of India but still be as bitter as ever. . . ."*

To those who know and accept her, who wrestle with themselves as she has wrestled with herself, Jean Wharton's thoughts and intentions are clear and unmistakable. They are so even when there is an element of apparent contradiction. Even when, so to speak, she seems to create a "cloud of unknowing." We know what has been made of the sayings of Jesus. Even of his behavior!

I have not brought up Jean Wharton's name, however, merely to eulogize her, though I think it altogether proper for me to do so since I am so very much in her debt and since I frequently go out of my way to pay tribute or homage to far inferior souls. No, I am compelled to speak of her because of an aspect of the singular struggle she has waged ever since she saw the light. I beg the reader to take it for granted that I am speaking of no ordinary person, no ordinary struggle. It is perhaps unfortunate, or misleading, that I suggested the name of Mary Baker Eddy in connection with hers. That Christian Science played a part in her life is undeniable; I would even venture to call it a very valuable part. But all that belongs to the past. Whoever takes the trouble to read her *Blueprints for Living* will discover that there are drastic differences between Jean Wharton's present viewpoint and Mary Baker Eddy's.

It seems inevitable that anyone who possesses a unique point of

---

* *The Gospel of Ramakrishna,* published by the Vedanta Society, N. Y.

view is bound to cause disturbance. One cannot have a definite, positive view concerning the meaning and purpose of life without its affecting one's behavior, which in turn affects those about one. And, sad as the truth may be, it usually affects people unpleasantly. The great majority, that is. As for the few, the disciples so-called, all too often their behavior lends itself to caricature. The innovator is always alone, always subject to ridicule, idolatry and betrayal.

In reading the lives of the great spiritual leaders of the past— Gautama, Milarepa, Jesus—or even figures like Lao-tse and Socrates—we profess to understand their tribulations. We understand with our minds, at least. But let a new figure appear in our midst, one armed with new vision, greater awareness, and the problem begins all over again. Men have an ingrained tendency to regard these irruptions of the spirit as closed dramas. Even the most enlightened men sometimes.

Should the new spirit happen to be embodied in a woman the situation becomes even more complex. *"It is not a woman's role!"* As if the realm of spirit were man's alone.

But it is not merely because she was a woman that Jean Wharton found herself involved, it was because she was a person, a very human person. I must confess, in passing, that it was with her own sex that she encountered the greatest difficulties. Which is not so strange perhaps, considering the efforts men have made over the centuries to warp women's minds.

But to get back to the heart of the matter. . . . The whole problem is heartrendingly set forth in the second volume of Wasserman's trilogy, which begins with *The Maurizius Case*. In the English translation this second volume is called *Dr. Kerkhoven*. The man, Kerkhoven, is an extraordinary healer who happens to be an analyst instead of a spiritual healer. His very gift is his undoing. In saving others he crucifies himself. Not willingly and deliberately, but because being what he is, doing what he does (for others) involves him in a drama which is beyond his or any man's powers to cope with. Kerkhoven had no intention of "saving the world." He was a man of passion, of deep insight, of pure, unselfish motives. He became the victim of his own compassionate nature. One has to read the book to be convinced of his almost flawless character.

In a way, the reading of this trilogy, together with my long and most fruitful talks with Renée Nell in Beverly Glen, prepared me for at least a partial, and certainly a most sympathetic, understanding of Jean Wharton's own inner drama. As I interpreted the situation, she had reached a point where the futility and absurdity of helping others had become a flagrant reality. She had broken away from the Church, from any and every kind of organization, in fact, just as earlier in life she had parted from home and parents. Extremely sensitive to the sorrow and suffering of others, aware of the ignorance and the blindness which is the cause of all our ills, she was virtually compelled to accept the roles of mentor, comforter, healer. She fell into it naturally and unassumingly, more as an angelic being than as a doer of good deeds. In performing her duties she innocently believed that she was awakening the afflicted to the nature and existence of the true source of power and health, of peace and joy. But, like all who have made the experiment, she gradually came to perceive that people are not interested in the divine power which is theirs but only in finding an intermediary who will undo the havoc which they have wrought through stupidity or meanness of soul. She discovered what others know only too well in a cynical way, that people prefer to believe in and worship a god who is remote rather than live out the godlike nature which is their inherent being. She found that people prefer the easy path, the lazy, irresponsible path, of confession, repentance and sinning anew to the hard but direct path which leads, not to the Cross, but to life more abundant, life everlasting.

"Old hat!" you say? But have you dismissed it with your intellect or from bitter personal experience? It makes a difference. No one elects to be a martyr, however much it may seem that way to those who are immune to heroic ordeals. And no one sets about saving the world unless he has first experienced the miracle of personal salvation. Even the ignorant are capable of distinguishing between a Lenin and a Francis of Assisi, between a Franklin D. Roosevelt and a Ramakrishna, or even a Gandhi. As for Jesus the Nazarene or Gautama the Buddha, who would even dream of comparing them to any historical figure?

When she had demonstrated to her own satisfaction that she *could* cure people of their physical ills, when she discovered that it was not so much a doing as a seeing, she devoted her energies to the task of convincing others that she herself was but an instrument—"Not I but the Father!"—that this same healing power was within everyone's reach, if one would but open his eyes. This honest endeavor only brought confusion and misunderstanding. And increasing alienation. Not that people ceased calling on her for aid (of every sort), but that the very ones she had made well again were the hardest to convert to her way of thinking. As for the outsiders, those who watched from the sidelines, it was all a foregone conclusion. They saw the ridiculous in the sublime. They saw ego where there was only self-effacement.

In touching on these problems I used to urge her to employ greater detachment. It was easy for me to recognize how she fell into the same trap over and over, how she allowed herself, all unwittingly, to be used and exploited. How a simple question, which she thought to be sincere, could lead her into explanations which were exhausting. Sometimes in her compulsive behavior, in her eagerness to set things right, leave no stone unturned, I would accuse her (silently) of meddling. To even hint of such a contingency would have distressed her. She was totally unaware, or seemed to be, that she was perpetually hovering over others in readiness to be of service. Ever on the alert, she was like a sentinel fighting off fatigue. Her very nature decreed that it could not be otherwise. Her efforts to correct this attitude must, I know, meet with indifference in the minds of those who can readily close their eyes where the afflictions and misfortunes of others are concerned. But to those who are aware, supremely aware, the problem is not one of shutting the eyes or of keeping them open, it is one of refraining from intervention. "Fools rush in where angels fear to tread," goes the saying. Obviously, angels see farther and deeper than ordinary mortals; if angels give pause it is assuredly from no thought of self-protection.

When should one lend oneself to action? What constitutes an *act*? And may it not be that not to act is sometimes a higher form of action? Jesus was silent before Pontius Pilate. The Buddha delivered his greatest sermon by holding a flower up to the multitude to behold.

"Jean," I once ventured to say, "you have declared that all is good, that evil is but the negative of that which is all positive, that the plan is perfect, that light triumphs over darkness, that truth must and does prevail. . . . But can you forbear to succor the weak, can you forbear to straighten out crooked souls, can you respond to foolish questions, or imperious demands, with silence? Can you just *be* what you are, confident that nothing more is demanded of you? Is not *being* the all? Or, as you put it, *seeing*? Seeing through the false, the illusory, the unreal?"

There was never the slightest doubt in my mind as to her sincerity. The one defect, if I dare call it that, which I could detect in her was an inordinate sense of compassion. And yet, what greater link can there be between the human and the divine? The compassionate nature is awakened precisely when the heart and mind become as one, when the human will surrenders in absolute trust. In true compassion there is neither attitude nor involvement. Nor is there any relinquishing or deplenishment of powers. Quite the contrary, indeed. When compassion is manifested, all discordant elements are instantly attuned. But it can only make itself felt, only become operative and work its magic, when there is absolute certitude, absolute accord with truth. When "I and the Father are one."

What I detected in her now and then was a wavering, or indecisiveness, which prompted her in weak moments to give that little push which only the "master" can refrain from giving—or give because he is certain of the outcome. Formerly she had given many an exhausting push, and had paid the price for doing so. There was little danger of her relapsing. The question was how to go forward, how to be of greater service without creating new temptations, new traps, which the ego ever lies in wait to exploit. With every ounce of wisdom she possessed she schooled herself anew each day to banish even the most innocent kind of intercession. Aware that self-exhortation is but a reminder of hidden failings, she also disciplined herself to do whatever her inner promptings urged. Fighting to leave herself open, to avoid making decisions, to eliminate opinions, use no will, meet each situation as it arose *when* it arose and not before, fighting not to fight, struggling not to struggle, deciding not to decide, she was indeed making herself a battleground. Outwardly there was little trace of this many-sided conflict; she was always serene, confident, optimistic, and therapeutic, even without meaning to be so. Inwardly, however, she was consumed. She had a role to play in life but the nature of this role was becoming more and more elusive. The more she evolved, the deeper her insight, the less there was for her to do. And she had always been a very active, very energetic person. She scarcely knew what is called fatigue. Moreover, she had done her utmost to make herself as anonymous as possible. She had surrendered even the desire to surrender. But her life— to those who watched her anxiously—only seemed to become more hectic, more involved. Her comings and goings were as erratic as the quivering of a compass needle in the presence of hidden ore. Everyone had a different explanation for her behavior, but no explanations hit the mark. Not even her own.

To cut short the *déroulement* of her personal history, as I soon shall, is not to pique the reader's curiosity nor to arouse interest in an exceptional personality—the world is full of remarkable "personalities"—but to draw attention to a problem which vitally concerns us all, however little we may think about it. It is sometimes said about this transitional period we are passing through that *this* time there will be no world figure to emerge and lead us out of the wilderness. *This* time we will be obliged to save ourselves. (Which is, of course, what every great teacher struggled to make man understand.) Given the dire circumstances in which the world at large is now enmeshed, it is strikingly noticeable that there is no one recognizable figure on the horizon capable of inspiring us as a world leader. Neither is there any new doctrine whose message, if followed, would deliver us from our inertia. That the Kingdom of Heaven is within—or "within our reach," as scholars now insist the translation should be—that man needs no intermediary, that he cannot be saved except by his own efforts, that the abundance of the earth is inexhaustible—these ineluctable truths now stare us in the face implacably and incontrovertibly. There is indeed a cruel, ironic validity to our stubborn refusal to be saved. The contemptuous, scornful way in which we treat would-be saviours is not altogether a reflection of our imperviousness. We *know* today that the "do-gooders" and the "fixer-uppers" are capable of doing more damage than the carefree, heedless sinners.

As a people, we Americans have submitted to some perilous experiments. Ever since 1914 we have been trying to patch things up for the world. Not with a clear, clean conscience, it is true, but not entirely in hypocritical fashion either. In brief, we have behaved as a people would who have had more than their share of the good things of life, who have not been crippled morally, physically and spiritually by successive invasions and revolutions. Yet we have failed completely to ameliorate the harrowing conditions which beset the rest of the world. Not only that, but we ourselves have deteriorated and retrogressed. We have lost much of the character, the independence, the buoyancy and resiliency, to say nothing of the courage, faith and optimism, of our forefathers. Still a young nation, we are already weary, filled with doubts and misgivings, and absolutely at sea as to what course to pursue in world affairs.

All we seem able to do is to give ourselves more injections and arm to the teeth. When we do not truculently threaten or menace, we wheedle, cajole and appease as best we know how. It is clear to all the world that all we really care about is to enjoy our huge piece of pie in peace and tranquillity. But we know now beyond all doubt, and it is this which disturbs us profoundly, that we cannot enjoy our pie while the rest of the world starves. We cannot even have our piece of pie unless we aid others to have theirs too. (Assuming that they want pie and not something more substantial.)

If it is abundance we worship, then common sense would dictate that we cease wasting our time and energy on the manufacture of destructive products and destructive thoughts. Imagine a man who is strong and healthy, who wants nothing of his neighbor because he has more than enough at home, and who insists on taking pills, donning a full coat of armor when he goes to work, and then proceeds to build walls around his dwelling place so that nobody will break in and rob him of so much as a crust of bread. Or who says: "Yes, I shall be happy to sit down to the table with you, but first you must change your ideas." Or who goes even further and says: "The trouble with you is that you don't know how to live!"

I don't pretend to know how the other half lives, but I do know something about the way this half lives. I don't even have to stir from the tiny community in which I have my abode. With all the good that I see in the neighbors about me, with all the valiant efforts I observe them making to live up to the good life, to do right by one another, to make the most of the paradise in which they find themselves, still, if I am honest and truthful, I must declare that they have only one foot in this new world which is begging to be opened up. I mean the world of full and harmonious relationship—with God, man, Nature, children, parents, husband or wife, brother or sister. I say not a word, you observe, about art, culture, intellect, invention. The world of play, yes! A vast and perhaps the most profitable world of all, next to that of sheer idleness. But first things first. . . .

No, as a writer, I cannot help but look upon the immediate scene with different eyes than would a mere friend or neighbor. I can see all that Jean Wharton saw—and perhaps more. I have chosen to dwell on the "interesting" things which happened to me here, whether good or bad, whether wholesome or unwholesome. I am not taking a moral survey of the environment. It doesn't matter to me that a few hundred yards in this direction or that I can come face to face with an ornery bastard or a God-given son of a bitch or a filthy miser or a vain and arrogant fool. "It takes all kinds to make a world." *Ouais!* If I stray from the cowpath on my daily walk through the hills and come home bristling with thistles and burrs, who's to blame? In a casual conversation with a neighbor you sometimes get overtones and reverberations of your own private misery which give you an inkling of conditions round about which you had ignored or overlooked. That so-and-so, who seems so well-adjusted, so at peace with the world, so tolerant and gracious, should have a wife who is literally driving him crazy may come as a startling revelation. Or that so-and-so, who seems so happy and content in his field of work and whom every one looks upon as a "success," regards himself as a miserable failure and thinks of nothing but the great mistake he made in refusing to become a judge, a diplomat, or whatever it may be. No matter what the one in question be—judge, politician, artist, plumber, day laborer or farm hand—if you look deep into his life you will find an unhappy, unfulfilled individual. And if *he* in his own soul is a miserable creature, you can almost count on it that his wife is an even more miserable one. In the home that seems to you so snug and cozy, so warm, so inviting, there are ghosts and skeletons, tragedies and calamities brewing, far greater, far more subtle and complex, than our dramatists and novelists ever give us. No artist has sufficient genius to touch bottom, where the private life of the individual is concerned. "If you are unhappy," says Tolstoy, "and I *know* that you are unhappy. . . ." Those words ever ring in my ears. Tolstoy himself, grand old man that he was, genius that he was, good Christian that he was, was unable to avoid unhappiness. His domestic life reads like a sad joke. The greater he grew in soul the more ridiculous a figure he cut at home. A classic situation, yes, but when repeated on a trivial scale and universally, something to weep about. The husbands are doing their best, the wives are doing *their* best, yet nothing jells. Firecrackers but no fireworks. Petty quarrels, stupid brawls, jealousy, intrigue, increasing estrangement, hysterical anxiety, followed by more wrangling, more intrigues, more gossip, more vilification and recrimination, after which divorce, alimony, division of progeny, division of chattels, and then a new go at it, whereupon a new failure, a new setback. Finally it's old John Barleycorn, bankruptcy, cancer or a dash of schizophrenia. Then suicide, moral, spiritual, physical, nuclear and etheric.

Such is the picture which doesn't always come clear through the televistic screen. The negative, in other words, from which all that is positive, good and everlasting will eventually come through. Easy to recognize because no matter where your parachute lands you it's always the same: the everyday life.

With this setup I am almost as familiar as Jean Wharton who has spent so much time, so much effort, developing positives for those who see only negatives, or rather are unable to read negatives, for if they could they would have no more need for positives than for negatives. Why is it we cannot hold the positive, once it has been shown us? The answers are many, varying with school and dogma. In any case, do we not resemble those myopic individuals who, during a train ride in which they have fallen sound asleep, their spectacles safely in their pockets, suddenly open their eyes and, for a fraction of time, see everything sharp and clear, as sharp and clear as if they enjoyed perfect vision? Let us not quibble. Their vision *was* perfect—for just a few instants. What made it so? Do they ask themselves the question? No! They calmly wipe their eyes, now blurred again, and put on their specs. With these, so they tell themselves, they can see as well as the next man. But they do *not* see as well as the man with normal eyesight. They see as cripples.

It is all of a piece—the look in the eye, the posture, the stance, the gait, and "the angle of vision," as Balzac says. The angel in man is ready to emerge whenever that dread human will to have it one's own way can be kept in abeyance. Things not only *look* different, they *are* different, when perfect sight is restored. To see things whole is to be whole. The fellow who is out to burn things up is the counterpart of the fool who thinks he can save the world. The world needs neither to be burned up nor to be saved. The world is, we are. Transients, if we buck it; here to stay, if we accept it. Nothing is solid, fixed or unalterable. All is flux, because everything created is also creative. If you are unhappy—"and I *know* you are!"—take thought! You can spend the rest of your life fighting it out on every front, in every vector—and get nowhere. Give up, throw in the sponge, and possibly you will look at the world with new eyes. More than possibly you will see your friends and enemies in a new light—even your wife, or that rascally, inconsiderate, hardheaded, ill-tempered, gin-soaked devil of a husband.

Is there a discrepancy between this realistic picture, which I have just sketched, and the attractive positive which I painted when the "oranges" were in bloom? No doubt there is. Have I contradicted myself? No! Both pictures are true, even though colored by the temperament of the writer. We are always in two worlds at once, and neither of them is the world of reality. One is the world we think we are in, the other is the world we would like to be in. Now and then, as if through a chink in the door—or like the myopic who falls asleep in the train—we get a glimpse of the abiding world. When we do, we know better than any metaphysician can expostulate, the difference between true and false, the real and the illusory.

Several times now I have stressed the fact that whatever "it" is one gets here at Big Sur, one gets it harder, faster, straighter than one would elsewhere. I come back to it again. I say, the people here are fundamentally no different from people elsewhere. Their problems are basically the same as those who inhabit the cities, the jungles, the desert or the vast steppes. The greatest problem is not how to get along with one's neighbor but how to get along with one's self. Trite, you say. But true, nevertheless.

What is it that makes one's problems (here in Big Sur) assume such a dramatic aspect? Almost melodramatic at times. The place itself has much to do with it. If the soul were to choose an arena in which to stage its agonies, this would be *the* place for it. One feels exposed—not only to the elements, but to the sight of God. Naked, vulnerable, set against an overwhelming backdrop of might and majesty, one's problems become magnified because of the proscenium on which the conflict is staged. Robinson Jeffers is unerring in high-lighting this aspect of his narrative poems. His figures and their manner of behavior are not falsely exaggerated, as some believe. If his narratives smack of Greek tragedy, it is because Jeffers rediscovered here the atmosphere of the gods and fates which obsessed the ancient Greeks. The light here is almost as electric, the hills almost as bare, the community almost as autonomous as in ancient Greece. The rugged pioneers who settled here needed only a voice to make known their secret drama. And Jeffers is that voice.

But there is another factor which enters into play here. Though not cut off, in the strict sense, Big Sur receives, as through a filter, the violent waves which agitate the world. Living here, whether at the edge of the sea or on top of a mountain, one gets the feeling that it is all happening "out there" somewhere. One is not obliged to read the daily paper over his morning coffee nor tune in on the radio for the latest shock injection. One can live with or without, take it or leave it, and not feel out of step with the rest of the community. One does not rush to work in a crowded, ill-smelling subway; one is not on the telephone all day; one is not confronted with picket lines or police hurling tear bombs into a panic-stricken mob. One isn't obliged to buy a television set for the children. Life can pursue its course here free of so many disturbing elements which are accepted as normal by the rest of America.

On the other hand, when things get tough, when one is at his wit's end, when one's patience is tried to the breaking point, there is no one to go to, no movie to stultify the mind, no bar to lap it up in (there *are* drinking places, yes, but one would soon be excommunicated if they were used for this purpose), no pavements to pound, no store windows to stare at, no bastards to pick a fight with. No, you are completely on your own. If you insist on gnashing your teeth you can gnash them at the wild waves, at the silent forest, or at the stony hills. One can get desperate here in a way that no city man understands. Sure, you can run amok . . . but where would it lead you? You can't slash mountains to ribbons, nor cut the sky to pieces, nor flatten a wave with the broadest sword. You can get the screaming meemies all right, but what would Mother Nature say if you took to acting up that way?

I recall one period—right here on Partington Ridge—in which I went through all the demi-quivers of real desperation. It was during the time when my then wife was easing herself out of a hopeless situation. She had taken the children back East, ostensibly to become acquainted with their grandparents whom they had never seen. Some time after they were due back her letters suddenly stopped coming. I waited, wrote a few unanswered letters, one of which was returned unopened (indicating that the addressee had left for parts unknown, or died), and then, as the silence thickened, I suddenly grew panicky. I wasn't so much concerned for my wife, though perhaps I ought to have been, as I was about the children. *"Where in hell are my children?"* I kept asking myself. I kept asking myself the question louder and louder, until it seemed to me that I was shouting it for all to hear. Finally I sent my wife's sister a wire, to which I got a response two days later, informing me that "they" had left by train some days ago and were probably in Los Angeles. It was small comfort, because as I figured then (in my innocence), if she intended to bring the children home, Los Angeles was not home. Besides, how could I know that Los Angeles was her point of destination? Maybe that was only a jumping off place? Maybe they were over the border by now and

deep in the heart of Mexico. And then and there I realized that
"home" had come to mean some other place—for her. Now I had
no way of communicating with her. I was cut off, just as sharp and
neat as if by a razor blade. A day passed, two days, three days.
Still no word. My pride prevented me from wiring her sister again.
"I'll sit and wait," I told myself. "I'll sit till hell freezes over." Oh
yeah? Try it! There are twenty-four hours in a day, and these can
be broken down into minutes, seconds, and fractions of seconds
which last an eternity. And all you can think of, all you can repeat
to yourself over and over and over, is—"Where, where, *where?*"
Yes, one can always go to the police or hire a private detective . . .
a man of action can think of a thousand things to do in such an
emergency. But I am not that type. I sit on a rock and think. Or
I think I am thinking. No man can say he "thinks" after he has
subjected his mind to all the questions and answers his conscience
puts him. No, my mind was just a blank, a blank piece of blubber
that had been mercilessly pounded by alternate doubts and hopes,
alternate recriminations and confessions.

What does one do in such a case—the wild waves going up and
down, the gulls screaming at you, the buzzards sniffing at you as
if you were already so much tripe, and the sky so full of glory
yet empty of hope? I'll tell you what you do, if you have an ounce
of sense left in you. I'll give it to you the way William Blake
answered when a visitor once asked him what he did in moments
of dire extremity. William Blake calmly turned to his good wife
Kate, his helpmate, and he said to her: "Kate, what *do* we do in
such cases?" And his dear Kate replied: "Why, we get down on
our knees and pray, don't we, Mr. Blake?"

That's what I did, and that's what every bleeding mother's son
has to do when things get too unbearable.

8.

If ever I should find time hanging heavy on my hands I know what to do: hop in my car, drive to Los Angeles, and search out the files which are kept in steel cabinets in the Special Collections Division of the University Library there. In these files are the thousands of letters which, at their urgent request, I have been turning over to the library ever since I have been in Big Sur. They are for posterity, I suppose. Unfortunately, some of the best ones, the maddest, the craziest, I burned (at my wife's instigation) shortly before the library made its request. Before that, in New York, and again in Paris (when leaving for Greece), I got rid of a short ton of correspondence which I then thought of no importance, even for "posterity."

With the letters, *bien entendu,* arrive manuscripts, beautifully printed poems, books of indescribable variety, checks, wedding and funeral announcements (why not divorce notices also?), photos of newborn infants (the spawn of my fans), theses (dozens of them), lecture programs, excerpts from books, clippings, reviews in a dozen different languages, requests for photos or autographs, plans for a new world, appeals for funds, pleas to help stop the execution of this or that innocent one, pamphlets and monographs ranging in subject matter from dietary cures to the true nature of Zoroastrianism.

It is assumed that I am vitally interested in all these subjects, projects and proposals. What I am most interested in, naturally, is checks. If I see an envelope which bears promise of containing a check, that is the one I open first. Next in order come those which bear the postmark of exotic countries. The ones I put away to read some rainy day are the thick envelopes which I know in advance contain abortive stories, essays or poems which I am generally told that I may consign to the waste basket if I choose—the sender never has the courage to do this himself! On the other hand, a real fat one from someone I adore I may save until I go to the sulphur baths, there to enjoy it in peace and quiet. But how rare are these in comparison with the slew of crap which pours in day in and day out!

Sometimes it is a very brief letter, in an exquisite or else an execrable hand, which will "send" me. It is usually from a foreigner who is also a writer. A writer I have never heard of before. The short letters which exasperate me are from ultralucid spirits to whom I have presented a knotty, complicated, usually legal or ethical, problem, and who are adept in cutting through fog and grease with three or four scimitar-like lines which always leave me exactly where I was before posing the problem. The type I have in mind is the judicial type. The better the lawyer, the bigger the judge, the briefer and more bewildering the reply.

Let me say at the outset that the most vapid letter writers are the British. Even their handwriting seems to reveal a paucity of spirit which is glaring. From a calligraphic standpoint, they appear to be crouching behind their own shadows—skulking like poltroons. They are congenitally incapable of coming out with it, whatever it may be that impelled them to write me. (Usually I discover that it is about themselves, their spiritual poverty, their crushed spirits, their lowered horizon.) There are exceptions, to be sure. Splendid, remarkable exceptions. As epistolary virtuosi, no one can equal Lawrence Durrell, the poet, or John Cowper Powys, the returned Welshman. Durrell's letters awaken the same sure delight which comes with viewing a Persian miniature or a Japanese wood-block print. I am not thinking of the physical aspect of his letters, though this too plays a part, but the language itself. Here is a happy master of prose whose style is pure and limpid, whose lines sing, bubble, effervesce, whether writing a letter or writing a treatise. From wherever he sits penning his letter there is wafted the fragrance, the wonder and the eternality of landscape, to which is added the spice of fable and myth, of legend and folklore, of customs, ritual and architecture. He has written me, Lawrence Durrell, from such places as Cos, Patmos, Knossus, Syracuse, Rhodes, Sparta, Delphi, Cairo, Damascus, Jerusalem, Cyprus. The very names of these stopping places make my mouth water. And he has put them all in his books and in his poems. . . .

As for "Friar John," as Powys sometimes styles himself, the very look of his letters puts me in ecstasy. He probably writes with a pad on his knee, a pad which is pivoted on invisible ball bearings. His lines flow in a labyrinthian curve which permits them to be read upside down, swinging from a chandelier or climbing a wall. He is always exalted. Always. Trifles become monumental. And this despite the fact that he has lost the use of one eye, has no teeth to chew with, and until fairly recently—he is now in his eighties—suffered unremittingly from gastric or duodenal ulcers. The oldest of all my correspondents (excepting Al Jennings), he is also the youngest and the gayest, the most liberal, the most tolerant, the most enthusiastic of all. Like William Blake, I feel certain that he will die singing and clapping his hands.

Few are they who are able to write freely and effortlessly about anything and everything—as Chesterton and Belloc did. The name of the sender usually apprises me of the nature of the contents of a letter. One writes perpetually about his ailments, another about his financial difficulties, another about his domestic problems, another about his run-ins with publisher or dealer; one guy is hepped on pornography and obscenity, can never get off the subject; another talks only about Rimbaud or about William Blake; another about the Essenes; another about the stratospheric complexities of Indian metaphysics; another about Rudolf Steiner or the "masters" in the Himalayas; some are Dianetic bloodhounds, others Zen enthusiasts; some write only of Jesus, Buddha, Socrates and Pythagoras. You might suppose the latter breed to be stimulating minds. On the contrary, they are the dullest, the windiest, the dryest of all. Genuine "gaseous vertebrates." They are only surpassed in dullness by the nimble wits who are always ready to relay the latest joke overheard at the office or in a public toilet.

The letters that really set me up for a few days are the "isotopes" which come by carrier pigeon—from cranks, freaks, nuts and plain lunatics. What a splendid insight into an author's life we would have if such missives were collected and published occasionally. Whenever a celebrated author dies there is a stampede to unearth the correspondence exchanged between him and other world-wide celebrities. Sometimes these make good reading, often not. As a devotee of French literary weeklies, I often find myself reading snatches of correspondence between men like Valéry and Gide, for example, and wondering all the while why I am so sleepy.

Some of those I roughly classify as "nuts" are not wacky at all but eccentric, raffish, perverse and, being genuine solipsists, all of them, of course at odds with the world. I find them most humorous when they are pathetically whining about the cruelty of fate. This may sound malicious, but it is a fact that nothing is more hilarious to read about than the troubles of a person who is "somehow" always in trouble. What seem like mountains to this type are always molehills to us. A man who can enlarge on the tragedy of a hangnail, who can elaborate on it for five and six pages, is a comedian from heaven sent. Or a man who can take your work apart with hammer and tong, analyze it to nothingness, and hand you the missing members in an old-fashioned *bidet* which he normally uses for serving spaghetti.

There was one sly coyote who used to write me direct from the asylum, a chap to whom in a moment of weakness I had sent a photograph and who for weeks thereafter bombarded me with letters ten, twenty, thirty pages long, in pencil, crayon and celery stalks—always about my supposed kidney trouble. He had noticed the pouches under my eyes (an inheritance from Franz Josef on the paternal side) and he had deduced that I was destined for a speedy end. *Unless* I followed his recommendations for the care and preservation of the bladder, which required a number of instalments to elucidate. The regimen he prescribed began with physical exercises of a highly unorthodox character and were to be performed without the slightest deviation six times a day, one of these times being in the middle of the night. Any one of these exercises would have tied the perfect gymnast into a sailor's knot. The exercises were to be accompanied by dietary feats which only a madman could think up. For example. . . .

"Eat only the stem of the spinach plant, but grind first with a pestle, then mix in chickweed, parsley, dandelion that has gone to seed, nutmeg and the tail of any rodent which has not been domesticated.

"Eschew all meats except the flesh of the guinea pig, the wild boar, the kangaroo (now put up in tins), the onager of Asiatic origin—not the European variety!—the muskrat and the garter snake. All small birds are good for the bladder, excepting the finch, the dart and the miner bird."

He counseled strongly against standing on one's head, which he described as an atavistic praxis of supernatural origin. Instead, he recommended walking on all fours, particularly over precipitous terrain. He thought it advisable, nay indispensable, to nibble between meals, particularly to nibble minute particles of caraway seeds, sunflower seeds, watermelon seeds, or even gravel and bird seed. I was not to take much water, nor tea, coffee, cocoa and tisanes, but to drink as much whiskey, vodka, gin as I could—a teaspoonful at a time. All liqueurs were taboo, and sherry, no matter what the origin, was to be shunned as one would a witch's brew. He explained in a footnote that he had to be stringent in this regard because, after years of research (in a laboratory, supposedly) he had discovered that sherry, however and wherever manufactured, contained traces of the arnica root, liverwort and henbane, all poisonous to the human organism though rarely deleterious when given to convicts in the death-cell or to micro-organisms employed in approved formulae for the making of antibiotics. Even if I were at the point of death, I was not to resort to any of the sulfa drugs, penicillin or any of the allied miracle drug family based on mud, urine and fungus.

Aside from the rapidity with which time flies, unbelievably so!, there is another aspect of life at Big Sur which always stupefies me, *viz.,* the amount of trash which accumulates daily. The trash has to do with my correspondents. For, in addition to photographs, theses, manuscripts and so on which accompany the letters, come articles of clothing, stationery, talismans and amulets, albums of records, rare coins, rubbings *(frottages),* medallions, ornamental trays, Japanese lanterns and Japanese gimcrackery, art supplies, catalogues and almanacs, statuettes, seeds from exotic blooms, exquisite tins of cigarettes, neckties galore, hand-winding phonographs, carpet slippers from Jugoslavia, leather pantouffles from India, pocketknives with multiple accessories, cigarette lighters (none that ever work!), magazines, stock market reports, paintings (huge ones sometimes, which cost time and money to return), Turkish and Greek pastries, imported candies, rosaries, fountain pens, wines and liqueurs, occasionally a bottle of Pernod, pipes which I never smoke (but never cigars!), books of course, sometimes complete sets, and food: salami, lachs, smoked fish, cheeses, jars of olives, preserves, jams, sweet and sour pickles, corn bread (the Jewish variety), and now and then a bit of ginger. There is hardly a thing I need which my correspondents cannot supply me with. Often, when short of cash, they send me postage stamps— filched from the till, no doubt. The children also receive their share of gifts, from toys of all kinds to delicious sweets and exquisite items of wearing apparel. Whenever I make a new friend in some outlandish part of the world I invariably remind him to send the children something "exotic." One such, a student in Lebanon, sent me the Koran in Arabic, a diminutive volume in fine print, which he urged me to teach the youngsters when they came of age.

One can easily see, therefore, why we always have plenty with which to start a fire. Why we always have enough paper, cardboard and twine to wrap books and parcels. In the old days, when I had to walk up and down the hill, the gift business presented a problem. Now, with a Jeep station wagon, I can haul a cartload if need be.

Certain individuals who write me regularly never fail to repeat like a refrain—"Be sure to let me know if you need anything. If I don't have it or can't get it, I know someone who can and will. Don't hesitate to call on me—for anything!" (Only Americans write this way. Europeans are more conservative, so to speak. As for the Russians—the exiled ones—they will offer you heaven too.) In this group there are certain individuals who by any standard of measurement are exceptional. One is a radio operator for an air line, another is a biochemist who runs a laboratory in Los Angeles, another is a student of Greek parentage, another is a young script writer from Beverly Hills. When a package comes from V., the radio operator, I am apt to find literally anything in it, barring an elephant. The main item in the package is always carefully wrapped in wads of newspaper (newspapers from India, Japan, Israel, Egypt, anywhere he happens to be at the time) together with French, German and Italian illustrated weeklies. In the French weeklies I am always certain to find at least one text on a subject which I happen to be interested in at that moment. It's as if he divined my need! Anyway, sandwiched in and around the precious object he has sent will be Turkish delight, fresh dates from the Orient, sardines from Portugal, smoked Japanese oysters and other little delicacies he thought up at the last minute. . . . F., the laboratory man, when shipping typewriter paper, carbon or ribbons that I am in need of, never fails to include a newfangled pen or pencil, a bottle of extra-ultra vitamins, a jar of lachs, a huge salami and a loaf or two of genuine corn bread, the one and only bread, as far as I am concerned, and now getting to be as scarce, and almost as expensive, as sturgeon. He would send sweet butter, too, if it traveled well. . . . K. and M., the other two, always offer to type my scripts or get things printed for me. If I ask for one or two tubes of water colors they send me a year's supply, to say nothing of blocks of excellent water-color paper. K. used to keep his grandmother busy knitting socks and sweaters for me—and making loukoumi for the children.

Some, like Dante Z., render service by doing research work for me. Dante will go through the thickest tomes and give me a summary of the contents, or track down a buried passage which, at the moment, I deem important to have on tap in my files, or translate difficult passages from obscure works, or find out if such and such an author wrote such and such a work and why, or dig into ancient medical treatises for data which I may never use but which I like to have on hand in the event that I engage in dispute with some learned ass.

Or there is a great soul like Dr. Leon Bernstein who will, if I ask it, take a plane to visit a poverty-stricken devil who is in need of treatment, and not only will he do everything that is needed (gratis) but he will see to it that the poor devil is provided for during the long period of convalescence.

Is it any wonder that John Cowper Powys is forever extolling the Jews and the Negroes? Without the latter, as I have often remarked, America would be a joyless, immaculate, superabundant museum of monotonous specimens labelled "the white race." Without the Jews, charity would begin at home and stay there. Every artist, in America certainly, must be indebted a hundred times over to his Jewish friends. And indebted not for material services only. Think, *chers confrères,* who is the first among your friends to give encouragement, to read your work, look at your paintings, show your work around, *buy* your work (on the instalment plan, if necessary). *Buy* it, I say, and not beg off with the lame excuse— "If only I could afford it!" Who lends you money to carry on, even when he has no money to spare? Who else but the Jew will say: "I know where to borrow it for you, don't you do a thing!" Who is it thinks to send you food, clothing, and the other vital necessities of daily life? No, the artist—in America, at least—cannot avoid coming into contact with the Jew, becoming friends with him, imitating him, imbibing from him the courage, the patience, the tolerance, the persistence and the tenacity which this people has in its blood, because, to be an artist is to lead a dog's life, and most Jews begin life that way. Others do too, certainly, but they seem to forget it as they rise in life. The Jew seldom forgets. How can he, living in the midst of a drama which is endlessly repeated?

And now I think of the letters which come regularly from Palestine, from Lilik Schatz, son of Boris, who has become my brother-in-law. Lilik lived for several years at Krenkel Corners, which is a sunken hollow midway between Partington Ridge and Anderson Creek. While living in Berkeley he made a trip to Big Sur one day expressly to induce me to do a silk-screen book with him, which we did, after much labor and struggle, and from scratch.* This book, *Into the Night Life,* the conception, the making, and its sale (which remains steadily at zero), was the beginning of a great friendship. It was only after he had returned to his home in Jerusalem that I got to know his wife's sister, Eve, and married her. If I hadn't found Eve I would be a dead duck today.

But the letters. . . . To begin with, know ye all that Lilik, the son of Boris, who was the son of Bezalel as built the Ark, has the extraordinary gift of being able to talk in any tongue. Not that he is a linguist, though he does know half a dozen languages moderately well, including his native Hebrew. It is not knowledge of a language that he needs in order to communicate with his neighbor, be that man a Turk, an Arab, a Ceylonese, a Peruvian of the Andes, a pygmy or a Chinese mandarin. Lilik's procedure is to start talking at once—with tongue, hands, feet and ears—explicating mimetically as he goes along by grunts and squeals, dance steps, Indian signs, Morse code and so on. It's all sustained and borne along by an overflowing current of sympathy, empathy, identity, or whatever you wish to call that fundament of good will, good nature,

---

* See his account of this enterprise in the illustrated brochure dealing with the production of the book.

brotherhood, sisterhood, divine benevolence and understanding which is his special heritage. Yes, Lilik can talk to a stone wall and get a response from it. Some of the living tombstones I have seen him plead with, when he desperately needed to sell a painting or an *objet d'art* from his father's collection, were more deaf, more impenetrable, than any stone wall. There are human beings, as we all know, who freeze at the mere mention of a painting for sale. There are some who turn to stone whenever there is the slightest hint that they may be called upon to relinquish so much as a moldy crust of bread.

If Lilik had a rough time of it in Big Sur, he's having an equally rough time of it in his home town, Jerusalem. But his letters never sound that way. No, Lilik begins—invariably—with himself seated on the terrace of a noisy café and some poor devil begging to shine his shoes or sell him a rug which he doesn't need. (It varies . . . sometimes it's the dessicated toenail of a saint that's being offered to him.) Even if it's raining, the sun is always out (in his heart) and he, the professor *(cher maître, cher ami)*, is in particularly fine fettle, either because he is just about to tackle a new series of oils or because he has just ended a bout of work. His letters start with the place, the moment, the immediate thought, the way he feels—whether short of breath, constipated, or delighted with his warm beer. In a few lines he manages to evoke the atmosphere of the crowd, the market place, the cemetery hard by, the waiters running to and fro, the peddlers and mendicants wheedling and whining, the chickens being plucked (by toothless hags), the mountebanks performing their stunts, the smell of food, grime, sweat and drink, the clove he just swallowed by mistake, yesterday's delicious garlic (we used to airmail him a clove of garlic at a time), the juicy colors which he will squeeze on to his palette the moment he gets home. *Und so weiter*.

Every other word is mispelled, whether written in English, German, Russian or French. It would take a mental acrobat to deliberately distort, or transmogrify, words the way Lilik does unwittingly. Only a homely word like fart comes off intact, so to say. And there is lots of farting in his jubilant epistles—on his own part and on the part of those around him. The Israelis apparently do not blush or hasten to excuse themselves when they "break wind," as we say in polite literature.

"At this moment," he will write, "we are having trouble again with the Arabs, or the Arabs with us." Homeward bound, he may have to duck into a doorway several times in order to escape stray bullets. Every time he leaves the house his wife, Louise, wonders if he will come back dead or alive. But Lilik, from all accounts, doesn't give much heed to these goings on; it's all part of the daily routine. What interests him, what makes him *chuckle*—there's a word he could never succeed in spelling if he went to school for three solid years!—is the news from the outside world. Perhaps getting it in Hebrew makes it appear even more complicated than it does to us. From that sunny café (even if it's raining) where he sits leisurely sipping his warm beer, leisurely nibbling at a piece of stale cheese, the world outside seems what it truly is—absolutely cockeyed. Sure, he says, we may be having our troubles with the Arabs—he never says "with the bloody Arabs"—but what about Formosa, what about China, Indonesia, Russia, Japan, North Africa and South Africa, West Germany and East Germany, and so on, meaning up and down, back and forth, round and about the grisly gridiron on which the "civilized" nations of the world are matching wits, stoking fires, pushing each other around, shoving, grabbing, scrambling, lying to one another and insulting one another, jeering or menacing, patching up coalitions here, breaking down alliances there, disarming some nations and arming others to the teeth, talking peace and progress and preparing to murder *en masse,* promising this group of devil dogs the latest models in all-out destruction while cautiously limiting others to obsolete fleets, tanks, bombers, rifles, machine guns, hand grenades and flame-throwers, which were once effective in "saving civilization" but are now scarcely more destructive than Fourth of July firecrackers, and firecrackers may soon be eliminated altogether, even for Fourth of

July celebrations, because they are dangerous for children to handle, whereas atom bombs, when kept neatly in stockpiles, wouldn't hurt a fly. As he slyly puts it, quoting Professor Slivovitz, "the analects of logistics, when fed through I.B.M. machines, add up to little more than matzoth balls." What Lilik implies, talking through his dummy professor, is that the voice of insanity can be heard above the evening call to prayer. What we need, as the professor would say, are not more amplifiers, or better amplifiers, but reductors, filters, screens, which will enable us to distinguish between the maudlin ravings of a statesman and the cooing of a turtle dove. . . . I must leave him, dear Lilik, in the peace and serenity of four in the afternoon when bullfighters meet their death and diplomats stab us in the back over their atom bomb cocktails.

(So you grew a peenus, Mrs. Feitelbaum? *Nu,* what else is new?)

Other voices, other rooms; other worries, other microbes. I don't know why, but speaking of the lack of garlic brings to mind the image of that forlorn Basque girl whom I found standing on the road outside our house one late afternoon in winter, her thin, busted shoes waterlogged, her hands numb with cold, too timid to knock at the door but determined to see me if she had to stand there in the rain all night.

What was her urgent mission? To inquire if I were acquainted with Nietzsche's philosophy of "peace and disarmament" as given in the second volume of *Thoughts Out of Season.* The poor girl, what she needed was nourishment, not more "peace and dismemberment." I brought her in, sat her by the fire, dried her skirt and stockings, and had my wife throw a good meal into her. Then, after I had listened to as much as I could take for one evening, I drove her down to Emil White's and begged him to put her up for the night and see that she got a lift in the morning. (She was headed for L.A. No money, no car. All the nuts and crackpots seem headed for L.A. And they all travel light, like the birds of the air.)

Finding the atmosphere congenial at Anderson Creek—the old

story!—she lingered on for a week before hitting the road. She offered Emil a lay before leaving, to show her gratitude, but he wasn't tempted. Too much "peace and dismemberment."

Three or four weeks later I received a letter from her—she was now in Montana—giving me a detailed account of the troubles which a certain tribe of Indians was having with our Federal government and conveying an earnest message from the head of the tribe to come immediately so that I might be informed at first hand of the complicated situation. She stated that they, the headmen of the tribe, would endeavor to persuade me to act as intermediary for them in Washington, D. C. I *of course* immediately chartered a private plane and, flying low over Duck Creek, impressed into my service a secretary, interpreter and full-fledged stenotypist.

Lying awake that night, I thought of a humorous episode which took place in that make-believe world of Washington, D. C., shortly after my return from Europe. Someone in the upper circles, whose acquaintance I had made by hazard in another part of the world, had invited me to a luncheon at a famous club in the heart of our spotless capital. I thought I would be dining with a few of his intimate friends, the usual devotees of "tropical" literature. As one guest after another swept through the revolving door, I noticed that they all had under their arms packages which looked suspiciously alike. It also seemed to me that these guests were one and all men of standing. They were, indeed, as I soon learned. Each one was an official from those departments of the government whose duty it is to be on the lookout for, track down, and bring to just punishment the culprits who deal in pornographic literature. As I was at that time the chief culprit in the government's eye, these representatives of truth and enlightenment were paying me a signal honor in bringing the offending books to be autographed. I must say that they all seemed like good fellows well met, not one of them deranged or undermined, damaged or deteriorated, by my "filthy" books. After apologies for being engaged in such unclean work—apologies given sincerely and accepted sincerely—they pressed me, each in turn, to think of something "original" to inscribe above my signature.

When I thought I had signed them all, an official more imposing looking than the others unwrapped a special package and, dumping a few copies (of this same "tropical" literature), said to me in low tones: "This one, if you will be so kind, I would like inscribed to Secretary So-and-So." When I had faithfully done as bidden, he murmured in an even lower tone of voice: "And this one is for President So-and-So." As he reached for the third copy, I said to myself: "This must be for his Most Holy Eminence, the Pope of Rome!" But it wasn't. It was for one of the nonentities in the Cabinet. The last one he asked me to inscribe, always with the same polite "if you will be so kind!", was destined for the Ambassador from Soviet Russia. It developed that this emissary had requested his wife, who was then visiting Washington, to bring back the most obscene work of mine she could lay hands on. She was to bring it back in person, not entrust it to the diplomatic pouch. At this point, my gorge rising, I excused myself and went to the men's room to throw up. I succeeded only in bringing up some bile. . . .

Not a word of all this is true, of course. Just the ravings of "a Brooklyn boy."

Speaking of this same "tropical" literature, I must add a word about the filthy, tattered, chewed up copies which are sent me from time to time by fans who, in the course of dumping antiquated phonographs and water pistols upon the unsuspecting aborigines of the hinterlands, make occasional visits to bordels and other "slaughterhouses of love" in order, no doubt, to wash away their sins. Since living here in Big Sur I must have received at least a dozen copies of the banned books which these nonchalant marauders filched from the private libraries which are (naturally) to be found in these unorthodox retreats. One wonders who the readers are—the madam, the girls, or the clients? Whoever had read the copies sent me had read them attentively, assiduously and often with a critical eye. Some corrected my spelling, some improved my punctuation, some added phrases here and there which would have thrilled a James Joyce or a Rabelais by their inventiveness. Others, under the influence of drink, no doubt, littered the margins with epithets such as I have never seen anywhere, neither in our own public toilets nor in the toilets of French newspapers, where invention and ribaldry run riot.

Of all the tidbits which pop up in the mail the ones which excite me the most, which leave me dreaming longest, are the picture postcards from the assholes of creation. Imagine getting a postcard from a digger attached to some archaeological expedition in the dreary wastes of Asia Minor who says he has just stumbled on a copy of *Sexus* in the village of Christ knows what name! Or a cryptic message from a celebrated artist whom you have worshipped all your life but never dared write, though in your head you've written him letters yards long, and he says: "Having lunch here (on the banks of the Nile, the Ganges or the Brahmaputra) with some devoted followers of yours"; and there follow the signatures of the starry members of the Pleiades. Or from some atoll in the far Pacific a message scrawled with a broom handle states that the Colonel or the Brigadier-General lifted "my only copy of *Capricorn*, please get me another!" Adding, not entirely for effect—"before I am liquidated." Or comes a letter in a language unknown to you, informing you that the sender has just run across a wonderful passage in a manuscript—a passage about *Capricorn* again—written by a man who died alone on a coral reef. Or an elderly gentleman, once a reviewer and one of the first to acclaim you, writes on crested stationery from his castle in the Hebrides, inquiring if you are still alive, have you written anything since and what is it, adding (sorrowfully): "You see, I've been knighted since!" Since what? Possibly since writing the review which cost him his job!

All these messages, inquiries, fond wishes and tokens of affection and remembrance create an elation which may last for days, not because you're puffed up but because, just as when you were very young and very much in love with a will-o'-the-wisp, some bedraggled Gypsy, reading your hand, drove you to fever pitch telling you all the things you already knew when all you wanted to hear were those three magic words—*"She loves you!"*

When the Armenian soothsayer, in Athens, was predicting the varied and exciting voyages I was yet to undertake, when he was indicating the general directions of these voyages, one indubitably toward the Orient, another unmistakably toward the South Pacific, and so on, the question which was hammering in my brain was: "Be specific! Tell me if I shall ever get to Lhasa, to Mecca, to Timbuctoo!" Today I realize that if I do not get there in person one of my "emissaries" will, and I'll one day know everything I long to know, not in the life to come but in this life here on earth.

9.

They say you can chop off a lizard's tail and he'll grow a new one just as fast as you please. But why chop the poor creature's tail off? Similarly, it's useless to vanquish, or even liquidate, your enemies since the morrow will only bring you new ones. Do we want peace or do we simply want to be spared a horrible end?

I think in much the same fashion about what we style our needs. Not what we *crave,* for to crave (even sainthood) only piles up more Karma. In Dianetics they speak of "clears" and of those who have not yet been "cleared," which means the vast majority of us. The only "clears" I have met thus far are men and women who never heard of Dianetics. When you're a "clear," no matter what school of thought you belong to—a genuine "clear" would belong to none—you usually get what you want when you need it. Neither too soon nor too late, neither too much nor too little. You and your needs go through the clearing house together, so to speak. With neurotics it's the other way round: a neurotic is always on the outside looking in, or, if he *is* on the inside, he's like a fish in an aquarium.

I don't wish to pretend that I'm a "clear," but I do know that things are clarifying for me more and more every day. I didn't have to reach the age of forty-five to realize that man is an angelic as well as a diabolic being; but it wasn't until I reached my forties that I was able to put the two elements of our being together and regard them as happily wedded. As soon as I ceased to look for the devil in a man (or woman) I found the angel, and vice versa. Finally I was able to see a human being for what he is—not two but one. And when I reached that point I was able to understand many things which before I had conveniently labeled as white magic or black magic. I became aware eventually only of magic, pure magic, nothing but magic. If it were used for selfish purposes it worked disastrously; if used unselfishly the effect was beyond all expectation. But it was the same one substance, no matter how used.

Today the whole world has been made aware of this simple truth through the frightening presence of the atom bomb. The difference between thinking in terms of atomic energy and thinking in terms of magic is the same as between examining a micro-organism through a microscope and piercing the multiverse with a high-powered telescope. In the one case you tend to concentrate on nothingness and in the other on infinitude.

When you begin to differentiate between "shadow and substance" you're already toying with magic. Or, to put it another way, you have the lamp in your hands but you haven't yet learned to wish for the right thing. You rub it absent-mindedly now and then. And, "just like magic," things happen. What an odd word—

happen! Things happen, just like you yourself happened. It takes time to catch on to just what it is that happens each time, but by dint of repetition you gradually discover—the speed depending on the ratio between clear and foggy—that "to happen," which is only an infinitive, is exactly the right expression, and that you are not dealing with an intransitive verb (the Chinese have no "intransitives") but with a thought symbol mysteriously related to the most potent, continuous energy imaginable, what in good, old-fashioned parlance is called "the will of God." Lifted out of the gibberish in which it's generally wrapped, these four words simply mean that the Intelligence which directs the universe, or the Mind which is the Universe, is there to draw on, there to collaborate with, when *you* stop trying to run the show.

To give a problematic example, here is how this perennial magic works. . . .

Instead of bucking your head against a stone wall (why do we get headaches so often?), sit quietly with hands folded and wait for the wall to crumble. If you're willing to wait an eternity, it may happen in the twinkling of an eye. For walls often give way quicker than the proud spirit which rules us. Don't sit and *pray* that it will happen! Just sit and *watch* it happen. Sit thus, indifferent to everything that has been said and taught about walls. From dwelling on the headache which you will notice has departed, dwell on the emptiness between things, and finally on the emptiness *of* things. When this vast emptiness is filled with nothing but emptiness you will awaken to the fact that what you regarded as a wall is not a wall at all, but a bridge possibly, or a ladder of fire. The wall will still be there, of course, and if you had only ordinary vision it would be much like any other wall, but now you've lost that kind of vision and with it the difficulty that a bricklayer has in understanding what a scientist means when he explains what the elements of a wall really are. You have an edge over the scientist because you feel no need to explain anything. What is, *is*.

The foregoing is paregorical. Those who understand will understand. Those who don't will still have a bellyache—or a headache. Let me put it yet another way. . . .

We have all observed how our friends turn themselves over to the surgeon when the physician's efforts have failed. Or to the analyst—for psychic surgery—when there is no other way out. Or to a disciple of the Bates method when the eye specialist confesses his helplessness. Or to a Christian Scientist practitioner when the only other resort seems suicide. In one way or another we all, when we get truly desperate, fling ourselves "into the arms of Jesus."

Now then. . . . Throughout the sad history of medicine there are marginal figures (beside whose names a great question mark is always affixed) who have worked miracles which the medicos (of all ages) endeavor to nullify, with nothing more, sometimes, than a shrug of the shoulders. Generally speaking, it is only the hopeless cases which are served up to this type of healer. It is said of Paracelsus, for example, that in several instances he resuscitated the dead. Jesus waited three days before raising Lazarus from the grave. And in Jesus' own time there lived an even more astounding miracle worker than himself, if we are to believe the accounts given of his life and work. I refer to Apollonius of Tyana. As for Cabeza de Vaca, who led an altogether charmed life, until the moment that he was commanded to heal or die he had no knowledge whatever of his healing powers.

The annals of folklore abound in spectacular cures by men and women whose names are now forgotten. One of the striking features of these heretical performances is what might be called the technique of nonrecognition. Just as Gandhi successfully exploited the doctrine of nonresistance, so these "aberrants" practiced nonrecognition: nonrecognition of sin, guilt, fear and disease . . . even death.

The medico, on the other hand, is a type who is not only on the alert for the slightest symptoms of malaise but who instills in us his predilection for and obsession with maladies which are Hydra-headed, which increase in the measure that he so "successfully" copes with them. We pay a heavy price for the dubious benefits which our authorized "healers" confer. For the privilege of being repaired by a professional expert we are expected to sacrifice the rewards of years of labor. Those who are unable to afford the luxury of being carved to pieces by an expert butcher must die or cure themselves. The curious thing about these expensive overhaulings is that one is offered no guarantee of immunity (after the event) against other, often worse, ailments. Indeed, it seems to work the other way round. The more we are patched up the more dilapidated we become. One may continue to exist, but only as a walking cadaver.

Today the physician, as we once thought him to be, is becoming obsolete. In his place there rules a queer triumvirate: the diagnostician, the laboratory worker, and the pharmacist. The holy family which doles out miracle drugs. The surgeon is now getting only the scraps, juicy scraps, I must say, since he is still extremely prosperous and always on the point of drinking himself to death.

Now and then, at the sulphur baths, I meet a perfect specimen of health and vitality who was given up by the doctors years ago. They all tell the same story: they forgot about their ailments, they ignored them, they found something to do—something of a serviceable nature—which made them forget themselves.

I wouldn't be dwelling on this painful subject if it were not for the fact that I receive so many letters dealing with it, if it were not one of the most frequent topics of conversation when visitors arrive. Perhaps I attract people who are given to experimentation. Perhaps I attract individuals who are struggling manfully to pierce the hocus-pocus which envelops and obstructs our march through life. People are constantly supplying me with startling facts, amazing events, incredible experiences—as if I were another Charles Fort. They struggle, they rebel, they experiment, they get glimpses of truth, they are raised up by spasmodic gusts of self-confidence—and yet they are hopelessly enmeshed. "Dear fellow-sufferers," I feel like saying, "I *know* you are perplexed and bewildered, I *know* you are riddled with doubts, I *know* you are searching and struggling, but would it not be wiser to stop struggling (even against struggling), wiser to give way to doubt completely, test everything in the light of your own conscience, and abide by the answer?" One will tell you that the stars are against him, another that his job is driving him crazy or that his boss is a bloodsucker, another that he had a bad start in life or that his wife is the cause of all his misery, another that he is not fit to cope with a world as rotten as ours, and so on and so on.

However true these statements may be—God knows, they may be each and every one all too true!—however much we feel the need to justify our inexplicable behavior, the fact remains that once we have decided to live, once we have decided to enjoy life, none of these disturbing, distressing, crippling factors is of the least importance. I have known cripples and invalids who were radiant sources of joy and inspiration. And I have known "successful" men and women who were like running sores. Had we the power to resurrect the dead, what could we offer that life itself has not already offered, and continues to offer, in full measure? What *is* one to say to young people who, at the very threshold of manhood or womanhood, throw themselves like dogs at your feet and beg for a crust of comfort? What has come over these youngsters who, instead of upsetting the world with their fiery thoughts and deeds, are already seeking ways of escape from the world? What is happening to make the young old before their time, frustrated instead of liberated? What is it gives them the notion that they are useless and unfit for life's struggles?

What is happening? Life is making new demands upon us. The cosmic cataclysms which ancient man had to face have given way to moral cataclysms. The cyclotron not only smashed atoms, it smashed our moral codes. The day of wrath is upon us, but in an unexpected guise. Conveniences have been converted to scourges: only the gods know how to handle thunder and lightning. And yet, a truly young man, a product of the age, as we say—a Tamerlane, an Alexander, a Napoleon—would be fixing to throw a bomb which would restore us to sanity. He would not be thinking of ways of escape but of how to kill off his elders and all they represent. He would be thinking how to give this tired world a new lease on life. He would already be writing his name in the sky.

There is a young French Canadian I know whose brain is seething with just such thoughts. He smells of genius a mile off. His letters are packed with extraordinary pickings and gleanings from every imaginable realm. He seems to be acquainted with all the doctrines and dogmas, even the most hairsplitting ones, which man has ejected from his tortured brain. He can write in the tone of a sage, a poet, a madman, or like "Jesus the Second." In one letter he will lift me to the heavens, in the next crush me like a worm. He can take Freud and Einstein apart, put them together again, and make lamb fries of them. He can analyze his imaginary ailments with the skill and dexterity of a Hindu pundit. He can almost walk on water but he can't swim worth a duck. He is at once the most endearing, the most lovable, the most promising young man *and* the most pestiferous. He can be cantankerous to such a degree that you feel like taking the axe to him. And when he chooses, he will woo you like a turtledove. In one letter he's found the solution to the world's problems, his own included, and in the following letter he's impatiently marking time until his next incarnation. If today he's avid about Ramakrishna or Krishnamurti, tomorrow he may be even more so about the Marquis de Sade or Gilles de Rais.

The question which agitates my young friend most is: what role shall I play in life? Joseph Delteil, in an early work, says simply: *"Sois potentat!"* In the chapter called *"Toi d'abord!"* he begins thus: *"Fouille-toi les tripes: là sont toute puissance et toute vérité! La vertu est un mot romain qui signifie estomac."* He continues— I am lifting phrases here and there: *"Tu as droit de volupté. La vie est ta femme: baise-la à ta guise.... Méfie-toi des penseurs: ce sont des paralytiques. De doux et tristes impuissants. . . . Méfie-toi des* *rêveurs: ce sont des aveugles. . . . Sous prétexte qu'ils ne voient pas le monde, ils le nient."**

Chesterton, in his book on Dickens, has much to say about playing the fool, or rather, being the fool. Above all, about appreciating the fool. In the chapter called "The Great Dickens Characters" we get passages like the following:

"He [Dickens] declared two essential things about it [life]— that it was laughable, and that it was livable. The humble characters of Dickens do not amuse each other with epigrams; they amuse each other with themselves.

"The key to the great characters of Dickens is that they are all great fools. . . . The great fool is a being who is above wisdom rather than below it. . . . A man can be entirely great while he is entirely foolish. We see this in the epic heroes, such as Achilles. Nay, a man can be entirely great because he is entirely foolish.

"It may be noticed that the great artists always choose great fools rather than great intellectuals to embody humanity. Hamlet does express the aesthetic dreams and the bewilderment of the intellect; but Bottom the Weaver expresses them much better.

"There is an apostolic injunction to suffer fools gladly. We always lay the stress on the word 'suffer,' and interpret the passage as one urging resignation. It might be better, perhaps, to lay the stress upon the word 'gladly,' and make our familiarity with fools a delight, and almost a dissipation."†

There is not such a world of difference between being a "potentate," as Delteil urges, and being a great, a sublime fool. In a later work called *Jesus II*,‡ Delteil, writing with all the fire and enthusiasm of youth, plus the divine wisdom of the fool, gives us a profound and hilarious piece of writing, profound because it is so hilarious. It is something like the Sunday of Creation, this book, and the message it conveys is one which could only be given on the

---

* *De J.-J. Rousseau à Mistral* by Joseph Delteil (Paris: Editions du Capitole, 1928).

† *Charles Dickens* (New York: Dodd, Mead and Co., 1906).

‡ *Jesus II*, by Joseph Delteil (Paris: Flammarion, 1947).

Seventh Day. In it Jesus the Second runs around like a chicken with its head cut off. *"Sauve qui peut!"* he screams as he gallops from one corner of the earth to another, warning of the imminent destruction which threatens. Toward the end, somewhere in the vague vicinity of Mt. Ararat, he runs into a rum, staid fellow, none other than old Adam himself. There ensues a delicious dialogue about the wicked ones, "they" who are responsible for all our ills. As this Jesus enumerates the great crimes being committed in the name of humanity (the book was written with the war fresh in mind), old Adam scoffingly says: "Pooh! *Nada, supernada!*" It is apparent that this Jesus is at the end of his rope, and what is worse, at the end of his wits. Old Adam has blandly dismissed all the horrors, all the crimes, all the atrocities with a—*"Gestes que tout cela. . . . Jeux de mains, ombres chinoises, phénomenologie."*

"The evil's not there," says old Adam, in a suave, secretive voice, a voice as *"inouie"* as the first almond blossom. "The evil is within." It is not act but state, he explains. *Being,* and not doing. "Evil is in the soul!"

There was a Biblical silence. One heard the centuries clicking away beyond the sky . . . then a salvo of machine-gun fire somewhere . . . military laughs, boots. . . .

"Each man for himself! Scram!" cries Jesus.

"Child!" says the other. . . . "The earth is round. . . . 'They' are everywhere. . . . Even in the Garden of Eden."

Jesus is speechless.

"So what!" says Adam. "I've been here, calm and tranquil, since the beginning. . . . *Incognito,* my son: that's the great secret. . . . I've taken to the underground . . . the underground of the soul. *(le maquis de l'âme)."*

When you put the book down you feel as if God's own angels had made pipi in your hair. The raciness of the language, the exuberance of spirit, the hilarious blaphemy and obscenity, the reckless freedom of invention, give it a magical quality. Nobody is spared, nothing is left sacred. Yet the book is an act of pure reverence—reverence for life. When your stomach muscles cease twitching, when you have wiped the last tear away, you realize not that you have been made a fool of (which is what the critics would have you believe) but that you have just parted company with a fool of the first magnitude, a fool who scuttled your addled pate and, in lieu of wisdom, in lieu of salvation, took you for a ride "to laughter unending."

And this, if I possessed the gift, is what I would offer my young Canadian friend who passed his bleak youth in an even bleaker atmosphere but who is now, thank God, living a life of sin in that delightful city of vice and corruption, Paris. He has not yet taken his soul to the underground—but give him time! After the imaginary ailments come the real ailments. After inoculation, immunity. After immortality, eternity. After Jesus first, second, third and last, old Adam remains. Adam Cadmus. Aren't the hollyhocks just glorious? And have you seen those Johnny-jump-ups? Why did you take that crucifix down from the wall? Put it back! Haven't I said that every crucifixion worth the name is a rosy one? *"Suave qui peut?"* Poouah! Try this Liederkranz . . . it's sublime. . . .

10.

One of the subjects frequently discussed in these parts is discipline, the discipline which children should or should not be given. No subject, not even the atom bomb, can create more divergence of opinion, more conflict, between good neighbors. Pressed to the wall, every one will agree that the only discipline worth the name is self-discipline. But, and here's where the fireworks commence— "children have to be taught how to behave!"

How does one go about teaching children to behave? (*Properly,* of course.) Off-hand one would think that there was but one answer: *by example.* But anyone who has participated in such a discussion knows that this is the last thin line of defense. The power of example seems to be regarded as a minor technique in the strategy of daily warfare. It's the reply of a saint, not of a harassed, bewildered parent or teacher. Somewhere in the course of an interminable argument you are sure to be informed that saints didn't have children of their own, or that Jesus, who said, "Suffer the little ones to come unto me for of such is the Kingdom of Heaven," might have spoken otherwise had he known what are called domestic problems. In other words, that Jesus was talking through his hat.

The other day, getting my shoes shined, I had a most interesting conversation with the colored bootblack, William Greenwell. I always patronize the Reverend Greenwell because with the shoe-shine I receive a few gratuitous words of wisdom. My friend, who is a trustee of the Baptist Church and a lecturer and critic of Bible teachings, is probably well known in Monterey. One can't help noticing his stand, which is in the hallway of a rooming house, because at the entrance there is always a pair of high boots from which calla lilies are sprouting.

From morning till night the Reverend Greenwell is at his stand shining shoes. And always in the same attire: a shabby army coat and pants, a dingy apron, and a battered-looking fedora dating from the Civil War. No matter how the conversation starts, it's sure to finish with the Bible. My friend *knows* his Bible. He quotes from it freely, and often at length, giving chapter and verse together with commentary and exegesis. In his mouth the words sound pungent and provocative, alive and immediate.

The other day, as I took my place on the throne, he inquired after my boy, who usually wants a shoeshine too. That started the conversation. *Youth!* The Reverend Greenwell's eyes lit up when he pronounced the word. He has four sons of his own, all grown men now, whom he had done his best "to raise the right way." But it was the grandson, he remarked, who opened his eyes. This little fellow was *different*. He had a way of his own, and at times he presented a problem.

He went on to say that this grandson had awakened his curiosity. Instead of correcting him, instead of pushing him around, he had set himself to study the boy's ways and to discover, if possible, why he behaved as he did.

"You can shout and threaten and punish all you like," he observed, "but the truth is that each and every one of us is unique, has a nature all his own. It's no use saying 'Don't do this,' or 'Don't do that!' Find out *why* it is he chooses to do this instead of that, or that instead of this. You can't push people around, especially not little people. You can only *guide* them. And that's an art! Yes *sir!*" He looked at me with a gleam in his eye.

"Now look at Nature. Nature has her own way of handling problems. When a man's old, Nature takes him and she stretches him out in death. 'You're finished,' she says. 'Give the young ones a chance!' The world belongs to the young, not the old. As soon as a man comes of age he hardens and stiffens. He *rigidifies,* that's what. Nature *never* grows old. Nature stands for life, for growth, for flexibility, for experimentation. With Nature it's all give and take. Nature is all one substance; she's not at war with herself. We too are members of the one body." He paused a moment and held his arm aloft. "Mutilate *that* and the whole body suffers!"

Another pause to expectorate. He's a tobacco-chewing man.

"No, my friend, man is full of pride and conceit. Full of arrogance. Always wanting it *his* way, not God's way. Look at the world! Look at these young people milling about—they're all at sea. No one to tell them which way to go, which road to take. It's all wrong from the start—I mean our system of education. We fill their minds with a lot of things that are of no use to them and we tell them nothing about the things they ought to know. We stuff them with false knowledge. We try to bend them and twist them to *our* way of thinking. We never, teach them to think for themselves. We're on their backs all the time. *'Don't do this, don't do that!* Not *that* way, *this* way!' It's no good, it won't work. It's not Nature's way, or God's.

"Every child that's born into the world has the power to open our eyes, to give us a new vision of life. And what do we do? Try to make him over, make him into our own image. And who are we? *What* are we? Are we models of wisdom and under-standing? Because a man has wealth or fame, because he com-mands an army or has invented a new weapon of destruction, does that make him a better man than you or I? Does that make him a better father, a better teacher?

"Most of us know little more than we were told. That isn't very much, is it? Nothing to brag about, anyway. Now a child is born innocent. A child brings with it light and love . . . and a hunger to learn. The adult is looking toward the grave, or else toward the past. But the child lives in the present, in the spirit of the eternal. No, we're not *educating* our children: we're driving them, pushing them, shoving them around. We're teaching them to make the same foolish mistakes we made—and then we punish them for imitating us. That's not Nature's way. That's *man's* way . . . *the human way.* And it leads to sin and death."

I often think of Greenwell's words when my own two youngsters get to plying me with questions I can't answer. As a rule I tell them the truth—"I don't know." And if they say, "Mommy would know," or "Harrydick knows," or "God knows, doesn't He?" I say, "Fine! You ask him (or her) next time."

I try to convey the idea that ignorance is no sin. I even hint, softly, to be sure, that there are questions which nobody can answer, not even Mommy or Harrydick. I hope in this way to prepare them for the revelation which is sure to come one day that acquiring knowledge is like biting into a cheese which grows bigger with every bite. I also hope to instill the thought that to answer a question oneself is better than having someone answer it for you. Even if it's the wrong answer! Only on quiz programs do we get the "correct" answers—but what do they add up to?

The gulf between knowledge and truth is infinite. Parents talk a lot about truth but seldom bother to deal in it. It's much simpler to dispense ready-made knowledge. More expedient too, for truth demands patience, endless, endless patience. The happiest expedient of all is to bundle kids off to school just as soon as they can stand the strain. There they not only get "learning," which is a crude substitute for knowledge, but discipline.

I've said a number of times, and I say it again—as a boy I led a happy life. A very happy life. I only remember being "disciplined" once, and that was at my mother's bidding. Evidently I had misbehaved the whole day, to the point of exasperation. When my father came home from work that evening he was informed that he was to give me a sound thrashing. I could see from the expression my father assumed that he wasn't overjoyed to perform this humiliating task. I felt sorry for him. When therefore he took off his leather slipper and whacked me with it, I pretended that it hurt and I bawled just as loud as I could. I hoped that would make him feel better. He was not a man to mete out punishment to anyone, let alone his own son. And so I collaborated to the best of my ability.

In the eyes of the neighbors here I don't rate very high as a father. For one thing, I don't "lower the boom" often enough. I have a reputation for being too lenient, too indulgent. Now and then, when I've lost my temper, I *have* clobbered the kids. When they pushed me too far, as we say. When this happens I immediately feel repentant and I try to forget the incident as quickly as possible. I never harbor any feelings of guilt, nor do I promise myself that I will be more strict with them in future—so as to avoid a recurrence of these disgraceful scenes. The child lives in the moment, and I do my best to follow his example.

When I particularly loathe myself is when I catch myself saying: "If you don't watch out you're going to catch it again!" I feel that a threat is worse than a blow. The healthier children are, the more bounce they have, the more frequent are the threats hurled at them. Normal, healthy children are natural-born hell-raisers. They were not made for the life we offer them, we who have given up the ghost, who conform every step of the way. Well-behaved children may be a delight to live with but they rarely make outstanding men and women. I make exception where the parents are themselves unusual, where they have created an atmosphere of harmony through the everyday practice of goodness, kindness and understanding. But how many homes radiate this kind of atmosphere? In the Western world the home is a battleground where husband fights wife, brother fights sister, and parents fight the children. The din is only drowned by the radio, which echoes the same situation, only on a bigger, more brutal, more perverted, more despicable scale. And if it isn't drowned that way, it's drowned in alcohol. Such is "home" for the child of today. In the civilized world, at any rate.

Acting the doting father, I was the boy who remembered the wonderful, riotous times he had doing all the things he was not supposed to do. I cannot recall ever being seriously unhappy until the pangs of *Weltschmerz* set in.

As a father I've also been somewhat of a mother, because not having a job like other honest citizens—writing is only a pastime!— I was always within earshot, always within reach, when the kids got out of hand. As a father who was also unhappily married, I had often to act as arbiter when there should have been no need for an arbiter. Whatever decisions I made, they were wrong, and they were subsequently used against me. At least, so it seemed to me.

One of the minor aspects of this tragicomic dilemma was the fact that my wife believed that she was protecting *me*. Protecting me, I mean to say, from the annoyances which children are prone to inflict upon fathers who have nothing more important to do than write books. Since she did everything by the book, and to the extreme, the protection she was offering me usually worked more harm than good. Or so I regarded it. (I know I didn't always see straight!)

Anyway, it went something like this. . . . No matter what happened, they were not to disturb me at work. If they fell and hurt themselves, they were not to make a fuss about it. If they had to weep or scream, they were to do it out of earshot. (It never occurred to her, I suppose, that I would have felt much better if they had come and wept on my shoulder.) Whatever it was they wanted, they were to wait until I was ready to give them my attention. If, in spite of all injunctions, they knocked at my studio door—and they did, of course!—they were made to feel that they were guilty of committing a small crime. And, if I were foolish enough to open the door and give them a moment's attention, then I was abetting the crime. Worse, I was guilty of sabotage. If I took a breather, and profited by it to see what the kids were up to, then I was guilty of encouraging them to expect things of me which they had no right to expect.

By midafternoon I usually had but one thought—to get as far away from the house as possible, and take the kids with me. Often we would return home exhausted. And when children get exhausted they are not the most amenable creatures in the world.

It was an endless circle. *Punkt!*

When the separation came about I made a forlorn and desperate effort to be a father *and* mother. The girl had just started school, but the boy, her junior by three years, was too young to attend school. What he needed was a nurse or a governess. Now and then a neighbor—and here I think especially of that kind soul, Dorothy Herbert—came and lent a hand. In a short time I realized that there was nothing to do but to entrust the boy to his mother's care, which I did, with the understanding that she would return him to me as soon as I found someone capable of providing him with the proper care and attention.

Shortly thereafter an attractive-looking woman knocked at the door and said she had been told that I was looking for someone to take care of my children. She had two children of her own, about the same age as ours, and she had separated from her husband. All she wanted was room and board in exchange for her services. As she expressed it, she didn't care what was demanded of her, if only she might live in Big Sur.

Her arrival coincided with the arrival of my wife and boy, who had come to celebrate the girl's birthday. What a stroke of fortune, I thought, as I explained the situation. To my astonishment my wife agreed that the young woman seemed suitable for the task, and after a few tears, consented to leave the boy in my care.

It was a hectic day. From miles around the kids had come to celebrate and jubilate. Some of them brought their parents along.

I forgot to say that a few days previous to this event my friend Walker Winslow had installed himself in the studio above. He had driven all the way from Topeka with his left hand, having cracked his right shoulder blade some weeks before. Knowing of my plight, Walker had volunteered his services as cook and part-time "governess," hoping, no doubt, that he would find a few hours a day in which to work in peace and quiet. (He had received a commission from a big publisher to do a book on the founder of the Menninger Foundation, where he had been staying.*) He also looked forward, no doubt, to repeating the pleasant experiences we had shared while at Anderson Creek.

In the course of the merrymaking the young woman, Ivy was her name, discreetly withdrew from sight. She was shy and somewhat embarrassed, knowing no one present and having no particular role to fill. Strolling about by her lonesome she ran into Walker.

---

* *The Menninger Story* (New York: Doubleday, 1956).

As Walker related it to me afterwards, Ivy was on the point of leaving then and there. She was depressed, confused, and thoroughly ill at ease. However, after a cup of coffee and a quiet chat in the studio, he had succeeded in restoring her self-confidence. Walker is easy to talk to, and women particularly find him very understanding, very comforting.

Later that day he took me aside to explain that I might have difficulties with Ivy, that she was emotionally disturbed because of her own unhappy life, and somewhat intimidated by the responsibility she was assuming. The situation was aggravated, for her, by the fact that she would be obliged to leave her own two children in her husband's care.

"I felt I ought to tell you this," he said. Then he added: "But I think she deserves a tryout. She means well, I know that."

Walker was of the opinion that if the arrangement didn't work out well he and I should be able to look after the children. I could take care of Tony in the morning and he in the afternoon. He would do all the cooking and the dish-washing too. But it would be better if Ivy proved equal to the task.

Ivy lasted just about twelve hours. She quit cold, giving as her reason that my kids were "impossible." My wife, of course, had already left and I was in no hurry to inform her of the turn of events. Walker had to drive Ivy and her two youngsters to town and rush home to prepare the evening meal.

After dinner we had a short talk. "Are you sure you want to keep the children now?" he asked. I told him I felt up to it, if he would carry out his end of the bargain.

The very next day the fun began. To devote a whole morning to a three-year-old boy full of piss and vinegar is a job for someone with six hands and three pairs of legs. No matter what we decided to play, the jig lasted only a few minutes. Every toy in the place had been taken out, used, and thrown aside in less than an hour. If I suggested that we go for a walk he was too tired. There was an old tricycle he liked to ride, but before the morning was out a wheel had come off and, though I sweated blood, I simply could not make it stay on again. I tried playing ball but his co-ordination wasn't good enough; I almost had to stand on top of him and put the ball in his hands. I got out his building blocks too—several bushel baskets full—and tried, as they say, to have him do something "constructive," but his interest in this pastime lay exclusively in kicking the house, or the bridge, apart after I had built it. That was fun! I tied all his choo-choo cars together, added a few tin cans and other noise-makers to them, and ran about like a zany while he sat and watched me. This bored the shit out of him in no time.

At intervals Walker showed up to see how we were making out. Finally—it couldn't have been later than ten o'clock, if that late—he said: "Go up and work a while. I'll take over. You need a break."

More to recover myself than to work, I reluctantly obeyed. There I sat, in my den, poring over the pages I had just finished, but too dead to squeeze out another line. What I wanted, early as it was, was a nap! I could hear Tony shouting and screaming, shrieking and wailing. Poor Walker!

When Val arrived, after school, the difficulties increased. It was nothing but fight, fight, fight. Even if it were nothing more than a rock which one of them had picked up, the other one immediately claimed it. *It's mine, I saw it first! You did not! I did too see it first. Caca pipi head, caca pipi head!* (Their favorite expression.) It now demanded the full time of the two of us to handle the situation. By dinnertime we were always pooped out.

It was the same old story every day. No improvements, no progress. An absolute standstill. Walker, being an early riser, managed to get some work done before breakfast. He was up at five, regular as a clock. After he had made himself a pot of strong coffee he would sit down to the machine. When he wrote, he wrote fast. He did everything fast. As for me, I would remain in bed till the last horn, hoping to store up an extra supply of nervous energy. (I didn't know, in those days, about "rose hips," nor about calcium and phosphorus tablets, nor about tiger's milk.) As for getting any writing done, I dismissed the idea once and for all. Even a writer has first of all to be, and to feel like, a human being. My problem was—to survive. Always I nourished the illusion that someone would turn up to rescue me, someone who loved children and knew how to handle them. Whatever I needed usually came my way, when sorely pressed. Why not the perfect governess? In my dreams I always pictured my savior in the guise of a Hindu, Javanese or Mexican, a woman of the people, simple, not too intelligent, but definitely possessed of that one great prerequisite: *patience.*

Evenings, after the kids had been put to bed, poor Walker would endeavor to engage me in talk. It was hopeless. I had only one thought in mind—to get to bed as soon as possible. Every day I would say to myself: "It can't go on this way forever. *Courage,* you poor imbecile!" Every night, on climbing into bed, I would repeat: "Another day! Patience, *patience!*"

One day, after he had been to town to fetch supplies, Walker quietly announced that he had looked up Ivy. "Just wanted to see how she was getting along." I thought it was very kind of Walker to do that. Just like him, of course. The sort of man who looks after every one who is in trouble. And always getting himself into trouble.

What I didn't know, until after the next trip to town, was that he and Ivy had become close friends. Or, as he put it: "Ivy seems to have a yen for me." In the interim Ivy's problems had taken a new twist. Having no means of support, she had been obliged to surrender her children to her husband. She was supposed to be quite cut up about this.

I had made the mistake of telling Walker that I never wanted to see Ivy again. She had left me in the lurch after a half-hearted effort and, like the elephant, I found it hard to forgive her. If her own children were well behaved, I said, it was only because their mother was a cold, ruthless bitch.

Walker defended her as best he could, assuring me that I would change my mind once I got to know her. "She has her troubles too," he said. "Don't forget that." But I was thoroughly unimpressed.

Winter had set in and with it the rains. Ivy showed up unannounced one afternoon and remained a few days. She made no effort to help with the children, or even with the cooking and cleaning. Knowing that I disliked her, she kept out of bounds. Occasionally she would pop in toward dark to sit by the little stove and poke the fire. For some reason she had fallen in love with this stove, so much so that she kept it clean and polished.

How the two of them managed in the studio above was beyond me. It was altogether without conveniences of any kind; there wasn't even a sink in it. The woodstove, which I had found somewhere, smoked continually. The floor was of cement and over it, to keep his feet dry, Walker had strewn some filthy, discarded rugs, potato sacks and torn sheets. The sliding door, which used to be the entrance (when it was a garage), gaped at both ends, thus providing an unwelcome circulation of air. Overhead, between the plaster-boards and the roofing, the squirrels and the rats made merry night and day. What was particularly exacerbating was the sound of nuts rolling back and forth up there. Not only did the roof leak but the windows too. When it rained a pool of water collected on the floor in no time. Hardly a "love nest," I must say.

Ivy had hardly returned to town when the rains came down in earnest. Never have I seen it rain as it did that winter. For days on end it deluged us, like a punishment from above. During this period it was impossible for Val to go to school; the school was about ten miles away and the road from our house to the highway was virtually unnavigable. This meant that I had to keep the two of them indoors—and keep them happy.

We worked at it in relays, Walker and I. When it came nap time I lay down with them. I hoped by doing so to replenish my

powers for the second half of the day. What a delusion! All we
did at nap time was to toss to and fro. When I thought "we" had
enough, I would tell them to scram—and that they would do, like
kittens scrambling out of a sack. Usually I was more exhausted
after the nap than I had been before. The hours that lay ahead
moved like lead.

The room in which all the shenanigans went on was of ordinary
size and fortunately not too cluttered with furniture. The main
obstructions were the bed, the table and the little stove. I say
"obstructions" because to make their joy unconfined I had given
them permission to use their bikes indoors. The bikes were brought
into play whenever they grew tired of games. To clear the deck
(from front door to back door) for the races the floor had first to
be cleared of all obstacles. Everything was thrown on the bed and
the table. The table was piled with chairs, toys, tools and imple-
ments, and the bed with games, bugles, swords, rubber dolls, balls,
klaxons, building blocks, rifles and toy soldiers. The rugs I rolled
up and shoved against the big French windows where the rain
water always collected. In the middle of the room, where the bed
and the stove faced each other, there was always danger of traffic
congestion. From whichever end of the room they began the racing
they always collided between the stove and the bed. Naturally they
engaged in the usual abusive arguments which traffic snarls provoke.

They could keep it up for an hour or more at a time, the bike
races. I had no place to sit or lie, so I stood first in one spot, then
another, like a referee at a boxing match. Now children who are
having fun hate to see a grownup idling his time away. It didn't
take them long to suggest that, since I had chosen to stand and
watch, I might as well be a traffic cop. I was provided with a club,
a rifle and a diminutive bobby's hat which someone had made
Tony a gift of. Oh yes, and a whistle! My job was to wait till
they rode a few paces, blow the whistle, put my hand up—vertically
or horizontally—and then blow again. Sometimes the change of

pace was so abrupt that one of us would accidentally get conked with a club or a rifle butt. As to whether they were genuine accidents was always a matter of hot dispute.

From the bike performance we generally moved into the clown and tumbling act. At this point Walker would be summoned. Walker was a good head taller than I, and when he put them on his shoulders and started trotting and bucking they were in seventh heaven. When Walker had had enough of it, I would get down on the floor and engage them in the snake act. This meant squirming and struggling, with one on top and the other below, until someone got flattened. It had no other purpose than to use up energy quickly. To get a breather, I would suggest we roll dice or shoot marbles. We played dice for pennies, for chips, for buttons and for matches. They were on the way to becoming real good crap-shooters, I must say. When that gig was up, Walker or I would play the clown.

The act they loved the most was an imitation of Red Skelton advertising some famous brand of beer and getting drunk in the process. Red Skelton had been to the house some months before and he had put on this skit as the crowning touch to a long and most hilarious afternoon. The kids had not forgotten it. Never would. Nor I either.... To do it properly, one has to have a suit of old clothes and a battered slouch hat, preferably a size too big. The reason is simple. Aside from the beer which one has to guzzle, and which must trickle freely over one's chin, throat and chest, there comes a fall at the end which, taken on a floor slippery with beer and pieces of bread and cheese, plays havoc with one's clothes. (Oddly enough, what my kids remember most vividly about that afternoon when Skelton came is the fact that he himself, he, the great Red Skelton, had insisted on mopping up the mess he made!) Anyway, as all television fans know, it's a sloppy, goofy, hiccoughing, sidesplitting performance. Anything goes, so long as you keep on guzzling, spilling the beer, sticking bread into your eyes and ears, and rocking back and forth on your heels. Sometimes I actually felt drunk after giving one of these imitations. The kids would get even drunker. Just watching, I mean. At the end we would all be flopping around like double-jointed crowbars. If I happened now and then to slide under the bed, I would lie there as long as possible, to recuperate.

Then dinner. Time for a general cleanup. Had a visitor walked in at this hour he would have thought himself in a lunatic asylum. For one thing, we had to work fast. Because, when Walker starts cooking, he cooks like lightning. Every evening he would cook a full course meal, beginning with soup and salad and including meat, potatoes, gravy, vegetables, biscuits and pie or custard pudding.

Of course everyone was famished by dinnertime. What objects we had failed to allocate during the cleaning up period we left on the floor—for later. Later meant after the kids had retired for the night, when, so to speak, there was nothing more to do. It was only a half-hour's work, this mopping up. A pleasant fillip to a gruelling day. Bending, stooping, sorting, wiping, disentangling, arranging and rearranging—child's play, you might say. I used to think how lucky I was that we had no pets to take care of, no livestock in the house, no bird cages to clean out.

A word about the meals. . . . To me they were delicious. Every day I blessed Walker for being the excellent cook he was. Not the kids, however! Hungry though they were, it was not the sort of cooking they had been used to. One didn't like gravy, the other didn't like fat. "I *hate* Brussels sprouts," Tony would say. "I can't eat macaroni any more, it makes me vomit." This from Val. It took days to discover, by the trial and error system, what they did like, what they would eat. Even pie and puddings were no longer to their taste. They wanted jello.

Walker was not only at his wit's end but plumb disgusted. From a chef he had been reduced to a short-order cook. I did nothing but apologize for their behavior throughout the meal. Often I was driven to assume the ridiculous role of the anxious parent who feels that his only recourse is to plead with the child, beg it to try this, taste that—just a weeny, teeny little bit! Spearing a piece of juicy roast pork with a succulent rim of fat around it, spearing it from Tony's plate, I would hold it a few inches from my mouth a moment, admire it, examine it, make clucking sounds with tongue and palate, dribble a bit into the bargain, then, just before gobbling it, say: "Ooooooh! How delicious! Ooooooh! you don't know what you're missing!" All to no effect, naturally.

"It stinks!" he would say. Or, "It makes me puke!"

And then with a sigh, the sigh of a weary *grande dame,* Val would push her plate aside and in a languid, bored tone inquire what the nature of the dessert might be this evening.

"Jello, my dear!" I would say, putting all the venom and sarcasm into my voice that I could command.

"Jello? I'm sick of that stuff."

"O.K. How about frogs' nests then? Or a bowl of rusty nails with sliced cucumbers on the side? Listen, kid, tomorrow we're having pea soup with finnan haddie and smoked oysters. And you're going to like it!"

"Oh yeah?"

"Yes, and don't throw that crust of bread to the birds either! We're serving it up for breakfast tomorrow morning, sprinkled with honey, mustard and garlic sauce. I know you *love* mustard. Did I ever tell you, my finicky little sweetheart, that when bread gets old enough, moldy enough, it breeds worms? And out of little worms come tapeworms. You know what I'm talking about, don't you?" (Brief pause, to observe effect.) "Do you remember that restaurant I once told you about . . . on the rue de la Gaîeté . . . where I used to go for snails? It was a smelly old place but every-thing tasted good there. If you didn't like the food, they threw you out on your. . . ."

"Oh, Daddy, cut it out! We don't want to listen to that stuff."

From Tony: "Daddy, you're not talking right. You don't mean it, do you?"

"I do too mean it, Tony me boy. I'm just working into it. You kids talk puke and vomit; I talk snails and turtle soup. Get me?"

Val, sort of haughtily: "We don't like that kind of talk, Daddy. Mommy never talks that way. . . ."

"That's what's the matter. . . ." I check myself just in time. (Ahoy, mate! Up with the jib!) "What was I saying now? Oh yeah, about the mock turtle. There are three kinds of turtle, you know: the mock, the hard shell, and the Ojibway. . . ."

"Daddy, you're drunk!"

"I am not drunk neither!" (I sure would like to have been.) "No, I'm just feeling feisty. That's a new one for you. Wrap it up, it's yours for the asking."

"Aw, *shit!*" says Tony.

(Now where in the world could he have picked up a word like that?)

"You mean caca, don't you, son? Or *manure?*"

"I said *shit,*" says Tony.

"And I say caca-pipi head!"

"And I say you're goofy," says Val.

"Good, now we can start all over again. But how about a piece of pie first . . . with some nice Yogurt smeared over it? I say now, did you ever have a go at limburger? No? Well, you've got a treat in store for you. . . . Walker, why don't you bring us home some limburger next time you go to town? Or Liederkranz . . . the soft, runny kind. . . . Now if you'll all join me in a piece of pie I'll have another cut of salami and a swig of Haig and Haig. How's that?"

(Delivering this little spiel, a most bizarre thought entered my head. What if, when the divorce proceedings came up, I were to hand the judge a stenographic copy of these post-prandial *divertissements?* Wouldn't that be a stunner?)

A lull. I'm holding my head in my hands, doing my damndest to keep my eyes open. Walker's already washing the dishes, scraping the pans. I ought to make an effort to toss the garbage, but I'm glued to the chair. I look at the kids. They have that groggy look of a pug trying to fall into a clinch after a swift one in the guts.

"You gotta read us a story, Daddy."

"The hell I do."

"You promised."

"I did not neither."

"If you don't read us a story we won't go to sleep."

"Ich gebibble."

To jerk them out of it I make a reference to the frying pan. "How would you like me to conk you with *that?*"

A few more pippa passes and I've got them as far as the bathroom. I've cajoled them into washing their faces, but not into brushing their teeth.

What an ordeal that was—getting them to brush their teeth! I'd sooner drink a pint of Sloan's Liniment than go through that routine again. And, despite all the bloody fussing and fuming at the wash basin, today they've got cavities galore. The wonder is that I, the taskmaster, haven't got chronic laryngitis, what with all the coaxing, pleading, wheedling and threatening I indulged in.

One fine day Walker lost his temper. The incident made a deep impression on me. I had never believed it possible for Walker to say so much as a cross word. He was always calm, amiable, yielding, and as for patience, well, he had the patience of a saint. With dangerous psychopaths Walker could hold his own. As an attendant in lunatic asylums he had kept things under control without ever resorting to strap, club or truncheon.

But the kids had found his Achilles heel.

It was in the middle of a long, exasperating morning when he exploded. I was indoors puttering around when he called me out. "You've got to do something," he yelled, his face red as a beet. "These kids are completely out of hand."

I didn't even ask what they had done. I knew that he had taken more than his share right from the start. I didn't even try to apologize. I felt thoroughly humiliated, and absolutely desperate. To see Walker in such a state was the last straw.

That evening, after the kids were out of the way, he talked to me quietly and soberly. He made it clear that I was not only punishing myself but the kids as well. He talked not only as a friend but also as an analyst might talk to a patient. In the course of his talk he opened my eyes to a twist in the situation which I had been blind to. He said that I should endeavor to find out—for my own good—whether my desire to keep the children was based on love for them and concern for their welfare or on a hidden desire to punish my wife.

"You're not getting anywhere this way," he said. He spoke so gently and reasonably. "I came here to help you. If you insist on going through with it, I won't desert you. But how long can you hold out? You're a bundle of nerves now. Frankly, Henry, you're licked—but you won't admit it to yourself."

Walker's words had their effect. I slept on it, thought it over another twenty-four hours, then announced the decision.

"Walker," I said, "I'm throwing in the sponge. You're right. I'll send her a wire to come and fetch them."

She came immediately. Relieved as I was, I was nevertheless heartbroken. And with the dull ache came exhaustion and loss of spirits. The place now seemed like a morgue to me. A dozen times a night I would wake with a start, thinking that they were calling me. There is no emptiness like the emptiness of a home which your children have flown. It was worse than death. And yet it had to be.

Did it, though? Did I really try hard enough? Couldn't I have been more flexible, more ingenious, more inventive, more this, more that? I made myself the most bitter accusations. I was a fool to have listened to Walker, wise and well meaning though he had been. He had caught me in a moment of weakness. Another day and I would have had the courage and the will to resist his suggestion. Though I couldn't deny the truth of his words, I would nevertheless say to myself: "But he's not a *father!* He doesn't know what it means to be a father."

Wherever I strayed I stumbled over something that they had dropped and forgotten. There were toys everywhere, despite all that my wife had carted with her. And tops and marbles. And spoons and dishes. Each little object brought the tears to my eyes. With each passing hour I wondered aloud what they were doing. Did they like their new school? (Tony was being put in a nursery school.) Had they found new playmates? Did they fight as much as ever, or were they too despondent now to think of fighting? Every day I had the impulse to go down the road and telephone them, but I resisted the urge for fear of upsetting them. I tried to resume the writing, but I had no thoughts except for them. If I took a walk, hoping to shake off my black thoughts, I was reminded at every turn of some little incident, some escapade, we had shared together.

Yes, I missed them. I missed them like sin. I missed them the more for all the difficulties we had gone through together. Now there was only Walker. And what good was I to Walker, or he to me? I wanted to be alone with my grief, my bereavement. I wanted to go up into the hills and bellow like a wounded bull. I had been a husband, I had been a father, I had been a mother—and a governess and a playmate and a fool and an idiot. Now I was nothing, not even a clown. As for being a writer, I wanted no more of it. What could I possibly say that would be of interest or of value to anyone? The mainspring was broken, the clock had stopped. If only a miracle would happen! But I couldn't think of any solution that would have the remedial virtues of a miracle. I would have to learn to live again as if nothing had happened. But if you love your children you can't learn to live that way. You wouldn't *want* to live that way.

Life, however, says: *"You must!"*

I went back to the bathroom, as I had the morning they left, and I wept like a madman. I wept and sobbed and screamed and cursed. I carried on like that until there wasn't another drop of anguish left in me. Until I was like a crumpled, empty sack.

11.

Ephraim Doner is the father of that little genius, Tasha. I have been wanting to say something about him ever since I began this potpourri.

This is a testimonial, long-deferred, in the key of *Ut-mineur*. I began it, to be truthful, many months ago, while sitting for a portrait he did of me on rising from my bed of sorrow.

Some believe that the man and the artist are one; others hold a different view. No doubt it depends on who you are as to whom you meet and what you find of perfection or imperfection in the one you meet.

And, let me ask before we start—can you put together what has been torn asunder?

There are times, I must say, when I see in Doner only the father, or only the friend. There are times when I see in him the artist and nothing but the artist. Usually I see all the ninety-eight elements of which he is composed, and I see them combined to a degree which is not only exciting but inspiring. For when he is at par, this incredible Ephraim, he is the apotheosis of the one and only: man in the image of the Creator. When I see him thus I feel like weeping. And I do weep occasionally—a tender, affectionate weep, *dans les coulisses,* so to speak.

What is it about the man that moves me so at times? The fact, or the realization of the fact, that he neglects absolutely nothing. Or, to put it positively, that he shows concern, genuine concern, for everybody and everything.

Every time I take leave of him the word ritual comes to my mind. For there is something about this loving concern which he manifests, something of awareness in it, perhaps, which lends to all his actions the flavor of ritual observance. As soon as I think in this wise I perceive why it is I am always so happy in his company. I know then that every act of Doner's is a demonstration of the truth, as Eric Gutkind puts it, that the supreme gift which life offers us is the chance to know eternal life. To put it more mundanely, when Doner adds a little seasoning to the food he serves he is putting another touch of God in it, nothing less.

Ephraim Doner has had a hard life, and a gay one. Only the gay dog knows how to be tough, how to butter his bread with caviar, so to say, when there's nothing but mustard to be had. Concerning his struggle to live the life of an artist, Doner has a thousand and one stories up his sleeve. The best one is the one about sleeping with the donkey—in Cagnes-sur-Mer. All his stories are variations on a single theme, to wit, that to become an artist one must first *be* an artist. No one is born an artist. One elects for it! And when you elect to be the first and last among men you find nothing strange about sleeping with a donkey, putting your paws in the garbage pail, or swallowing reproaches and insults from all the near and dear ones who regard your way of life as a grave mistake.

I believe it was Santayana who wrote at length about "the good life." What he said I am still ignorant of, because I am congenitally incapable of reading Santayana. I do know, however, what is meant by the good life, and why the artist's life is a preparation for the good life. The reason, in a word, is this: the good life is the holy life. (Wholly living, wholly dying.) It is the kind of life in which you do your utmost every day, not for art, not for country, not for family, not for yourself even, but because it's the *only* thing to do. Life is being, which includes doing and not doing. Art is making. To be a poet of life, though artists seldom realize it, is the *summum*. To breathe out more than one breathes in. To walk two miles when asked to walk one. Thus to honor, obey and worship the Creator. "The full Name over the full world," as Gutkind says. This the poet of life heralds every day of his life.

To divagate. . . . When I ask Maître Ephraim, as I fondly call him, whether I should learn to do precipitations (in the water-color medium) by the technical route or by the intuitive-experimental method, he answers: "Use more parsley!" Now there is good reason why parsley—"more parsley"—constitutes a full and just answer. Parsley, as everyone knows, is an herb. The herb, like the ritual, has been sadly neglected in our progressive, work-a-day world. Though the herbs belong to the vegetable kingdom, they are nearer to the mineral than the animal kingdom. Which is to say that, as an enclave, they also form a hegemony. They are autonomous and autochthonous. Wholly aside from these attributes, they possess an elixir which is a source of health and vitality. A sprig of parsley, consequently, has the same inspirational quality for the devout water-colorist as does the shamrock for the Irish bard.

But let me not forget! With the parsley always goes a bit of the *Shilchan Aruch,* the *Kabbala,* and the Book of Daniel. The parsley is thrown in at the last minute, as when making a good omelette. What really sustains me, fortifies me, guides my hand, whether for precipitations, sunbursts or sandstorms, is the crystallized wisdom of those huge, soaring birds—the anonymous prophets—who hovered for generations over the cosmological riddle.

To make it still more clear, Doner will take me by the hand. "It's like this, Henry. . . ." *Like this* means that he is preparing to dive into the labyrinth. "A full answer," he says, "is always in the nature of a riddle. If someone asks, 'Why the Sphinx?' the answer must contain the Sphinx as well as other things. Some people regard this sort of answer as evasive. The trouble with such people is, they never put the right questions. A full answer may omit facts and figures, but it always includes God. Now water-color problems are not cosmological problems. Nor even epistemological problems. Why waste time, then? *More parsley!* That settles it."

There is a self-portrait of Doner's which will probably hang in a museum one day. It is a superb painting as well as a superb portrait. The shirt is as alive as the expression on his face, and the background is of a texture rich enough to support the sins of a saint—or an ephah of barley. Doner is there widespread, like the Pentateuch itself under the rays of the noonday sun. He is there agape, if I may put it thus, for he has caught that fugitive look which the mirror renders when we catch a glimpse of ourselves off guard. Doner sees himself looking at himself but without knowing that it is himself he is looking at. In this fleeting glimpse of his unknown self he has contrived to introduce an element of the *cocasse*. As if Jacob, waking from his dream, beheld a fly on the end of his nose. One ought not to say that he is looking at himself; but then neither is he looking at the world, for the world has dissolved momentarily. It is just a glance that he has given us, but in this glance is contained the wonder of life.

A detail. . . . If you look closely you will observe that one ear is spread fan-wise. There is something verging on the ridiculous in the way this ear protrudes. Only an adept could have balanced the hypnotic glance with this bizarre appendage. It *is* an ear, however. An ear that has caught something from afar. *What?* The wheeling of the constellations? The croaking of a frog? Perhaps only the whispering of time babbling of eternity. Whatever it was, the owner heard it with his whole being. For an instant he was the sea shell. The *mysterium*.

To do a good portrait, it goes without saying, one must be able to see into the soul of the sitter. To do a good self-portrait, one must look into the ashes. Man builds on the ruins of his former selves. When we are reduced to nothingness, we come alive again. To season one's destiny with the dust of one's folly, that is the trick. In the ashes lie the ingredients for portrayal of self.

Now the spirit of Doner is large and boisterous. There is a roar to it, as the surf in an empty shell. It is the roar of the universe, the same which splits the soul of man in moments of revelation. And who, in his right senses, would attempt to make a canvas roar? Yet Doner has done just that. And he has done it with a cigarette glued to his lips.

That cigarette! A link, not with reality, but with the art of badinage. Only with cigarette to lip does he really talk. Talk persiflage and camouflage. *Pythagoras plus Aquinas equals Jonah and the whale.* Or—*Micah is to Isinglass what Job is to Jehovah.* With that cigarette glued to his lips, Doner can take the measure of any man—and his ancestral tree to boot. To use his own language—"It was thus that Mordecai made a shambles of Belshazzar."

Ephraim Doner and Bezalel Schatz: of all my friends these are the only two whose educational background I envy. Schatz was educated in his father's school, in Jerusalem: the Bezalel School of Arts and Crafts. He learned nothing but arts and crafts; all the other subjects which we cram down our children's throats he learned on the side, and learned them better that way. As for Doner, who was born and raised in Vilna, he had the fortune to have for a grandfather a famous rabbi, known not only as a great scholar but as a man of wisdom. They are blessed, these two friends. They are free spirits. They were not indoctrinated, they were taught to think for themselves. Theirs is still an insatiable curiosity—about everything. Coupled with a healthy disregard for mundane facts. As a reader, Doner is omnivorous. He reads with equal facility in Hebrew, Polish, German, French, Spanish, Italian. Every year he rereads *Don Quixote*. He is one of the half-dozen Americans I know who also reads everything that issues from the pen of Blaise Cendrars.

Almost every time we go to town we stop at the Doners for dinner. And whenever the Doners make their trip to the sulphur baths they invariably stop at our place for dinner. While waiting for the duck to brown we usually play a few rounds of ping-pong. By the time dinner is ready to be served Tasha has made a half-dozen pictures.

When we are not talking books, food, education (the insanity of it), herbs or painting, we are talking and drinking wine. The leitmotif which runs through all our talk is France. It was in 1931 or '32 that I met Doner in Paris. Just once. We did not meet again until he took up residence in the Carmel Highlands, about seven years ago. To hear us talk, you would think that we had spent the greater part of our lives in France. We did, of course, spend the *best* years of our lives there. And we have never forgotten it.

Doner's acquaintance with France began at Villefranche. He was on a cruise of the Mediterranean, taking a fling with the last few dollars he had saved working as a furrier in a New York sweatshop. A friend of his who was playing the stock market had already lost half of Doner's savings when, sailing down Broadway one day, he, Doner, espied a poster announcing that he too might enjoy a three months' cruise in the Mediterranean—if he had what it took. He looked in his bank book and he found that he had exactly the right amount. When the boat put in at Villefranche he went ashore to have a drink. The spot so enchanted him that he decided then and there to forgo the rest of the trip. For a year he wandered on foot through France, Spain, Italy, Portugal, Yugoslavia and neighboring countries. The few dollars he had cashed in on his ticket didn't last very long. But he eked out an existence by sketching portraits in bars and restaurants. When he returned to New York he went back to the fur trade for another year, saving what money he could. At the end of that time he destroyed all his tools, so as not to be tempted ever again, and shipped to France where he was determined to live as a painter. He remained abroad four or five years, during which time he taught himself to paint. Today he is one of the best painters on the peninsula and, more than I can say about most painters, an artist from head to toe.

Doner is one of the most gregarious individuals I have ever met. One can hardly ever go to his home without running into visitors. In spite of interruptions, he not only turns out a respectable number of canvases but also finds time to do the chores, run errands for his friends, listen to their problems, make trips to the beach, the desert, the wineries, the ranches, add wings to his house, build rock walls, care for the garden, lay tiles, give painting lessons, instruct his daughter, help his wife with the cooking and cleaning, do the shopping, go for abalone, mussels and snails, nurse his alcoholic friends, bail them out of jail when they run amok, borrow and lend money (he's as good at the one as at the other), and a thousand and one things that would drive the ordinary artist raving mad.

His talk reflects his protean activities. (He takes no vitamins, by the way, not even blackstrap molasses or brewer's yeast.) He is just as alive and captivating when discussing the merits of a new sauce he has thought up as when talking chess, herbs, Napoleon or his beloved Cervantes. Like myself, he seems destined to attract misfits, neurotics, psychopaths, alcoholics, dope fiends, vagabonds, eccentrics and plain downright bores. Now and then he sells a painting; to seal the bargain, he generally forces the buyer to take one of my books. He also intercepts the "nuisances" who are en route to Partington Ridge and who, for unaccountable reasons, stop off to see him first. If it is someone who turns out to be interesting after all, he will drive him down to my place himself—a mere jaunt of seventy miles there and back. He always makes certain before they start that the newcomer load up with good things to eat and drink. *A friend,* what!

These visitors he brings are usually fellows who have traveled far and wide. He knows that he has only to say—"Henry, this chap has just come back from Burma," or "This man has been to Yemen" —to put me in my most receptive mood. Or just: *"C'est un français, mon vieux!"* (At the Big Sur Post Office, where visitors without "proper passports" are frequently turned back, it is understood that if the person seems like a Frenchman he is to be sent ahead with all the courtesy and attention due a visiting potentate.)

Stay put and watch the world go round!

Listening to the fascinating tales of these globe-trotters, I often think of my father, who virtually never set foot outside the place

he was born in. Marooned in his tailoring establishment, he nevertheless gave the impression that he had seen all the strange places
which his customers had visited and loved to talk about. He had
a retentive memory, a passionate interest in all that was alien, and
an ability to identify himself with the person to whom he was
listening. He could reel off the names of streets, bars, shops,
celebrities, monuments and so on, belonging to the most unheard
of places. Now and then he would fib about these towns, villages
and cities which he had never set foot in: I mean, aberrate in an
elaborate way. No one ever took it amiss. He was a genuine
voyageur imaginaire. And I am very much like him in this respect.
A picture postcard of some remote place is sufficient to make me
think I know the place intimately. (Sometimes I surprise myself
making strange and acute observations about these far off places.
True things, which I only discover later through chance references
in books.) With regard to certain cities in China, Burma, India,
I have such strong mental pictures of them that, if I do visit them
one day, I doubt that the real picture will be strong enough to
erase the imaginary one.

But to come back to Doner. . . . Because of his background,
because of his blood, because of his trials and tribulations, and perhaps mostly because he is an artist first and foremost, he is and
always will be an incorrigible giver. The first thing he asks, when
we meet, is if I am in need of anything. "I just sold a sketch,"
he will say. "Can't I lend you something?" If I don't say No
promptly, he will add: "I can make it twenty, if you like." (As if
he feared I thought he intended to hand me only a measly five
spot.) "I can always borrow," he says. "That is, if you need
more. . . . By the way, don't forget to let me give you some wine
before you leave. I've got four cases of the most delicious. . . ."
and here he will mention a wine he knows I adore.

Sometimes I come across him standing on the highway beside
the Chevron gas station near his home. What's he doing? Waiting. Just waiting. Waiting and hoping that someone will come

along whom he can touch for a few bucks. He's never depressed about lack of funds. Simply active and alert. Taking a stand beside him, to lend him moral support, it has happened more than once that a "friend" just happens along . . . and what has this good friend brought for Maître Ephraim but a beautiful salmon fresh caught or a fine Italian salami with an equally gorgeous, savory Italian cheese, sometimes a case of French wine into the bargain. All this without even rubbing the *kmeya* which I gave him expressly for use in such emergencies.

Aside from his generosity, Doner is just about the most indulgent person I have ever known, particularly where children are concerned. (We have a secret understanding, the two of us, that visitors who pay no heed to children or animals are taboo.) Rosa, his wife, is even more indulgent where children are in question. She absorbs children just as blood absorbs the oxygen in the air. The degree to which she caters to them is almost alarming. It is her profession to instruct mothers and teachers in the art of handling children. A most difficult profession, needless to say, particularly in a community which nurtures spoiled brats.

To see to it that Tasha's little friends have all the advantages which (theoretically) they deserve, Rosa unwittingly puts a burden on Doner's shoulders which most men would resent. Their household centers around children—noisy children, demanding children, spoiled children, most of them. Fortunately, Maître Ephraim's studio is some twenty yards from the house; here Doner locks himself in every morning to work until late noon. (It seems to be the common routine among artists hereabouts to get as much done as possible by noon each day; after that hell is apt to break loose.)

The school which Tasha attends is located near a beautiful cove opposite a Carmelite nunnery. It is probably one of the last of its kind in America. There are only a handful of pupils, and what learning they receive is painless. During recesses they play on the beach, only a stone's throw away from the schoolhouse. Here the nuns often come to frisk and scamper, piously. The more daring ones occasionally wet their feet in the sea. Paddling about in full mourning, they give the impression of demented haddocks trained to stand upright.

The contrast between this country school and the typical city school is remarkable. Here the children are happy, carefree and eager to be taught. They are not drilled, disciplined and mechanized. Indeed, they behave as if they owned the school. The atmosphere of the concentration camp is completely missing. Should a pupil desire to bring a pet to school with her, she may, provided it's not a horse or cow. If she brings a little friend along, the friend is made welcome by pupils and teachers alike. In fact, they may stop everything and do a sing in her honor.

When Tasha was a very young child she took a fall from a second-story window. That was the beginning of the special education which she has been receiving ever since. There is little likelihood that Tasha will take another fall, even from grace. She is guided, counseled and directed from both ends with all the skill, tact, cunning and superior insight which her loving parents can muster. Sooned or later she gets most everything she asks for. If she is a little spoiled in the process, no one gets hysterical. Time will unspoil her. If Tasha wants liver and onions for breakfast, she gets it. Why not? Whose stomach is it? If she wants a shoulder bird, she gets it. Once she wanted a beautiful goat, and she got it, but abandoned it shortly in favor of a horse. As a supplement, she gets all the milk she can down, all the vitamins, brewer's yeast and blackstrap molasses. To say nothing of herbs! At present she has a bike which Tony has his eye on and which we all pray she will abandon in favor of an M.G. or a Jaguar.

In any other household such tactics would produce a monster. With any other parents Tasha's demands would smell of blackmail. But Ephraim and Rosa are more than equal to the test. They have freedom in their blood and a recklessness for consequences which can only spring from a firm belief in the triumph of love. The problems which arise from their indulgence, and of course problems do arise, they dismiss as transitory. The are never concerned with what Tasha may demand of them next, but only what she may grow into in response to love, understanding and forbearance. They observe and direct her growth much as an expert gardener would a delicate plant. They shield her only to give her strength.

The interesting thing about this experiment is that it works. The mother is not a nervous wreck, as most mothers are, but flourishing. As for the father, he becomes more and more creative every day. It is as if the more they lavished on the child the more is lavished on them, in unexpected ways. "Free flow" is the unwritten motto above their door. The result is that the reservoir (of natural affection) is always full. From this hub of bedlam, indulgence and indiscriminate hospitality there filters through to friends, neighbors and playmates a current of sanity, joyousness and prodigality which acts like a leaven.

Is it not somewhat strange that two immigrants of lowly origin should have such an effect upon their surroundings? Whatever they may owe to America, America owes much more to them. Whatever was worth while in the American tradition they have accepted and exploited to the fullest. They remain—Americans in the making. For the American is only an American when he perpetuates the experiment begun by his forefathers. He is only an American if he carries on the work of making his country the melting pot which it was destined to be. Ironically, it is in the *American* home today, not the immigrant's, that we find prejudice and intolerance rampant. It is in the household of the Hundred Percenter that we find a spirit of inertia, a lack of healthy curiosity and native enthusiasm, to say nothing of a frightening tendency to conform for the sake of ease and comfort. It is Mr. Slivovitz, not Mr. Mayflower, who is nearer to Daniel Boone, Thomas Paine, John Brown and their ilk.

The extraordinary indulgence which the Doners manifest does not spring from weakness or mere compliance. It is born of superabundant spirit. It is directed towards everything capable of growth, whether plant, creature, child, artist or idea. In obeying this impulse to nurture and sustain the life spirit, they grow in like measure and are nurtured, sustained and fortified by the very powers they have called into play.

I said of Doner a while back that he is the type who, if asked to go a mile, goes with you twain. This attitude is hardly one of indulgence. True, there is in it sympathy and compassion, and an understanding which surpasses the ordinary. But the essence of it is reverence for life. Or perhaps simply—*reverence*. Those who do more than is asked of them are never depleted. Only those who fear to give are weakened by giving. The art of giving is entirely a spiritual affair. In this sense, to give one's all is meaningless, for there is no bottom where true giving is concerned.

Now and then I take Doner to task for spreading himself too far afield. One might as well reprove Niagara Falls for shedding so much water! It is both the weakness and the virtue of the Jew to spill over in all directions. What seems chaotic to the Gentile appears normal to the Jew. He has a superendowment of energy, a superabundance of enthusiasm. He is strikingly interested in others. His innate love of justice, his compassion, his gregariousness and his burning desire to be of service, mark him as a firebrand in any community of Gentiles.

The more I see of Doner the more I understand the Diaspora. The fate of the Jew is not nearly as tragic as the fate of the Gentile who dispersed him far and wide, drove him underground, forced him to sharpen his wits and develop his inner powers. All the obstacles we have put in his path, all the handicaps we have imposed, have only strengthened him. Incapable of making him adapt to *our* way of life, we are finally beginning to adapt ourselves to *his* way of life. We are even beginning to admit that the Christian way of life was practiced by the Jew long before the first Christian appeared. In clinging stubbornly to his ways, the Jew is converting us to a Christianity which we have never put into practice.

In Doner it is the Chassidic strain which predominates. This
ecstatic element reveals itself in his work. If it is a scene from Nature
which he paints, the canvas sings. In some of his seascapes the bare
rocks, shrouded in guano, leap exultantly from the foam and mist
like personifications of joy and abiding strength. The sea is always
a mirror of supernal light, a restless, piercing light, which issues
from the depths of the unknowable. All the chaos of water, wind
and sky is subdued, or subjugated, by a poetic manipulation of the
brush which seeks only to evoke the essential mystery of the scene.
The horizon line, thin, wavering, semiobscure, bends under the
impalpable weight of the heavens, but with the delicacy of a muscle
yielding to a bidden urge.

Contemplating such a painting, I know that there has been no
undue dispersal of the artist's forces. I realize, when I study the
painting, that the conflicting interests which I had feared would
pull him this way and that were but healthy seductions which he
survived and made use of in alchemical fashion. The elasticity of
soul which makes the giver is the supreme protection of the creator.
When he returns to his rock, his sky, his sea, he puts into them all
that he has endured, sacrificed and discovered through identification
with the sorrows and sufferings of his fellow-men. The meaning
of the diaspora shines through his work like a rainbow.

If the first Christian was a Jew, it is quite possible that the last
one will also be a Jew, for there is nothing in the history of the
uncircumcised to indicate that they are capable of bridging the gap
between man and man-god, or as the Chinese say, between
"*l'homme* and *l'homme-humain*."

12.

On the surface there is something not only quixotic but paradoxical about "the part of fortune." One always likes to think he *earned* his good fortune, or that he made the most of the breaks which chance presented. Myself, I have come to believe that through being receptive, keeping one's mind and heart open—showing faith and trust, in other words—one's desires, or prayers, are realized. By prayer I do not mean asking, hoping, begging or bartering for that which one desires but, without formulating it, living the thought— "Thy will be done!" In short, acknowledging wholeheartedly to ourselves that, whatever the situation we find ourselves in, we are to regard it as an opportunity and a privilege as well as a challenge.

Up to a certain point in my life I have known more ups and downs, I do believe, than fall to the lot of the ordinary man. About the time I moved into the Villa Seurat (1934), I became aware that the seismographic disturbances, so to speak, were diminishing. A definite rhythm and order was beginning to manifest itself, though outwardly my life was still hectic, troubled and confused. The realization that there *was* a pattern to my life, one which made sense, came about in a curious way. Shortly after moving into the Villa Seurat I had begun to record my dreams. And not only the dreams but the associations which the act of transcribing them induced. Doing this over a period of several months, I suddenly began to see. "To suddenly see," as Saroyan says somewhere. A pregnant phrase—to anyone who has had the experience. An expression which has only one meaning: to see with new eyes.

About this same time, through a concatenation of events, "haphazard" encounters, the reading of certain books—books that were thrown into my lap, as it were—things began to jell. I became more and more aware of a curious phenomenon, hitherto conspicuous by its absence: the realization of one dream after another. I soon developed an attitude of caution with regard to *what* I desired, having come to realize that we generally desire either what is unimportant or else what is actually harmful. At this point, as everyone knows who has had the experience, enter the subtle temptations.

The trip to Greece (1939-40), which came about through an unforeseen friendship with Lawrence Durrell, clinched things. It was a "break" in a triple sense, for not only was it a stroke of good fortune—the very best thing that could have happened to me at the time—but it was also the means of breaking with a life which had already come to an end in the Villa Seurat. Above and beyond all this, however, is the fact that the Greek adventure was an eye-opener: from then on the world no longer looked the same to me. Even the expulsion from Greece, due to the war, was a blessing which I had not the wisdom at the time to comprehend. Finally, the rediscovery of America,* a then seemingly futile and unpleasant business, led to the discovery of Big Sur.

From here on (Big Sur) things began to happen in earnest. If I did not succeed in finding the "peace and solitude" I had hoped to find, I most certainly found other things which have more than compensated for my disappointment. Once again, I might say that I found what I needed to find, experienced what I needed to experience.

Of all the many fruitful experiences which I fell heir to since anchoring in Big Sur, the discovery of certain books holds as much, possibly more, importance, I find in retrospect, as the "coincidences," *rencontres hasardeux* and other "unpredictables." Of the "meetings" with these books I hope to have more to say later on.†

Where to begin in this web which stretches out in all directions—

* Recounted in *The Air-conditioned Nightmare* (New York: New Directions, 1945).

† In the second volume of *The Books in My Life.*

vertically as well as horizontally—and which is apparently without limits? The first thing one realizes when one begins to examine into such a mysterious thing as "fortune" is the fact, and it is a stupendous one, that there is neither beginning nor end. All is interconnected and of a piece. When we put the parts together, like a puzzle, the good and the bad seem equally "the part of fortune." Trifles particularly assume an importance altogether disproportionate to size or weight. Everything falls into whack, and to a degree which nullifies the vain assumptions of the ego. When I spoke of rhythm and order a while ago, what I meant was a matching of inner and outer, or—"as above so below." If I read the stars, it was not to find out what was going to happen tomorrow but to seek confirmation in what was taking place at the moment.

Stay put and watch the world go round!

Aye, but like a tightrope walker, not a slug. Treading softly, eyes front. A miss is as good as a mile. This side of Paradise and that side of Paradise. One thing as good as another. Alert and relaxed; empty and wide awake. In step, but not in uniform. The revolver always handy, but loaded with blank cartridges. A weather eye open for weeds, thistles, burrs, nettles and thorns. To arms! when the bugle calls, but minus a trigger finger.

Never pray for money! If you send out an S.O.S., ask for chicken feed. Otherwise you'll be cruelly deceived. Never mention the filthy lucre except in terms of what it can buy. Take commodities and light your pipe with the greenbacks! Remember, if you can't make money, make friends. Not too many either, because one real friend is all you need to protect you against the blows of outrageous fortune.

I said at the beginning of this potpourri that it started like a haemorrhage—with Cingria. And who put Cingria under my nose? Gerald Robitaille of the 19th Arrondissement. Answer this —how did Gerald know that what I needed to start the merry-go-round was a copy of the *N.R.F.* with its *"couronne"* for the recently departed and sorely beloved Charles-Albert Cingria? And how could any mortal foresee that the remembrance of a single meeting with the said Charles-Albert would galvanize these last eleven years of my life?

What is Hecuba to me or I to Hecuba?

A potpourri, did I say? Why yes. Or—point-counter-point. Hearts are trumps. Win or lose, it's the same two-handed game of pinochle.

Ever since I began writing I have been compelled at intervals to send out letters begging for help. The intervals between these cries of distress grow bigger with the years, *heureusement*. Of late— the last seven years or so—I have noticed something strange and interesting taking place. No sooner have I had the letters mimeo- graphed, and the first batch off in the mail, than a check arrives which makes the whole thing seem ridiculous. Not a check in answer to my appeal, mind you, but a check from the blue. Usually it's for a debt which I had written off as hopeless or payment for royalties which I had forgotten all about.

"Should I not have displayed a little more patience?" I ask myself. "Or, is it possible that, in taking action, I gave fate a little push in the right direction?"

Oddly enough, the important thing turns out to be not the money but the discovery of a friend I didn't know I had. Yes, it's good to send out an appeal, even if at the last moment it turns out to have been unnecessary. Why? Because, aside from discovering your real friends, the ones who send you their widow's mite, you learn what you have always known—that the rich are generally the last to respond. My last experience in this realm, an over- whelming one, revealed the fact that the four individuals (out of a hundred or more) who failed to respond, even with a "No thank you!" were the very wealthiest ones on my list. The aid which one of these alone might have offered without batting an eye- lash. . . . But why go into it? The sad thing, the ironic thing, about this quartet, is that they all regard themselves as great friends of mine. One of them always slaps me on the back when we meet and, in his blithe, jovial way, says: "Henry, you're a saint!" I ought to ask him sometime just what he means by this remark—whether he's grateful because I don't hound him or whether it takes a saint to live on nothing.

When I was getting ready to go to Greece I gave into the hands of a friend for safekeeping a trunk containing the notebooks and manuscripts I thought precious enough to keep. The war broke out, I lost contact with my friend, and soon I resigned myself to the thought that the trunk was lost. In fact, after a few years I thoroughly forgot that there was such a trunk. Then, shortly after I was installed at Partington Ridge, I received word from an officer in the merchant marine that he was holding two trunks consigned to me. He added that he was one of my readers and that it was a pleasure to be of service—no charge for the transportation.

When the trunks arrived I saw to my amazement that one of them belonged to the man I call Fillmore in *Tropic of Cancer*. (Those who know the story will recall how I packed him off to America, *sans cheapeau, sans bagage*.) For a good two years, after he got back to his town town, Fillmore, who was somewhat of a lawyer as well as a "bohemian," drove the customs officials and the railway officials (at the Gare St. Lazare where he had left his trunk *en consigne*) crazy. I believe he even went so far as to address a letter of abuse to the President of the Republic. And now, here it was, intact. I opened it out of curiosity: it contained nothing but law books, family albums and souvenirs of his days at Yale. I opened the other one, which was mine, and found that nothing had been tampered with. Everything I had put in it was there, and in good condition. Among the contents was the original voluminous script of the *Tropic of Cancer,* an item which may one day fetch a small fortune.

Where had these trunks been all the time? Who had sent them to me? *A déménageur* from a village outside Paris, a man whom I had met only twice and with whom I had exchanged but a few brief words. When I wrote to thank him I inquired what I could possibly give him in return for the great gift he had made me. I made it very clear that I considered the recovery of the trunk a priceless boon. He replied: "Nothing! Nothing at all! It was a pleasure to be of service." I wrote again, several times in fact, hoping that I could induce him to suggest, if not money, something which he and his family might have need of. (The French at that time were still sorely in need of many things.) But no, not a thing did he crave. His last reply was to the effect that, if I would be so kind, I might send him an autographed copy of one of my books—nothing more. In the course of correspondence I learned that the trunks had been entrusted to him when my friend left France at the outbreak of war. But how this conscientious moving man discovered my whereabouts is still a mystery. And how Fillmore's trunk, along with my own, happened to find its way into the cellar of the good Marius Battedou is also a mystery.

Had the trunk contained the Dead Sea scrolls, I feel certain the good man would have made the same reply.

Voilà un chic type!

Money—and how it gets that way! During the first months on Partington Ridge I toyed with the idea of going to Mexico to finish *The Air-conditioned Nightmare*. I drew up an "appeal for funds"—sufficient to last me a year, I specified—and begged Frances Steloff, of the Gotham Book Mart, N. Y., to post it on her bulletin board. I had little expectation of getting results from this appeal. It was worded rather flippantly, I thought, probably because in the bottom of my heart I really did not want to go to Mexico. All I wanted, truly, was a little hard cash.

A few weeks later there came a letter, postmarked New York, containing a cashier's check for $250.00. The sender, who gave his name as Harry Koverr, gave me to understand that he wished to keep his identity secret. He promised to send me a like sum every month, for a year. He added that he had read everything of mine he could get hold of and wished me to know that he was a warm admirer. It was rather a strange letter, couched in perfect English

but with a foreign tinge to it which aroused my curiosity. I made
no effort, however, to discover who the man was. (Never look a
gift horse in the mouth!)

The instalments came regularly, as he had promised. In the
meantime, a young woman with whom I had been corresponding
for some time came to stay with me. She was a dancer and she
made it a habit to go through her routine every day, rain or shine.
Now and then, strolling through the forest, I would come upon
her clad in leotards and swinging from limb to limb like a chim-
panzee. All part of her training. . . .

One day as we were trudging up the hill, loaded with mail and
supplies, a car pulled up behind us and the driver leaned out to ask
if I might be Henry Miller.

"I'm Harry Koverr," he said.

I looked at him blankly, failing to make the proper association.

"I'm the man who sends you those checks. Don't you recognize
a friend?"

For a moment I was too embarrassed to make reply. I blushed
crimson. And then it clicked.

"Haricot Vert!" I shouted. "So that's it?"

Only then had it dawned on me that he had been using as an
alias the French for "string bean."

"So you're French?"

"Not really," he replied. "I'm Swiss. Or rather, I was born in
Switzerland." He then gave me his real name.

When we got to the cabin and unloaded the food and wines he
had brought along, I asked as discreetly as I could what had
brought him all the way to Big Sur.

His reply amused me. "I wanted to see how you were getting
along." He then proceeded to give the cabin (which belonged to
Keith Evans) a hasty inspection, pressed his nose against the big
plate-glass window facing the sea, took a step or two outdoors to
glance at the hills which were all gold, and, heaving a genuine sigh,

exclaimed: "I see now why you didn't go to Mexico. This is the next thing to Heaven."

We sampled the Pernod he had brought and soon began exchanging confidences. I was surprised to learn that he was not a rich man, though he was making a comfortable living as an insurance agent. The son of wealthy parents, who had encouraged him to live the life of a playboy, he had spent most of his bohemian life abroad, in France for the most part.

"I couldn't resist helping you," he said, "because I've always hankered to be a writer myself." He added quickly: "But I lack your guts. To starve is not in my line."

As he continued to fill out the story of his life I discovered that his present position was anything but rosy. He had made a bad marriage, was living beyond his means, and hadn't the slightest interest in the racket he had chosen for a livelihood. I began to suspect that he had come to tell me that he would not be able to continue helping me much longer. But I was wrong.

"What I'd really like to do," he suddenly remarked, "is trade places with you."

I was utterly unprepared for such a statement. I must have jibbed a bit.

"I mean," he continued, "that you're one man who seems to know how fortunate he is. As for me, I'm all mixed up."

The visit lasted only a few hours. We parted the best of friends.

As for the payments, they lasted another few months and then a dead silence. A prolonged silence. I thought possibly he had committed suicide. (He was the type to do it.) When I finally heard from him again a year or more had passed. It was a pathetic, desperate letter I received. He, the reckless benefactor, begged me to send him a substantial sum—and the balance just as soon as I possibly could.

For once I kept my promise. I immediately sent him a good round sum and, in the space of a few weeks, cleaned up the balance.

On receipt of the last payment he wrote me a long and fervent letter, a letter which unnerved me somewhat. The gist of it was to the effect that he could hardly believe what had happened. He confessed that he had never expectd me to come through—and definitely not with such dispatch. Not very flattering, thought I to myself, and, picking the letter up, I began rereading it. I stumbled on a passage which made me sit up. It was where he was explaining that only since he had lost everything had he begun to see the other fellow's point of view. In searching for help he had naturally turned to his friends, especially to those he had succored when in need. And they had failed him, every one of them. It was in sheer desperation that he had finally written *me*. And I had come across! He couldn't get over it. He thanked me again—and threw in a blessing.

I put the letter down to ruminate on it, and then I noticed that a postscript had been scrawled on the back of the last page. It said that now that he had touched bottom he was going to stay there ... *and write*. If I could do it, he could do it too. He had no use for the world, no desire to ever make money again. Though miserable, he was glad things had turned out the way they did. Anyway, I had restored his faith in human kind. It was now his turn to prove that he was a man. . . .

I can't say that I felt flattered, reading these words. Nor did I have much faith in his becoming a writer overnight. No, but what did interest me, and vitally, was the admission he made that only when he had reached the end of his rope, when he had come to the last among men, did he get a response. For many, many years now I have known and acted on the belief that when truly desperate you must turn to the least of your fellow-men. You must address yourself to the one who seems least likely to have what you are in need of. If we realized what we were doing, in acting thus, we would know that we were taking ourselves to a magician. The man with no resources is the one who possesses most resources. Or shall I say, who possesses *real* resources? Such a man is never frightened by an unexpected demand. Nor is he appalled or dismayed because you are in a state of penury. For *him* it is a matter of rejoicing. Now he can demonstrate what it means to be a friend. He behaves as if a privilege had been conferred upon him. He literally leaps to the bait.

"A hundred dollars, you say?" (A fabulous sum to a man who hasn't a pot to piss in.) He scratches his head. "Let me think a moment!"

He does a think, then a smile lights up his face. Eureka! And he dismisses the problem with a flourish, as if to say: *"A mere hundred?* I thought you were going to say a thousand!"

With this he gives you a bite to eat, stuffs a few shekels in your pocket, and tells you to go home and rest easy.

"You'll have it in the morning. Ta-ta!"

During the night . . . let me say it in French, it sounds more concrete . . . *le mirâcle se produit.*

Now to act with delicacy! To refrain from asking where the money came from, how it happened, when must it be returned, etc., etc., etc. Take the money, bless the Lord, embrace your friend who performed the miracle, shed a tear or two, and be off!

This is a homeopathic prescription for which no charge is made. . . .

Money isn't all. . . . The day Raoul Bertrand turned up was a red-letter day in my life. Not because he unlocked the door to my dwindled "fortune," though that was a timely performance, not because he made it a point to bring friends whom I enjoyed meeting as well as rare victuals which his old French housekeeper prepared especially for these occasions, not because he talked of things which were close to my heart and in a language I love to hear, but because he was that rare sort of individual who knows how to create just the right ambiance, an ambiance in which everything flourishes, sprouts, burgeons and promises never to fade. Whenever he appeared, *ce cher* Raoul Bertrand, somewhere deep inside me the music started up. Everything I had learned to appreciate in connection with the French way of life he seemed to exemplify; everything I had cherished as a result of my ten-year sojourn in France he resuscitated, as if with a magic wand. It mattered little whether we began with the bike races at the Vel d'Hiv, the dog cemetery at St. Ouen, Napoleon's last days at St. Helena, the mystery of the Basque tongue or the tragic history of the *Albigeois* . . . it was always a symphonic journey which brought us nearer to the heart and core of France.

I believe it was through Raoul Bertrand that Monsieur de Carmoy, of the Office d'Echanges, Paris, came to visit me one day. It is through this bureau that payments to foreign authors are controlled and regulated. Monsieur de Carmoy's visit, though altogether unofficial, made a deep impression on me: it was like receiving a visit from the government itself. As he handed me his card, on leaving, this kind and gracious emissary of the Republic of France informed me that if I ever encountered any difficulties in obtaining royalties due me, I was to drop him a line. He said it as if it would give him great pleasure to jump a plane and bring the money to me in person.

A few months later I had to take him at his word. The response was immediate, almost electrical.

Merci encore une fois, cher Monsieur de Carmoy!

But to come back to Raoul Bertrand. The day he paid me that first visit he was accompanied by a French journalist whom I had known in the Villa Seurat. Little more than a boy at the time, he was now a roving correspondent for a big Paris newspaper. When they were getting ready to leave, the journalist, who was flying back to Paris, asked if there was anything he could do for me when he got back. Without a moment's hestitation, I said: "Yes, there is." It was something which had popped into my head unbidden and which gushed out like a jet of water. It had to do with that nest egg which was getting addled, that "fortune" which had become a joke. It formulated itself in the shape of a question. The Pachoutinsky brothers: Eugene, Anatol and Leon: what had become of them? had they survived the war? were they in want? All one big question mark in my mind. The next thought, a corollary, was simple: Why not give them the key to the vault?

"Look," I said, "there's a little service you could render me. Put a small ad in a few of the Paris newspapers saying that Henry Miller, author of the *Tropic of Cancer,* wishes to locate his old friends, the Pachoutinsky brothers. Run it until there is an answer."

I then explained to him what these three brothers once meant to me, what they had done for me in my hour of need.

Hardly a month elapsed before I received an airmail letter from Eugene, with whom I had been the closest, telling me that they were all alive, in good spirits, and not in dire need. As for himself, all he was praying for was that the government—always the bloody government!—would give him the pension which he was entitled to for his services during the war. He had a touch of tuberculosis, among other things, but after a year or two in a "sana" he hoped to be his old self again.

I will skip the story of how he eventually received his pension—it sounds too incredible—but will give the epilogue.

In Versailles he made the acquaintance of an elderly gentleman who wanted to sell his home and remove to the provinces. Should Eugene succeed in finding a buyer, he promised to give Eugene sufficient with which to buy himself a home in the country. Eugene already had his eye on a village in the Midi called Rocquecor (Tarn-et-Garonne). By some incredible fluke, Eugene, who knew nothing about real estate, netted a buyer for the house in Versailles. The next thing I knew, he had purchased an abandoned schoolhouse in the village of Rocquecor. It was a building with thirteen rooms and looked somewhat like an ancient fortress converted into an insane asylum. On the picture postcard showing the schoolhouse, which was jauntily perched on an eminence, he indicated the two rooms which he said he was remodelling and setting aside for the use of my wife and self. They were to be ours exclusively—and forever. A way of saying that thus we would always have a second home—in our beloved France.

A *"pleurnicheur,"* as my friend Alf dubs me, I could not resist shedding a few warm tears looking at the site of our new home. Again I thought of that day when first I came upon Eugene outside the Cinema de Vanves: he was standing on top of a tall ladder pasting up a billboard announcing the coming of a film starring Olga Tchekova. Again I beheld the wretched piece of cardboard, properly *timbré* as even the most humble, wretched *"annonce"* must be in France, staring at me from the window of the *bistrot* opposite the cinema, where Eugene and I frequently repaired for a *"java"* and a game of chess. The announcement, which he had written in his own hand, informed the passer-by that Henri Miller, of the Hotel Alba (a few doors away) was available to teach English for the modest sum of ten francs an hour. Those who have read the *Tropic of Cancer* will recall this good friend Eugene and his "old world garden." What a euphemism, *his garden!* It was a dump somewhere near the Impasse du Thermopyle which they occupied, if I remember rightly. What connection there could be between that celebrated battleground and the narrow, smelly, dingy alley named after it baffles me. As for that "old world garden," it was in Eugene's heart, not outdoors anywhere.

As I sat there shedding a few warm tears, I thought how natural, logical and inevitable it was that Eugene, who never had a sou except when I needed a coffee, should be the man to make me such a royal gift. . . .

And now let us pass on to *The Thirteen Crucified Saviours* and *The Keys to the Apocalypse.* Such are the titles of two works I have been unable to lay hands on, though I have been promised them again and again by friends who claimed they could obtain them for me.

The first named is by Sir Godfrey Higgins, author of the celebrated *Anacalpysis.* Copies exist, I am told, but are difficult to find and exorbitant in price. I no longer want it, thank God.

As for the other, by the extraordinary Lithuanian poet, Oscar Vladislas de Lubicz Milosz (Milasius, in Lithuanian), there hangs a curious tale. What little I had read of and about Milosz intrigued me enormously.* I never spoke of my interest in him to anyone; indeed, there was no one I knew to whom I might speak of him.

About five years ago, while trying to collect certain books which were necessary for the work in hand,† I received a telegram signed Czeslaw Milosz, who turned out to be the nephew of the deceased poet. The letter which followed had nothing to do with the writer I was interested in; it was about the proposed visit of the director of the Warsaw Museum of Art. There followed an exchange of two or three letters which threw cold water on my enthusiasm for the poet's work. Czeslaw Milosz, then an attaché of the Polish Legation at Washington, was probably already at work upon the great novel which has since earned him fame.

Time passed. While on a vacation in Europe (1953), my wife

---

* I give just a few snatches of those aspects of Milosz which fired me: (1.) *"Pendant toute sa vie, Milosz tiendra Don Quichotte pour le synonyme de l'homme."* (2.) *"Il commença ses études (1896) à l'Ecole du Louvre et à l'Ecole des Langues Orientales. Il y étudia l'art phénicien et assyrien, ainsi que l'épigraphie orientale sous la direction du célèbre traducteur de la Bible, Eugène Ledrain. . . . Avec une passion innée, il apprit la cryptographie des langues palestino-mesopotamiennes. Etudiant la préhistoire, il songe à l'origine même de l'humanité, à celle du cosmos et à sa cause primordiale."* (3.) *"Milosz qui avait une vocation spirituelle indéniable, vivait dépaysé dans ce monde auquel il ne s'adaptait pas; il sentit toujours qu'il n'était créé pour le bonheur humain, que sa naissance avait déjà été une chute, et que son enfance était comme le souvenir de l'époque où il prit conscience de la gravité de cette chute."* (4.) *"La Nature (si belle aux yeux de la plupart des hommes), cette nature, au sein de laquelle nous vivons depuis des millénaires, et des millénaires, est une sorte d'absolu de la laideur et de l'infamie. Nous ne la supportons que parce que, tout au fond de nous-mêmes, survit le souvenir d'une* première nature *qui est* divine et vraie. *Dans cette nature* séconde, *qui nous environne, tout est mauvais indiciblement."* (Milosz' own words.) These citations are taken from a book called *O. V. de L. Milosz: sa vie, son oeuvre, son rayonnement,* by Geneviève-Irène Zidonis: Olivier Perrin, Editeur, 198 Boulevard Saint-Germain, Paris, 1951. (A gift from the French Consulate at Los Angeles, California.)

† *The Books in My Life* (New York: New Directions, 1952).

Eve and I stopped off at the Guilde du Livre in Lausanne to meet the director, Albert Mermoud, with whom I had been corresponding for several years. During a pause in the midst of a protracted conversation, Monsieur Mermoud, exactly like that friend of Raoul Bertrand, suddenly asked me if there was anything he could do for me while we were in Lausanne. And, just as in the other instance, I replied without a moment's hesitation and without previous thought—"Yes! Find me a book called *Les Clefs de l'Apocalypse* by Milosz!" I explained that I had been told by various friends that a definitive edition of Milosz's works had been published in Switzerland.

Mermoud gave me a strange smile and replied at once: "Nothing easier. I'll telephone the publisher immediately. He's a friend of mine, he lives here in Lausanne."

He picked up the receiver, got his friend whose name I failed to catch, and launched into an explanation for making his strange request. I heard him repeat my name several times—"Yes, he's sitting right here in my office!"—then he looked at me grinningly as if to say, "He knows you!" and went on talking. It was a lengthy conversation. Not to embarrass him, I turned to the friends who had come with us and began conversing with them in low tones.

After a time I became aware that the conversation over the telephone was unusually drawn out. Mermoud had ceased to talk; he was merely nodding and grunting now. He seemed to be listening most intently.

Finally he hung up, turned to me, and said: "I'm sorry. I can get you any of Milosz' books except the one you want."

He sat back in his chair and began giving me a lengthy account of the publisher's life, a most unusual one, and of the latter's relations with the poet. It appeared that the publisher had been not only a great friend but a genuine benefactor. If I am not mistaken, he himself had begun writing poetry as a result of reading Milosz. Yes, he had printed everything Milosz had ever written, including the book in question. But of this work—*The*

Keys to the Apocalypse—he had printed only *one* copy, which was exclusively for himself. He would not even let anyone borrow it. He did not want anyone to read it. Not even Henry Miller, whom he adored *(sic)*. Why this attitude? Because he regarded the book as unworthy of the author. I had the impression, from Mermoud's words, that there had been a disagreement between the two regarding the religious aspect of the work. I could be mistaken about this, because there was so much he rattled off and with such speed that I was left somewhat dazed.

A few months later, seated in a modest restaurant near the Senate (Paris), a man came up to our table and introduced himself as Czeslaw Milosz, the same who had written me from Washington. How he recognized me I can't explain; perhaps he had overheard my name. At any rate, after making apologies for something of no consequence which he had written in one of his letters, he sat down and engaged us in conversation. The Lausanne incident still fresh in my mind, I proceeded to relate what had occurred at the office of the Guilde du Livre. He seemed thoroughly nonplussed, shook his head several times as if it were beyond all comprehension, then exclaimed: "Why, it's ridiculous! I can get you the book. But I doubt that you will want to read it."

"Why?" said I.

"Because it's not really a book . . . it's only a page and a half long!"

You might have pushed me over with a feather. All this folderol over a page and a half! I was stunned.

"Do get it for me," I begged. "Now I want more than ever to read it."

He sssured me that he would, at the very first opportunity. To date it has not shown up. Will it ever? And what will that page and a half contain?

Restif de la Bretonne is a horse of quite another color! For years the name had been familiar to me, largely because of references made to his work by the French Surrealists, André Breton in particular. Why I never made an effort to read him I cannot say. The name itself was so intriguing, perhaps I feared to be deceived. Every now and then his name would crop up in a review of my own work. (At various times the critics have bracketed my name with such as Petronius, Rabelais, Swift, Sade, Whitman, Dostoevsky —and Restif de la Bretonne.)

One day I received a letter from our then minister to Ethiopia, J. Rives Childs. It informed me that the writer had read everything of mine that was available and thought that there were great affinities between my writings and those of the famous Restif. Had I ever read Restif? He felt certain I must have. I replied that I had never read a line of his. Whereupon I received a second letter, urging me to do so by all means. If I couldn't lay hands on the books I was to notify him and he would see to it that I received copies. He then informed me that he had given considerable time to the study of his life and work and was now busy compiling a bibliography of Restif.

In this letter he had urged me to make a point of reading *Monsieur Nicolas* and *Les Nuits de Paris*. He omitted telling me the size of these works. When I discovered that *Monsieur Nicolas* alone comprised some fourteen volumes my enthusiasm quickly abated. Meanwhile, from Cairo, N. Y., a Dante Zaccagnini, a scholar and voracious reader, also began to bombard me with eulogies of Restif de la Bretonne. To sharpen my appetite, he sent me a much abridged one-volume edition, by an English publisher, of *Les Nuits de Paris*. I read it with interest but was not fired. Moreover, from this brief taste I found only a frail connection between Restif's literary ways and my own. I decided, rather foolishly, that I had had enough of Restif for the time being.

Then one day the huge work on which our ambassador to Ethiopia had been working for so long arrived in the mail. A monumental work, indeed, for which all lovers of Restif must feel indebted. The vast range which it covered appalled me. "It's not up my alley," said I to myself. Besides, I had just put myself on record as saying that my purpose was to read less and less, not more and more.

It may be of interest, at this point, to know that Childs himself, as he relates in the Introduction to his vast compendium,* was almost discouraged in pursuing his task to the end when he discovered that the complete works of his beloved Restif numbered over fifty titles comprising some 200 volumes! The reading of Restif's entire output, however, represented only a fraction of the immense labor involved in the production of this massive tome.

To indicate the prodigious nature of this extraordinary creature, Restif, let me quote a few lines from Childs' Introduction:

"Pour moi, malgré toutes ses faiblesses—et il en avait beaucoup —Restif est un caractère sympathique pour de nombreuses raisons. Et tout d'abord une essentielle bonté de coeur, une large humanité accompagnée d'un sens toujours présent de l'inhumanité de l'homme envers son semblable, un désir passionné d'améliorer le sort de l'humanité, une grande vision du monde, un but absorbant d'être utile à ses contemporains et, plus encore, à la posterité, enfin une franchise foncière dans l'aveu de ses fautes. Il convient de souligner que, dans une époque où, du moins en France, il était de mode de mépriser Shakespeare et Jeanne d'Arc, Restif vantait leurs mérites. Il pensait élargir les horizons intellectuels des hommes et, dans ce but, il agissait sans prudence. Son oeuvre présente d'innombrables aspects, d'infinis méandres, de sorte qu'une seule vie suffirait à peine à en suivre tous les contours. Imparfait comme tous les hommes, il n'a jamais eu la prétention d'être ce qu'il n'était pas. Il était humain, peut-être trop humain, et par là nous lui sommes redevables de grandes dettes qui deviendront de plus en plus apparentes dans les années à venir." (Djeddah, Arabie Saoudite, *le 27 février*, 1948.)

Just when I thought the subject to be closed came a letter from

---

* *Restif de la Bretonne: Témoignages et Jugements: Bibliographie;* Au dépens de l'auteur. En vente à la Librairie Briffaut, 4, rue de Furstemburg, Paris (6), 1949.

Cairo saying that he, Dante, had now finished reading the fourteen volumes comprising the complete and unexpurgated French edition of *Monsieur Nicolas*—and that he was shipping them to me that same day. In a week or so the books arrived. I felt as if I had been shipped a coffin containing the remains of the incredible Restif!

What to do? First of all, put them in order, which I did. Then I scanned a page or two here and there, choosing volumes at random. Then I hoisted them up to the top shelf of my bookcase and ranged them beside the slim, unobtrusive volume called *The Round,* by Edward Santiago, saying to myself: "I'll dip into them some day when I'm stricken with paralysis." And so saying, I gathered the books which had been displaced by this new addition to my library, threw them into a carton and, hitching the horse to the buggy, I drove to the garbage dump which lies along the scenic route from Alaska to Tierra del Fuego and tossed them into the ocean.

And now for the Essenes, whom I finally came to grips with in Santa Monica. I had gone there at the invitation of my friend, Robert Fink, to see the paintings of Abe Weiner. Here I was introduced to Weiner's friend, Lawrence Lipton, a resident of Venice.

It was only toward the end of a long and delightful evening that I struck up a conversation with Lawrence Lipton. As a writer of mystery stories known to all America—by pen name, at least— he seemed the last man in the world that I would think to call upon for data about the mysterious sect called the Essenes.

The tête-à-tête which we launched into at full gallop, and minus the usual preliminaries, was more like an inspired game than an exchange of thought. The last time I had entered into a similar dance was in a little village in New Hampshire. I mention it because it is the sort of thing which happens but a few times in one's life. The event I refer to occurred on a winter's day after a conference which I had attended with Professor Herbert West, of Dartmouth, in a distant town. We were driving back to Professor

West's home in Hanover. It was late afternoon when Herb West suddenly decided that we ought to pay a visit to a friend of his in the village we were approaching.

He pulled up at the door of a modest house and there, standing in the doorway waiting to greet us, was his friend. I had been told nothing about the man, nor did I catch his name on being introduced. But the moment we greeted one another, it was as if I had known the man all my life. We began talking, right at the doorstep, as if continuing a conversation we had abandoned a short few thousand years ago in a previous incarnation. The only mundane thing I am able to recall in connection with this friend of West's is that he had served in the British Army in India for many years.

Our stay lasted about two hours, during which time the "Major" and I covered the most amazingly incongruous and seemingly disconnected subjects. Frequently it happened that we would mention the title of an obscure book or the name of some little-known historical figure or an outlandish department of knowledge, only to exchange a meaningful smile and pass on. Never once did we press the wrong button, so to speak. It was as if we were working an I.B.M. which threw out the correct answers without fail and without effort. Indeed, the atmosphere was one of pushing buttons, sliding into grooves, locking and interlocking, engaging and disengaging. The subjects touched on appeared to be nothing more than pretexts for the unraveling of something vastly more important, though what this something might be we never even tried to formulate.

Add this—that the man's life had nothing whatever in common with my own. We were from totally dissimilar worlds. Moreover, I've never made any attempt to communicate with him since that meeting. No need to. When we do meet again—and are we not bound to, perhaps in another life?—we will undoubtedly resume where we left off. . . .

But this Lawrence Lipton. . . . Physically, and I was aware of it immediately, he reminded me violently of someone I dislike intensely. He even talked like this person whom I still loathe and despise. Yet everything he touched on—he had a habit of drifting from one subject to another without transition—drew me to him like a magnet. He had already skirted a dozen themes the very mention of which always affects me like a dose of adrenalin. Suddenly I thought I heard him pronounce the word "Essenes." He had pronounced it correctly, which threw me off.

"Did you say the Essenes?" I asked.

"Yes," he replied. "Why? Are you interested in the subject?" He seemed surprised.

I explained that for years I had been tracking down whatever I could find regarding their customs, rituals and way of life. I mentioned certain similarities I thought I had discovered between their ways and those of the Albigensians. I made a passing reference to that strange book called *The Unknown Life of Jesus.* I cited Gerald Heard's book, *Time, Pain and Sex,* in which there is an exciting chapter dealing with this strange sect.

Yes, yes, he seemed to say, I'm familiar with all that—and much more. But have we time to go into it now? He was spilling over with names, dates, citations, all manner of strange, hermetic references.

"If you would really like to know more," he said, "I'll have my wife copy some of the more salient data which I've accumulated on the subject these last ten years or more."

"I wouldn't think of it . . ." I began.

"It's nothing at all," said he. "She'll be happy to do it, won't you, dear?"

She had to say Yes, of course.

A few weeks later I received the data he had promised me. Included were his own reflections and interpretations, extremely sagacious and pertinent.

Time passed and the subject of the Essenes dropped back into its accustomed niche. Then, just ten days ago, a physician back from Palestine, and bearing a message from my old friend Lilik, called my attention to an article, a lengthy one, on "The Dead Sea Scrolls," which he "thought" had appeared in *The New Yorker*. He said it was a very important article, written by Edmund Wilson. I was a bit sceptical, thought he had things mixed up. As I rarely read *The New Yorker* I knew nothing about this event, for such it turned out to be.

Two days later there appeared in the mail the issue of *The New Yorker* which my visitor had spoken of. It was sent me by Lawrence Lipton whom I had not heard from for months. In his letter Lipton stated that he thought it quite possible I had overlooked Wilson's article and, recalling my interest in the subject, deemed it imperative to dispatch it to me.

A coincidence? Possibly. I prefer to think otherwise.

At some point in his life most everyone ponders over the meaning of the word "coincidence." If we face the question courageously, for it *is* a disturbing one, we are forced to admit that mere happenstance is no answer. If we use the word "predestination" we feel defeated. And rightly so. It is only because man is born free that these mysterious conjunctions of time, place and event *can* take place. In the horoscopes of those men and women marked by destiny we observe that mere "incidents" become highly significant events. Perhaps because these individuals were able to realize more of their potential being than ordinary mortals, the correlation between inner and outer, micro and macro, is striking and diamond clear.

In grappling with the mystery of "chance" we may be unable to render suitable explanation but we cannot deny that we are made aware of laws beyond the reach of human understanding. The more aware we become the more we perceive that there is a relation between right living and good fortune. If we probe deep enough we come to realize that fortune is neither good nor bad, that what matters is the way we take our (good or bad) fortune. The common saying runs: "To make the most of one's lot." Implicit in this adage is the idea that we are not equally favored or disfavored by the gods.

The point I wish to stress is that in accepting our fate we are not to think that things were *destined* thus or that *we* were singled out for special attention, but that by responding to the best in ourselves we may put ourselves in rhythm with higher laws, the inscrutable laws of the universe, which have nothing to do with good or bad, you and me.

This was the test which the great Jehovah put to Job.

I could run on indefinitely with examples of these coincidences and "miracles," as I freely call them, which crop up in my life. Numbers, however, mean nothing. If only *one* had occurred, it would have the same shocking validity. Indeed, what baffles me more than almost anything, in human affairs, is man's ability to ignore or bypass events or happenings which do not fit into his pattern of thought, his unquestioned logic. In this respect civilized man is just as primitive in his reactions as the so-called savage. What he cannot account for he refuses to look squarely in the face. He dodges the issue by employing words like accident, anomaly, fortuitous, coincidence, and so on.

But each time "it" happens he is shaken. Man is not at home in the universe, despite all the efforts of philosophers and metaphysicians to provide a soothing syrup. Thought is still a narcotic. The deepest question is *why*. And it is a forbidden one. The very asking is in the nature of cosmic sabotage. And the penalty is—the afflictions of Job.

Every day of our lives we are presented with evidences of the vast, most complicated interconnection between the events which govern our lives and the forces which rule the universe. Our fear in pursuing the flashes of insight which they provoke is that we may come to know what will "happen" to us. The one thing we are given to know from birth is that we will die. But even this we find hard to accept, certain though it be.

Now what "happens" always carries this flavor of being unpredictable, of coming from without, of disregarding our wishes, our plans, our hopes. But those to whom things "happen" may be of two different orders. The one may regard these occurrences as normal and natural, the other as phenomenal or freakish and insulting to his intelligence. The one responds with his true self, the other with his petty ego. The former, who is truly religious-minded, finds no need to introduce the word God. The other, who is a religionist, though he may call himself a sceptic or an atheist, will deny vehemently that there is any intelligence in the universe greater than his own limited one. He has an explanation for everything except what is inexplicable, and his way of disposing of inexplicable phenomena is to pretend that they are beneath his attention. In the animal world his brother is the ostrich.

Let me close the subject—for the time being—with a citation from a book which has just been put into my hands. The book was lent me by a man whom I would have referred to (unthinkingly) as the last man in the world to be drawn to such a book. The connection between the author's words and the foregoing may not be instantly apparent. But there *is* one, and the reason for quoting this passage is that I consider it one of the best answers which could be made to the question which must already be forming itself in the reader's mind. It is taken from the Apologia to a biography of the celebrated Kahlil Gibran.*

"It was after much hesitation that I decided to write this book. For I believe that no man can faithfully, accurately and fully describe a single instant of his own life in all its intricate meanings and its infinite connections with the universal life. How, then, is one, no matter what his talents, to put between the two covers of a book the life of another man, be he an idiot or a genius! In that respect everything that men relate of men under the name of 'History' is, in my judgement, but so much froth breaking over the surface of that sea which is human life; the depths remain too

---

* *Kahlil Gibran: A Biography*, by Mikhail Naimy (New York: Philosophical Library, 1950). (Translated from the Arabic.)

deep, and the horizons too distant for any pen to plumb, or any brush to paint. Until this day we have not been able to write the 'history' of any man or of anything at all. Had we written the history of but a single man *in full,* we should be able to read in it the history of all men; and had we recorded *faithfully* the story of but one thing, we should discover in it the story of all things."

13.

If there is a genuine need, it will be met.

This thought, which Jean Wharton expressed over and over again, and in a hundred different ways, is one of those statements which can either be ridiculed into meaninglessness or accepted at face value and proved or disproved. That it has proved true in my own case, innumerable times, never ceases to astonish me. The thing to ask one's self first of all is—are we truly aware of our real needs? "It" knows, but not us. "We" are usually bringing up the rear, often absent altogether. We abdicate before the throne we might occupy is even offered us. There is a white charger, champing at the bit, ever ready to carry us to the most undreamed of goals. But do we mount him? Those who do leave a trail of fire behind them.

The question is, where do we want to go? And, do we want to take our baggage with us or travel light? The answer to the second question is contained in the first. Wherever we go, we must go naked and alone. We must each of us learn what no other can teach us. We must do the ridiculous in order to touch the sublime.

Who can say what the other's needs really are? No one can really aid another except by urging him to move on. Sometimes one must move on without stirring from the spot. To detach yourself from your problems, that is the idea. Why try to solve a problem? *Dissolve it!* Bathe it in a saline solution of neglect, contempt and indifference. Fear not to be a coward, a traitor, a renegade. In this universe of ours there is room for all, perhaps even *need* for all. The sun does not inquire about rank and status before shedding its warmth; the cyclone levels the godly and the ungodly; the government takes your tax money even though it be tainted. Nor is the atom bomb a respecter of persons. Perhaps that's why the righteous are squirming so!

What makes the fanatic sound so ridiculous is that he has a way of uttering profound truths, profound second-hand truths, which he proceeds to demonstrate in the realm of trivia. But if you can make a straw behave in an unprecedented way, the chances are you can do the same with a human being. The laboratory work of the scientist is all sure-fire stuff. Hazards are either ruled out or exploited to prove what was intended to be proved. The man of reason disdains to use the word miracle. He sweats to prove that there is no such thing, and all the while he is but proving that he is a miracle of incomprehension. There are miracles and miracles: it depends on who uses the word and how. But the man who claims to be a mere cog in the machine (the mind machine) has a way of talking like God when contradicted. Frequently he contradicts himself.

Let us leave God out for the moment. Shut all the doors and windows, seal the cracks! Now we can talk common sense. Let's see, what was it again . . . the atom bomb? Now I remember—it was coffee. Coffee's gone up again, did you know that? How on earth did we get on to *that?* How? Why, we were talking about money . . . what people will do for money, how money makes money, that sort of thing. We were saying that when it comes to

earning a living there are men who will take any kind of job
rather than go without. *Monsieur le Paris,* for instance. You might
think that nobody on earth would want to make a living chopping
other people's heads off. Admirable if he would chop his own head
off, whether for money or just for the hell of it. But other people's
heads . . . and at so much per head? Fantastic! A general, for
example, has men who do the dirty work for him. He never soils
his hands. After some special deed of valor (which may have cost
the lives of a hundred thousand men) he is usually decorated. But
Monsieur le Paris is always shunned by the "populance." Yet he
hardly ever chops off more than one head a month. Often he's a
solid member of the church. Takes communion and all that business. Drinking the blood of Jesus, he makes a mental note to
sharpen his axe. A conscientious worker, as we say. Believes in
doing a clean job, whether it be executions or dish-washing. As for
the blood, that's another matter. (Now and then he gets a squirt
in the eye.) If it were an ox he were felling, the blood would
fetch money. But human blood—no demand. Yet it has all the
vitamins, from A to Izzit. Curious, these taboos.

Interruption.

The other day I was out on the trail with my son Tony. Just as
we reached the mystery spot we named "Arizona" (where Colum-
bine makes love with Brother Onyx unmolested), he says to me:
"I'm *never* going to go to war!"

"How's *that?*" says I.

"I'll cut off my finger first, like Bennie Bufano."

What put this idea into his head I don't know. Probably a
remnant of one of our postprandial conversations.

To go on. . . .

If a woman looking like Salvation Nell should happen to knock
at your door, don't send her about her business *toute de suite.* Let
her bend your ear, if that's what she's a mind to do. People often
speculate on what the Saviour would look like should he decide to

pay us another visit. (I can tell you confidentially that he won't look like a da Vinci portrait! This is *ex cathedra,* of course.)

About Salvation Nell now. . . . If her lingo sounds sort of goofy, just say to yourself: "Maybe it's our dear Jesus come back to earth peddling vacuum cleaners. Come back as a woman, to take us by surprise."

(Dr. Bernstein, the noted brain surgeon, happened on us one day in much this way. We were in the midst of a spring cleaning. The first thing he says, taking off his coat, is: "Let me help you!" He didn't say, "I'm Dr. Bernstein, late of the Veterans' Winter Hospital, Topeka." He said: "Let me help you! I've done it many times before.")

And our dear Saviour, if determined to try it again, might very well say, while fumbling with her dress: "Take it easy, dearie, this vacuum cleaner will earn you a lot of free time. It's just the coolest, gonedest, sweetest gig you ever laid eyes on. Try it, won't you?"

And how would you know, without taking thought, that this thingamajig, this here chromium-plated, everlasting vacuum cleaner was not the very thing you were in need of, the answer to your silent prayers?

Even if you are naturally of a suspicious turn, even if you are preternaturally circumspect and wholly eaten away by reason and logic, you should be able to sense the difference between the Saviour in the guise of a vacuum peddler and an executioner in the guise of a servant of the State. When a general says, "Men, I want that position taken if it costs the lives of every man in this division," he means that no bullet, no bayonet, is going to pierce *his* hide. *You* are to cover yourselves with glory. As for *him,* he's got other divisions to throw in, other battles to fight, other wars to win. *"Forward!"* he shouts. "I'm going back for reinforcements."

Jesus had no reinforcements. He had only his own tender flesh. And we know how it was desecrated. There He hung on the cross, and when the agony was too great, He cried out: "My God, why hast Thou forsaken me?" Then darkness fell upon the land, the earth trembled and vomited forth the dead, and the sky was full of portents. Then three days and nights. Then forty more days. Then Peter and Paul. Then the acts of the apostles. Then Jerome and Augustine. And after many a moon, Francis, dear Francis of Assisi. Between times one doctrine after another, one church after another, one crusade after another, one inquisition after another. All in the name of Jesus.

And some people imagine that He's going to climb down from Heaven and repeat the performance.

For all we know He may.

In Bruges, where they have preserved a few drops of the precious blood shed on Calvary, something happens each year—on the very same day!—to make that coagulated blood liquefy. Nobody else's blood has ever behaved in this manner.

Wouldn't it be a surprise if next time, instead of handing Jesus over to be crucified, they handed Him over to be beheaded? If the blood of our Lord and Saviour, when it bubbled forth, suddenly spoke with tongues of fire?

FOOL, I AM INDESTRUCTIBLE. MAN IS INDESTRUC-TIBLE. THE WORLD IS INDESTRUCTIBLE. GIVE OVER, YOU IMBECILE! ENOUGH! IT HAS BEEN REHEARSED 79, 457, 648, 325, 496, 721 TIMES. IN THE NAME OF THE GREAT JEHOVAH, PUT DOWN THAT AX!

If there is a geuine need, it will be met. Not through the vain creation of robots, not by unlocking the sluices of memory, not through the coming of little men from outer space nor by bombarding the enemy from platforms in the sky. Not by eliminating all the dangerous germs and viruses, nor even by virtue of the second coming of Christ and the awakening of the dead.

First you will have to prove that your need *is* genuine. (And not by non-Euclidean logic!) Second, you will have to produce a certificate of sanity whereby to substantiate your sincerity. Third, you will have to be vaccinated against possible irruption of undue pride and egotism.

This accomplished, you will then be ready to undergo initiation: an ordeal imposed by the Brotherhood of Fools and Simpletons. Three questions will be put to you. Just three. The first: "How would you order the world if you were given the powers of the Creator?" The second: "What is it you desire that you do not already possess?" The third: "Say something which will truly astonish us!"

If you answer these satisfactorily you are then to return to your birthplace, sit quietly with hands folded, and meditate on the needs of all God's creatures, including the germs, the bacilli and the viruses. When you know what it is they need—down to the last cockroach!—you are to report back to the Brotherhood and dissolve the order.

Now isn't this much simpler than trying to squeeze yourself back into your mother's womb or trying to find an equation that will yield a bomb guaranteed not to backfire nor disturb other planetary beings? The earth reveals its wonders daily. We've only begun to scratch the surface. Patience! If time lacks, there is always eternity. And it's always on hand—like that pale, cool, refreshing beer advertised over the radio.

This is an interlude. It may be off-key, but that's because my throat is dry. Any contradictions which may have arisen thus far —I know how touchy you are!—can be ironed out on the piano clavier where there is absolutely no difference between sharps and flats, though some keys are white and others black. Besides, all this is preliminary and by way of coming to grips with a lacuna. To explain. . . .

As I went to the edge of the cliff a few minutes ago to void a little urine—it's vulgar to say "take a leak"—I suddenly realized that I have said almost nothing about *The Millennium of Hieronymus Bosch*. If you purchase the book, as I know you will, I would like you to turn to Plate 23, the last in the book, which you will find opposite page 147. It is called "The Cave of Pythagoras." If what meets the eye doesn't electrify you at once, send the book to the nearest insane asylum where it will be kept in a strait jacket.

The last five words on the page from which I am about to quote (page 127) read thus: ". . . *the task of genuine love.*" Let me repeat it:

THE TASK OF GENUINE LOVE

Don't look for the passage immediately, I beg you. Sit down, wherever you are, and let your mind dwell on these words. Ask yourself if, in all the years you have been dwelling on this planet, you have ever given a moment's thought to such a problem. Assume, if only for a moment, that there may be a problem which outweighs all the problems which now burden you. (Including the problem of not having any problems.) Don't put yourself in Sunday school to establish the proper frame of mind. Take it for granted that you are able to think your own thoughts. Then, allowing for deflation, ask yourself the question: *what is the task of genuine love?*

The author of the book I am about to quote from had, on the previous page, been speaking about the *"unum necessarium* of Adamite eugenics." As to who the Adamites were, their connection with the "Millenium," and other more disturbing conundrums, I beg leave to refer the reader to the book itself. But first a quick glance at the world. At the state of affairs, as it's called.

Once the radio is out of order, or the television set, and you enjoy a day or two of no news, you are bound to ask yourself what all the hubbub was about. What was it they were shouting and screeching about the other day at the U.N.? *Was it the other day or ten thousand years ago?* Seems to me they've been talking law and order, peace and harmony, the brotherhood of man, since eternity. Now they're in earnest, of course. Or so they would have us believe. ("Waiter, another stack of wheat cakes, please! With honey and cream, yes.") There's a genuine need and it's going to be met. Everyone has agreed that we must stop fighting; the trouble is, no one wants to surrender his weapons. As it stands now, those who are against wholesale destruction are opposed by those in favor of piecemeal destruction. Virtually all the natural-born citizens of this one and only world are represented at the U.N. except for a handful of savages in Africa and Australia, the American Indians, and the few million Chinese, who, though they are the descendants of the most ancient, the most cultured people that ever was, are not to be trusted. (Not today, at any rate. Tomorrow we may sing another tune. Today it's thumbs down.)

When you witness one of these epoch-making sessions in which nothing ever happens except more vetoes, more referenda, more adjournments, more protocol, more full-dress regalia, more banquets, more airplane trips, more threats, more preparedness, more panic, more hysteria, more stockpiles, more and better bombers, more and more battleships, cruisers, submarines, tanks, flame throwers, you know quite definitely that the millennium is not being ushered in. You know that two lascivious monkeys at the zoo, two monkeys picking fleas off one another's backside, are doing just as good a job.

One could settle the issue in a jiffy—what *is* the issue, by the way?—by bringing together three men of undisputed wisdom and benevolence and having them meet in a rice paddy clad only in loin cloths. They wouldn't have to be interplanetary diplomats either. Just normal human beings, on the order, say, of Lao-tse, Gautama, Jesus. Practical-minded men, not statesmen, not politicians, not dreamers. Men of good will, in other words.

One of the traits which distinguished the above-mentioned trio was this—they spoke only when they had something to say. When they were silent they were even more succinct.

Try to imagine the honeyed words of wisdom which would flow from the lips of our distinguished representatives at the U.N. if tomorrow there were slated for discussion—*the task of genuine love*. Contrast this imaginary scene with the following description of a scene (page 127) from *The Millennium of Hieronymus Bosch:*

". . . These fair-headed people of both sexes are all so alike that they could hardly be told apart, and their attitudes are anonymous and selfless. They are a single family, reminding us of a plant family all the more in that their expression is confined to a silent dreaminess and mute gazing. Theirs is a stillness as of vegetation, so that the fine-drawn, groping hands appear like tendrils seeking neighboring flowers for support.

"And they seem to grow up out of the ground as much at random as wild flowers in a meadow. For the vague uniformity of this naked life is not subjected to any formal discipline. Yet however arbitrarily the pattern of the moving bodies may be concentrated and condensed in one place and may loosen and scatter in another, there is nowhere any overcrowding and nowhere any random emptiness. However free each may be to follow his own inclination, there remains an invisible bond holding them all together. This is the *tenderness* with which all these inhabitants of the heavenly meadows cling together in brotherly and sisterly intimacy."

14.

The English man of letters has his club to repair to, the millionaire his yacht, the muezzin his minaret. As for me, there are the hot sulphur baths at Slade's Springs.

If I am lucky and no one is there, I share the delicious solitude with the rocks, the sea otters, a passing whale, the drifting clouds, mist and fog, the floating islands of kelp and the screeching gulls.

If the tide is out, I commune with a two-faced rock out of which the blazing sun and pounding surf have sculpted a king and queen of the Ptolemaic line. Under the rays of a slanting sun their features are as clear cut as those of the king and queen of spades. Curiously enough, I have never observed a gull defile their features.

It is rare that I enjoy the baths alone. Usually I find the tubs and sunning tables occupied. Those who derive the most from the baths are the ones who hold their tongues. (What was it Goethe said? "I personally should like to renounce speech altogether.") The wise ones have no need for talk. They are simply grateful to the powers that be for the privilege of steaming in the curative waters and basking in the sun.

The patrons are of all stripes and colors, from idiots who delight in taking pot shots at the seals to busy executives who work frantically at crossword puzzles while broiling themselves like lobsters. When the men from Gilroy invade the place it's like splashing about with a herd of water buffaloes. Astonishing physiques they have, all patterned after Apis the bull. The visitors who come most regularly are those with skin disorders and sufferers from arthritis, lumbago, gout, rheumatism and bursitis. One of these, a querulous bastard with the seven-year itch, has a backside so raw that it looks like a flaming sun. Another chap, who refuses to wear a truss, brings with him a monstrous pair of testicles which could just barely be squeezed into a wheelbarrow. As for varicose veins, there is every variety under the sun; the ones that look like rock candy colored blue and purple are the most intriguing.

On certain days the members of the ancient order of hermaphrodites take over. ("Oh Ron, I just love the way you wear your hair now!") Most of them are built like ephebes; many of them are artists, all of them are dancers, and idle conversation is something they adore. They're always discussing impersonal things in a very personal way. And they're always very busy—manicuring their nails, waving their hair, flexing their muscles, primping themselves, admiring themselves in their pocket mirrors. Delightful creatures, really. Especially when they let their hair down. When they get confidential with you. Often when observing them at their toilette I am reminded of the valiant Spartans—just before the battle of Thermopylae. I doubt, however, that the Slade's Springs type would be ready to die to the last man. ("It's sort of silly, don't you think?") Occasionally there will pop up a smart, dapper-looking European of dubious vintage accompanied by a handsome French poodle towards whom he behaves as a gallant fellow would with his mistress. This type of individual, usually a globe-trotter and more often than not a perfumer, is a delight to talk to. He can talk with equal felicity about anything, everything and nothing. The dog is his chief preoccupation; if he has anything of importance to communicate, it is to the dog he addresses himself.

I've met every conceivable type at the baths, or thought I had, until the other day. Then I stumbled on a new one, probably the first of his line. It was of a day when I had been alone and at peace. The sea was calm, almost glassy, the tide at low ebb; the coral-colored gums of the boulders that line the shore stuck out prominently. Gazing at the charred, bleached rocks that dotted the water line, their flaky, scaly surfaces glittering like mica, I almost fell into a trance. Everything was just falling into whack. Even the old bathtubs which had been flung over the cliff seemed a part of nature and at one with the jungle of kelp, the ribbon of fog on the horizon and the motionless motion of the hills. I was a ripe prey for "the alligator of ecstasy."

When I turned round—I had been standing at the guard rail—I saw a dark-skinned man of enormous girth who looked as though he were made of blubber covered with India rubber. His piercing black eyes glittered like anthracite. Restless eyes that struck at you like fangs. With him was a lad of ten or so, white, whom he ordered about as if he were his Number One Boy.

Soon we were joined by some old-timers just back from the hills with little bags of gold dust. A few minutes later my friend Bob Fink appeared. After a few words all around I climbed back into

my tub to soak some more. Meanwhile the roly-poly fellow soaped
himself vigorously, snorted like a bull, stood up in the tub, shook
himself, pounded his chest, then stepped out to sun himself. He
looked at everyone searchingly, then made for a table where he
stretched himself out full length, face forward. His uptilted head
was just about two feet away from mine.

The conversation, desultory and good-humored, had begun with
the subject of rattlers—and how they never bother the Indian.
From this it had switched to hoboes and the meaning of anarchism.
One of the men from the hills had a brother who was a confirmed
hobo, that is, a man of principle. He had been explaining his
brother's philosophy at some length. I noticed that the dark man
with the India-rubber skin had a mania for interrupting to ask for
more precise details. He seemed to be a born sceptic, knew everything better than the next fellow, and with it all had the air of
being a colossal ignoramus. His queries were brazen and defiant,
more like taunts and gibes. In addition, his voice was anything
but pleasing. When he grew excited, and everything that was said
seemed to drive him to the point of exasperation, though no one
ever addressed him, he would slide off the table, strut and swagger
like a little Hercules, a comical one, then plant himself squarely in
front of you and ask—"What makes the waves go up and down?
Can you answer that?"

If you simply said No, he would give you a look of utter disappointment. What he wanted was for you to say: "No, can you
tell me?"

All the while I was calmly floating on my back, quietly studying
him, wondering where on earth he came from and what could
possibly be his occupation. Now and then I sat up and gave him
a straight answer. He took it as if he had been given a jab in the
jaw. Finally I decided to put *him* a question.

"Are you Egyptian . . . or perhaps a Turk?"

"I'm from *India*," he replied, his eyes aflame, his head swaying
from left to right, and, as if to manifest his own super-satisfaction,

accompanying the words with a cooing, clucking sound which even the peacock would have difficulty in imitating.

"Very good," I said. "But you're not a Hindu, are you? What part of India do you come from?"

"Near Bombay . . . Poona," he replied.

"Then you speak Gujarati."

"No, Hindi." His eyes lit up again. They danced with fire.

"Do you know Sanskrit?"

"No, but I can write it."

"Perhaps you're a rajah."

"A *maharajah!*" he countered.

"Not a mahatma?"

"No, nor a yogi either."

Pause while we study each other amusedly.

"What's the difference, can you tell me, between a yogi and a mahatma?"

"A yogi thinks only of himself."

(*Very* good, thought I to myself.)

Aloud—"And how did you find that out?"

"I know lots of things that are not written in books," he replied with a smirk. "I travel. I travel around the world."

Another pause. He looks at me as if to say—"And your next question, please?"

"In September . . . *this* September . . . I will be in England. Do you know London?"

Before I could so much as nod my head he continued. "From London I will go to Paris, from Paris to Berlin, then to Vienna, and then to Rome, Athens, Damascus, Jerusalem, Cairo. . . ."

"In September . . . *this* September . . ." said I, "I shall be in Japan. After that Cambodia, Burma, India. . . ."

"You have been to India before?"

"No."

"You must go to India!" He said it as if it were a command.

More to lead him on than anything else, I told him it needed a little thinking. "It costs money, a trip like that. Especially to travel around in *your* country."

He gave a jackal-like laugh, threw back his head and screeched: "*Money?* What do you need money for?" He paused a moment, then asked: "What's your business?"

"I'm not in business. I write."

"You write articles, I suppose?"

"No, books."

Immediately he was all animation. Squatting on his well-padded haunch, assuming the air of a buttered Buddha, he leaned slightly forward and fixed me with his glittering eyes.

"You write an article . . . a *good* article . . . and I will get you five thousand dollars for it. *More* even. . . . How much do you need?"

Before I could make reply he was on his feet and grasping my arm, as if to pull me out of the tub. "I'll get you all the money you want, plus a free trip to Java, Burma, India, Ceylon, Bali. . . ." He pulled himself up short. "Look," he said, now fairly dancing with excitement, "I want you to write about Nature, not *people*— do you understand?" He took a few steps backward, pointed to the hills above us, then beckoned for me to get out of the tub. I did. "You see those trees up there . . . and that dark spot over there?" He indicated the area with an arclike motion of his hand. I looked searchingly, wondering what he saw there of particular interest. To my eye there was just the usual sweep of hills, the usual undulations, the usual trees, rocks, brush.

He dropped his arm, looked at me as if he were giving me a *koan* to solve, then exclaimed: "Can you write about *that*, just *that*"—he indicated the area once again with a sweep of the arm —"without describing it?"

Involuntarily my jaw dropped. *Without describing it!* (Sic)

"What you must do," he continued, "is to talk about such things as . . . how do you call it? . . . *earth-quavers!* about caves and grottoes, volcanoes, the waves, sea lions, sharks and whales . . .

not people. You must give it *symbology,* do you understand? That's what we are interested in."

(*We!* Who did he mean by "we"?)

"By the way," he said, as if it were practically settled now, the contract signed, my bags packed. "By the way, do you know any languages—*besides English?* You have to speak a few other languages too."

To please him I said: "I know a little French, a little . . ."

"Speak French to me!"

"What would you like me to say?"

"Anything! I understand everything. I speak French, Italian, German, Spanish, Greek, Russian, Persian . . ."

"T'es bien calé!" I barked.

"What language is that?" he snarled.

"Du français, espèce de con! Démerde-toi!"

(Naturally he didn't know I was making a prick of him.)

"Où avez-vous apprendi le français?" he demanded.

"Comme toi, à Paris. Panam!"

"I speak only correct French. *Polite* French." He looked at me askance as he muttered this. Apparently he was getting the drift of it.

To which I replied: *"A quoi bon continuer? Sprechen Sie Deutsch?"*

"Ja wohl!" he exclaimed. *"Je vous dite que je parle Arabe, Espagnol . . .* and Greek and Turkish. A little Armenian too."

"Fabelhaft!"

"Was meint das?"

"Das meint extraordinary . . . fabulous. *Kennen Sie nicht ein Wort wie fabelhaft? Vielleicht kennen Sie wunderbar."*

"Wunderbar, ja! That's German. . . . Now I will tell you another language I can speak—*Dar-goon!"*

"Never heard of it."

He grinned. For just one moment I thought he was going to break down and say, "Neither did I!" But he didn't.

He looked away, as if studying the sea, the heaving kelp. When he turned around there was a blank look on his face.

After what was meant to be an impressive pause, he asked: "Do you believe in a Creator?"

"I do," said I.

"Good! Are you a Christian then?"

"No," I replied, "I have no religion."

"Are you a Jew?"

"Not that I know of."

"But you believe in God?"

"Yes."

He looked at me squintingly. It was obvious he didn't believe me. "What do *you* believe in?" I asked.

"The Creator!" he replied.

"Have you a religion?"

"No. I belong to the Bahai movement. That's the *only* religion."

"So!" I made a clucking noise and preened my feathers.

"You must get to know the Creator! Jesus Christ was just a man, not a god. Would God allow Himself to be crucified? All nonsense!" He turned abruptly and gazed straight up at the sun. He pulled me violently by the arm. "Look up there!" he commanded, pointing to the fiery orb. "Tell me, can you see what's behind it?"

"No," said I. "Can you?"

"Behind the sun, behind the stars and all the planets, behind everything that man can see with his telescopes, is the Creator. Nobody has eyes good enough to see Him. But he's there. . . . You must believe in Him. It's necessary. Otherwise——."

"Otherwise what?"

"Otherwise you're lost. In India we have many religions, many worships, many idols, many superstitions . . . *and many fools.*"

Full stop. I said nothing. Blank for blank.

"Have you heard speak of the Nile?"

"The what?"

"The Nile! It's a river . . . in Egypt."

"Oh, the *Nile!* Why, of course. Everybody knows the Nile."

He gave me a disdainful sidelong glance.

"Yes, everybody knows the Nile, as you say, but do they know how many Niles there are?"

"What do you mean by that?" said I.

"Did you know that there is a white Nile, a blue Nile and a black Nile?"

"No," I replied, "I know only the green Nile."

"I thought so," he said. "And now tell me, what *is* the Nile?"

"You just told me . . . it's a river."

"But what does it mean?"

"What, *river?*"

"No, *the Nile!*"

"If you mean etymologically," said I, "I must confess my ignorance. If you mean symbolically, I must again confess ignorance. If you mean esoterically, then I am thrice ignorant. We're at the quincunx now. *Your serve!*"

Just as if I had said nothing at all, he informed me in his most pedantic manner that Nile meant—*in Egyptian!*—wisdom and fecundity. "Do you understand now?" he added.

"I think so." I murmured it most humbly.

"And the reason for that (for what?) is that it lies quiet like a snake and then it vomits. I have been up and down the Nile many times. And I've seen the Sphinx and the Pyramids. . . ."

"Didn't you tell me a while ago that you had been to Damascus?"

"I said I was *going* there. Yes, I've been to Damascus too. I go everywhere. Why should we stay in one spot?"

"You must be a rich man," said I.

He shook his head from side to side, rolled his eyes, made the cooing, clucking noise as before, and answered: "Tsch, tsch! I'm an artist, that's what I am."

"An artist? What, a painter?"

"I paint too. *Sculptor,* that's what I am."

Wunderbar! thought I to myself. *Fabelhaft!* If he's a sculptor, I'm an octoroon.

"Do you know Bennie Bufano?" I gave it to him like a test question.

Cautiously he replied: "I heard of him." Then he added quickly: "I know all the sculptors—including the dead ones."

"How about Lipschitz?"

"He's not a sculptor!"

"What is he then?"

"An ironworker."

"And Giacometti?"

"Tutti-frutti!"

"And Picasso?"

"A house painter! Doesn't know when to stop."

I wanted to steer him back to Damascus. Had he been to Lebanon, I wanted to know.

He had.

"And Mecca?"

"Yes! Medina too. And Aden and Addis Ababa. *Any more places?*"

At this point my friend Fink intervened to ask for a light. The look he gave me said—how long are you going to keep up this game? He turned to Mr. Know-it-all and offered him a cigarette.

"Not *now!*" said the latter, holding up his palms and making a mue of disgust. "When I am dry I shall ask you for one. It's better to wait."

I could hear Fink mumbling "Fuck yourself!" as he walked away. Meanwhile, possibly in answer to my last question—or his own— his nibs had begun spouting. I missed the first few sentences. Tuned in just as he was saying ". . . they have no stores, no salesmen, nothing to buy, nothing to sell. Everything you want is free. Whatever you raise you bring to the square and put it there. If you want fruit, you take it from the tree. As much as you like. But you mustn't fill your pockets. . . ."

Where in hell *is* this? I wondered to myself, but refrained from breaking his train of thought.

"Very few people ever get there. At the border they stopped me. Took away my passport. While they were gone I made a portrait of the man I was going to see. When they came back I handed them the portrait. They saw that it was a very good resemblance. 'You are a good man,' they said. 'We can trust you not to rob anybody.' So they let me in. I didn't need a penny. Whatever I asked for they gave me free. Most of the time I lived in the palace. I could have women too, if I wanted. But you shouldn't ask for such things. . . ."

At this point I couldn't resist asking what he was talking about. "What country *is* this?"

"I told you—*Arabia!*"

"*Arabia?*"

"Yes. And who was my friend?"

"How should I know?"

"King Sa-oud." He paused to let this sink in. "The richest man in the world. Every year he sells to America 500,000,000 barrels of oil. To England 200,000,000. To France 150,000,000. To Belgium 75,000,000. He *sells* it. He doesn't *deliver* it. They have to come and get it. All he asks"—he threw me a weak smile— "is a dollar a barrel."

"You mean they have to bring the barrels with them?"

"No, he pipes it out. The barrel is free. He charges only for the oil. A dollar a barrel. No more. *No less.* That's his profit."

My friend Fink hove to again. He was getting fidgety. He pulled me to one side. "How much more of this can you take?"

Our friend scuttled back to his tub. We collected our things and made ready to go. A sea otter poked its head through the glassy sea below us. We stayed a moment to watch its antics.

"I say!" shouted our India-rubber friend.

We turned around.

"I want you to brush up on your German!"

"Why?" I shouted.

"Because you should know a few languages. Especially German."

"But I know German."

"Then study Arabic. It may come in handy."

"And what about Hindi?"

"Yes, Hindi too . . . and Tamil."

"Not Sanskrit?"

"No, nobody speaks it any more. Only in Tibet."

Silence for a moment. He's splashing about like a walrus.

"Remember what I said before—put more symbology into your writing!"

"I'll try," I said. "And I should believe in the Creator, isn't that it?"

I waited for a retort but he said nothing. He was soaping the cracks between his toes.

I gave a shout, just as loud as I could.

He looked up, cupped his ear, as if someone were whispering to him.

"Now smile for me!" I said.

He drew his lips back.

"No, not that way. The way you did before. Roll your eyes. Move your head back and forth." Then I went—"Tsch, tsch, tsch. Like *that*," I said. "Come on now, do it for me before we go."

To my surprise, he did just as I wished.

"Good!" I said. "I think now maybe you *are* a Hindu. I know lots of Hindus. I had many Hindu friends once—in New York. Good boys, all of them. A little wacky, some of them. . . . Did you ever hear of Mazumdar?"

"Who?"

"Mazumdar. Haridas Mazumdar. He was a genius."

"What is his first name again?"

"Haridas."

"That's not a Hindu name!"

"No? Well, it isn't Czech either. Let's say it's Bulgarian."

Pause.

"By the way," said I, "you never told me *your* name."

"It's not important," he replied. "Nobody knows me. I use any name I like—if it pleases me."

"That's ducky. Just ducky. Tomorrow I am going to take the name Hounaman. Did you ever hear that name before? Tomorrow I'm going to call myself Sri Hounaman . . . and I'm going to have a hole cut in the seat of my trousers so that I can wag my tail if I feel like it. I want you to remember that! *Do you understand me?*"

He put his head under water so as not to hear any more.

"Come on, Bob," I said, "let's go. I've got to deliver a barrel of oil to the Prince of Monaco."

As we came alongside his tub he looked up, raised a forefinger, and with the solemnity of an ape, said: "You must not forget to go to India. I give you seven years to make up your mind. If you don't go before that time you never will."

On that dixit we exeunted.

15.

"If you do not know where you are going, any road will take you there."*

There are days when it all seems as simple and clear as that to me. What do I mean? I mean with regard to the problem of

* *Out of Confusion,* by M. N. Chatterjee (Yellow Springs, Ohio: Antioch Press, 1954).

living on this earth without becoming a slave, a drudge, a hack, a misfit, an alcoholic, a drug addict, a neurotic, a schizophrenic, a glutton for punishment or an artist *manqué*.

Supposedly we have the highest standard of living of any country in the world. Do we, though? It depends on what one means by high standards. Certainly nowhere does it cost more to live than here in America. The cost is not only in dollars and cents but in sweat and blood, in frustration, ennui, broken homes, smashed ideals, illness and insanity. We have the most wonderful hospitals, the most gorgeous insane asylums, the most fabulous prisons, the best equipped and the highest paid army and navy, the speediest bombers, the largest stockpile of atom bombs, yet never enough of any of these items to satisfy the demand. Our manual workers are the highest paid in the world; our poets the worst. There are more automobiles than one can count. And as for drugstores, where in the world will you find the like?

We have only one enemy we really fear: the microbe. But we are licking him on every front. True, millions still suffer from cancer, heart disease, schizophrenia, multiple sclerosis, tuberculosis, epilepsy, colitis, cirrhosis of the liver, dermatitis, gall stones, neuritis, Bright's disease, bursitis, Parkinson's disease, diabetes, floating kidneys, cerebral palsy, pernicious anaemia, encephalitis, locomotor ataxia, falling of the womb, muscular distrophy, jaundice, rheumatic fever, polio, sinus and antrum troubles, halitosis, St. Vitus's Dance, narcolepsy, coryza, leucorrhea, nymphomania, phthisis, carcinoma, migraine, dipsomania, malignant tumors, high blood pressure, duodenal ulcers, prostate troubles, sciatica, goiter, catarrh, asthma, rickets, hepatitis, nephritis, melancholia, amoebic dysentery, bleeding piles, quinsy, hiccoughs, shingles, frigidity and impotency, even dandruff, and of course all the insanities, now legion, *but*—our men of science will rectify all this within the next hundred years or so. *How?* Why, by destroying all the nasty germs which provoke this havoc and disruption! By waging a great preventive war —not a cold war!—wherein our poor, frail bodies will become a battleground for all the antibiotics yet to come. A game of hide and seek, so to speak, in which one germ pursues another, tracks it down and slays it, all without the least disturbance to our usual functioning. Until this victory is achieved, however, we may be obliged to continue swallowing twenty or thirty vitamins, all of different strengths and colors, before breakfast, down our tiger's milk and brewer's yeast, drink our orange *and* grapefruit juices, use blackstrap molasses on our oatmeal, smear our bread (made of stone-ground flour) with peanut butter, use raw honey or raw sugar with our coffee, poach our eggs rather than fry them, follow this with an extra glass of superfortified milk, belch and burp a little, give ourselves an injection, weigh ourselves to see if we are under or over, stand on our heads, do our setting-up exercises—if we haven't done them already—yawn, stretch, empty the bowels, brush our teeth (if we have any left), say a prayer or two, then run like hell to catch the bus or the subway which will carry us to work, and think no more about the state of our health until we feel a cold coming on: the incurable coryza. But we are not to despair. Never despair! Just take more vitamins, add an extra dose of calcium and phosphorus pills, drink a hot toddy or two, take a high enema before retiring for the night, say another prayer, if we can remember one, and call it a day.

If the foregoing seems too complicated, here is a simple regimen to follow: Don't overeat, don't drink too much, don't smoke too much, don't work too much, don't think too much, don't fret, don't worry, don't complain, above all, don't get irritable. Don't use a car if you can walk to your destination; don't walk if you can run; don't listen to the radio or watch television; don't read newspapers, magazines, digests, stock market reports, comics, mysteries or detective stories; don't take sleeping pills or wakeup pills; don't vote, don't buy on the instalment plan, don't play cards either for recreation or to make a haul, don't invest your money, don't mortgage your home, don't get vaccinated or inoculated, don't violate the fish and game laws, don't irritate your boss, don't say

yes when you mean no, don't use bad language, don't be brutal
to your wife or children, don't get frightened if you are over or
under weight, don't sleep more than ten hours at a stretch, don't
eat store bread if you can bake your own, don't work at a job you
loathe, don't think the world is coming to an end because the wrong
man got elected, don't believe you are insane because you find
yourself in a nut house, don't do anything more than you're asked
to do but do that well, don't try to help your neighbor until you've
learned how to help yourself, and so on. . . .

Simple, what?

In short, don't create aerial dinosaurs with which to frighten
field mice!

America has only one enemy, as I said before. The microbe. The
trouble is, he goes under a million different names. Just when you
think you've got him licked he pops up again in a new guise. He's
the pest personified.

When we were a young nation life was crude and simple. Our
great enemy then was the redskin. (He became our enemy when
we took his land away from him.) In those early days there were
no chain stores, no delivery lines, no hired purchase plan, no
vitamins, no supersonic flying fortresses, no electronic computers;
one could identify thugs and bandits easily because they looked
different from other citizens. All one needed for protection was a
musket in one hand and a Bible in the other. A dollar was a dollar,
no more, no less. And a gold dollar, or a silver dollar, was just
as good as a paper dollar. Better than a check, in fact. Men like
Daniel Boone and Davy Crockett were genuine figures, maybe not
so romantic as we imagine them today, but they were not screen
heroes. The nation was expanding in all directions because there
was a genuine need for it—we already had two or three million
people and they needed elbow room. The Indians and the bison
were soon crowded out of the picture, along with a lot of other
useless paraphernalia. Factories and mills were being built, and
colleges and prisons and insane asylums. Things were humming.

And then we freed the slaves. That made everybody happy, except the Southerners. It also made us realize that freedom is a precious thing. When we had recovered from the loss of blood we began to think about freeing the rest of the world. To do it, we engaged in two world wars, not to mention a little war like the one with Spain, and now we've entered upon a cold war which our leaders warn us may last another forty or fifty years. We are almost at the point now where we may be able to exterminate every man, woman and child thoughout the globe who is unwilling to accept the kind of freedom we advocate. It should be said, in extenuation, that when we have accomplished our purpose everybody will have enough to eat and drink, be properly clothed, housed and entertained. An all-American program and no two ways about it! Our men of science will then be able to give their undivided attention to other problems, such as disease, insanity, excessive longevity, interplanetary voyages and the like. Everyone will be inoculated, not only against real ailments but against imaginary ones too. War will have been eliminated forever, thus making it unnecessary "in times of peace to prepare for war." America will go on expanding, progressing, providing. We will plant the Stars and Stripes on the moon, and subsequently on all the planets within our comfy little universe. One world it will be, and American through and through. *Strike up the band!*

Now when I watch Howard Welch, a neighbor, going about his business I wonder if the glorious future I have just depicted may not be the flip and froth of dream. I look at Howard, who's a plain, handsome, ordinary fellow from Missouri, a chap full of energy, full of integrity, full of good will, and it seems to me that this program of progress and expansion doesn't jibe with his simple, sensible, straightforward view of things. Not that Howard isn't a hundred percent American. He's more than that, indeed. He's a hundred and twenty proof. But his notion of an all-American program is somewhat different from the one I have just outlined.

It's not as grandiose perhaps, but it's more foolproof than the star-spangled Utopia of our deluded dipsydoodlers.

When Howard came here, about four years ago, all he had in mind was to find work for his two hands and a place to flop. He wasn't choosy about the jobs that might be offered him. Nor was he fussy about what he wore or what he ate. He needed only a pair of pants, a shirt and a jacket; he knew how to get along on Mexican beans, squash, New Zealand spinach, wild mustard greens and similar pabulum. What really drew Howard to Big Sur was the hope of finding a small community of neighborly people in whose midst he could become self-sustaining, self-sufficient. He had no bizarre *Weltanschauung,* no ideological notions whatever, and no crusader's itch. "A little land and a living"—that was his dream. He came like a lone ranger in search of green pastures. Something just as simple and ordinary as that.

Why do I single Howard out? Not because I regard him as unique but because, to my way of thinking, he is a genuine American type. Tall, lean, muscular, alert, quick-witted, eyes a-twinkle, toes sparkling, slow of speech, musical voice, dry, kindly humor, fond of the banjo, the guitar, the harmonica, capable of working like a fiend if need be, spry as a leprechaun, good-natured, peaceably inclined but quick to flare up if provoked, always minding his own business, always pretending to be less than he is, ever ready to lend a hand, eccentric in attire but in a pleasing, dashing way, scrupulously conscientious, punctilious as well as punctual, sentimental but not sloppily so, idealistic, slightly cantankerous, neither a follower nor a leader, sociable yet chary of ties, and, where the other sex is concerned, just a trifle difficult to live with. A man, in short, who would lend spice to any community. A man to rely on, as a worker, as a helper, as a friend, as a neighbor.

This is the lone-American type I admire, the kind I believe in, can get along with, and whom I vote for even though he's never nominated for office. The democratic man our poets sang of but who, alas, is being rapidly exterminated, along with the buffalo, the moose and the elk, the great bear, the eagle, the condor, the mountain lion. The sort of American that never starts a war, never raises a feud, never draws the color line, never tries to lord it over his fellow-man, never yearns for a higher education, never holds a grudge against his neighbor, never treats an artist shabbily and never turns a beggar away. Often untutored and unlettered, he sometimes has more of the poet and the musician in him, philosopher too, than those who are acclaimed as such. His whole way of life is aesthetic. What marks him as different, sometimes ridiculous, is his sincerity and originality. That he aspires to be none other than himself, is this not the essence of wisdom?

Howard is one of those young men I spoke of earlier when gathering the oranges of the millennium. The type who is content to live *en marge*: the sort who believes in picking up the bread crumbs. I've run across a number of these individuals these last few years. They may not agree with all I say about them, but to my mind they all have something in common. They all arrived here by different paths, each with his own purpose, and one as different from the other as marbles from dice. But all "naturals." All somewhat "peculiar" in the eyes of the ordinary run. All of them, to my mind, men of service, men of good will, men of strong integrity. The ideal material for the making of community. Each and every one of them fed up with the scheme of things, determined to free themselves of the treadmill, lead their own lives. And ever willing to give of their best. None of them demanding anything more fantastic of life than the right to live after his own fashion. None of them adhering to any party, doctrine, cult or ism, but all imbued with very strong, very definite ideas as to how life may and can be lived even in these evil times. Never crusading for their ideas, but doing their utmost to put them into practice. Making compromises now and then, when compelled to, but always cleaving to the line. Adapting themselves to the ways of their neighbors but not necessarily to their views. The first to criticize themselves, laugh at themselves, humble themselves. Putting above everything

—human dignity. Difficult sometimes, especially where "trifles" are concerned, yet always available in genuine emergencies. Stone deaf when asked to toe the line.

All of them have demonstrated that it is possible to live happily on next to nothing. All are married, or have been. All are extremely capable, in many ways. As cabinet ministers they would be perfect. Under their guiding hand there would be no need for revolution, they would run the country into the ground in no time.

Whether they know it or not, that is precisely what they are trying to do. Their goal is not a bigger and better America but a world made for man. What they are seeking is a new old way of life, one consonant with human aspirations and equated with human proportions. Not back to the safety and security of the womb, but—*out of the wilderness!*

When I said a while ago that the aim of these individuals is to become self-sufficient, I hope I made myself clear. What they are after is to become as *un*dependent as possible. Interdependent would be more like it. Hudson Kimball, who pushed the idea furthest, found it extremely difficult. In attempting to live his own life he grew a vegetable garden, raised goats, chickens, rabbits, geese, kept bees too, if I am not mistaken, yet his wife had to give music lessons and he himself had to work in town a few days a week in order to raise the indispensable cash needed to meet the exigencies of even the simplest mode of life. He had no vices, no indulgences. He neither smoked nor drank, neither did his wife. They lived just about as frugally as two people can, with a child of eight or nine, but they couldn't make a go of it.

Jack Morgenrath, on the other hand, does pretty well. In fact, I would say very well. He works as little as possible—at anything. Just enough to earn the few dollars needed to provide for a wife and three children. Jack has two cars, whereas the Kimballs had none. (When the latter went to town, they had first to walk almost two miles to the highway, then grub a ride. They went to bed at dark, to avoid the expense of fuel and kerosene.) When his car breaks down, Jack takes the motor apart himself; I believe he could build a new body for it if he had to. Jack needs a car—and a truck —in order to hire himself out. Otherwise he wouldn't dream of owning one.

As for Warren Leopold, an architect, a builder, a painter, a fine carpenter, he has a wife and four children, probably the best behaved and the most contented children in the whole community. (Aside from the Lopez family.) His idea, or ideal, is to so manage that they won't need a house—they will all live together in a tent— or under a rock. Warren loves to build houses but loathes his profession. And with good reason. For, until one can establish himself as another Frank Lloyd Wright, one is condemned to design homes that will suit the taste of people who have no understanding of architecture whatever. In short, one must do the very opposite of what one believes in. To circumvent this dilemma, Warren had the very sensible idea of building a house according to his own ideas, living in it for a while, then selling it to anyone who took a fancy to it. Once he got a contract to design a house for a wealthy woman who paid him a handsome retaining fee. Warren didn't altogether approve of the kind of home the woman demanded, but he decided to do the best he could. He had two children then, one of whom had to undergo several very expensive operations. (It was just before the child was stricken that we met on the street in Monterey one day. Warren was still dazed by the amount of money he had collected as a retaining fee. He would have preferred no fee and a free hand in carrying out his architectural ideas. But here's how he greeted me. "Can't I give you a few hundred dollars? I don't know what to do with all this money." It never occurred to him to improve his standard of living. He wasn't even tempted to do so. When I refused his offer he said: "Look, you're always sending food and clothes to Europe"—it was right after the war— "Take the money and give it to those who need it." I refused again, this time with less conviction. . . . But that's the sort of chap Warren is.)

Warren can earn good money as a first-class carpenter. He doesn't want to. He wants a little piece of land, just enough to raise some fruit and vegetables, rabbits and chickens, and to hell with your $12.50 per day—or is it $20.00 a day that first-class carpenters now earn?

But perhaps I can better convey the feeling of frustration and disillusionment which carpenters, bricklayers, engineers and architects in America are prone to by quoting a few passages of a letter I once received from an Egyptian student whom I had hired to serve as a messenger when I was hiring and firing for the Cosmococcic Telegraph Company. It was in the spring of 1924 and Mohamed Ali Sarwat had left our employ to seek a better position in Washington, D.C.

ESTEEMED AND MOST HONOURABLE SIR:

I must write and let you know what sorrow's hand has done in my heart, and it grieves me very much to overburden you with my internal pains, but I feel extremely gratified to know that you are a rare and gracious soul.

Here I am, a wrecked ship dashed and broken into pieces, by the huge rocks in the wide, dark and rolling ocean of America. My dear sir, I have often heard people speak highly of this country, that its imaginary beauty had infatuated me and drew me hither from the calm East very vehemently.

Very shortly after I had landed here I found what I have taken for granted is but a mere poetic sentiment; and the magnificent and gigantic mansions of hopes were but dreams and foundationless. I am very much disappointed, dear sir. There is a quotation of a Persian poet that runs:

"And there must be a humanitarian soul in which you have to deposit your pains and sufferings, and in which you will find a balsam to relieve your ulcerated heart."

You know I left New York City as I was unsuccessful to earn the means of my livelihood there. I found myself lost among the crowds of the Materialistic rush in the very busy streets of the Western Metropolice. Then I have carried my knapsack of travel in the psychological attitude of Jean Valjean, the hero personage of *Les Miserables,* by the French Hugo and stepped forward hither with the absolute hope to earn easily the means of my living, but to my ill luck and misfortune I found all of Washington is like what I have previously had an introduction. What a pity! A man like me unable to eat his bread in the alleged garden-spot of the world. That is a great disaster. Whenever I think of the existing circumstances in this great country the lines of Longfellow run into my memory:

"Something, something done
has earned a night's repose."

And I also think of America according to Shakespeare's words in *Hamlet*: "Something is rotten in the State of Denmark!"

What can I say more, my dear sir? The flourishing rose of my hopes had already faded. Conditions are awfully bad here. Capitalism is enslaving Labour in the midst daylight of the twentieth century, and Democracy is but a word of no meaning.

He who has money is terribly tormenting he who has not, simply because he has to feed him, and he who has money is degraded from his spiritual sentiments. That is the main point of weakness. That the mistake of society.

Kindly write me whenever you have a chance to do so. Advise me what to do. Shall I be patient, and my patience come to its limits? Will conditions be continuously bad in the United States as they are now? Is there any hope of the sun shining to kill the dark clouds and enlighten the obscurity? I hardly believe so. Here is what I am thinking of: I find it a black spot in the white page of my life to come to America and return back to Egypt with failure, and I would rather die than so do.

My soul is very ambitious, and it is imprisoned within the cage of clay, the body! Shall I release it to enjoy liberty and boundless freedom? I like to return back to New York and shall not do so unless I know what my determination there will be. I want to be employed by you as a sergeant to look after the clothes, no matter what long my hours of work will be, as long as I shall be under your direction and will be leading a sedentary life. I am sure your heart will sympathize with my state and you will resume your endeavorings to put me in some position and see me settled. Do help me, please.

I shall come back to New York when you will be able to put me in such a work and send me a word to report myself to your kindness. Don't care much about the people, as I have no faith in them. I have only a very unshaking faith in *you*. You will be able yourself to solve my problem.

Don't hesitate to help me as much as you can. I want you to employ me as a sergeant, or elsewhere in a decent work. I am unable to afford being out of work for such a long time. I cannot exist. *Read this letter again!* Read it over in your spare time and write an answer please.

I have taken a very long time from yours. I must close. With very good wishes and kindest regards, I beg to lay under your feet my most respectful homage.

Your obedient servant always,
(*signed*) MOHAMED ALI SARWAT

As often as I've read the Gospels I've never run across a single reference to the baggage that Jesus toted around. There is not even mention of a satchel, such as Somerset Maugham made use of when walking about in China. (Bufano, the sculptor, travels lighter than any man I know, but even Bennie is obliged to carry a shaving kit in which he stuffs a change of linen, a toothbrush and a pair of socks.) As for Jesus, by all accounts he didn't own a toothbrush. No baggage, no furniture, no change of linen, no handkerchief, no passport, no identity card, no bankbook, no love letters, no insurance policy, no address book. To be sure, he had no wife, no children, no home (not even a winter palace) and no correspondence to look after. As far as we know, he never wrote a line. Home was where-ever he happened to be. Not where he hung his hat—because he never wore a hat.

He had no wants, that's the thing. He didn't even have to think about such a menial job as wardrobe attendant. After a time he ceased working as a carpenter. Not that he was looking for bigger wages. No, he had more important work to do. He set out to prove the absurdity of living by the sweat of one's brow. *Behold the lilies in the field. . . .*

The other day, glancing through one of our illustrated weeklies, I noticed an advertisement for a new Lincoln. The caption read: "For those who are never satisfied with the ordinary." The new car was described as one suitable for "modern living and magnificent driving." Further on, in this same weekly, there was a photograph of a great new bridge, a railroad bridge, I believe, in the city of Calcutta—or was it Bombay?—and on the riverbank, right in the shadow of this engineering triumph, a yogi could be seen standing on his head, clad only in a loincloth. He gave the impression of being able to stand in that position forever, if he chose to. Obviously, he had no need of that new bridge, nor of the new Lincoln "suitable for modern living." Whatever his needs, they were, like Jesus', few and far between.

"The world problem," said Krishnamurti once, "is the individual problem; if the individual is at peace, has happiness, has great tolerance, and an intense desire to help, then the world problem as such ceases to exist. You consider the world problem before you have considered your own problem. Before you have established peace and understanding in your own hearts and in your own minds, you desire to establish peace and tranquillity in the minds of others, in your nations and in your states; whereas peace and understanding. will only come when there is understanding, certainty and strength in yourselves."*

If I were running the World Order of Human Merit, I would

---

* *The Pool of Wisdom,* by J. Krishnamurti (Holland: Star Publishing Trust, 1928).

make Warren Leopold a Chevalier. When Warren has to pack and move (with a wife and four children), and he's done it time and again, he can do it in an hour or two. After he quit building houses according to other people's ideas, Warren traveled up and down the Coast a number of times. Always on the lookout for "a little land and a living." As he said to me once—"There's so much land everywhere, surely someone ought to be willing to part with a little. All we need is a half-acre." In one of the northern counties of this glorious state he one day found a spot of land. The man told him he could have it—for free. With wife and kids helping, Warren cleared the land, built a cabin to live in, started a vegetable patch, and just when everything seemed to be under control he had to clear out. The neighbors didn't like him. He wasn't their kind: he wore a beard, he refused to join the Grange, he chummed with the Indians and other no-good people, his ideas were too radical, and so on. Finally it turned out that the man who had given him the land didn't own it. He only thought he owned it. So they moved on. And always it was the same story: *"You don't belong."*

Well, nobody belongs who's trying to simplify his life. Nobody belongs who isn't trying to make money, or trying to make money make money. Nobody belongs who wears the same suit of clothes year in and year out, who doesn't shave, who doesn't believe in sending his children to school to be miseducated, who doesn't join up with Church, Grange and Party, who doesn't serve "Murder, Death and Blight, Inc." Nobody belongs who doesn't read *Time, Life,* and one of the Digests. Nobody belongs who doesn't vote, carry insurance, live on the instalment plan, pile up debts, keep a check account and deal with the Safeway stores or the Great Atlantic and Pacific Tea Company. Nobody belongs who doesn't read the current best sellers and help support the paid pimps who dump them on the market. Nobody belongs who is fool enough to believe that he is entitled to write, paint, sculpt or compose music according to the dictates of his own heart and conscience. Or who wants to be nothing more than an artist, an artist from tip to toe.

When Bob Nash left Wild Cat Canyon to go to Furnace Creek, Death Valley, he made application for a Guggenheim fellowship. I happened to read the outline of his "project" because I was one of several who sponsored his candidacy. I doubt if the Guggenheim people ever received an application such as the one Bob Nash sent in. It was simple, genuine, sincere. It ended like this: "I suppose my ultimate goal is simply to remain on the road which I am now on, to comprehend the universe."

To comprehend the universe! How those words must have bounced in the plush surroundings of a foundation dedicated to throwing money out the window!

What I like about Bob Nash is that he went ahead with his project "irregardless" of the Guggenheim award. If he gets it, I'll stand on my head for a month—like that yogi in the shadow of the railroad bridge.

Jesus did his work, and it was a mighty work, without a grant. So did Lincoln, and John Brown, and William Lloyd Garrison. If their efforts were crowned with failure, as some believe, it was not because they lacked financial support, or academic support. Can you picture Jesus receiving an honorary degree—LL.D., D.D., or M.D.—the last in recognition of his healing powers? Of all the degrees, "Doctor of Divinity" would have suited him least, what? Today, of course, if you wish to do God's work, you must first have a degree. Then, in lieu of doing the work of the Lord, you preach. Social security solves all the ugly problems.

To simplify one's life! It seems the most natural thing in the world to undertake, yet it's just about the most difficult. Everything stands in the way. Literally everything. How did Thoreau put it? "I am convinced that to maintain one's self on this earth is not a hardship, but a pastime, *if we will live simply and wisely.*"*

That "if"! The whole nation seems dead set against living simply

* Italics mine.

and wisely. Our leaders talk about making common effort, but what do they mean by it? Do they mean common effort towards the attainment of peace and understanding? Hardly.

Socrates defied his judges thus: "I am certain, O men of Athens, I should have perished long ago, and done no good either to you or myself. . . . He who will really fight for the right, if he would live even for a little while, must have a private station and not a public one."*

To create community—and what is a nation, or a people, without a sense of community—there must be a common purpose. Even here in Big Sur, where the oranges are ready to blossom forth, there is no common purpose, no common effort. There is a remarkable neighborliness, but no community spirit. We have a Grange, as do other rural communities, but what is a "Grange" in the life of man? The real workers are outside the Grange. Just as the "real men of God" are outside the Church. And the real leaders outside the world of politics.

Oddly enough, these lone travelers whom I've been talking about —fellows like Jack, Bob, Hudson, Warren, Howard—have more real community spirit than those who talk community. They think for themselves, they know where they stand, they travel light, and they're always available. They are not laboring to "establish peace and tranquillity in the minds of others." But neither are they indifferent to the plight of those about them. They do not overlook, do not ignore, those who are less fortunate than themselves. (I am not implying that they are unique in this respect; few, if any, here are capable of assuming such an attitude.) What I wish to stress is that it is easy to get at them, easy to enlist their support, moral or physical. They do not make problems of small issues. Nor do they make lame excuses. (As do the rich.) They answer Yes or No.   In addition, you know in advance what their answer will be. You know it will be the right answer, whether Yes or No.

---

* Taken from the editorial, "Socrates for Europe," *Manas*, Los Angeles, California, Dec. 7, 1955.

I spoke earlier as though they were guilty of undermining the fabric of our commonwealth. In reality, along with thousands of other unknowns, they are assisting in the creation of a new fabric, a simple, viable one, better able to stand the stress and strain, the wear and tear of time. In practicing their own way of life they point up the unessentials which make *our* way of life so absurd and futile.

Our tourists returning from abroad dwell on the poverty and misery of the great masses in Europe, Asia, Africa. They speak with pride of the abundance which we in America share. They talk of efficiency, sanitation, home comforts, high wages, the freedom to move about and to speak one's mind, and so on. They speak of these privileges as if they were *American* "inventions." (As if there had never been a Greece, a Rome, an Egypt, a China, an India, a Persia.) They never speak of the price we pay for these comforts, for all this progress and abundance. (As if we were free of crime, disease, suicide, infanticide, prostitution, alcoholism, addiction to drugs, military training, armament races and the obsession with lethal weapons.) They speak of motorcars, of the latest fashions in clothes, of superabundant produce, of refrigerators and deepfreezes, of washing machines, vacuum cleaners, of vitamins and barbiturates, of dry cereals, of pocketbooks, and so forth. Or of social security, pensions, dietary fads, automation, jet-propelled rockets, trips to the moon, libraries, hospitals, universities. Or of the marvels of psychoanalysis and Dianetics. Or, sentimentally, of the vanishing sea otter. They never speak of the degrading, senseless, undermining labor which must be performed in order to meet food and rent bills, keep a car, wear the proper clothes, pay the insurance companies, meet the tax levies with which to build tanks, battleships, submarines, jet bombers and create more stockpiles of this bomb and that. They are insured and secured, so they believe, against every emergency, every contingency. They may or may not have money in the bank, but they are certain to be in debt, mortgaged to the ears. They have, so they think, the most wonderful medical service in the world, yet they will succumb in the end to one of a thousand horrible ailments which even *American* citizens are heir to. Countless are those who will be maimed and mangled in factories and mills, in mines and laboratories; more still will be injured, crippled or killed in automobile accidents. More by the automobile than by the juggernaut of Mars. Disease alone will carry off more than all the other fatalities combined. Many will be rendered *hors de combat* through excessive drinking, or through the use of drugs. And almost as many from excessive eating, or from eating food products which have been robbed of their natural nourishment. Legions die through fear and anguish, nothing more.

And, to continue the story . . . those who were lucky enough to make a fortune will, if they live long enough, see their clever gains pissed away by their children. Those who have three cars, where only one was necessary, will end up in wheel chairs. Those who save their money will see it eaten up by those who want to make money make money. Those who work hard all their lives will receive in their old age a pension barely sufficient to keep a dog alive. As for the worker, he fares no better than the drone. The hobo, almost nonexistent now, lives a luxurious life by comparison. People are living on longer, but they are no match, in health, vitality or longevity, for the poor, hardy mountaineers of the Balkans. How many, in this land of plenty, are living to be eighty, ninety or a hundred, in full possession of their faculties, not chronically ill, and possessed of a full set of teeth, their own? How many of those who hang on until three score and ten may be said to be "living"? (Have you seen the fantastic valetudinarians of southern California and Florida who scoot along in motorized wheelchairs? Have you watched them idling the day away at cribbage, checkers, casino, dominoes?)

And how do writers, painters, sculptors, musicians, actors, dancers, to speak of the creative few, end their days? On a bed of roses? Does ever one of them look as Goethe did on his deathbed? Notice how the poets fade out of the picture. No man in his sound senses would elect to be a poet in this land of kingdom come!

Yes, Hemingway leads a grand life, seemingly. Name a few thousand other authors who do likewise!

It might be edifying to take time out and read how the great Milarepa died. (After a vain attempt to kill him with poison.) Or how Ramakrishna, succumbing to the ravages of cancer, comforted and cheered his disciples on his deathbed. Or how William Blake passed away singing.

Strange, but despite all the benefits of science, people are not dying the way these men did. They are dying miserably, here in America, though they have forked out the most exorbitant sums to doctor, surgeon and hospital. They may be given wonderful funerals, but no one has yet succeeded in making them die peacefully, nobly, serenely. Few enjoy the luxury of dying in their own beds.

"The human body is not a happenstance. It was created on purpose and by design. True, 'it comes forth like a flower and is cut down; it fleeth like a shadow and continueth not.' This is the way of all material things. But the creative forces and the natural laws that govern them are omnipotent, omniscient, omnipresent and eternal.

"The body springs from a cell less than one-hundredth of an inch in diameter, which contains nothing of which it is built. Soon it grows into a material entity, of which 62,500 miles of blood vessels are only a small part. It lives and functions until abuse, disease or some other force destroys it.

"Some bodies enter the world already dead. Others live various periods, the average life expectancy now being about fifty-nine years. Some live to be one hundred or more. . . .

"Of the nine primary functions of the body, those of growth and repair are most necessary to longevity. Creative processes resulting in growth appear to cease at maturity but we . . . have found that they do not. They only go into partial retirement. To the extent that basic body materials have to be replaced for the maintenance of life, they remain active. But without proper inducement they apparently grow tired and lag in their work. When creative processes are in full predominance over body decay, 140,000,000 cells are created every minute. This means an 8% replacement of basic body constituents every month, or a 96% new body every year.

"Could this creative rate be maintained, the average life expectancy might well be several times what it is today. In fact, one might live almost indefinitely. . . ."*

The great hoax which we are perpetuating every day of our lives is that that we are making life easier, more comfortable, more enjoyable, more profitable. We are doing just the contrary. We are making life stale, flat and unprofitable every day in every way. One ugly word covers it all: waste. Our thoughts, our energies, our very lives are being used up to create what is unwise, unnecessary, unhealthy. The stupendous activity which goes on in forest, field, mine and factory never adds up to happiness, contentment, peace of mind, or long life for those engaged in it. Very, very few Americans enjoy the work they are obliged to perform day in and day out. Most of them look upon their work as stultifying and degrading. Few ever find a way out. The vast majority are condemned, just as much as any slave, any convict, any half-wit. The work of the world, as it is so nobly called, is performed by drudges. That so many of them are well-educated only makes the picture that much worse. How little it matters whether one be lawyer, doctor, preacher, judge, chemist, engineer, teacher or architect. One might just as well have been hod-carrier, stevedore, bank clerk, ditch digger, gambler or garbage collector. Who really loves what he is doing day in and day out? What holds one to job, trade, profession or pursuit? Inertia. We are all locked together, as in a vise, feeding on one another, preying on one another. Talk of the

* Taken from "Reasons Why Longer Life Is Possible," by Dr. Leo L. Spears, of the Spears Chiropractic Sanitarium and Hospital, Denver, Colorado. Dr. Spears has since died of a heart attack.

insect world, by comparison we resemble their degenerate offspring!

Dominating the show, supervising and regulating it, stands a government composed of elected representatives of the people, which, for a collection of bunglers, misfits, jokesters and miscreants, would be hard to match.

And our millionaires—are they happy? *They,* at least, should be gay, jovial, light of heart. Is not the goal of all our striving to have even more than one wants? Look at them, our poor millionaires! The sorriest specimens of humanity on earth. How I wish the starving Asiatics could become millionaires overnight, all of them! How quickly they would realize the futility of the American way!

Then there are the middle classes—the bulwark of the nation, as we blithely say. Sober, steady, reliable, educated, conservative, self-respecting. You can count on them to steer a middle-of-the-road course. Could there be any emptier souls than these? All living like stuffed cadavers in a wax museum. Weighing themselves morning and night. Saying Yes today, No tomorrow. Weather vanes, shuttlecocks, noisy amplifiers. Have kept up a good front all their lives. Behind this front—nothing. Not even sandbags.

And the workers—the highest paid in all the world, as we proudly boast. Own their own cars, their own homes. (Some of them.) But all loaded with insurance, war bonds, cemetery plots. Children educated free of charge, schools equipped with playgrounds and recreation centers, food approved by the Pure Food inspectors. Factories air-conditioned. Toilets sanitary and always in good working order. Forty hours a week, double pay for overtime. At a hundred a week they find it difficult to make ends meet. The government robs them, the banks rob them, the merchants rob them, the labor leaders rob them, the boss robs them, everybody robs them. They rob one another. I speak of the de luxe workers, who sometimes make de luxe soldiers or de luxe politicians. As for the unwashed, the un-unionized, the unheard of variety, they live like rats. They are a disgrace to the nation. This is one nation which will *not* subscribe to poverty, filth, vice, illiteracy, mendicancy, or idleness and shiftlessness!

Except for the gangsters, who are getting smarter every day, more efficient, more cunning, more business-like, more progressive, more honorable, so to speak, and who are indoctrinating the young (through comics, movies, radio, television), infiltrating the ranks, so that sometimes it is difficult to tell whether the man seated next to you is one of them or just a lawyer, judge, banker, congressman or minister of the gospel ... except for the gangsters, I say, the ones who really seem to have it best, who know perfectly well what they are doing and like it, who show the least wear and tear, who get the most enjoyment out of life, are the fifty-, and one-hundred-dollars-per-call call girls, most of them highly intelligent, well educated, pleasant to look at, always well dressed, well read, simple and unaffected in deportment, less noisy, vulgar and vain-glorious, very much so, than the wives or mistresses of the men they cater to. Even a Supreme Court judge would find it pleasant, profitable and instructive to spend an hour or two with one of their calling. The pity is that they are not available to the rank and file!

As a minnesinger of the lumpen proletariat, I know that no respectable American will take the foregoing seriously. Any more than he will take seriously that fact that, by the latest count, 13,976,238 men and women, including a percentage of children as well, are rotting away in prisons, reformatories, hospitals, insane asylums, institutions for the mentally defective and similar establishments throughout the land. I may be off on my figures this way or that, but the facts are correct. As Lord Buckley says: "You lay it down, Nazz, and we'll pick it up!"

These are the kind of facts, needless to say, that one would hate to rub under a kitten's nose by way of house-breaking it. Even a whiff of such facts would give a plover or an osprey mental diarrhea. Better not present them to your children until they are ready for their master's degree. Better keep the young on lemons and lavender until they've reached the age of discretion.

REFERENCE TABLE FOR THE PRECEDING POTPOURRI

PART THREE

PARADISE LOST

Conrad Moricand

Born in Paris, January 17, 1887, at 7:00 or 7:15 P.M.

Died in Paris, August 31, 1954.

It was Anaïs Nin who introduced me to Conrad Moricand. She brought him to my studio in the Villa Seurat one day in the fall of 1936. My first impressions were not altogether favorable. The man seemed somber, didactic, opinionated, self-centered. A fatalistic quality pervaded his whole being.

It was late afternoon when he arrived, and after chatting a while, we went to eat in a little restaurant on the Avenue d'Orléans. The way he surveyed the menu told me at once that he was finicky. Throughout the meal he talked incessantly, without its spoiling his enjoyment of the food. But it was the kind of talk that does not go with food, the kind that makes food indigestible.

There was an odor about him which I could not help but be aware of. It was a mélange of bay rum, wet ashes and *tabac gris,* tinctured with a dash of some elusive, elegant perfume. Later these would resolve themselves into one unmistakable scent—the aroma of death.

I had already been introduced to astrologic circles before meeting Moricand. And in Eduardo Sanchez, a cousin of Anaïs Nin, I had found a man of immense erudition, who, on the advice of his analyst, had taken up astrology therapeutically, so to speak. Eduardo often reminded me of the earthworm, one of God's most useful creatures, it is said. His powers of ingestion and digestion were stupendous. Like the worm, his labors were primarily for the benefit of others, not himself. At the time Eduardo was engrossed in a study of the Pluto-Neptune-Uranus conjunctions. He had delved deep into history, metaphysics and biography in search of material to corroborate his intuitions. And finally he had begun work on the great theme: Apocatastasis.

With Moricand I entered new waters. Moricand was not only an astrologer and a scholar steeped in the hermetic philosophies, but an occultist. In appearance there was something of the mage about him. Rather tall, well built, broad shouldered, heavy and slow in his movements, he might have been taken for a descendant of the American Indian family. He liked to think, he later confided, that there was a connection between the name Moricand and Mohican. In moments of sorrow there was something slightly ludicrous about his expression, as if he were consciously identifying himself with the last of the Mohicans. It was in such moments that his square head with its high cheek bones, his stolidity and impassivity, gave him the look of anguished granite.

Inwardly he was a disturbed being, a man of nerves, caprices and stubborn will. Accustomed to a set routine, he lived the disciplined life of a hermit or ascetic. It was difficult to tell whether he had adapted himself to this mode of life or accepted it against the grain. He never spoke of the kind of life he would have liked to lead. He behaved as one who, already buffeted and battered, had resigned himself to his fate. As one who could assimilate punishment better than good fortune. There was a strong feminine streak in him which was not without charm but which he exploited to his own detriment. He was an incurable dandy living the life of a beggar. And living wholly in the past!

Perhaps the closest description I can give of him at the outset of our acquaintance is that of a Stoic dragging his tomb about with him. Yet he was a man of many sides, as I gradually came to discover. He had a tender skin, was extremely susceptible, particularly to disturbing emanations, and could be as fickle and emotional as a girl of sixteen. Though he was basically not fair-minded, he did his utmost to be fair, to be impartial, to be just. And to be loyal, though by nature I felt that he was essentially treacherous. In fact, it was this undefinable treachery which I was first aware of in him, though I had nothing on which to base my feelings. I remember that I deliberately banished the thought from my mind, replacing it with the vague notion that here was an intelligence which was suspect.

What I looked like to him in those early days is a matter of conjecture on my part. He did not know my writings except for a few fragments which had appeared in translation in French revues. He, of course, knew my date of birth and had presented me with my horoscope shortly after I became acquainted with him. (If I am not mistaken, it was he who detected the error in my hour of birth which I had given as midnight instead of noon.)

All our intercourse was in French, in which I was none too fluent. A great pity, because he was not only a born conversationalist but a man who had an ear for language, a man who spoke French like a poet. Above all, a man who loved subtleties and nuances! It was a dual pleasure I enjoyed whenever we came together—the pleasure of receiving instruction (not only in astrology) and the pleasure of listening to a musician, for he used the language much as a musician would his instrument. In addition there was the thrill of listening to personal anecdotes about celebrities whom I knew only through books.

In brief, I was an ideal listener. And for a man who loves to talk, for a monologist especially, what greater pleasure could there be for him than in having an attentive, eager, appreciative listener?

I also knew how to put questions. Fruitful questions.

All in all, I must have been a strange animal in his eyes. An expatriate from Brooklyn, a francophile, a vagabond, a writer only at the beginning of his career, naive, enthusiastic, absorbent as a sponge, interested in everything and seemingly rudderless. Such is the image I retain of myself at this period. Above all, I was gregarious. (He was anything but.) And a Capricorn, though not of the same decan. In age we were but a few years apart.

Apparently I was something of a stimulant to him. My native optimism and recklessness complemented his ingrained pessimism and cautiousness. I was frank and outspoken, he judicious and reserved. My tendency was to exfoliate in all directions; he, on the other hand, had narrowed his interests and focused on them with his whole being. He had all the reason and logic of the French, whereas I often contradicted myself and flew off at tangents.

What we had in common was the basic nature of the Capricorn. In his *Miroir d'Astrologie** he has summed up succinctly and discriminatingly these common factors to be found in the Capricorn type. Under *"Analogies"* he puts it thus, to give a few fragments:

"Philosophers. Inquisitors. Sorcerers. Hermits. Gravediggers. Beggars.

"Profundity. Solitude. Anguish.

"Chasms. Caverns. Abandoned places."

Here are a few Capricorns of varying types which he gives: "Dante, Michelangelo, Dostoevsky, El Greco, Schopenhauer, Tolstoy, Cézanne, Edgar Allan Poe, Maxim Gorky. . . ."

Let me add a few of the more common qualities they possess, according to Moricand.

"Grave, taciturn, closed. Love solitude, all that is mysterious, are contemplative.

"They are sad and heavy.

"They are born old.

"They see the bad before the good. The weakness in everything leaps immediately to their eyes.

"Penitence, regrets, perpetual remorse.

"Cling to the remembrance of injuries done them.

"Seldom or never laugh; when they do, it is a sardonic laugh.

"Profound but heavy. Burgeon slowly and with difficulty. Obstinate and persevering. Indefatigable workers. Take advantage of everything to amass or progress.

"Insatiable for knowledge. Undertake long-winded projects. Given to the study of complicated and abstract things.

"Live on several levels at once. Can hold several thoughts at one and the same time.

"They illumine only the abysses."

There are the three decans or divisions to each house. For the first decan—I was born the 26th of December—he gives this:

---

* Paris: Au Sans Pareil, 1928.

"Very patient and tenacious. Capable of anything in order to succeed. Arrive by dint of perseverance, but step by step. . . . Tendency to exaggerate the importance of earthly life. Avaricious of self. Constant in their affections and in their hatreds. Have a high opinion of themselves."

I quote these observations for several reasons. The reader will discover, each in his own way, the importance which may or may not be attached to them.

But to get on. . . . When I first met him, Moricand was living—*existing* would be better—in a very modest hotel called the Hotel Modial in the rue Notre Dame de Lorette. He had but recently weathered a great crisis—the loss of his fortune. Completely destitute, and with no ability or concern for practical affairs, he was leading a hand-to-mouth existence. For breakfast he had his coffee and croissants in his room, and often he had the same for dinner too, with no lunch in between.

Anaïs was a godsend. She aided him with modest sums as best she could. But there were others, quite a few indeed, whom she likewise felt compelled to aid. What Moricand never suspected was that, in presenting him to me, Anaïs hoped to unload some of her burden. She did it gently, tactfully, discreetly, as she did all things. But she was definitely finished with him.

Anaïs knew quite well that I was unable to support him, unless morally, but she also knew that I was ingenious and resourceful, that I had all manner of friends and acquaintances, and that if I was sufficiently interested I would probably find a way to help him, at least temporarily.

She was not far wrong in this surmise.

Naturally, from my standpoint, the first and most important thing was to see that the poor devil ate more regularly, and more abundantly. I hadn't the means to guarantee him three meals a day, but I could and did throw a meal into him now and then. Sometimes I invited him out to lunch or dinner; more often I invited him to my quarters where I would cook as bountiful and delicious a meal as possible. Half-starved as he was most of the time, it was small wonder that by the end of the meal he was usually drunk. Drunk not with wine, though he drank copiously, but with food, food which his impoverished organism was unable to assimilate in such quantities. The ironic thing was—and how well I understood it!—that by the time he had walked home he was hungry all over again. Poor Moricand! How very, very familiar to me was this ludicrous aspect of his tribulations! Walking on an empty stomach, walking on a full stomach, walking to digest a meal, walking in search of a meal, walking because it is the only recreation one's pocketbook permits, as Balzac discovered when he came to Paris. Walking to lay the ghost. Walking instead of weeping. Walking in the vain and desperate hope of meeting a friendly face. Walking, walking, walking. . . . But why go into it? Let's dismiss it with the label—"ambulatory paranoia."

To be sure, Moricand's tribulations were without number. Like Job, he was afflicted in every way. Altogether devoid of the latter's faith, he nevertheless displayed remarkable fortitude. Perhaps all the more remarkable in that it was without foundation. He did his best to keep face. Rarely did he break down, in my presence at least. When he did, when tears got the better of him, it was more than I could bear. It left me speechless and impotent. It was a special kind of anguish he experienced, the anguish of a man who is incapable of understanding why he of all men should be singled out for punishment. He led me to believe, always indirectly, that never had he done his fellow-man an injury with intent and deliberation. On the contrary, he had always tried to be of help. He liked to believe, and I have no doubt he was sincere, that he harbored no evil thoughts, bore no one any ill will. It is true, for example, that he never spoke ill of the man who was responsible for his comedown in the world. He attributed this misfortune entirely to the fact that he was too trusting. As though it were his own fault and not the fault of the one who had taken advantage of his confidence.

Using what little wits I possessed, for I was scarcely more capable than he in practical matters, I finally hit upon the idea of asking my friends to have Moricand do their horoscopes for a modest fee. I believe I suggested a hundred frances as a fee, but it may only have been fifty. One could then get a very decent meal for from twelve to fifteen francs. As for Moricand's room rent, it could not have been more than three hundred francs per month, possibly less.

All went well until I exhausted my list of friends and acquaintances. Then, not to let Moricand down, I began inventing people. That is to say, I would give him the name, sex, date, hour and place of birth of individuals who did not exist. I paid for these horoscopes out of my own pocket, naturally. According to Moricand, who had not the least suspicion of the turn things had taken, these imaginary subjects comprised an astounding variety of characters. Occasionally, faced with a most incongruous chart, he would express a desire to meet the subject, or would press me for intimate details which of course I would offer with the ease and nonchalance of one who knew whereof he spoke.

When it came to reading personalities, Moricand impressed one as possessing certain powers of divination. His sixth sense, as he called it, served him well in interpreting a chart. But often he had no need of a chart, no need of dates, places, and so on. Never shall I forget the banquet given by the group sponsoring the revue *Volontés* which was directed by Georges Pelorson. Eugene Jolas and I were the only Americans in the group, the rest were all French. There must have been about twenty of us at table that evening. The food was excellent and the wine and liqueurs plentiful. Moricand sat opposite me. On one side of him sat Jolas and on the other, I believe, Raymond Queneau. Every one was in excellent spirits, the conversation running high.

With Moricand in our midst, it was inevitable that sooner or later the subject of astrology must come up for discussion. There he was, Moricand, cool as a cucumber, and filling his breadbasket to the best of his ability. Lying in wait, as it were, for the jeers and derision which he doubtless anticipated.

And then it came—an innocent question by an unsuspecting nobody. Immediately a sort of mild insanity pervaded the atmosphere. Questions were being hurled from all directions. It was as if a fanatic had suddenly been uncovered—or worse, a lunatic. Jolas, who was a little under the weather by now and consequently more aggressive than usual, insisted that Moricand give demonstrable proofs. He challenged Moricand to single out the various zodiacal types seated about him. Now Moricand had undoubtedly made such classification in his head during the course of his conversation with this one and that. He could not help doing so by virtue of his calling. It was everyday routine with him, when talking to an individual, to observe the person's manner of speech, his gestures, his tics and idiosyncrasies, his mental and physical build, and so on. He was acute enough, adept enough, to distinguish and classify the more pronounced types present at the table. So, addressing himself to one after another whom he had singled out, he named them: Leo, Taurus, Libra, Virgo, Scorpio, Capricorn, and so on. Then, turning to Jolas, he quietly informed him that he believed he could tell him the year and day of his birth, perhaps the hour too. So saying, he took a good pause, raised his head slightly, as if studying the look of the heavens on the appointed day, then gave the exact date and, after a further pause, the approximate hour. He had hit it right on the nose. Jolas, who was dumbfounded, was still catching his breath as Moricand went on to relate some of the more intimate details of his past, facts which not even Jolas' close friends were aware of. He told him what he liked and what he disliked; he told him what maladies he had suffered from and was likely to suffer from in the future; he told him all manner of things which only a mind-reader could possibly divulge. If I am not mistaken, he even told him the location of a birthmark. (A shot in the dark like this was a trump card that Moricand loved to play when he had things well in hand. It was like putting his signature to a horoscope.)

That was one occasion when he ran true to form. There were others, some of them more eerie, more disturbing. Whenever it happened it was a good act. Far better than a spiritualistic séance.

Thinking of these performances, my mind always reverts to the room he occupied on the top floor of his hotel. There was no elevator service, naturally. One had to climb the five or six flights to the attic. Once inside, the world outside was completely forgotten. It was an irregular shaped room, large enough to pace up and down in, and furnished entirely with what belongings Moricand had managed to salvage from the wreck. The first impression one had, on entering, was that of orderliness. Everything was in place, but exactly in place. A few millimeters this way or that in the disposal of a chair, an *objet d'art,* a paper knife, and the effect would have been lost—in Moricand's mind, at least. Even the arrangement of his writing table revealed this obsession with order. Nowhere at any time was there ever any trace of dust or dirt. All was immaculate.

He was the same about his own person. He always appeared in clean, starched linen, coat and pants pressed (he probably pressed them himself), shoes polished, cravat arranged just so and to match his shirt of course, hat, overcoat, rubbers and suchlike neatly arranged in the clothes closet. One of the most vivid remembrances he had of his experience in the First World War—he had served in the Foreign Legion—was of the filth which he had been obliged to endure. He once recounted to me at great length how he had stripped and washed himself from head to toe with wet snow (in the trenches) after a night in which one of his comrades had vomited all over him. I had the impression that he would far rather have suffered a bullet wound than an ordeal of this nature.

What sticks in my crop about this period, when he was so desperately poor and miserable, is the air of elegance and fastidiousness which clung to him. He always seemed more like a stockbroker weathering a bad period than a man utterly without resources. The clothes he wore, all of excellent cut as well as of the best material, would obviously last another ten years, considering the care and attention he gave them. Even had they been patched, he would still have looked the well-dressed gentleman. Unlike myself, it never occurred to him to pawn or sell his clothes in order to eat. He had need of his good clothes. He had to preserve a front were he to maintain even interrupted relations with *le monde*. Even for ordinary correspondence he employed good stationery. Slightly perfumed too. His handwriting, which was distinctive, was also invested with the traits I have underlined. His letters, like his manuscripts and his astrological portraits, bore the stamp of a royal emissary, of a man who weighed every word carefully and would vouch for his opinions with his life.

One of the objects in this den he inhabited I shall never forget as long as I live. The dresser. Towards the end of an evening, usually a long one, I would edge toward this dresser, wait for a pro-pitious moment when his glance was averted, and deftly slip a fifty- or hundred-franc note under the statuette which stood on top of the dresser. I had to repeat this performance over and over because it would have embarrassed him, to say the least, had I handed him the money or sent it to him in the mail. I always had the feeling, on leaving, that he would give me just time enough to reach the nearest Métro station, then duck out and buy himself a *choucroute garnie* at a nearby *brasserie*.

I must also say that I had to be very careful about expressing a liking for anything he possessed, for if I did he would thrust it on me in the manner of a Spaniard. It made no difference whether I admired a cravat he was wearing or a walking stick, of which he still had a number. It was thus I inadvertently acquired a beautiful cane which Moïse Kisling had once given him. On one occasion it demanded all my powers of persuasion to prevent him from giving me his only pair of gold cuff links. Why he was still wearing starched cuffs and cuff links I never dared ask him. He would probably have answered that he had no other kind of shirts.

On the wall by the window, where he had arranged his writing table caticornered, there were always pinned up two or three charts of subjects whose horoscopes he was studying. He kept them there at his elbow just as a chess player keeps a board handy on which he has a problem arranged. He believed in allowing time for his interpretations to simmer. His own chart hung beside the others in a special niche.

He regarded it at frequent intervals, much as a mariner would a barometer. He was always waiting for an "opening." In a chart, he told me, death manifested itself when all the exits were blocked. It was difficult, he averred, to detect the advent of death in advance. It was much easier to see it after a person had died; then everything became crystal clear, dramatic from a graphic standpoint.

What I recall most vividly are the red and blue pencil marks he employed to indicate the progress or regression of the span of chance in his chart. It was like watching the movement of a pendulum, a slow moving pendulum which only a man of infinite patience would bother to follow. If it swung a little this way, he was almost jubilant; if it swung a little the other way, he was depressed. What he expected of an "opening" I still do not know, since he was never prepared to make any apparent effort to improve his situation. Perhaps he expected no more than a breather. All he could possibly hope for, given his temperament, was a windfall. Certainly nothing in the way of a job could have meant anything to him. His one and only desire was to continue his researches. Seemingly, he had reconciled himself to his limitations. He was not a man of action, not a brilliant writer who might some day hope to liberate himself by the pen, nor was he flexible and yielding enough to beg his way. He was simply Moricand, the personality so clearly revealed by the chart which he himself had drawn up. A "subject" with a bad Saturn, among other things. A sad wizard who in moments of desperation would endeavor to extract a thin ray of promise from his star Regulus. In short, a victim doomed to live a dolorous, circumscribed life.

"We all get a break some time or other," I used to say to him.

"It can't rain all the time! And what about that saying—'It's an ill wind that blows no one some good'?"

If he was in a mood to listen I might even go further and say: "Why don't you forget the stars for a while? Why not take a vacation and act *as if* fortune were yours? Who knows what might happen? You might meet a man in the street, an utter stranger, who would be the means of opening these doors you regard as locked. There is such a thing as grace too. It could happen, you know, if you were in the right mood, if you were prepared to let something happen. And if you forgot what was written in the sky."

To a speech of this sort he would give me one of those strange looks which signified many things. He would even throw me a smile, one of those tender, wistful smiles which an indulgent parent gives a child who poses an impossible problem. Nor would he rush to offer the answer which he had ever at his disposal and which, no doubt, he was weary of stating when thus cornered. In the pause which followed he gave the impression that he was first testing his own convictions, that he was rapidly surveying (for the thousandth time) all that he had ever said or thought about the subject, that he was even giving himself an injection of doubt, widening and deepening the problem, giving it dimensions which neither I nor anyone else could imagine, before slowly, ponderously, coldly and logically formulating the opening phrases of his defense.

"Mon vieux," I can hear him saying, "One must understand what is meant by chance. The universe operates according to law, and these laws obtain as much for man's destiny as for the birth and movements of the planets." Leaning back in his comfortable swivel chair, veering slightly round to focus better on his chart, he would add: "Look at *that!*" He meant the peculiar and particular impasse in which he was fixed at the moment. Then, extracting my chart from the portfolio which he always kept handy, he would beg me to examine it with him. "The only chance for me at this moment," he would say most solemnly, "is *you*. There *you* are!" And he would indicate how and where I fitted into the picture.

"You and that angel, Anaïs. Without you two I would be a goner!"

"But why don't you look at it more positively?" I would exclaim. "If we are there, Anaïs and I, if we are all that you credit us with being, why don't you put all your faith and trust in us? Why don't you let us help you to free yourself? There are no limits to what one person can do for another, is that not so?"

Of course he had an answer to that. His great failing was that he had an answer for everything. He did not deny the power of faith. What he would say quite simply was that he was a man to whom faith had been denied. It was there in his chart, the absence of faith. What could one do? What he failed to add was that he had chosen the path of knowledge, and that in doing so he had clipped his own wings.

Only years later did he offer me a glimpse into the nature and origin of this castration which he referred to as lack of faith. It had to do with his boyhood, with the neglect and indifference of his parents, the perverse cruelty of his schoolmasters, one in particular, who had humiliated and tortured him in inhuman fashion. It was an ugly, woeful story, quite enough to account for his loss of morale, his spiritual degradation.

As always before a war, there was fever in the air. With the end approaching, everything became distorted, magnified, speeded up. The wealthy were as active as bees or ants, redistributing their funds and assets, their mansions, their yachts, their gilt-edged bonds, their mine holdings, their jewels, their art treasures. I had at the time a good friend who was flying back and forth from one continent to another catering to these panicky clients who were trying to get out from under. Fabulous were the tales he told me. Yet so familiar. So disgustingly familiar. (Can anyone imagine an army of millionaires?) Fabulous too were the tales of another friend, a chemical engineer, who would turn up at intervals for dinner, just back from China, Manchuria, Mongolia, Tibet, Persia, Afghanistan, wherever there was deviltry afoot. And always with the same story—of intrigue, plunder, bribery, treachery, plots and projects of the most diabolical sort. The war was still a year or so away, but the signs were unmistakable—not only for the Second World War but for the wars and revolutions to follow.

Even the "bohemians" were being routed out of their trenches. Amazing how many young intellectuals were already dislocated, dispossessed, already being pushed about like pawns in the service of their unknown masters. Every day I was receiving visits from the most unexpected individuals. There was only one question in every one's mind: *when?* Meanwhile make the most of it! And we did, we who were hanging on till the last boat call.

In this merry, devil-may-care atmosphere Moricand took no part. He was hardly the sort to invite for a festive evening which prom-ised to end up in a brawl, a drunken stupor, or a visit from the police. Indeed, the thought never entered my head. When I did invite him over for a meal I would carefully select the two or three guests who were to join us. They were usually the same ones each time. Astrological buddies, so to speak.

Once he called on me unannounced, a rare breach of protocol for Moricand. He seemed elated and explained that he had been stroll-ing about the quays all afternoon. Finally he fished a small package out of his coat pocket and handed it to me. "For *you!*" he said, with much emotion in his voice. From the way he said it I under-stood that he was offering a gift which only I could appreciate to the full.

The book, for that's what it was, was Balzac's *Seraphita*.

Had it not been for *Seraphita* I doubt very much that my adven-ture with Moricand would have terminated in the manner it did. It will be seen shortly what a price I paid for this precious gift.

What I wish to stress at this point is that, coincident with the feverishness of the times, the increased tempo, the peculiar derange-ment which everyone suffered, writers more than others perhaps, there was noticeable, in my own case at any rate, a quickening of the spiritual pulse. The individuals who were thrown across my path, the incidents which occurred daily and which to another would have seemed like trifles, all had a very special significance in my mind. There was an *enchaînement* which was not only stimulating and exciting but often hallucinating. Just to take a walk into the outskirts of Paris—Montrouge, Gentilly, Kremlin-Bicêtre, Ivry—was sufficient to unbalance me for the rest of the day. I enjoyed being unbalanced, derailed, disoriented early in the morning. (The walks I refer to were "constitutionals," taken before breakfast. My mind free and empty, I was making myself physically and spiritually prepared for long sieges at the machine.) Taking the rue de la Tombe-Issoire, I would head for the outer boulevards, then dive into the outskirts, letting my feet lead me where they would. Coming back, I always steered instinctively for the Place de Rungis, which in some mysterious way connected itself with certain phases of the film *L'Âge d'or*, and more particularly with Luis Bunuel himself. With its queer street names, its atmosphere of not belonging, its special assortment of gamins, urchins and monsters who hailed from some other world, it was for me an eerie and seductive neighborhood. Often I took a seat on a public bench, closed my eyes for a few moments to sink below the surface, then suddenly opened them to look at the scene with the vacant stare of a somnambulist. Goats from the *banlieue,* gangplanks, douche bags, safety belts, iron trusses, *passerelles* and *sauterelles* floated before my glazed eyeballs, together with headless fowl, beribboned antlers, rusty sewing machines, dripping ikons and other unbelievable phenomena. It was not a community or neighborhood but a vector, a very special vector created wholly for my artistic benefit, created expressly to tie me into an emotional knot. Walking up the rue de la Fontaine à Mulard, I struggled frantically to contain my ecstasy, struggled to fix and hold in my mind (until after breakfast) three thoroughly disparate images which, if I could fuse them successfully, would enable me to force a wedge into a difficult passage (of my book) which I had been unable to penetrate the day before. The rue Brillat-Savarin, running like a snake past the Place, balances the works of Eliphas Lévi, the rue Butte aux Cailles (farther along) evokes the Stations of the Cross, the rue Félicien Rops (at another angle) sets bells to ringing and with it the whir of pigeon wings. If I was suffering from a hangover, as I frequently was, all these associations, deformations and interpenetrations became even more quixotically vivid and colorful. On such days it was nothing to receive in the first mail a second or third copy of the *I Ching,* an album of Scriabin, a slim volume concerning the life of James Ensor or a treatise on Pico della Mirandola. Beside my desk, as a reminder of recent festivities, the empty wine bottles were always neatly ranged: Nuits Saint-Georges, Gevrey-Chambertin, Clos-Veugeot, Vosne Romanée, Meursault, Traminer, Château Haut-Brion, Chambolle-Musigny, Montrachet, Beaune, Beaujolais, Anjou and that *"vin de prédilection"* of Balzac's—Vouvray. Old friends, even though drained to the last drop. Some still retained a slight bouquet.

Breakfast, *chez moi.* Strong coffee with hot milk, two or three delicious warm croissants with sweet butter and a touch of jam. And with the breakfast a snatch of Segovia. An emperor couldn't do better.

Belching a little, picking my teeth, my fingers tingling, I take a quick look around (as if to see if everything's in order!), lock the door, and plunk myself in front of the machine. Set to go. My brain afire.

But what drawer of my Chinese cabinet mind will I open first? Each one contains a recipe, a prescription, a formula. Some of the items go back to 6,000 B.C. Some still further back.

First I must blow the dust away. Particularly the dust of Paris, so fine, so penetrating, so nearly invisible. I must submerge to the root taps—Williamsburg, Canarsie, Greenpoint, Hoboken, the Gowanus Canal, Erie Basin, to playmates now moldering in the grave, to places of enchantment like Glendale, Glen Island, Sayville, Patchogue, to parks and islands and coves now transformed into garbage dumps. I must think French and write English, be very still and talk wild, act the sage and remain a fool or a dunce. I must balance what is unbalanced without falling off the tightrope. I must summon to the hall of vertigo the lyre known as the Brooklyn Bridge yet preserve the flavor and the aroma of the Place de Rungis. It must be of this moment but pregnant with the ebb of the Great Return. . . .

And it was just at this time—too much to do, too much to see, too much to drink, too much to digest—that, like heralds from distant yet strangely familiar worlds, the books began to come. Nijinsky's *Diary*, *The Eternal Husband*, *The Spirit of Zen*, *The Voice of the Silence*, *The Absolute Collective*, the *Tibetan Book of the Dead*, *l' Eubage*, the *Life of Milarepa*, *War Dance*, *Musings of a Chinese Mystic*. . . .

Some day, when I acquire a house with a large room and bare walls, I intend to compose a huge chart or graph which will tell better than any book the story of my friends, and another telling the story of the books in my life. One on each wall, facing each other, impregnating each other, erasing each other. No man can hope to live long enough to round out these happenings, these unfathomable experiences, in words. It can only be done symbolically, graphically, as the stars write their constellated *mysterium*.

Why do I speak thus? Because during this period—too much to do, too much to see, taste, and so forth—the past and the future converged with such clarity and precision that not only friends and books but creatures, objects, dreams, historical events, monuments, streets, names of places, walks, encounters, conversations, reveries, half-thoughts, all came sharply into focus, broke into angles, chasms, waves, shadows, revealing to me in one harmonious, understandable pattern their essence and significance.

Where my friends were concerned, I had only to think a moment in order to evoke a company or a regiment. Without effort on my part they ranged themselves in order of magnitude, influence, duration, proximity, spiritual weight and density, and so on. As they took their stations I myself seemed to be moving through the ether with the sweep and rhythm of an absent-minded angel, yet falling in with each in turn at exactly the right zodiacal point and at precisely the destined moment, good or bad, to tune in. What a medley of apparitions they presented! Some were shrouded in fog, some sharp as sentinels, some rigid as phantom ice-bergs, some wilted like autumn flowers, some racing toward death, some rolling along like drunks on rubber wheels, some pushing labor-iously through endless mazes, some skating over the heads of their comrades as if muffled in luminol, some lifting crushing weights, some glued to the books in which they burrowed, some trying to fly though anchored with ball and chain, but all of them vivid, named, classified, identified according to need, depth, insight, flavor, aura, fragrance and pulse beat. Some were suspended like blazing planets, others like cold, distant stars. Some burgeoned with frightening rapidity, like novae, then faded into dust; some moved along discreetly, always within calling distance, as it were, like beneficent planets. Some stood apart, not haughtily but as if waiting to be summoned—like authors (Novalis, for example) whose names alone are so freighted with promise that one post-pones reading them until that ideal moment which never arrives.

And Moricand, had he any part in all this scintillating turmoil? I doubt it. He was merely part of the décor, another phenomenon pertinent to the epoch. I can see him still as he then appeared in my mind's eye. In a penumbra he lurks, cool, gray, imperturbable, with a twinkle in his eyes and a metallic *"Ouais!"* shaping his lips. As if saying to himself: *"Ouais!* Know it all. Heard it before. Forgot it long ago. *Ouais! Tu parles!* The labyrinth, the chamois with the golden horns, the grail, the argonaut, the *kermesse à la* Breughel, the wounded groin of Scorpio, the profanation of the host, the Areopagite, translunacy, symbiotic neurosis, and in a wilderness of pebbles a lone katydid. Keep it up, the wheel is softly turning. A time comes when. . . ." Now he is bent over his *pantâcles*. Reads with a Geiger counter. Unlatching his gold foun-tain pen, he writes in purple milk: Porphyry, Proclus, Plotinus, Saint Valentin, Julian the Apostate, Hermes Trismegistus, Apollonius of Tyana, Claude Saint-Martin. In his vest pocket he carries a little phial; it contains myrrh, frankincense and a dash of wild sarsparilla. *The odor of sanctity!* On the little finger of his left hand he wears a jade ring marked with yin and yang. Cautiously he brings out a heavy brass watch, a stem-winder, and lays it on the floor. It is 9:30, sidereal time, the moon on the cusp of panic, the ecliptic freckled with cometary warts. Saturn is there with her ominous milky hue. *"Ouais!"* he exclaims, as if clinching the argument. "I say nothing against anything. I observe. I analyze. I calculate. I distillate. Wisdom is becoming, but knowledge is the certainty of certitude. To the surgeon his scalpel, to the gravedigger his pick and shovel, to the analyst his dream books, to the fool his dunce cap. As for me, I have a bellyache. The atmosphere is too rarefied, the stones too heavy to digest. *Kali Yuga.* Only 9,765,854 years to go and we will be out of the snake pit. *Du courage, mon vieux!"*

Let us take a last look backward. The year is 1939. The month is June. I am not waiting for the Huns to rout me out. I am taking a vacation. Another few hours and I shall be leaving for Greece.

All that remains of my presence in the studio at the Villa Seurat is my natal chart done in chalk on the wall facing the door. It's for whomever takes over to ponder on. I'm sure it will be an officer of the line. Perhaps an erudite.

Oh yes, and on the other wall, high up near the ceiling, these two lines:

> *Jetzt müsste die Welt versinken,*
> *Jetzt muszte ein Wunder gescheh'n.*

Clear, what?

And now it is my last evening with my good friend Moricand. A modest repast in a restaurant on the rue Fontaine, diagonally opposite the living quarters of the Father of Surrealism. We spoke

of him as we broke bread. *Nadja* once more. And the "Profanation of the Host."

He is sad, Moricand. So am I, in a faint way. I am only partly
there. My mind is already reaching out for Rocamadour where I
expect to be on the morrow. In the morning Moricand will once
again face his chart, observe the sway of the pendulum—undoubtedly it has moved to the left!—see if Regulus, Rigel, Antares or
Betelgeuse can aid him just a wee, wee bit. Only 9,765,854 years
before the climate changes. . . .

It's drizzling as I step out of the Métro at Vavin. I've decided
I must have a drink all by my lonesome. Does not the Capricorn
love solitude? *Ouais!* Solitude in the midst of hubbub. Not
heavenly solitude. Earthly solitude. *Abandoned places.*

The drizzle turns into a light rain, a gray, sweetly melancholy
rain. A beggar's rain. My thoughts drift. Suddenly I'm gazing at
the huge chrysanthemums my mother loved to raise in our dismal
back yard in the street of early sorrows. They are hanging there
before my eyes, like an artificial bloom, just opposite the lilac bush
which Mr. Fuchs, the hundski picker, gave us one summer.

Yes, the Capricorn is a beast of solitude. Slow, steady, persevering. Lives on several levels at once. Thinks in circles. Fascinated
by death. Ever climbing, climbing. In search of the edelweiss,
presumably. Or could it be the *immortelle?* Knows no mother.
Only "the mothers." Laughs little and usually on the wrong side of
the face. Collects friends as easily as postage stamps, but is unsocia-
ble. Speaks truthfully instead of kindly. Metaphysics, abstractions,
electromagnetic displays. Dives to the depths. Sees stars, comets,
asteroids where others see only moles, warts, pimples. Feeds on
himself when tired of playing the man-eating shark. A paranoiac.
An *ambulatory* paranoiac. But constant in his affections—*and his
hatreds. Ouais!*

From the time the war broke out until 1947 not a word from
Moricand. I had given him up for dead. Then, shortly after we
had installed ourselves in our new home on Partington Ridge, a

thick envelope arrived bearing the return address of an Italian princess. In it was enclosed a letter from Moricand, six months old, which he had requested the princess to forward should she ever discover my address. He gave as his address a village near Vevey, Switzerland, where he said he had been living since the end of the war. I answered immediately, telling him how glad I was to know that he was still alive and inquiring what I could do for him. Like a cannon ball came his reply, giving a detailed account of his circumstances which, as I might have guessed, had not improved. He was living in a miserable pension, in a room without heat, starving as usual, and without even the little it takes to buy cigarettes. Immediately we began sending him foodstuffs and other necessities of which he was apparently deprived. And what money we could spare. I also sent him international postal coupons so that he would not be obliged to waste money on stamps.

Soon the letters began to fly back and forth. With each succeeding letter the situation grew worse. Obviously the little sums we dispatched didn't go very far in Switzerland. His landlady was constantly threatening to turn him out, his health was getting worse, his room was insupportable, he had not enough to eat, it was impossible to find work of any kind, and—in Switzerland you don't beg!

To send him larger sums was impossible. We simply didn't have that kind of money. What to do? I pondered the situation over and over. There seemed to be no solution.

Meanwhile his letters poured in, always on good stationery, always airmail, always begging, supplicating, the tone growing more and more desperate. Unless I did something drastic he was done for. That he made painfully clear.

Finally I conceived what I thought to be a brilliant idea. Genial, nothing less. It was to invite him to come and live with us, share what we had, regard our home as his own for the rest of his days. It was such a simple solution I wondered why it had never occurred to me before.

I kept the idea to myself for a few days before broaching it to

my wife. I knew that it would take some persuading to convince
her of the necessity for such a move. Not that she was ungenerous,
but that he was hardly the type to make life more interesting. It
was like inviting Melancholia to come and perch on your shoulder.

"Where would you put him up?" were her first words, when
finally I summoned the courage to broach the subject. We had
only a living room, in which we slept, and a tiny wing adjoining it
where little Val slept.

"I'll give him my studio," I said. This was a separate cubicle
hardly bigger than the one Val slept in. Above it was the garage
which had been partly converted into a workroom. My thought
was to use that for myself.

Then came the big question: "How will you raise the passage
money?"

"That I have to think about," I replied. "The main thing is,
are you willing to risk it?"

We argued it back and forth for several days. Her mind was
full of premonitions and forebodings. She pleaded with me to
abandon the idea. "I know you'll only regret it," she croaked.

What she could not understand was why I felt it imperative to
assume such a responsibility for one who had never really been an
intimate friend. "If it were Perlès," she said, "it would be different;
he means something to you. Or your Russian friend, Eugene. But
Moricand? What do you owe *him*?"

This last touched me off. What did I owe Moricand? Nothing.
And everything. Who was it put *Seraphita* in my hands?

I endeavored to explain the point. Halfway along I gave up.
I saw how absurd it was to attempt to make such a point. A mere
book! One must be insane to fall back on such an argument.

Naturally I had other reasons. But I persisted in making
Seraphita my advocate. Why? I tried to get to the bottom of it.
Finally I grew ashamed of myself. Why did I have to justify my-
self? Why make excuses? The man was starving. He was ill.
He was penniless. He was at the end of his rope. Weren't these

reason enough? To be sure, he had been a pauper, a miserable pauper, all the years I had known him. The war hadn't changed anything; it had only rendered his situation more hopeless. But why quibble about his being an intimate friend or just a friend? Even if he had been a stranger, the fact that he was throwing himself on my mercy was enough. One doesn't let a drowning man sink.

"I've just got to do it!" I exclaimed. "I don't know how I'm going to do it, but I will. I'm writing him today." And then, to throw her a bone, I added: "Perhaps he won't like the idea."

"Don't worry," she said, "he'll grab at a straw."

So I wrote and explained the whole situation to him. I even drew a diagram of the place, giving the dimensions of his room, the fact that it was without heat, and adding that we were far from any city. "You may find it very dull here," I said, "with no one to talk to but us, no library to go to, no cafés, and the nearest cinema forty miles away. But at least you will not have to worry anymore about food and shelter." I concluded by saying that once here he would be his own master, could devote his time to whatever pleased him, in fact he could loaf the rest of his days away, if that was his wish.

He wrote back immediately, telling me that he was overjoyed, calling me a saint and a savior, et cetera, et cetera.

The next few months were consumed in raising the necessary funds. I borrowed whatever I could, diverted what few francs I had to his account, borrowed in advance on my royalties, and finally made definite arrangements for him to fly from Switzerland to England, there take the *Queen Mary* or *Elizabeth,* whichever it was, to New York, and fly from New York to San Francisco, where I would pick him up.

During these few months when we were borrowing and scraping I managed to maintain him in better style. He had to be fattened up or I would have an invalid on my hands. There was just one item I had failed to settle satisfactorily, that was to liquidate his back rent. The best I could do, under the circumstances, was to send a letter which he was to show his landlady, a letter in which I promised to wipe out his debt just as soon as I possibly could. I gave her my word of honor.

Just before leaving he dispatched a last letter. It was to reassure me that, as regards the landlady, everything was jake. To allay her anxiety, he wrote, he had reluctantly given her a lay. Of course he couched it in more elegant terms. But he made it clear that, disgusting though it was, he had done his duty.

It was just a few days before Christmas when he landed at the airport in San Francisco. Since my car had broken down I asked my friend Lilik (Schatz) to meet him and put him up at his home in Berkeley until I could come and fetch him.

As soon as Moricand stepped off the plane he heard his name being called. "Monsieur Moricand! Monsieur Moricand! *Attention!*" He stopped dead and listened with open mouth. A beautiful contralto voice was speaking to him over the air in excellent French, telling him to step to the information desk, where someone was waiting for him.

He was dumbfounded. What a country! What service! For a moment he felt like a potentate.

It was Lilik who was waiting for him at the information desk. Lilik who had coached the girl. Lilik who whisked him away, fixed him a good meal, sat up with him until dawn and plied him with the best Scotch he could buy. And to top it off he had given him a picture of Big Sur which made it sound like the paradise which it is. He was a happy man, Conrad Moricand, when he finally hit the hay.

In a way, it worked out better than if I had gone to meet him myself.

When a few days passed and I found myself still unable to get to San Francisco, I telephoned Lilik and asked him to drive Moricand down.

They arrived the next day about nine in the evening.

I had gone through so many inner convulsions prior to his

arrival that when I opened the door and watched him descend the garden steps I was virtually numb. (Besides, the Capricorn seldom reveals his feelings all at once.)

As for Moricand, he was visibly moved. As we pulled away from an embrace I saw two big tears roll down his cheeks. He was "home" at last. Safe, sound, secure.

The little studio which I had turned over to him to sleep and work in was about half the size of his attic room in the Hotel Modial. It was just big enough to hold a cot, a writing table, a chiffonier. When the two oil lamps were lit it gave off a glow. A Van Gogh would have found it charming.

I could not help but notice how quickly he had arranged everything in his customary neat, orderly way. I had left him alone for a few minutes to unpack his bags and say an Ave Maria. When I returned to say goodnight I saw the writing table arranged as of yore—the block of paper resting slantwise on the triangular ruler, the large blotting pad spread out, and beside it his ink bottle and pen together with an assortment of pencils, all sharpened to a fine point. On the dresser, which had a mirror affixed to it, were laid out his comb and brush, his manicure scissors and nail file, a portable clock, his clothes brush and a pair of small framed photographs. He had already tacked up a few flags and pennants, just like a college boy. All that was missing to complete the picture was his birth chart.

I tried to explain how the Aladdin lamp worked, but it was too complicated for him to grasp all at once. He lit two candles instead. Then, apologizing for the close quarters he was to occupy, referring to it jokingly as a comfortable little tomb, I bade him goodnight. He followed me out to have a look at the stars and inhale a draught of clean, fragrant night air, assuring me that he would be perfectly comfortable in his cell.

When I went to call him the next morning I found him standing at the head of the stairs fully dressed. He was gazing out at the sea. The sun was low and bright in the sky, the atmosphere extremely clear, the temperature that of a day in late spring. He seemed entranced by the vast expanse of the Pacific, by the far off horizon so sharp and clear, by the bright blue immensity of it all. A vulture hove into sight, made a low sweep in front of the house, then swooned away. He seemed stupefied by the sight. Then suddenly he realized how warm it was. "My God," he said, "and it is almost the first of January!"

"C'est un vrai paradis," he mumbled as he descended the steps.

Breakfast over, he showed me how to set and wind the clock which he had brought me as a gift. It was an heirloom, his last possession, he explained. It had been in the family for generations. Every quarter of an hour the chimes struck. Very softly, melodiously. He handled it with the utmost care while explaining at great length the complicated mechanism. He had even taken the precaution to look up a watch-maker in San Francisco, a reliable one, to whom I was to entrust the clock should anything go wrong with it.

I tried to express my appreciation of the marvelous gift he had made me, but somehow, deep inside, I was against the bloody clock. There was not a single possession of ours which was precious to me. Now I was saddled with an object which demanded care and attention. "A white elephant!" I said to myself. Aloud I suggested that *he* watch over it, regulate it, wind it, oil it, and so on. "You're used to it," I said. I wondered how long it would be before little Val—she was only a little over two—would begin tinkering with it in order to hear the music.

To my surprise, my wife did not find him too somber, too morbid, too aged, too decrepit. On the contrary, she remarked that he had a great deal of charm—and *savoir-faire*. She was rather impressed by his neatness and elegance. "Did you notice his hands? How beautiful! The hands of a musician." It was true, he had good strong hands with spatulate fingers and well-kept nails, which were always polished.

"Did you bring any old clothes?" I asked. He looked so citified in his dark business suit.

He had no old clothes, it turned out. Or rather he had the same good clothes which were neither new nor old. I noticed that he was eyeing me up and down with mild curiosity. I no longer owned a suit. I wore corduroy pants, a sweater with holes in it, somebody's hand-me-down jacket, and sneakers. My slouch hat—the last I was to own—had ventilators all around the sweat band.

"One doesn't need clothes here," I remarked. "You can go naked, if you want."

"*Quelle vie!*" he exclaimed. "*C'est fantastique.*"

Later that morning, as he was shaving, he asked if I didn't have some talcum powder. "Of course," I said, and handed him the can I used. "Do you by chance have any Yardley?" he asked. "No," I said, "why?"

He gave me a strange, half-girlish, half-guilty smile. "I can't use anything but Yardley. Maybe when you go to town again you can get me some, yes?"

Suddenly it seemed as if the ground opened under my feet. Here he was, safe and secure, with a haven for the rest of his life in the midst of "*un vrai paradis,*" and he must have Yardley's talcum powder! Then and there I should have obeyed my instinct and said: "Beat it! Get back to your Purgatory!"

It was a trifling incident and, had it been any other man, I would have dismissed it immediately, put it down as a caprice, a foible, an idiosyncrasy, anything but an ominous presage. But of that instant I knew my wife was right, knew that I had made a grave mistake. In that moment I sensed the leech that Anaïs had tried to get rid of. I saw the spoiled child, the man who had never done an honest stroke of work in his life, the destitute individual who was too proud to beg openly but was not above milking a friend dry. I knew it all, felt it all, and already foresaw the end.

Each day I endeavored to reveal some new aspect of the region to him. There were the sulphur baths, which he found marvelous

—better than a European spa because natural, primitive, unspoiled. There was the "virgin forest" hard by, which he soon explored on his own, enchanted by the redwoods, the madrones, the wild flowers and the luxuriant ferns. Enchanted even more by what he called "neglect," for there are no forests in Europe which have the unkempt look of our American forests. He could not get over the fact that no one came to take the dead limbs and trunks which were piled crisscross above one another on either side of the trail. So much firewood going to waste! So much building material lying unused, unwanted, and the men and women of Europe crowded together in miserable little rooms without heat. "What a country!" he exclaimed. "Everywhere there is abundance. No wonder the Americans are so generous!"

My wife was not a bad cook. In fact, she was a rather good cook. There was always plenty to eat and sufficient wine to wash the food down. California wines, to be sure, but he thought them excellent, better in fact than the *vin rouge ordinaire* one gets in France. But there was one thing about the meals which he found difficult to adjust to—the absence of soup with each meal. He also missed the suite of courses which is customary in France. He found it hard to accommodate himself to a light lunch, which is the American custom. Midday was the time for the big meal. Our big meal was at dinner. Still, the cheeses weren't bad and the salads quite good, all things considered, though he would have preferred *l'huile d'arachide* (peanut oil) to the rather copious use of olive oil which we indulged in. He was glad we used garlic liberally. As for the *bifteks,* never had he eaten the like abroad. Now and then we dug up a little cognac for him, just to make him feel more at home.

But what bothered him most was our American tobacco. The cigarettes in particular were atrocious. Was it not possible to dig up some *gauloises bleues,* perhaps in San Francisco or New York? I opined that it was indeed but that they would be expensive. I suggested that he try Between the Acts. (Meanwhile, without telling him, I begged my friends in the big cities to rustle up some

French cigarettes.) He found the little cigars quite smokable. They reminded him of something even more to his liking—cheroots. I dug up some Italian stogies next time I went to town. Just ducky! Good! We're getting somewhere, thought I to myself.

One problem we hadn't yet solved was stationery. He had need, he maintained, for paper of a certain size. He showed me a sample which he had brought with him from Europe. I took it to town to see if it could be matched. Unfortunately it couldn't. It was an odd size, a size we had no demand for apparently. He found it impossible to believe that such could be the case. America made everything, and in abundance. Strange that one couldn't match an ordinary piece of paper. He grew quite incensed about it. Holding up the sample sheet, flicking it with his fingernail, he exclaimed: "Anywhere in Europe one can find this paper, exactly this size. And in America, which has everything, it can't be found. *C'est emmerdant!*"

To be frank, it was shitty to me too, the bloody subject. What could he be writing that demanded the use of paper precisely that size? I had got him his Yardley talc, his *gauloises bleues,* his eau de cologne, his powdered, slightly perfumed pumice stone (for a dentifrice), and now he was plaguing me about paper.

"Step outside a moment, won't you?" I begged. I spoke quietly, gently, soothingly. "Look out there . . . look at that ocean! Look at the sky!" I pointed to the flowers which were in bloom. A hummingbird had just made as if to alight on the rose bush in front of us. All its motors were whirring. *"Regardez-moi ça!"* I exclaimed. I allowed a due pause. Then, in a very even tone of voice I said: "When a man has all this, can he not write just as well on toilet paper if he has to?"

It registered.

"Mon vieux," he began, "I hope you don't think I am exigent...."

"I do indeed," said I.

"You must forgive me. I'm sorry. Nobody could be more grateful than I for all you have done."

"My dear Moricand, I am not asking for gratitude. I'm asking for a little common sense." (I wanted to say "horse sense" but couldn't think of the equivalent in French immediately.) "Even if we had no paper at all I would expect you to be happy. You're a free man now, do you realize that? Why, god-damn it, you're better off than I am! Look, let's not spoil all this"—I gestured loosely toward the sky, the ocean, the birds of the air, the green hills—"let's not spoil all this with talk of paper, cigarettes, talcum powder and such nonsense. What we should be talking about is—*God*."

He was crestfallen. I felt like apologizing then and there, but I didn't. Instead I strode off in the direction of the forest. In the cool depths I sat down beside a pool and proceeded to give myself what the French call an *examen de conscience*. I tried to reverse the picture, put myself in his boots, look at myself through *his* eyes. I didn't get very far, I must confess. Somehow, I just could not put myself in his boots.

"Had my name been Moricand," said I softly to myself, "I would have killed myself long ago."

In one respect he was an ideal house guest—he kept to himself most of the day. Apart from meal times, he remained in his room almost the entire day, reading, writing, perhaps meditating too. I worked in the studio-garage just above him. At first the sound of my typewriter going full blast bothered him. It was like the rat-a-tat-tat of a machine gun in his ears. But gradually he got used to it, even found it stimulating, he said. At lunch and dinner he relaxed. Being so much on his own, he seized these occasions to engage us in conversation. He was the kind of talker it is difficult to disengage once he has sunk his hooks into you. Lunch times I would often pull myself away abruptly, leaving him to work it out as best he could with my wife. Time is the one thing I regard as precious. If I had to waste time, I preferred to waste it in taking a nap rather than in listening to my friend Moricand.

Dinner was another matter. It was hard to find an excuse for terminating these sessions at my own time. It would have been a pleasure to glance at a book after dinner, since there was never any time for reading during the day, but I never got the chance. Once we were seated for the evening meal we were in for it till he had exhausted himself. Naturally, our conversations were all in French. Moricand had intended to learn a little English but after a few attempts gave it up. It was not a "sympathetic" language to him. It was even worse than German, he thought. Fortunately, my wife spoke some French and understood a lot more, but not enough to follow a man with Moricand's gift of speech. I couldn't always follow him myself. Every now and then I would have to halt the flow, ask him to repeat what he had just said in simpler language, then translate it for my wife. Now and then I would forget myself and give him a spate of English, soon arrested of course by his blank look. To translate these bursts was like sweating out a cold. If, as frequently happened, I had to explain something to my wife in English, he would pretend that he understood. She would do the same when he conveyed something confidential to me in French. Thus it happened that often the three of us were talking three different subjects, nodding, agreeing with one another, saying Yes when we meant No, and so on, until the confusion became so great that we all threw up our hands simultaneously. Then we would begin all over, sentence by sentence, thought by thought, as if struggling to cement a piece of string.

Nevertheless, and despite all frustration, we managed to understand one another exceedingly well. Usually it was only in the long, overembroidered monologue that we lost him. Even then, astray in the complicated web of a long-drawn-out story or a windy explanation of some hermeneutic point, it was a pleasure to listen to him. Sometimes I would deliberately let go my attention, facilitate the process of getting lost, in order to better enjoy the music of his words. At his best he was a one man orchestra.

It made no difference, when he was in the groove, what he chose to talk about—food, costume, ritual, pyramids, Trismegistus or

Eleusinian mysteries. Any theme served as a means to exploit his virtuosity. In love with all that is subtle and intricate, he was always lucid and convincing. He had a feminine flair for preciosities, could always produce the exact timbre, shade, nuance, odor, taste. He had the suavity, velleity and mellifluousness of an enchanter. And he could put into his voice a resonance comparable in effect to the sound of a gong reverberating in the deathlike silence of a vast desert. If he spoke of Odilon Redon, for example, his language reeked of fragrant colors, of exquisite and mysterious harmonies, of alchemical vapors and imaginings, of pensive broodings and spiritual distillations too impalpable to be fixed in words but which words could evoke or suggest when marshaled in sensorial patterns. There was something of the harmonium in the use he made of his voice. It was suggestive of some intermediate region, the confluence, say, of divine and mundane streams where form and spirit interpenetrated, and which could only be conveyed musically. The gestures accompanying this music were limited and stereotyped, mostly facial movements—sinister, vulgarly accurate, diabolical when restricted to the mouth and lips, poignant, pathetic, harrowing, when concentrated in the eyes. Shudderingly effective when he moved his whole scalp. The rest of him, his body, one might say, was usually immobile, except for a slight tapping or drumming with the fingers now and then. Even his intelligence seemed to be centered in the sound box, the harmonium which was situated neither in the larynx nor in the chest but in a middle region which corresponded to the locus empyrean whence he drew his imagery.

Staring at him abstractly in one of those fugitive moments when I caught myself wandering among the reeds and bulrushes of my own vagaries, I would find myself studying him as if through a reflector, his image changing, shifting like swift-moving cloud formations: now the sorrowful sage, now the sybil, now the grand cosmocrator, now the alchemist, now the stargazer, now the mage. Sometimes he looked Egyptian, sometimes Mongolian, sometimes Iroquois or Mohican, sometimes Chaldean, sometimes Etruscan. Often very definite figures out of the past leaped to mind, figures he either seemed to incarnate momentarily or figures he had affinities with. To wit: Montezuma, Herod, Nebuchadnezzar, Ptolemy, Balthasar, Justinian, Solon. Revelatory names, in a way. However conglomerate, in essence they served to coalesce certain elements of his nature which ordinarily defied association. He was an alloy, and a very strange one at that. Not bronze, not brass, not electrum. Rather some nameless colloidal sort of alloy such as we associate with the body when it becomes a prey to some rare disease.

There was one image he bore deep within him, one he had created in youth and which he was never to shake off: "Gloomy Gus." The day he showed me a photograph of himself at the age of fifteen or sixteen I was profoundly disturbed. It was almost an exact replica of my boyhood friend, Gus Schmelzer, whom I used to tease and plague beyond endurance because of his somber, morose, eternally somber and morose mien. Even at that age— perhaps earlier, who knows?—there were engraved in Moricand's psyche all the modalities which such terms as lunar, saturnian and sepulchral evoke. One could already sense the mummy which the flesh would become. One could see the bird of ill omen perched on his left shoulder. One could feel the moonlight altering his blood, sensitizing his retina, dyeing his skin with the pallor of the prisoner, the drug addict, the dweller on forbidden planets. Knowing him, one might even visualize those delicate antennae of which he was altogether too proud and on which he placed a reliance which overtaxed his intuitive muscles, so to speak. I might go further—why not?—and say that, looking deep into his sorrowful eyes, somber, simian eyes, I could see skull within skull, an endless, cavernous Golgotha illumined by the dry, cold, murderous light of a universe beyond the imaginative bounds of even the hardiest scientific dreamer.

In the art of resuscitation he was a master. Touching anything that smacked of death, he came alive. Everything filtered through to him from the tomb in which it was buried. He had only to wave his wand to create the semblance of life. But, as with all sorcery, even the most poetic, the end was always dust and ashes. For Moricand the past was rarely a living past; it was a morgue which at best could be made to resemble a museum. Even his description of the living was but a cataloguing of museum pieces. There was no distinction in his enthusiasms between that which is and that which was. Time was his medium. A deathless medium which had no relation to life.

It is said that Capricorns get on well together, presumably because they have so much in common. It is my own belief that there are more divergences among these earth-bound creatures, that they have more difficulty understanding one another, than is the case with other types. Mutual understanding between Capricorns is more a surface agreement, a truce, so to speak, than anything else. At home in the depths or on the heights, seldom inhabiting any region for long, they have more kinship with the roc and the leviathan than with one another. What they do understand, perhaps, is that their differences are altitudinal, due primarily to shifts of position. Capable of running the whole gamut, it is easy for them to identify as you or me. This is their bond and explains their ability to forgive but never to forget. They forget nothing, ever. Their memory is phantasmagorical. They remember not only their personal, human tribulations, but their prehuman and subhuman ones as well. They can slither back into the protoplasmic slime with the ease of eels slipping through mud. They also carry remembrances of higher spheres, of seraphic states, as if they had known long periods of liberation from earthly thralls, as if the very language of the seraphim were familiar to them. Indeed, one might almost say of them that it is earthly existence to which they, the earth-bound, are of all types least suited. To them the earth is not only a prison, a purgatory, a place of expiation but it is also a cocoon from which they will eventually escape equipped with indestructible wings. Hence their mediumship, their ability and desire to practice acceptance, their extraordinary readiness for conversion. They enter the world like visitors destined for another planet, another sphere. Their attitude is one of having a last look around, of perpetually bidding good-bye to all that is terrestrial. They imbibe the very essence of the earth, and in doing so prepare the new body, the new form, in which they will take leave of earth forever. They die innumerable deaths whereas others die but once. Hence their immunity to life *or* death. Their true locus is the heart of mystery. There all is clear to them. There they live apart, spin their dreams, and are "at home."

He was hardly with us more than a week when he called me to his cell one day for a "consultation." It was about the uses of codeine. Beginning with a long preamble about his sufferings and privations since the year one, he ended with a brief account of the nightmare he had lived through during his recent sojourn in Switzerland. Though he was a Swiss citizen, Switzerland was not his country, not his climate, not his bowl of soup. After all the humiliations he had suffered during the war (the second one) came even worse ones which the unfeeling Swiss had imposed. All this by way of leading up to the seven-year itch. He paused to roll up his trousers. I was horrified. His legs were nothing but a mass of sores. There was no need to dwell further on the subject.

Now if he could only get a little codeine, he explained, it would help to calm his nerves, allow him to get some sleep at least, even though it could not cure the itch. Wouldn't I try to get some for him, perhaps tomorrow when I went to town? I said I would.

I had never used codeine or any drug that puts one to sleep or wakes one up. I had no idea that codeine could only be had by doctor's prescription. It was the druggist who informed me of this. Not wishing to disappoint Moricand, I called on two doctors I knew to ask if they would furnish me with the necessary prescription. They refused.

When I informed Moricand of the situation he was almost beside himself. He acted as if there were a conspiracy on the part of American physicians to keep him in misery. "How absurd!" he cried. "Even in Switzerland it's sold openly. I would have more chance, I suppose, if I asked for cocaine or opium."

Another day or two passed, during which time he got no sleep at all. Then another consultation. This time to inform me that he had thought of a way out. Very simple, too. He would write to his druggist in Switzerland and ask him to mail him the codeine in very small particles. I explained to him that such importation would be illegal, no matter how small the quantity. I explained further that he would be incriminating me too should he do such a thing.

"What a country! What a country!" he exclaimed, raising his hands heavenward.

"Why don't you try the baths again?" I suggested. He promised he would. He said it as if I had requested him to swallow a dose of castor oil.

As I was about to leave he showed me a letter which he had just received from his landlady. It was about the bill he owed and my failure to keep my promise. I had completely forgotten about her and her bloody bill.

We never had any money in the bank, but I did have a few bills in my pocket. I fished them out. "Maybe this will quiet her for a while," I said, laying them on his table.

About a week later he called me to his room again. He was holding an envelope in his hand which he had just opened. He wanted me to look at the contents. It was a letter from his Swiss druggist say that he was happy to be of service. I looked up and saw the tiny pellets which he was holding in the palm of his hand.

"You see," he said, "there is always a way."

I was furious but tongue-tied. I could not deny that, were the situation reversed, I would probably have done the same. He was desperate, that was obvious. Besides, the baths had been no help.

They had aggravated his condition, if I was to believe him. At any rate, he was through with the baths: they were poison to his system.

Now that he had what he needed he took to roaming the forest regularly. Good, thought I, he needs the exercise. But he overdid it; the excessive walking made his blood boil. From another standpoint these excursions did him good. The forest bequeathed something which his Swiss spirit demanded. He always returned from his walks elated and physically exhausted. "Tonight," he would say, "I should be able to sleep without taking any pills."

He deceived himself. The itching grew worse. He continued to scratch himself furiously, even in deep slumber. The itch had traveled too. Now it had attacked his arms. Soon it would devastate his whole body, all but his genitals.

There were remissions, of course. If guests arrived, particularly French-speaking guests, his morale improved overnight. Or if he received a letter from a dear friend who was still doing a stretch in prison because of his activities during the Occupation. Sometimes an exceptionally good dinner was sufficient to change his mood for a day or two. The itching never ceased, apparently, but the scratching might be halted for a while.

As the days passed, he became more and more aware that I was a person upon whom it gave people pleasure to shower gifts. With the mail there came packages containing all manner of things. What astounded Moricand was that they were usually the very things we were in need of. If we ran out of wine a friend was sure to turn up with an armful of excellent bottles; if I needed wood, a neighbor would appear with the gift of a load of wood, enough to last several months. Books and magazines, of course, poured in steadily. Now and then I would receive postage stamps, whole sheets of them. Only money failed to pour in. That always came in a trickle, a trickle which often dried up altogether.

It was with a falcon's eye that Moricand eyed this steady influx of gifts. As for the steady flow of visitors, even the bores, the time

wasters, he observed, were instrumental in lightening our burdens.
"It's altogether natural," he would say. "It's there in your horoscope. Even when Jupiter deserts you at times you are never left
unprotected. Besides, with *you* misfortune only works to your
ultimate advantage. You can't possibly lose!"

I never dreamed of responding to such remarks by pointing out
the struggles and the sacrifices I had made throughout my life. But
to myself I would say: "It's one thing for 'it' to be in your horoscope; it's another to make it manifest."

One thing seemed to escape his notice entirely—the favors, the
services which my friends were constantly rendering him. He had
not the slightest notion how much everyone was concerned for his
welfare. He behaved as if it were all a matter of course, now that
he was in the land of plenty. Americans were like that, naturally
kind and generous, don't you know. They had no grave problems
to worry about They were born lucky, the gods looked after them.
A shade of contempt always crept into his voice when he referred
to the benevolence of the American. He lumped us with the huge
cauliflowers, carrots, squash and other monstrous-looking vegetables and fruits we produce in inexhaustible quantity.

I had asked only one little favor of Moricand when I invited him
to stay with us for the rest of his days. That was to teach my
daughter French, if possible. I had asked it more to relieve him
of an undue sense of gratitude than for any deep concern about
the child's acquisition of French. All she ever learned during his
stay with us was *Oui* and *Non,* and *Bon jour, Monsieur Moricand!*
He seemed to have no use for children; they annoyed him, unless
they were extremely well behaved. As with most people who stress
behavior, being well behaved meant keeping out of sight and reach.
He was utterly at a loss to understand my preoccupation with the
child, the daily walks we took, the efforts I made to amuse, entertain and instruct her, the patience with which I listened to her
idiotic questions, her excessive demands. He had no idea, naturally,
of the joy she gave me. It was obvious, but perhaps he did not wish

to recognize it, that she was my only joy. Val always came first. It irritated everyone, not only Moricand. And particularly my wife. The opinion roundabout was that I was an aging dolt who was spoiling his only child. Outwardly it did indeed seem so. The reality which underlay the situation, or the relationship, I hesitated to reveal even to my intimate friends. It was ironic, to be sure, that the very ones who levelled these reproaches were guilty of doing the same silly things, of showing the same exaggerated affection, for their pets. As for Val, she was my own flesh and blood, the apple of my eye; my only regret was that I could not give her more time and attention.

It was about this time that the little mothers all became interested in the dance. Some went in for singing too. Very fine. Commendable, as we say. But what about the children? Were they also taught to sing and dance? Not a bit. That would come later, when they were old enough to be sent to the ballet class or whatever the fad might be which the little mothers deemed indispensable in the cultural advancement of their progeny. The mothers were too busy at the moment cultivating their own latent talents.

There came a day when I taught Val her first song. We were marching home through the woods; I had hoisted her on my shoulders to save her weary little legs. Suddenly she asked me to sing. "What would you like?" I said, and then I gave her that feeble joke of Abraham Lincoln about knowing only two songs: one was "Yankee Doodle," the other wasn't.

"Sing it!" she begged.

I did, and with a vengeance. She joined in. By the time we arrived home she knew the verse by heart. I was supremely delighted. We had to sing it over and over, naturally. It was Yankee Doodle this and Yankee Doodle that. Yankee Doodle dandy and the Devil take the hindmost!

Moricand took not the slightest interest in such diversions. "Poor Miller!" he probably said to himself, meaning what a ridiculous figure I could cut.

Poor Val! How it cut me when, endeavoring to have a few words with him, she would get for rebuff: "I speak no English."

At table she annoyed him incessantly with her silly chatter, which I found delicious, and her poor table manners.

"She ought to be disciplined," he would say. "It's not good for a child to receive so much attention."

My wife, being of the same mind, would chime in like a clock. She would bemoan the fact that I frustrated all her efforts in this direction, would make it appear that I took a diabolical pleasure in seeing the child misbehave. She could not admit, naturally, that her own spirit was of cast iron, that discipline was her only recourse.

"He believes in *freedom*," she would say, making the idea of freedom sound like utter rubbish.

To which Moricand would rejoin: "Yes, the American child is a little barbarian. In Europe the child knows its place. Here the child rules."

All too true, alas! And yet. . . . What he forgot to add is what every intelligent European knows, what he himself knew only too well and had admitted many times, namely, that in Europe, especially *his* Europe, the child becomes an adult long before his time, that he is disciplined to death, that he is given an education which is not only "barbarous" but cruel, crazy, stultifying, that stern, disciplinary measures *may* make well-behaved children but seldom emancipated adults. He forgot, moreover, to say what his own childhood had been like, to explain what discipline, good manners, refinement, education had done for him.

To exculpate himself in *my* eyes he would wind up by explaining to my wife that I was a born anarchist, that my sense of freedom was a peculiarly personal one, that the very idea of discipline was abhorrent to my nature. I was a rebel and an outlaw, a spiritual freak, so to say. My function in life was to create disturbance. Adding very soberly that there was need for such as me. Then, as if carried away, he would proceed to rectify the picture. It was also a fact, he had to admit, that I was too good, too kind, too gentle, too patient, too indulgent, too forbearing, too forgiving. As if this balanced the violence, the ruthlessness, the recklessness, the treachery of my essential being. At this point he might even say that I *was* capable of understanding discipline, since, as he put it, my ability to write was based on the strictest kind of self-discipline.

"*C'est un être bien compliqué,*" he would conclude. "Fortunately, I understand him. I know him inside out." With this he would press his thumb against the table top, as if squashing a louse. That was *me* under his thumb, the anomaly which he had studied, analyzed, dissected, and could interpret when occasion demanded.

Often an evening that began auspiciously would end in an involved discussion of our domestic problems, something which I abhorred but which wives seem to enjoy, particularly when they have a sympathetic listener. Since I had long resigned myself to the futility of arriving at any understanding with my wife through discussion—I might as well have talked to a stone wall—I limited my participation to rectifying falsehoods and distortions of fact. For the most part I presented an adamant silence. Quite aware that there are always two sides to the picture, poor Moricand would struggle to shift the discussion to more fundamental grounds.

"One gets nowhere with a type like Miller," he would say to my wife. "He does not think in the way you and I do. He thinks in circular fashion. He has no logic, no sense of measure, he is contemptuous of reason and common sense."

He would then proceed to describe to her *her* virtues and defects, in order to demonstrate why we could never see eye to eye, she and I. "But I understand you both. I can act as arbiter. I know how to put the puzzle together."

As a matter of fact, he was quite correct in this. He proved to be a most excellent referee. In his presence, what might have ended in explosions ended only in tears or mute perplexity. Often, when I prayed that he would grow weary and take leave of us for the night, I could sense my wife doing the very opposite. Her only chance of talking with me, or at me, was in his presence. Alone we were either at one another's throats or giving each other the silence. Moricand often succeeded in lifting these furious and prolonged arguments, which had become routine, to another level; he helped us, momentarily at least, to isolate our thoughts, survey them dispassionately, examine them from other angles, free them of their obsessive nature. It was on such occasions that he made good use of his astrological wisdom, for nothing can be more cool and objective, more soothing and staying to the victim of emotion, than the astrological picture of his plight.

Not every evening was spent in argument and discussion, to be sure. The best evenings were those in which we gave him free rein. After all, the monologue was his forte. If by chance we touched on the subject of painting—he had begun life as a painter —we were sure to be richly rewarded for hearing him out. Many of the now celebrated figures in French art he had known intimately. Some he had befriended in his days of opulence. His anecdotes concerning what I choose to call the golden period—the two or three decades leading up to the appearance of *les Fauves*— were delicious in the sense that a rich meal is delicious. They were always spiced with uncanny observations that did not lack a certain diabolical charm. For me this period was fraught with vital interest. I had always felt that I was born twenty or thirty years too late, always regretted that I had not first visited Europe (and remained there) as a young man. Seen it *before* the First World War, I mean. What would I not give to have been the comrade or bosom friend of such figures as Apollinaire, Douanier Rousseau, George Moore, Max Jacob, Vlaminck, Utrillo, Derain, Cendrars, Gauguin, Modigliani, Cingria, Picabia, Maurice Magre, Léon Daudet, and such like. How much greater would have been the thrill to cycle along the Seine, cross and recross her bridges, race through towns like Bougival, Châtou, Argenteuil, Marly-le-roi, Puteaux, Rambouillet, Issy-les-Moulineaux and similar environs circa 1910 rather than the year 1932 or 1933! What a difference it

would have made to see Paris from the top of a horse-drawn omni-
bus at the age of twenty-one! Or to view the *grands boulevards*
as a *flâneur* in the period made famous by the Impressionists!

Moricand could summon all the splendor and misery of this
epoch at will. He could induce that *"nostalgie de Paris"* which
Carco is so adept at, which Aragon, Léon-Paul Fargue, Daudet,
Duhamel and so many French writers have given us time and
again. It needed only the mention of a street name, a crazy monu-
ment, a restaurant or cabaret which exists no more, to start the
wheels turning. His evocations were even more piquant to me
because he had seen it all through the eyes of a snob. However
much he had participated, he had never suffered as did the men
he spoke of. His sufferings were to come only when those who
had not been killed in the war or committed suicide or gone insane
had become famous. Did he ever imagine in his days of opulence,
I wonder, that the time would come when he would be obliged to
beg his poor friend Max Jacob for a few sous—Max who had renounced the world and was living like an ascetic? A terrible thing
to come down in the world when your old friends are rising on the
horizon like stars, when the world itself, once a playground, has
become a shabby carnival, a cemetery of dreams and illusions.

How he loathed the Republic and all it represented! Whenever
he made mention of the French Revolution it was as if he were
face to face with evil itself. Like Nostradamus, he dated the dete-
rioration, the blight, the downfall from the day *le peuple—la
canaille,* in other words—took over. It is strange, now that I come
to think of it, that he never once spoke of Gilles de Rais. Any more
than he ever spoke of Ramakrishna, Milarepa, or St. Francis.
Napoleon, yes. Bismarck, yes. Voltaire, yes. Villon, yes. And
Pythagoras, of course. The whole Alexandrian world was as
familiar and vivid to him as if he had known it in a previous incarnation. The Manichean world of thought was also a reality to him.
Of Zoroastrian teachings he dwelt by predilection on that aspect
which proclaims "the reality of evil." Possibly he also believed

that Ormuzd would eventually prevail over Ahriman, but if so it was an eventuality only realizable in a distant future, a future so distant as to render all speculation about it, or even hope in it, futile. No, the reality of evil was undoubtedly the strongest conviction he held. He was so aware of it, indeed, that he could enjoy nothing to the full; actively or passively he was always exorcising the evil spirits which pervade every phase, rung and sphere of life.

One evening, when we had touched on things close to his heart, he asked me suddenly if I had lost all interest in astrology. "You never mention it any more," he said.

"True," I replied. "I don't see what it would serve me to pursue it further. I was never interested in it the way you are. For me it was just another language to learn, another keyboard to manipulate. It's only the poetic aspect of anything which really interests me. In the ultimate there is only one language—the language of truth. It matters little how we arrive at it."

I forget what his reply to this was precisely, only that it conveyed a veiled reproach for my continued interest in Oriental thought. I was too absorbed in abstract speculations, he hinted. Too Germanic, possibly. The astrologic approach was a corrective I stood in need of. It would help to integrate, orient, and organize much in me that was *flou* and chaotic. There was always a danger, with a type like me, of becoming either a saint or a fanatic.

"Not a lunatic, eh?"

"*Jamais!*"

"But something of a fool! Is that it?"

His answer was—Yes and No. I had a strong religious strain, a metaphysical bent. There was more than a touch of the Crusader in me. I was both humble and arrogant, a penitent and an Inquisitioner. And so on.

"And you think a deeper knowledge of astrology would help overcome these tendencies?"

"I would not put it exactly like that," he said. "I would say simply that it would help you to see more clearly . . . see into the nature of your problems."

"But I have no problems," I replied. "Unless they are cosmological ones. I am at peace with myself—and with the world. It's true, I don't get along with my wife. But neither did Socrates, for that matter. Or. . . ."

He stopped me.

"All right," I said, "tell me this—what has astrology done for *you*? Has it enabled you to correct your defects? Has it helped you to adjust to the world? Has it given you peace and joy? Why do you scratch yourself like a madman?"

The look he gave me was enough to tell me that I had hit below the belt.

"I'm sorry," I said, "but you know that I'm often rude and direct for a good reason. I don't mean to belittle you or make fun of you. But here's what I would like to know. Answer me straight! What is the most important—peace and joy or wisdom? If to know less would make you a happier man, which would you choose?"

I might have known his answer. It was that we have no choice in such matters.

I violently disagreed. "Perhaps," said I, "I am still very much of an American. That is to say, naive, optimistic, gullible. Perhaps all I gained from the fruitful years I spent in France was a strengthening and deepening of my own inner spirit. In the eyes of a European, what am I but an American to the core, an American who exposes his Americanism like a sore. Like it or not, I am a product of this land of plenty, a believer in superabundance, a believer in miracles. Any deprivation I suffered was my own doing. I blame nobody but myself for my woes and afflictions, for my shortcomings, for my transgressions. What you believe I might have learned through a deeper knowledge of astrology I learned through experience of life. I made all the mistakes that it is possible for a man to make—and I paid the penalty. I am that much richer, that much wiser, that much happier, if I may say so, than if I had found through study or through discipline how to avoid the snares and pitfalls in my path. . . . Astrology deals in potentialities, does it not? I am not interested in the potential man. I am interested in what a man actualizes—or realizes—of his potential being. And what is the potential man, after all? Is he not the sum of all that is human? *Divine,* in other words? You think I am searching for God. I am not. God is. The world is. Man is. We are. The full reality, that's God—and man, and the world, and all that is, including the unnameable. I'm for reality. More and more reality. I'm a fanatic about it, if you like. And what is astrology? What has it to do with reality? Something, to be sure. So has astronomy, so has biology, so has mathematics, so has music, so has literature; and so have the cows in the field and the flowers and the weeds, and the manure that brings them back to life. In some moods some things seem more important than others. Some things have value, others don't, we say. *Everything* is important and of value. Look at it that way and I'll accept your astrology...."

"You're in one of your moods again," he said, shrugging his shoulders.

"I know it," I replied. "Just be patient with me. You'll have your turn. . . . Every so often I revolt, even against what I believe in with all my heart. I have to attack everything, myself included. Why? To simplify things. We know too much—and too little. It's the intellect which gets us into trouble. Not our intelligence. *That* we can never have enough of. But I get weary of listening to specialists, weary of listening to the man with one string to his fiddle. I don't deny the validity of astrology. What I object to is becoming enslaved to any one point of view. Of course there are affinities, analogies, correspondences, a heavenly rhythm and an earthly rhythm . . . *as above, so below.* It would all be crazy if it weren't so. But knowing it, accepting it, why not forget it? I mean, make it a living part of one's life, something absorbed, assimilated and distributed through every pore of one's being, and thus forgotten, altered, utilized in the spirit and the service of life. I abhor people who have to filter everything through the one language they know, whether it be astrology, religion, yoga, politics, economics or what. The one thing about this universe of ours which intrigues me, which makes me realize that it *is* divine and beyond all knowing, is that it lends itself so easily to any and all interpretations. Everything we formulate about it is correct and incorrect at the same time. It includes our truths and our errors. And, whatever we think about the universe in no way alters it. . . .

"Let me get back to where I started. We all have different lives to lead. We all want to make conditions as smooth and harmonious for ourselves as possible. We all want to extract the full measure of life. Must we go to books and teachers, to science, religion, philosophy, must we know so much—and so little!—to take the path? Can we not become fully awake and aware without the torture we put ourselves through?"

"Life is nothing but a Calvary," he said. "Not even a knowledge of astrology can alter that stern fact."

"What about the exceptions? Surely. . . ."

"There are no exceptions," he replied. "Everyone, even the most enlightened, has his private griefs and torments. Life is perpetual struggle, and struggle entails sorrow and suffering. And suffering gives us strength and character."

"For what? To what end?"

"The better to endure life's burdens."

"What a woeful picture! It's like training for a contest in which one knows in advance he will be defeated."

"There is such a thing as renunciation," he said.

"But is it a solution?"

"For some Yes, for others No. Sometimes one has no choice."

"In your honest opinion, do we ever really have what is called choice?"

He thought a moment before answering.

"Yes, I believe we do have a measure of choice, but much less than people think. Within the limits of our destiny we are free to choose. It is here precisely that astrology is of great importance: when you realize the conditions under which you have come into the world, which astrology makes clear, you do not choose the unchooseable."

"The lives of great men," said I, "would seem to tell us the opposite."

"As you say, *so it would seem*. But if one examines their horoscopes one is impressed by the fact that they could scarcely have chosen other than they did. What one chooses or wills is always in accordance with one's character. Faced with the same dilemma, a Napoleon would act one way, and a St. Paul another."

"Yes, yes, I know all that," I interrupted. "And I also know, or believe, that St. Francis would have been St. Francis, St. Paul St. Paul, and Napoleon Napoleon, even if they had had a profound knowledge of astrology. To understand one's problems, to be able to look into them more deeply, to eliminate the unnecessary ones, none of that really interests me any longer. Life as a burden, life as a battleground, life as a problem—these are all partial ways of looking at life. Two lines of poetry often tell us more, give us more, than the weightiest tome by an erudite. To make anything truly significant one has to poetize it. The only way I get astrology, or anything else, for that matter, is as poetry, as music. If the astrological view brings out new notes, new harmonies, new vibrations, it has served its purpose—for me. Knowledge weighs one down; wisdom saddens one. The love of truth has nothing to do with knowledge or wisdom: it's beyond their domains. Whatever certitude one possesses is beyond the realm of proof.

"The saying goes, 'It takes all kinds to make a world.' Precisely. The same does not hold for views or opinions. Put all the pictures together, all the views, all the philosophies, and you do not get a totality. The sum of all these angles of visions do not and never will make truth. The sum of all knowledge is greater confusion. The intellect runs away with itself. Mind is not intellect. The intellect is a product of the ego, and the ego can never be stilled, never be satisfied. When do we begin to know that we know?

When we have ceased to believe that we can ever know. Truth comes with surrender. And it's wordless. The brain is not the mind; it is a tyrant which seeks to dominate the mind.

"What has all this to do with astrology? Nothing perhaps, and yet everything. To you I am an illustration of a certain kind of Capricorn; to an analyst I'm something else; to a Marxist another kind of specimen, and so on. What's all that to *me*? What does it concern me how your photographic apparatus registers? To see a person whole and for what he is one has to use another kind of camera; one has to have an eye that is even more objective than the camera's lens. One has to see through the various facets whose brilliant reflections blind us to the real nature of an individual. The more we learn the less we know; the more equipment we have the less we are able to see. It's only when we stop trying to see, stop trying to know, that we really see and know. What sees and knows has no need of spectacles and theories. All our striving and struggling is in the nature of confession. It is a way of reminding ourselves that we are weak, ignorant, blind, helpless. Whereas we are *not*. We are as little or as much as we permit ourselves to think we are.

"Sometimes I think that astrology must have had its inception at a moment in man's evolution when he lost faith in himself. Or, to put it another way, when he lost his wholeness. When he wanted to know instead of to be. Schizophrenia began far back, not yesterday or the day before. And when man split he split into myriad fragments. But even today, as fragmented as he is, he can be made whole again. The only difference between the Adamic man and the man of today is that the one was born to Paradise and the other has to create it. And that brings me back to the question of choice. A man can only prove that he is free by electing to be so. And he can only do so when he realizes that he himself made himself unfree. And that to me means that he must wrest from God the powers he has given God. The more of God he recognizes in himself the freer he becomes. And the freer he becomes the fewer decisions he has to make, the less choice is presented to him. Freedom is a misnomer. Certitude is more like it. Unerringness. Because truthfully there is always only one way to act in any situation, not two, nor three. Freedom implies choice and choice exists only to the extent that we are aware of our ineptitude. The adept takes no thought, one might say. He is one with thought, one with the path.

"It seems as if I were straying far afield. I'm not, really. I'm merely talking another language. I'm saying that peace and joy is within everyone's province. I'm saying that our essential being is godlike. I'm saying that there are no limitations, either to thought or action. I'm saying that we're one, not many. I'm saying that we are there, that we never could be anywhere else except through negation. I'm saying that to see differences is to make differences. A Capricorn is a Capricorn only to another astrologer. Astrology makes use of a few planets, of the sun and the moon, but what of the millions of other planets, other universes, all the stars, the comets, the meteors, the asteroids? Does distance count, or size, or radiance? Is not all one, interactive, interpenetrating? Who dares to say where influences begin and leave off? Who dares to say what is important and what is not? Who owns this universe? Who regulates it? Whose spirit informs it? If we need help, guidance, directions, why not go straight to the source? And what do we want help, guidance and direction for? To make things more comfortable for ourselves, to be more efficient, to better achieve our ends? Why is everything so complicated, so difficult, so obscure, so unsatisfactory? Because we have made ourselves the center of the universe, because we want everything to work out as we wish it. What we need to discover is what *it* wishes, call *it* life, mind, God, whatever you please. If that is the purpose of astrology, I am all for it.

"There's something else I would like to say, to finish with the subject once and for all. It's about our everyday problems, principally the problem of getting along with one another, which seems to be the main problem. What I say is, if we are going to meet one another with a view or an awareness of our diversity and divergences we will never acquire enough knowledge to deal with one another smoothly and effectively. To get anywhere with another individual one has to cut through to the rock-bottom man, to that common human substratum which exists in all of us. This is not a difficult procedure and certainly doesn't demand of one that he be a psychologist or a mind reader. One doesn't have to know a thing about astrological types, the complexity of their reactions to this or that. There is one simple, direct way to deal with all types, and that is truthfully and honestly. We spend our lives trying to avoid the injuries and humiliations which our neighbors may inflict upon us. A waste of time. If we abandoned fear and prejudice, we could meet the murderer as easily as the saint. I get fed up with astrological parlance when I observe people studying their charts to find a way out of illness, poverty, vice, or whatever it may be. To me it seems like a sorry attempt to exploit the stars. We talk about fate as if it were something visited upon us; we forget that we create our fate every day we live. And by fate I mean the woes that beset us, which are merely the effects of causes which are not nearly as mysterious as we pretend. Most of the ills we suffer from are directly traceable to our own behavior. Man is not suffering from the ravages wrought by earthquakes and volcanoes, by tornadoes and tidal waves; he is suffering from his own misdeeds, his own foolishness, his own ignorance and disregard of natural laws. Man can eliminate war, can eliminate disease, can eliminate old age and probably death too. He need not live in poverty, vice, ignorance, in rivalry and competition. All these conditions are within his province, within his power, to alter. But he can never alter them as long as he is concerned solely with his own individual fate. Imagine a physician refusing his services because of danger of infection or contamination! We are all members of the one body, as the Bible says. And we are all at war with one another. Our own physical body possesses a wisdom which we who inhabit the body lack. We give it orders which make no sense. There is no mystery about disease, nor crime, nor war, nor the thousand and one things which plague us. Live simply and wisely. Forget, forgive, renounce, abdicate. Do I need to study my horoscope to understand the wisdom of such simple behavior? Do I have to live with yesterday in order to enjoy tomorrow? Can I not scrap the past instantly, begin at once to live the good life—if I really mean to? *Peace and joy.* . . . I say it's ours for the asking. Day by day, that's good enough for me. Not even that, in fact. Just today! *Le bel aujourd'hui!* Wasn't that the title of one of Cendrars' books? Give me a better one, if you can. . . ."

Naturally, I did not deliver this harangue all in one breath, nor exactly in these words. Perhaps much of it I merely imagine that I said. No matter. I say it now as of then. It was all there in my mind, not once, but repeatedly. Take it for what it's worth.

With the coming of the first good rain he began to grow despondent. It's true that his cell was tiny, that water leaked through the roof and the windows, that the sow bugs and other bugs took over, that they often dropped on his bed when he was asleep, that to keep warm he had to use an ill-smelling oil stove which consumed what little oxygen remained after he had sealed up all the cracks and crevices, stuffed the space beneath the door with sacking, shut all the windows tight, and so on. It's true that it was a winter in which we got more than our usual share of rain, a winter in which the storms broke with fury and lasted for days on end. And he, poor devil, was cooped up all day, restless, ill at ease, either too hot or too cold, scratching, scratching, and utterly incapable of warding off the hundred and one abominations which materialized out of the ether, for how else explain the presence of all these creeping, crawling, ugly things when all had been shut tight, sealed and fumigated?

I shall never forget his look of utter bewilderment and distress when he called me to his room one late afternoon to inspect the lamps. "Look," he said, striking a match and applying the flame to the wick. "Look, it goes out every time."

Now Aladdin lamps are quixotic and temperamental, as country people know. They have to be kept in perfect condition to function properly. Just to trim the wick neatly is in itself a delicate operation. Of course I had explained things to him a number of times, but every time I visited him I noticed that the lamps were dim or smoking. I knew too that he was too annoyed with them to bother keeping them in condition.

Striking a match and holding it against the wick, I was just about to say, "You see, it's simple . . . nothing to it"—when, to my surprise, the wick refused to ignite. I lit another and another, and still the wick refused to take fire. It was only when I reached for a candle and saw how it spluttered that I realized what was wrong.

I opened the door to let in some air and then tried the lamp again. It worked. "Air, my friend. You need air!" He looked at me in amazement. To get air he would have to keep a window open. And that would let the wind and rain in. *"C'est emmerdant!"* he exclaimed. It was indeed. It was worse than that. I had visions of finding him in bed one fine morning—suffocated.

Eventually he devised his own method of getting just enough air. By means of a string and a series of hooks inserted at intervals into the upper half of the Dutch door he could obtain as little or as much air as he chose. It was not necessary to open a window or remove the sacking beneath the door or dig out the putty with which he had sealed the various cracks and crevices in the walls. As for the bloody lamps, he decided that he would use candles instead. The candles gave his cell a mortuary look which suited his morbid state of mind.

Meanwhile the itch continued to plague him. Every time he came down for meals he rolled up his sleeves or the legs of his trousers to show us the ravages it had made. His flesh was by now a mass of running sores. Had I been in his boots I would have put a bullet through my brain.

Obviously something had to be done or we would all go crazy. We had tried all the old-fashioned remedies—to no avail. In desperation I begged a friend who lived some few hundred miles away to make a special trip. He was a capable all-round physician, a surgeon and a psychiatrist to boot. He also knew some French. In fact, he was an altogether unusual fellow, and generous and frank. I knew that he would give me good advice if he could not cope with the case.

Well, he came. He examined Moricand from head to toe and inside out. That done, he engaged him in talk. He paid no further heed to the running sores, made no further mention of the subject. He talked about all manner of things but not about the itch. It was as if he had completely forgotten what he had been summoned for. Now and then Moricand attempted to remind him of the object of his visit but my friend always succeeded in diverting his attention to some other subject. Finally he made ready to leave, after writing out a prescription which he left under Moricand's nose.

I escorted him to the car, eager to know what he really thought.

"There's nothing to do," he said. "When he stops thinking about it the itch will disappear."

"And in the meantime. . . ?"

"Let him take the pills."

"Will they really help?"

"That depends on *him*. There's nothing in them to hurt him, or to do him any good. Unless he believes so."

There was a heavy pause.

Suddenly he said: "Do you want my honest advice?"

"I certainly do," said I.

"Then get him off your hands!"

"What do you mean?"

"Just that. You might as well have a leper living with you."

I must have looked sorely puzzled.

"It's simple," he said. "He doesn't want to get well. What he wants is sympathy, attention. He's not a man, he's a child. A spoiled child."

Another pause.

"And don't worry if he threatens to do himself in. He'll probably pull that on you when everything else fails. He won't kill himself. He loves himself too much."

"I see," said I. "So that's how it stands. . . . But what in hell will I tell him?"

"That I leave to you, old pal." He started up the motor.

"O.K." I said. "Maybe I'll take the pills myself. Anyway, a thousand thanks!"

Moricand was lying in wait for me. He had been studying the prescription but could make nothing of it, the handwriting was too abominable.

In a few words I explained that in my friend's opinion his ailment was psychological.

"Any fool knows that!" he blurted out and in the next breath— "Is he really a doctor?"

"A quite famous one," I answered.

"Strange," said Moricand. "He talked like an imbecile."

"OH?"

"Asking me if I still masturbated."

"*Et puis. . .?*

"If I liked women as much as men. If I had ever taken drugs. If I believed in emanations. If, if, if. . . . *C'est un fou!*"

For a minute or two he was speechless with rage. Then, in a tone of utter misery, he muttered as if to himself: "*Mon Dieu, mon Dieu, qu'est-ce que je peux faire? Comme je suis seul, tout seul!*"

"Come, come," I murmured, "calm yourself! There are worse things than the itch."

"*Like what?*" he demanded. He said it with such swiftness that I was taken aback.

"*Like what?*" he repeated. "*Psychological . . . pouah!* He must take me for an idiot. What a country this is! No humanity. No understanding. No intelligence. Ah, if only I could die . . . die tonight!"

I said not a word.

"May you never suffer, *mon cher Miller,* as I am suffering! The war was nothing compared to this."

Suddenly his glance fell on the prescription. He picked it up, clenched it in his fist, then threw it on the floor.

"Pills! He gives *me,* Moricand, pills! Bah!" He spat on the floor. "He's a quack, your friend. A charlatan. An impostor."

Thus ended the first attempt to pull him out of his misery.

A week passed and then who should turn up but my old friend Gilbert. Ah, I thought, at last someone who speaks French, someone who loves French literature. What a treat for Moricand!

Over a bottle of wine I had no difficulty in getting them to talk to one another. It was only a matter of a few minutes before they were discussing Baudelaire, Villon, Voltaire, Gide, Cocteau, *les ballets russes, Ubu Roi,* and so forth. When I saw that they were hitting it off nicely I discreetly withdrew, hoping that Gilbert who had also suffered the afflictions of Job, would raise the other's morale. Or at least get him drunk.

An hour or so later, as I was sauntering down the road with the dog, Gilbert drove up.

"What, going so soon?" I said. It was unlike Gilbert to leave before the last bottle had been emptied.

"I've had a bellyful," he replied. "What a prick!"

"Who, Moricand?"

"Exactly."

"What happened?"

By way of answer he gave me a look of sheer disgust.

"Do you know what I'd do with him, *amigo?"* he said vengefully.

"No, what?"

"Push him over the cliff."

"That's easier said than done."

"Try it! It's the best solution." With that he stepped on the gas.

Gilbert's words gave me a shock. It was altogether unlike him to talk that way about another person. He was such a kind, gentle, considerate soul, had been through such hell himself. Obviously it hadn't taken long for him to see through Moricand.

Meanwhile my good friend Lilik, who had rented a shack a few miles down the road, was doing his utmost to make Moricand more at home. Moricand liked Lilik and had implicit faith in him. He could hardly feel otherwise, since Lilik did nothing but render him services. Lilik would sit with him by the hour, listening to his tales of woe.

From Lilik I gleaned that Moricand thought I was not paying him enough attention. "You never inquire about his work," he said.

"His work? What do you mean? What is he working at?"

"I believe he's writing his memoirs."

"That's interesting," I said. "I must have a look some time."

"By the way," said Lilik, "have you ever seen his drawings?"

"What drawings?"

"My God, haven't you seen them yet? He's got a whole stack of them in his portfolio. Erotic drawings. Lucky for you," he chuckled, "that the customs men didn't discover them."

"Are they any good?"

"Yes and no. They're certainly not for children to look at."

A few days after this conversation took place, an old friend turned up. Leon Shamroy. As usual, he was loaded with gifts. Mostly things to eat and drink.

This time Moricand opened his falcon eyes even wider.

"It's staggering," he murmured. He drew me to one side. "A millionaire, I suppose?"

"No, just the head camera man for the Fox Films. The man who wins all the Oscars."

"I only wish you could understand his talk," I added. "There's no one in all America who can say the things he says and get away with it."

Just then Leon broke in. "What's all the whispering about?" he demanded. "Who is this guy—one of your Montparnasse friends?

Doesn't he talk English? What's he doing here? Sponging on you,
I'll bet. Give him a drink! He looks bored—or sad."

"Here, let him try one of these," said Leon, fishing a handful
of cigars out of his breast pocket. "They only cost a dollar apiece.
Maybe he'll get a kick out of them."

He nodded to Moricand to indicate that the cigars were for
him. With that he threw away the half-finished Havana he had
allowed to go out and lit a fresh one. The cigars were almost a foot
long and thick as seven-year-old rattlers. They had a beautiful
aroma too. Cheap at twice the price, thought I to myself.

"Tell him I don't talk French," said Leon, slightly annoyed
because Moricand had expressed his thanks in long-winded French.
As he spoke he undid a package out of which spilled some luscious-
looking cheeses, some salami and some *lachs*. Over his shoulder:
"Tell him we like to eat and drink. We'll chew the rag later.
Hey, where's that wine I brought? No, wait a minute. I've got
a bottle of Haig and Haig in the car. Let's give him that. The
poor bugger, I'll bet he's never had a tumbler of whisky in his
life. . . . Listen, what's the matter with him? Doesn't he ever
crack a smile?"

He went on sputtering like that, opening more parcels, cutting
himself a hunk of corn bread, buttering it with delicious sweet
butter, spearing an olive, tasting an anchovy, then a sour pickle, a
little of this, a little of that, at the same time unearthing a box of
sweets for Val, together with a beautiful dress, a string of beads
and . . . *"Here,* this is for *you,* you bastard!" and he flung me a
tin, of expensive cigarettes. "I've got more for you up in the car.
By the way, I forgot to ask you—how are things going with you?
Haven't made your pile yet, have you? You and Bufano! A
couple of orphans. Lucky you have a friend like me . . . someone
who *works* for a living, what?"

Meanwhile Lilik had gone to the car and brought things down.
We opened the Haig and Haig, then a beautiful brand of Bordeaux
for Moricand (and for ourselves), looked appraisingly at the

Pernod and the Chartreuse which he had also thought to bring. The air was already thick with smoke, the floor littered with paper and string.

"Is that shower of yours still working?" asked Leon, unbuttoning his silk shirt. "I've got to take one soon. Haven't had any sleep for thirty-six hours. Christ, am I glad to get away for a few hours! By the way, can you bunk me for the night? Maybe two nights? I want to talk to you. We've got to make some real dough for you soon. You don't want to be a beggar all your life, do you? Don't answer! I know what you're going to say. . . . By the way, where are your water colors? Drag 'em out! You know me. I may buy a half dozen before I leave. If they're any good, I mean."

Suddenly he noticed Moricand was pulling on a cheroot.

"What's the matter with that guy?" he shouted. "What's he got that stink weed in his mouth for? Didn't we just give him some good cigars?"

Moricand explained blushingly that he was reserving the cigars for later. They were too good to smoke immediately. He wanted to fondle them a while before lighting up.

"Fuck that nonsense!" cried Leon. "Tell him he's in America now. We don't worry about tomorrow, do we? Tell him when he finishes those I'll send him a box from L.A." He turned his head away, lowered his voice a trifle, "What's griping him anyway? Has he been starved to death over there? Anyway, the hell with him! Look, I want to tell you a little joke I heard the other night. Translate it for him, will you? I want to see if he'll laugh."

My wife is making a vain attempt to set the table. Leon has already embarked on his little joke, a filthy one, and Lilik is farting like a stallion. In the middle of his tale Leon pauses to cut himself another hunk of bread, pour a drink, take off his shoes and socks, spear an olive, and so on. Moricand watches him goggle-eyed. A new specimen of humanity for him. *Le vrai type américain, quoi!* I have a suspicion he's really enjoying himself. Sampling the Bordeaux, he smacks his lips. The *lachs*

intrigues him. As for the corn bread, he's never seen or tasted it
before. Famous! *Ausgezeichnet!*

Lilik's laughing so hard the tears are rolling down his cheeks.
It's a good joke, and a filthy one, but difficult to translate.

"What's the trouble?" says Leon. "Don't they use that kind of
language where he comes from?"

He observes Moricand diving into the viands, sipping his wine,
trying to puff away at the huge Havana.

"O.K. Forget the joke! He's filling his belly, that's good enough.
Listen, what did you say he was again?"

"Among other things an astrologer," I said.

"He doesn't know his ass from a hole in the ground. *Astrology!*
Who wants to listen to that shit? Tell him to get wise to himself. . . . Hey, wait a minute, Ill give him my birth date. Let's
see what he makes of it."

I give the dope to Moricand. He says he's not ready yet. Wants
to observe Leon a little longer, if we don't mind.

"What did he say?"

"He says he wants to enjoy his food first. But he knows that
you're an exceptional type." I added this to relieve the tension.

"He said a mouthful there. You're damned right I'm an exceptional type. Anyone else in my place would go crazy. Tell him for
me that I've got his number, will you?" Then, turning directly
to Moricand, he says: "How's the wine . . . the *vin rouge?* Good
stuff, what?"

"*Epatant!*" says Moricand, unaware of all the innuendoes that
had passed under his nose.

"You bet your ass it's good," says Leon. "*I* bought it. I know
good stuff when I see it."

He watches Moricand as if his nibs were a trained otter, then
turns to me. "Does he do anything else beside read the stars?"
Giving me a reproachful look, he adds: "I'll bet he likes nothing
better than to sit on his fat fanny all day. Why don't you put
him to work? Get him to dig a garden, plant vegetables, hoe the

weeds. That's what he needs. I know these bastards. They're all alike."

My wife was getting uncomfortable. She didn't want Moricand's feelings to be hurt.

"He's got something in his room you'll enjoy seeing," she said to Leon.

"Yeah," said Lilik, "right up your street, Leon."

"What are you trying to pull on me? What's the big secret? Out with it!"

We explained. Leon seemed strangely disinterested.

"Hollywood's full of that crap," he said. "What do you want me to do—*masturbate?*"

The afternoon wore on. Moricand retired to his cell. Leon took us up to inspect his new car, which could do ninety per in nothing flat. Suddenly he remembered that he had some toys for Val in the back of the car. "Where's Bufano these days?" says he, fishing around in the trunk.

"Gone to India, I think."

"To see Nehru, I bet!" He chuckled. "How that guy gets around without a cent in his pockets beats me. By the way, what are *you* doing for money these days?"

With this he dives into his pants pocket, hauls out a wad of greenbacks fastened with a clip, and begins peeling off a few.

"Here, take this," he says, shoving the greenbacks in my fist. "I'll probably owe you money before I leave."

"Have you anything good to read?" he asks suddenly. "Like that Giono book you lent me, remember? What about that guy Cendrars you're always pissing in the pants about? Has any of his stuff been translated yet?" He threw another half-finished Havana away, crushed it under his heel, and lit a fresh one. "I suppose you think I never look at a book. You're wrong. I read plenty. . . . Some day you're going to write a script for me—and earn some real dough. By the way"—he jerked his thumb in the

direction of Moricand's studio—"is that guy taking you for a lot
of dough? You're a chump. How did you ever fall into the trap?"

I told him it was a long story . . . some other time.

"What about those drawings of his? Should I have a look? He
wants to sell them, I suppose? I wouldn't mind taking some—if
it would help *you* out. . . . Wait a minute, I want to take a crap
first."

When he returned he had a fresh cigar in his mouth. He was
looking roseate.

"There's nothing like a good crap," he said, beaming. "Now
let's visit that sad-looking bimbo. And fetch Lilik, will you? I want
his opinion before I let myself in for anything."

As we entered Moricand's cell Leon sniffed the air. "For Christ's
sake, make him open a window!" he exclaimed.

"Can't, Leon. He's afraid of draughts."

"Just like him, for crying out loud. O.K. Tell him to trot his
dirty pictures out—and make it snappy, eh? I'll puke up if we
have to stay here more than ten minutes."

Moricand proceeded to get out his handsome leather portfolio.
He placed it circumspectly before him, then calmly lit a *gauloise
bleue*.

"Ask him to put it out," begged Leon. He drew a pack of
Chesterfields from his pocket and offered Moricand one. Moricand
politely refused, saying he couldn't stand American cigarettes.

"He's nuts!" said Leon. *"Here!"* and he proffered Moricand a
big cigar.

Moricand declined the offer. "I like these better," he said, bran-
dishing his foul French cigarette.

"If that's how it is, fuck it!" said Leon. "Tell him to get going.
We can't waste the whole afternoon in this tomb."

But Moricand wasn't to be hurried. He had his own peculiar
way of presenting his work. He allowed no one to touch the
drawings. He held them in front of him, turning them slowly,
page by page, as if they were ancient papyri to be handled with a

shovel only. Now and then he drew a silk handkerchief from his breast pocket to remove the perspiration from his hands.

It was my first view of his work. I must confess the drawings left a bad taste in my mouth. They were perverse, sadistic, sacrilegious. Children being raped by lubricious monsters, virgins practicing all manner of illicit intercourse, nuns defiling themselves with sacred objects . . . flagellations, medieval tortures, dismemberments, coprophagic orgies, and so forth. All done with a delicate, sensitive hand, which only magnified the disgusting element of the subject matter.

For once Leon was nonplused. He turned to Lilik inquiringly. Asked to see some of them a second time.

"The bugger knows how to draw, doesn't he?" he remarked.

Lilik hereupon pointed out a few he thought were exceptionally well executed.

"I'll take them," said Leon. "How much?"

Moricand named a price. A stiff one, even for an American client.

"Tell him to wrap them up," said Leon. "They're not worth it, but I'll take them. I know someone would give his right arm to own one."

He fished out his wad, counted the bills rapidly, and shoved them back into his pocket.

"Can't spare the cash," he said. "Tell him I'll send him a check when I get home . . . *if he'll trust me.*"

At this point Moricand seemed to undergo a change of heart. Said he didn't want to sell them singly. All or nothing. He named a price for the lot. A whopping price.

"He's mad," shrieked Leon. "Let him stick 'em up his ass!"

I explained to Moricand that Leon would have to think it over.

"Okay," said Moricand, giving me a wry, knowing smile. I knew that in *his* mind the bird was in the bag. A handful of trumps, that's what he was holding. "Okay," he repeated as we took leave of him.

As we sauntered down the steps Leon blurted out: "If the bastard had any brains he'd offer to let me take the portfolio and show them around. I could probably get twice what he's asking. They might get soiled, of course. What a finicky prick!" He gave me a sharp nudge. "That'd be something, wouldn't it, *to dirty that smut!*"

At the foot of the steps he paused a moment and caught me by the arm.

"You know what's the matter with him? He's *sick*." He touched his cranium with his forefinger.

"When you get rid of him," he added, "you'd better disinfect the place."

Some few nights later, at the dinner table, we at last drifted into the subject of the war. Moricand was in excellent form and only too eager to relate his experiences. Why we had never touched on all this before I don't know. To be sure, in his letters from Switzerland he had given me an outline of all that had taken place since we parted that night in June of 1939. But I had forgotten most of it. I knew that he had joined the Foreign Legion, for the second time, joined it not out of patriotism but to survive. How else was he to obtain food and shelter? He lasted only a few months in the Legion, of course, being altogether unfit for the rigors of that life. Discharged, he had returned to his garret in the Hotel Modial, more desperate, naturally, than ever before. He was in Paris when the Germans marched in. The presence of the Germans didn't bother him as much as the absence of food. At the last ditch he ran into an old friend, a man who held an important post at Radio-Paris. The friend took him on. It meant money, food, cigarettes. An odious job, but. . . . At any rate, the friend was now in prison. A collaborator, evidently.

He rehearsed the whole period again, this evening, and in great detail. As though he felt compelled to get it off his chest. From time to time I lost the thread. Never interested in politics, in feuds, in intrigues and rivalries, I became utterly confused just at the crucial period when, by command of the Germans, he intimated that he had been forced to go to Germany. (They had even picked out a wife for him to marry.) Suddenly the whole picture got out of whack. I lost him in a vacant lot with a Gestapo agent holding a revolver against his spine. It was all an absurd and horrendous nightmare anyway. Whether he had been in the service of the Germans or not—he never defined his position clearly—was all one to me. I wouldn't have minded if he had quietly informed me that he had turned traitor. What I *was* curious about was—how did he manage to get out of the mess? How did it happen that he came off with a whole skin?

Of a sudden I realize that he's telling me of his escape. We're no longer in Germany, but in France . . . or is it Belgium or Luxembourg? He's headed for the Swiss border. Bogged down by two heavy valises which he's been dragging for days and weeks. One day he's between the French Army and the German Army, the next day between the American Army and the German Army. Sometimes its neutral terrain he's traversing, sometimes it's no mans land. Wherever he goes it's the same story: no food, no shelter, no aid. He has to get ill to obtain a little nourishment, a place to flop, and so forth. Finally he really is ill. With a valise in each hand he marches on from place to place, shaking with fever, parched with thirst, dizzy, dopey, desperate. Above the cannonade he can hear his empty guts rattling. The bullets whizz overhead, the stinking dead lie in heaps everywhere, the hospitals are overcrowded, the fruit trees bare, the houses demolishd, the roads filled with homeless, sick, crippled, wounded, forlorn, abandoned souls. Every man for himself! War! War! And there he is floundering around in the midst of it: a Swiss neutral with a passport and an empty belly. Now and then an American soldier flings him a cigarette. But no Yardley's talc. No toilet paper. No perfumed soap. And with it all he's got the itch. Not only the itch, but lice. Not only lice, but scurvy.

The armies, all sixty-nine of them, are battling it out around him.
They don't seem to care at all for his safety. But the war is definitely coming to an end. It's all over but the mopping up. Nobody
knows why he's fighting, nor for whom. The Germans are licked
but they won't surrender. Idiots. Bloody idiots. In fact, everybody's licked except the Americans. They, the goofy Americans,
are romping through in grand style, their kits crammed with
tasty snacks, their pockets loaded with cigarettes, chewing gum,
flasks, crap-shooting dice and what not. The highest paid warriors
that ever donned uniform. Money to burn and nothing to spend
it on. Just praying to get to Paris, praying for a chance to rape
the lascivious French girls—or old hags, if there are no girls left.
And as they romp along they burn their garbage—while starving
civilians watch in horror and stupefaction. *Orders*. Keep moving!
Keep liquidating! On, on . . . on to Paris! On to Berlin! On to
Moscow! Swipe what you can, guzzle what you can, rape what
you can. And if you can't, shit on it! But don't beef! Keep going,
keep moving, keep advancing! The end is near. Victory is in
sight. Up with the flag! Hourrah! Hourrah! And fuck the gen-
erals, fuck the admirals! Fuck your way through! Now or never!

What a grand time! What a lousy mess! What horripilating
insanity!

("I am that General So-and-So who is responsible for the death
of so many of your beloved!")

Like a ghost our dear Moricand, by now witless and shitless, is
running the gauntlet, moving like a frantic rat between the oppos-
ing armies, skirting them, flanking them, outwitting them, running
head on into them; in his fright speaking good English now and
then, or German, or just plain horseshit, anything to disengage
himself, anything to wiggle free, but always clinging to his saddle-
bags which now weigh a ton, always headed for the Swiss border,
despite detours, loops, hairpin turns, double-eagles, sometimes crawling on all fours, sometimes walking erect, sometimes smothered
under a load of manure, sometimes doing the St. Vitus dance.

Always going forward, unless pushed backward. Finally reaching the border, only to find that it is blocked. Retracing his steps. Back to the starting point. Double fire. Diarrhea. Fever and more fever. Cross-examinations. Vaccinations. Evacuations. New armies to contend with. New battle fronts. New bulges. New victories. New retreats. And more dead and wounded, naturally. More vultures. More unfragrant breezes.

Yet always and anon he manages to hold on to his Swiss passport, his two valises, his slender sanity, his desperate hope of freedom.

"And what was in those valises that made them so precious?"

"Everything I cherish," he answered.

"Like what?"

"My books, my diaries, my writings, my. . . ."

I looked at him flabbergasted.

"No, Christ! You don't mean to say. . . ."

"Yes," he said, "just books, papers, horoscopes, excerpts from Plotinus, Iamblichus, Claude Saint-Martin. . . ."

I couldn't help it, I began to laugh. I laughed and laughed and laughed. I thought I'd never stop laughing.

He was offended. I apologized.

"You lugged all that crap around like an elephant," I exclaimed, "at the risk of losing your own hide?"

"A man doesn't throw away everything that is precious to him —just like that!"

"I would!" I exclaimed.

"But my whole life was bound up in those encumbrances."

"You should have thrown your life away too!"

"Not Moricand!" he replied, and his eyes flashed fire.

Suddenly I no longer felt sorry for him, not for anything that had ever happened to him.

For days those two valises weighed me down. They weighed as heavily on my mind and spirit as they had on Moricand's when he was crawling like a bedbug over that crazy quilt called Europe. I dreamed about them too. Sometimes he appeared in a dream,

Moricand, looking like Emil Jannings, the Jannings of *The Last Laugh,* the Grand Hotel porter Jannings, who has been sacked, who has lost his standing, who furtively smuggles his uniform out each night after he has been demoted to attendant in the toilet and washroom. In my dreams I was forever shadowing poor Conrad, always within shouting distance of him yet never able to make him hear me, what with the cannonades, the blitz bombs, the machine-gun fire, the screams of the wounded, the shrieks of the dying. Everywhere war and desolation. Here a shell crater filled with arms and legs; here a warrior still warm, his buttons ripped off, his proud genitals missing; here a freshly bleached skull crawling with bright red worms; a child impaled on a fence post; a gun carriage reeking with blood and vomit; trees standing upside down, dangling with human limbs, an arm to which a hand is still attached, the remains of a hand buried in a glove. Or animals in stampede, their eyes blazing with insanity, their legs a blur, their hides aflame, their bowels hanging out, tripping them, and behind them thousands more, millions of them, all singed, scorched, racked, torn, battered, bleeding, vomiting, racing like mad, racing ahead of the dead, racing for the Jordan, shorn of all medals, passports, halters, bits, bridles, feathers, fur, bills and hollyhocks. And Conrad Moriturus ever ahead, fleeing, his feet shod in patent leather boots, his hair neatly pomaded, his nails manicured, his linen starched, his mustache waxed, his trousers pressed. Galloping on like the Flying Dutchman, his valises swinging like ballast, his cold breath congealing behind him like frozen vapor. *To the border! To the border!*

And that was Europe! A Europe I never saw, a Europe I never tasted. Ah, Iamblichus, Porphyry, Erasmus, Duns Scotus, where are we? What elixir are we drinking? What wisdom are we sucking? Define the alphabet, O wise ones! Measure the itch! Flog insanity to death, if you can! Are those stars looking down upon us, or are they burnt holes in a filament of sick flesh?

And where is General Doppelgänger now, and General Eisenhower, and General Pussyfoot Cornelius Triphammer? Where the enemy? Where is Jack and where is Jill? How I would like to put a message through—to the Divine Creator! But I can't remember the name. I'm so utterly harmless, so innocent. Just a neutral. Nothing to declare but two valises. Yes, a citizen. A quiet sort of madman, nothing more. I ask for no decorations, no monuments in my name. Just see that the bags get through. I'll follow afterwards. I'll be there, even if I'm only a trunk. Moriturus, that's my name. Swiss, yes. A *légionnaire. Un mutilé de la guerre.* Call me anything you like. *Iamblichus,* if you wish. Or just— "The Itch"!

Taking advantage of the rainy season, we decided to break ground for a vegetable patch. We chose a spot that had never been dug up before. I began with a pick and my wife continued with the spade. I suppose Moricand felt slightly conscience-stricken to see a woman doing such work. To our surprise, he offered to do some spading himself. After a half-hour he was all in. It made him feel good just the same. In fact, he felt so good that after lunch he asked if we would put on some phonograph records—he was dying to listen to a little music. As he listened he hummed and whistled. He asked if we had any of Grieg's music, *Peer Gynt* particularly. Said he used to play the piano long ago. Played by ear. Then he added that he thought Grieg was a very great composer; he liked him best of all. That knocked me for a loop.

My wife had put on a Viennese waltz. Now he really became animated. All of a sudden he went up to my wife and asked her if she would dance with him. I nearly fell off the chair. Moricand dancing! It seemed incredible. Preposterous. But he did, and with heart and soul. He whirled and whirled around until he got dizzy.

"You dance beautifully," said my wife, as he took a seat, panting and perspiring.

"You're still a young man," I threw in.

"I haven't done this since the year 1920 something," he said almost blushingly. He slapped his thigh. "It's an old carcass but it still has a bit of life."

"Would you like to hear Harry Lauder?" I asked.

For a moment he was perplexed. Lauder, Lauder. . .? Then he got it.

"Certainly," he said. Obviously he was in a mood to hear anything.

I put on "Roamin' in the Gloamin'." To my amazement he even tried to sing. I thought perhaps he had had a little too much wine at lunch, but no, it wasn't the wine or the food this time, he was just happy for once.

The horrible thing is that it was almost more pitiful to see him happy than sad.

In the midst of these pleasantries Jean Wharton walked in. She was living just above us now in a house which she had recently had built. She had met Moricand once or twice before, but merely to exchange greetings. This day, being in extraordinary good humor, he mustered enough English to carry on a little conversation with her. When she left he remarked that she was a very interesting woman, rather attractive too. He added that she had a magnetic personality, that she radiated health and joy. He thought it might be well to cultivate her acquaintance, she made him feel good.

He felt so good, indeed, that he brought his memoirs down for me to read.

All in all, it was a remarkable day for Moricand. The best day of all, however, was the day Jaime de Angulo came down from his mountain top to pay us a visit. He came expressly to meet Moricand. We had, of course, informed Moricand of Jaime's existence, but we had never made a point of bringing the two together. To tell the truth, I didn't think they would get along very well together, since they seemed to have so little in common. Besides, I was never certain how Jaime would behave after he had a few drinks under his belt. The occasions when he did visit us and leave without making a scene, without cursing, reviling and insulting everyone, were few and far between.

It was shortly after lunch that Jaime rode up, hitched his horse to the oak tree, gave it a punch in the ribs, and descended the steps. It was a bright, sunny day, rather warm for a day in February. As usual, Jaime wore a bright headband around his forehead—his dirty snotrag, probably. Brown as a walnut, gaunt, slightly bow-legged, he was still handsome, still very much the Spaniard—and still utterly unpredictable. With a feather in his headband, a little grease paint, a different costume, he might have passed for a Chippewa or a Shawnee Indian. He was definitely the outlaw.

As they greeted one another I could not help but remark the contrast they presented, these two figures (born only five days apart) who had passed their youth in a sedate, aristocratic quarter of Paris. Two "Little Lord Fauntleroys" who had seen the seamy side of life, whose days were now numbered, and who would never meet again. The one neat, orderly, immaculate, fussy, cautious, a man of the city, a recluse, a stargazer; the other the exact opposite. The one a pedestrian, the other a cavalier. The one an aesthete, the other a wild duck.

I was wrong in thinking they had so little in common. They had much in common. Aside from a common culture, a common language, a common background, a common love of books, libraries, research, a common gift of speech, a common addiction—the one to drugs, the other to alcohol—they had an even greater tie: their obsession with evil. Jaime was one of the very few men I ever met of whom I could say that he had a streak of the Devil in him. As for Moricand, he had always been a diabolist. The only difference in their attitude toward the Devil was that Moricand feared him and Jaime cultivated him. At least, it always seemed thus to me. Both were confirmed atheists and thoroughly anti-Christian. Moricand leaned toward the antique pagan world, Jaime toward the primitive. Both were what we would call men of culture, men of learning, men of elegance. Jaime, playing the savage or the sot, was still a man of exquisite taste; no matter how much he spat on all that was "refined," he never truly outgrew the Little Lord Fauntleroy he had been as a boy. It was only through dire necessity that Moricand had renounced *la vie mondaine;* at heart he remained the dandy, the fop, the snob.

When I brought out the bottle and the glasses—the bottle only half-full, by the way—I anticipated trouble. It did not seem possible that these two individuals, having traveled such divergent paths, could get along together for long.

I was wrong about everything this day. They not only got along, they scarcely touched the wine. They were intoxicated with something stronger than wine—the past.

The mention of the Avenue Henri-Martin—they had discovered in the space of a few minutes that they had been raised in the very same block!—started the ball rolling. Dwelling on his boyhood, Jaime at once began to mimic his parents, impersonate his schoolmates, re-enact his deviltries, switching from French to Spanish and back again, acting now as a sissy, now as a coy young female, now as an irate Spanish grandee, now as a petulant, doting mother.

Moricand was in stitches. Never did I believe that he could laugh so hard or so long. He was no longer the melancholy grampus, nor even the wise old owl, but a normal, natural human being who was enjoying himself.

Not to intrude on this festival of reminiscence, I threw myself on the bed in the middle of the room and pretended to take a nap.

But my ears were wide open.

In the space of a few short hours it seemed to me that Jaime succeeded in rehearsing the whole of his tumultuous life. And what a life it was! From Passy to the Wild West—in one jump. From being the son of a Spanish grandee, raised in the lap of luxury, to becoming a cowboy, a doctor of medicine, an anthropologist, a master of linguistics, and finally a cattle rancher on the crest of the Santa Lucia range here in Big Sur. A lone wolf, divorced from all he held dear, waging a perpetual feud with his neighbor Boronda, another Spaniard, poring over his books, his dictionaries (Chinese, Sanskrit, Hebrew, Arabic, Persian, to mention but a few), raising a little fruit and vegetables, killing deer in season and out, forever exercising his horses, getting drunk, quarreling with everyone, even his bosom pals, driving visitors away with the lash, studying in the dead of night, coming back to his book on language, *the* book on language, he hoped it would be!—and finishing it just before his death. . . . Between times twice married, three children, one of them his beloved son, crushed to death beneath him in a mysterious automobile accident, a tragedy which had a lasting effect upon him.

Odd to listen to it all from the bed. Strange to hear the so-called shaman talking to the sage, the anthropologist to the astrologer, the scholar to the scholar, the linguist to the bookworm, the horseman to the boulevardier, the adventurer to the hermit, the barbarian to the dandy, the lover of languages to the lover of words, the scientist to the occultist, the desperado to the ex-*Légionnaire,* the fiery Spaniard to the stolid Swiss, the uncouth native to the well-dressed gentleman, the anarchist to the civilized European, the rebel to the well-behaved citizen, the man of the open spaces to the man of the garret, the drunkard to the dope fiend. . . .

Every quarter hour the *pendule* gave out its melodious chimes. Finally I hear them speaking soberly, earnestly, as if it were a matter of grave concern. It is about language. Moricand says but little now. He is all ears. With all his knowledge, I suspect that he never dreamed that on this North American continent there once were spoken so many varieties of tongues, languages, not dialects merely, languages great and small, obscure and rudimentary, some extremely complicated, baroque, one might say, in form and structure. How could he know—few Americans know—that side by side there existed tribes whose languages were as far apart as is Bantu from Sanskrit, or Finnish from Phoenician, or Basque from German. The idea had never entered his head, cosmopolite that he was, that in a remote corner of the globe known as Big Sur a man named Jaime de Angulo, a renegade and a reprobate, was spending his days and nights comparing, classifying, analyzing, dissecting roots, declensions, prefixes and suffixes, etymologies, homologies, affinities and anomalies of tongues and dialects borrowed from all continents, all times, all races and conditions of man. Never had he thought it possible to combine in one person, as did this Angulo, the savage, the scholar, the man of the world, the recluse, the idealist and the very son of Lucifer. Well might he say, as he did later: *"C'est un être formidable. C'est un homme, celui-là!"*

Yes, he was indeed that, *a man,* dear Jaime de Angulo! A beloved, hated, detested, endearing, charming, cantankerous, pesky, devil-worshiping son-of-a-bitch of a man with a proud heart and a defiant soul, filled with tenderness and compassion for all humanity, yet cruel, vicious, mean and ornery. His own worst enemy. A man doomed to end his days in horrible agony—mutilated, emasculated, humiliated to the very core of his being. Yet even unto the end preserving his reason, his lucidity, his devil-may-care spirit, his defiance of God and man—and his great impersonal ego.

Would they ever have become bosom friends? I doubt it. Fortunate it was that Moricand never carried out his resolution to walk to the top of the mountain and offer a hand in friendship. Despite all they had in common they were worlds apart. Not even the Devil himself could have united them in friendship and brotherhood.

Reviewing their encounter that afternoon in my mind's eye, I see them as two egomaniacs hypnotized for a few brief hours by the mingling of worlds which overshadowed their personalities, their interests, their philosophies of life.

There are conjunctions in the human sphere which are just as fleeting and mysterious as stellar ones, conjunctions which seem like violation of natural law. For me who observed the event, it was like witnessing the marriage of fire and water.

Now that they have both passed beyond, one may be pardoned

for wondering if they will ever meet again, and in what realm. They had so much to undo, so much to discover, so much to live out! Such lonely souls, full of pride, full of knowledge, full of the world and its evils! Not a grain of faith in either of them. Hugging the world and reviling it; clinging to life and desecrating it; fleeing society and never coming face to face with God; playing the mage and the shaman, but never acquiring wisdom of life or the wisdom of love. In what realm, I ask myself, will they meet again? And will they recognize one another?

One bright day as I was passing Moricand's cell—I had just dumped some garbage over the cliff—I found him leaning over the lower half of the Dutch door as if in contemplation. I was in an excellent mood because, as always when dumping the garbage, I had been rewarded by a breath-taking view of the coast. This particular morning everything was bright and still; the sky, the water, the mountains stared back at me as if reflected in a mirror. If the earth weren't curved I could have gazed right into China, the atmosphere was that clean and clear.

"*Il fait beau aujourd'hui,*" said I, depositing the garbage can to light a cigarette.

"*Oui, il fait beau,*" said he. "Come in a minute, won't you?"

I stepped in and took a seat beside his writing table. What now? I wondered. Another consultation?

He lit a cigarette slowly, as if debating how to begin. Had I been given ten thousand guesses, I could never have guessed what he was about to say. However, I was, as I say, in a most excellent mood; it mattered little to me what was disturbing him. My own mind was free, clear, empty.

"*Mon cher Miller,*" he began in an even, steady tone, "what you are doing to me no man has a right to do to another."

I looked at him uncomprehendingly. "What I am doing to *you*. . . ?"

"Yes," he said. "You don't realize perhaps what you've done."

I made no reply. I was too curious to know what would follow to feel even the least indignation.

"You invited me to come here, to make this my home for the rest of my days. . . . You said I did not need to work, that I could do anything I pleased. And you demanded nothing in return. One can't do that to a fellow-man. It's unjust. It puts me in an unbearable position." It was undermining, he wanted to say.

He paused a moment. I was too flabbergasted to make reply immediately.

"Besides," he continued, "this is no place for me. I am a man of the city; I miss the pavement under my feet. If there were only a café I could walk to, or a library, or a cinema. I'm a prisoner here." He looked around him. "This is where I spend my days— and nights. Alone. No one to talk to. Not even you. You're too busy most of the time. Moreover, I feel that you're uninterested in what I am doing. . . . What am I to do, sit here until I die? You know I am not a man to complain. I keep to myself as much as I can; I occupy myself with my work, I take a walk now and then, I read . . . and I scratch myself continually. How long can I put up with it? Some days I feel as if I will go mad. I don't belong. . . ."

"I think I understand you," said I. "It's too bad it worked out this way. I meant only to do you a good turn."

"*Oui, je le sais, mon vieux!* It's all my fault. Nevertheless. . . ."

"What would you have me do? Send you back to Paris? That's impossible—at least right now."

"I know that," he said.

What he didn't know was that I was still struggling to pay back what I had borrowed to bring him to America.

"I was just wondering," he said, drumming his fingers on the table top, "how a city like San Francisco might be."

"Very good for a while," I said, "but how manage it? There's nothing you could work at, and I certainly couldn't support you there."

"Of course not," he said, "I wouldn't think of it. My God, you've done plenty already. More than enough. I shall never be able to repay you."

"Let's not go into *that!* The point is that you're unhappy here. Nobody is to blame. How could either of us have foreseen such an issue? I'm glad you spoke your mind. Perhaps if we put our heads together we can find a solution. It's true that I haven't given you or your work much attention, but you see what my life is like. You know how little time I have for my own work. You know, I too would like to walk the streets of Paris once in a while, feel the pavement under my feet, as you say. I too would like to be able to go to a café when I feel like it and meet a few congenial spirits. Of course, I'm in a different position from you. I'm not miserable here. Never. No matter what happens. If I had plenty of money I would get up and travel, I would invite my old friends to come and stay with me. . . . "I'd do all sorts of things I don't even dream of now. But one thing is certain in my mind—that this is a paradise. If anything goes wrong, I most certainly will not attribute it to the place. . . . It's a beautiful day today, no? It will be beautiful tomorrow when it pours. It's beautiful too when the fog settles down over everything and blacks us out. It was beautiful to *you* when you first saw it. It will be beautiful when you have gone. . . . Do you know what's wrong? (I tapped my skull.) *This up here!* A day like today I realize what I've told you a hundred different times—that there's nothing wrong with the world. What's wrong is our way of looking at it."

He gave me a wan smile, as if to say, "Just like Miller to go off on such a tangent. I say I'm suffering and he says everything is perfect."

"I know what you're thinking," I said. "Believe me, I feel for you. But you must try to do something for yourself. I did the best I could; if I made a mistake, then you must help me. Legally I'm responsible for you; morally you are responsible only to yourself. Nobody can help you but yourself. You think that I am indifferent to your suffering. You think I treat the itch too lightly. I don't. All I say is, find out what itches you. You can scratch and scratch, but unless you discover what's itching you you will never get relief."

"*C'est assez vrai,*" he said. "I've reached bottom."

He hung his head a few moments, then looked up. An idea had flashed through his mind.

"Yes," he said, "I am that desperate that I am willing to try anything."

I was wondering what exactly that might mean when he promptly added: "This woman, Madame Wharton, what do you think of her?"

I smiled. It was a rather big question.

"I mean, does she really have healing powers?"

"Yes, she does," said I.

"Do you think she could help *me?*"

"That depends," I replied. "Depends greatly on you, on whether you want to be helped or not. You could cure yourself, I believe, if you had enough faith in yourself."

He ignored this last. Began pumping me about her views, her methods of operation, her background, and so on.

"I could tell you a great deal about her," I said. "I could talk to you all day, in fact. But what would it matter? If you wish to put yourself in someone else's hands, you must surrender completely. What she believes in is one thing; what she can do for you is another. If I were in your boots, if I were as desperate as you pretend to be, I wouldn't care how the trick was accomplished. All I would care about would be to get well."

He swallowed this as best he could, remarking that Moricand was not Miller and vice versa. He added that he believed her to be highly intelligent, though he confessed he could not always follow her thoughts. There was something of the mystic or the occult about her, he suspected.

"You're wrong there," I said. "She has no use for mysticism *or* occultism. If she believes in magic, it's everyday magic . . . such as Jesus practiced."

"I hope she doesn't want to convert me first," he sighed. "I have no patience with that humbug, you know."

"Maybe that's what you need," I said laughingly.

"Non! Seriously," he said, "do you think I could put myself in her hands? My God, even if it's Christianity she's going to spout, I'm willing to listen. I'll try *anything.* Anything to get rid of this horrible, horrible itch. I'll *pray,* if she wants me to."

"I don't think she'll ask you to do anything you don't want to do, my dear Moricand. She's not the sort to force her opinions on you. But I do think this. . . . If you listen to her seriously, if you believe that she can do something for you, you may find that you will think and act in different fashion than you now believe possible. Anyway, don't think one way and act another—not with *her!* She'll see through you immediately. And, after all, you wouldn't be fooling *her,* only yourself."

"Then she does have definite views . . . *religious* views, I mean?"

"Of course! That is, if you want to put it that way."

"What do you mean by that?" He looked slightly alarmed.

"I mean, old chap, that she has no religious views whatever. She's religious through and through. She acts out her views or beliefs. She doesn't think *about,* she thinks. She thinks things through—and acts them out. What she thinks about life, God, and all that, is very simple, so simple that you may not understand it at first. She's not a thinker, in *your* sense of the word. To her, Mind is all. What one thinks, one is. If there's something wrong with you, it's because your thinking is wrong. Does that make sense?"

"C'est bien simple," he said, nodding his head dolorously. (Too simple! is what he meant.) Obviously he would have been more excited had I made it sound intricate, abstruse, difficult to follow. Anything simple and direct was suspect to him. Besides, in his mind healing powers were magical powers, powers acquired through study, discipline, training, powers based on mastery over

secret processes. Furthest from his mind was the thought that anyone could enter into direct communication with the source of all
power.

"There's a force in her," he said, "a vitality which is physical and
which I know can be communicated. She may not know from
where it derives, but she possesses it and radiates it. Some times
ignorant people have these powers."

"She's not ignorant, I can tell you that!" I said. "And if it *is*
a physical force you feel in her presence you will never capture
it for yourself, unless. . . ."

"Unless what?" he exclaimed eagerly.

"I won't say now. I think we've talked enough about her. After
all, no matter what I tell you, the result depends on *you,* not her.
Nobody has ever been cured of anything who did not want to be
cured. The converse is just as true, only it's more difficult to swallow. It's always easier to take a negative view than a positive one.
Anyway, whether the itch stops or not, it will be an interesting
experiment for you. But think about it before you ask her aid. And
you must ask her yourself, *compris?*"

"Don't worry," he replied. "I'll ask her. I'll ask her today, if
I see her. I don't care what she orders me to do. I'll get down on
my knees and pray, if that's what she wants. Anything! I'm at
my wit's end."

"Good!" said I. *"On verra."*

It was too wonderful a morning to surrender myself to the machine. I took myself to the forest, alone, and when I had come to
the usual halting place beside the pool, I sat down on a log, put
my head in my hands and began to laugh. I laughed at myself,
then at him, then at fate, then at the wild waves going up and
down, because my head was full of nothing but wild waves going
up and down. All in all, it was a lucky break. Fortunately, we
were not married to one another; there were no children, no compli-
cations. Even if he wanted to return to Paris, I believed I could
manage it somehow. That is, with a little cooperation on his part.

But what a lesson he had given me! Never, never again, would

I make the mistake of trying to solve someone's problems for him. How deceptive to think that by means of a little self-sacrifice one can help another overcome his difficulties! How egotistical! And how right he was to say that I had undermined him! Right and yet wrong! Because, making a reproach like that, he should have followed it up with—"I'm leaving. Leaving tomorrow. And this time I won't even take a toothbrush with me. I'll strike out on my own, come what may. The worst that can happen to me is to be deported. Even if they ship me back to Hell it's better than being a burden to someone. At least, I'll be able to scratch myself in peace!"

At this point I thought of a strange thing—that I too was suffering from the itch, only it was an itch one couldn't get at, an itch that didn't manifest itself bodily. But it was there just the same . . . there where every itch begins and ends. The unfortunate part about my ailment was that nobody ever caught me scratching. Yet I was at it night and day, feverishly, frantically, without let. Like Paul, I was constantly saying to myself: "Who shall deliver me from the body of this death?" What irony that people should be writing me from all over the world, thanking me for the encouragement and inspiration my work had given them. No doubt they looked upon me as an emancipated being. Yet every day of my life I was fighting a corpse, a ghost, a cancer that had taken possession of my mind and that ravaged me more than any bodily affliction possibly could. Every day I had to meet and battle anew with the person I had chosen as a mate, chosen as one who would appreciate "the good life" and share it with me. And from the very beginning it had been nothing but hell—hell and torment. To make it worse, the neighbors regarded her as a model creature—so spry, so lively, so generous, so warm. Such a good little mother, such an excellent housewife, such a perfect hostess! It's not easy to live with a man thirty years older, a writer to boot, and especially a writer like Henry Miller. Everyone knew that. Everyone could see that she was doing her utmost. She had courage, that girl!

And hadn't I made a failure of it before? Several times, in fact?

Could any woman on earth possibly get along with a man like me? That's how most of our arguments ended, on that note. What to answer? There was no answer. Convicted, sentenced, condemned to rehearse the situation over and over, until one or the other should fall apart, dissolve like a rotting corpse.

Not a day of peace, not a day of happiness, unless on my own. The moment she opened her mouth—*war!*

It sounds so simple: break it up! get a divorce! separate! But what about the child? Where would I stand, in court, claiming the right to keep my daughter? *"You?* A man with *your* reputation?" I could just see the judge foaming at the mouth.

Even to do away with myself would not remedy matters. We had to go on. We had to fight it out. No, that's not the word. Iron things out. (With what? A flatiron?) *Compromise!* That's better. It's not either! Then surrender! Admit you're licked. Let her walk over you. Pretend you don't feel, don't hear, don't see. Pretend you're dead.

Or—get yourself to believe that all is good, all is God, that there is nothing but good, nothing but God who is all goodness, all light, all love. *Get yourself to believe.* . . . Impossible! One has to just believe. *Punkt!* Nor is that enough. You have to *know.* More than that. . . . You have to *know* that you know.

And what if, despite everything, you find her standing before you, mocking, jeering, deriding, denigrating, sneering, lying, falsifying, distorting, belittling, calling black white, smiling disdainfully, hissing like a snake, nagging, backbiting, shooting out quills like a porcupine. . .? What then?

Why, you say it's good, it's God manifesting, it's love appearing —only in reverse.

And then?

You look *through* the negative . . . until you see the positive.

Try it sometime—as a morning exercise. Preferably after standing on your head for five minutes. If it doesn't work, get down on your knees and pray.

It *will* work, it's got to work!

That's where you're wrong. If you think it's got to, it won't.

But it must, eventually. Otherwise you'll scratch yourself to death.

What is it my friend Alan Watts says? "When it is clear beyond all doubt that the itch cannot be scratched, it stops itching by itself."

On the way home I stopped at the edge of the clearing, where the huge abandoned horse trough stood, to see if the pots and pans were in order. Tomorrow, the weather permitting, little Val would fix me another make-believe breakfast. And I would probably give her a few make-believe suggestions for improving the bacon and eggs, or the oatmeal, or whatever she might decide to serve me.

Make believe. . . . Make believe you're happy. Make believe you're free. Make believe you're God. Make believe it's all Mind.

I thought of Moricand. "I'll get down on my knees and pray, if that's what she wants." How idiotic! He might equally well have said: "I'll dance, I'll sing, I'll whistle, I'll stand on my head . . . if that's what she wants." *She* wants. As if she wanted anything but his welfare.

I got to thinking of the Zen masters, one old dog in particular. The one who said, "It's your mind that's troubling you, is it? Well then, bring it out, put it down here, let's have a look at it!" Or words to that effect.

I wondered how long the poor devil would continue scratching himself if every time he dug his nails into his flesh one of those gay old dogs would appear out of the ether and give him thirty-nine blows with a stout cudgel.

And yet you know that when you get home she'll be facing you and you'll lose your temper!

Scratch that!

She need only say: "I thought you were in your studio working."

And you'll say: "Must I work all the time? Can't I take a walk once in a while?"

And like that, the fur will fly, and you won't be able to see through the negative. . . . You'll see red, then black, then green, then purple.

Such a beautiful day! Did *you* make it? Did *she* make it?

Fuck who made it! Let's go down and see what she wants to fight about. God made it, that's who.

So I go down, bristling like a porcupine.

Fortunately, Jean Wharton's there. Moricand's already been to see her. And she's given her consent.

How different the atmosphere is when Jean's around! As if the sun were pouring through all the windows with intensified light and warmth and love. At once I feel normal. Like my real self. One couldn't possibly bicker and wrangle with a person like Jean Wharton. At least, *I* couldn't. I take a look at my wife. Does she look any different? To be honest, she does. For one thing, there's no fight in her now. She too looks normal. Like any other human being, I'd say.

I won't go so far as to say that I can see God in her. No.

Anyway, there's a lull.

"So you're going to take him on?" I say.

"Yes," says Jean, "he seems to be desperately in earnest. Of course, it won't be easy."

I was going to say, "What language will you talk?" but the question answered itself. God's language, of course!

With anyone else it was bound to work. With Moricand. . . ?

God can talk to a stone wall and make it respond. But the human mind can be thicker, harder to penetrate, than even a wall of steel. What is it the Hindus say? "If God wished to hide, He would choose man to hide in."

That evening, as I was going up the garden steps to have a last look around, I met Jean sailing through the gate. She had a lantern in one hand and what seemed like a book in the other. She seemed to be floating through the air. Her feet were on the ground all right, but her body had no weight. She looked more beautiful, more radiant, than I had ever seen her before. Truly an emissary of light and love, of peace and serenity. In the few years since I first met her, at the Big Sur Post Office, she had gone through a definite transformation. Whatever she believed in, whatever it was that she was practicing, it had altered her physically as well as mentally and spiritually. Had I been Moricand, at that moment, I would have been made whole instantly.

But it didn't work out that way. It didn't work at all, as a matter of fact. A fiasco from start to finish.

It was the next morning that I got a full report from Moricand. He was not only incensed, he was outraged. "Such nonsense!" he cried. "Am I a child, a fool, an idiot, that I should be treated thus?"

I let him rave. After he had calmed down I got the details, at least the important one to his way of thinking. The fly in the ointment, what was it but *Science and Health!* He had done his best, he said, to follow Jean Wharton's talk—apparently he had understood almost nothing. The talk was difficult enough to swallow but then, in taking leave, she had thrust this Mary Baker Eddy book under his nose, urging him to read a few passages and dwell on them. She had indicated the passages she thought best to concentrate on. To Moricand, of course, the *Key to the Scriptures* had about as much value as a child's primer. Less, indeed. He had spent his whole life denying, ridiculing, suppressing this kind of "nonsense." What he had expected of Jean Wharton was a laying on of hands, a magical rapport which would aid him in exorcising the demon that made him scratch night and day. The last thing on earth he wanted was a spiritual interpretation of the art of healing. Or shall I say what is nearer the truth—that he did not want to be told he could heal himself, that indeed he *must* heal himself!

When I met Jean, a little later, and related what he had told me, she explained that she had left the book with him, not with any intention of converting him to Christian Science, but simply to make him forget himself for a while. She had understood him, his French, clearly enough and she had been prepared to wrestle with him anew the next night and for as many nights as might be necessary. She confessed that perhaps it had been a mistake to give him Mary Baker Eddy to read. However, as she well said, had he been sincere, had he been willing to surrender just the least bit, he would not have been so outraged by the book. A man who is desperate can find comfort in anything, sometimes even in that which goes against the grain.

The discussion about the book incited me to have a look at it myself. I had read quite a little about Mary Baker Eddy but I had never, strangely enough, gone to the book itself. I discovered immediately that I was in for a pleasant surprise. Mary Baker Eddy became very real to me. My critical opinion of her fell away. I saw her as the great soul she was, human, yes, human to the core, but filled with a great light, transformed by a revelation such as might occur to any of us were we big enough and open enough to receive it.

As for Moricand, it was as if we had removed the last stepping stone from under his feet. He was depressed as never before. Absolutely despondent, wretched, miserable. Every night he wailed like a banshee. Instead of an *apéritif* before dinner he would treat us to an exhibition of his sores. "It's inhuman," he would say. "You've got to *do* something!" Then, with a sigh, "If only I could take a warm bath!"

We had no bath tub. We had no miracle drugs. We had nothing but words, empty words. At any rate, by now he was just a flaming wretch who had delivered himself to the mercy of the Devil.

Only one evening before the final breakdown stands out clearly. I remember it well because earlier that evening, while we were still eating, he had expressed his irritation with Val, who was sitting beside him, in a way I can never forget. Bored with the conversation, she had begun to play with the knives and forks, rattle the dishes, anything to gain attention. Suddenly, in a playful way, she had snatched the piece of bread lying beside him. Furious, he snatched it from her fist and placed it on the other side of his plate. It was not the gesture of annoyance so much as the look in his eyes which startled me. It was a look full of hatred, the look of a man so beside himself that he might even commit murder. I never forgot it and I never forgave it.

It was a hour or two later, after the child had been put to bed, that he launched into a lengthy tale which I shall recapitulate briefly. What provoked it I no longer remember. But it was about a child, a girl of eight or nine. The telling of it seemed to take up the entire evening.

As often happened, when beginning a yarn, he shrouded the opening in irrelevant wrappings. It was not until (following him down the *grands boulevards*) he made mention of the Passage Jouffroy that I was aware that he was spinning a tale. The Passage Jouffroy happens to be one of those arcades which are freighted with souvenirs for me. Many thing had happened to me, in years gone by, while strolling through that well-known landmark. I mean inner happenings, events one never thinks to write about because too fleeting, too impalpable, too close to the source.

And now here is Moricand suddenly shocking me into awareness of the fact that he is following on the heels of a woman and her daughter. They have just turned into the Passage Jouffroy, window shopping, seemingly. *When* he began following them, *why, how long,* has lost importance. It's the sudden inner excitement which his looks and gestures betray that takes hold of me, rivets my attention.

I thought at first it was the mother he was interested in. He had described her swiftly, deftly, much as a painter would. Described her as only Moricand could describe a woman of that type. In a few words he had stripped her of her nondescript garb, her pseudo-maternal air, her pretense of strolling the boulevards with her in-nocent little lamb. He had recognized her for what she was the moment she had turned into the Passage Jouffroy, that moment when she had hesitated just the fraction of a second, as if she were about to look back, but didn't. He knew then that *she* knew he was following.

It was almost painful to hear him rhapsodize about the little girl. What was it about her that so excited him? *The look of the perverted angel!*

His words were so graphic, so diabolically searching, that despite myself, I was ready to believe that the child was steeped in vice. *Or else so innocent that. . . .*

The thought of what was passing through his mind made me shudder.

What followed was mere routine. *He* took a stand before a window display of manikins dressed in latest sports models while a few feet away the woman and child dallied to gaze upon a virginal figure garbed in a beautiful Communion dress. Observing that the child was rapt in wonder, he threw the woman a quick glance and nodded meaningfully toward her charge. The woman responded with the barest perceptible sway of her head, lowered her eyes a moment, then, looking straight at him, through him, grasped the child's hand and led her away. He permitted them to get a respectable distance ahead, then followed in their wake. Near the exit the woman stopped a moment to buy some sweets. She made no further sign, except to turn her bowed head in the direction of his feet; she then resumed what was to all appearances an innocent promenade. Once or twice the little girl made as if to turn around, as would any child whose attention had been caught by the flutter of pigeon wings or the gleam of glass beads.

There was no increase in their pace. The mother and daughter sauntered along as if taking the air, enjoying the sights. Leisurely they turned down one street and up another. Gradually they approached the neighborhood of the Folies-Bergère. Finally they came to a hotel, a hotel with a rather flamboyant name. (I mention it because I recognized the name; I had spent a week in this hotel once, in bed most of the time. During that week, flat on my back, I had read Céline's *Voyage au bout de la nuit.*)

Even as they entered the woman made no visible effort to see if he were following. She had no need to look: it had all been worked out telepathically in the Passage Jouffroy.

He waited outside a few moments to collect himself, then, though his guts were still quivering, he walked calmly up to the desk and booked a room. As he filled out the *fiche* the woman laid her key down a moment to stuff something in her purse. He didn't even have to turn his head to catch the number. He gave the *garçon* a liberal tip and, since he had no bags, told him it was unnecessary to show him the way. By the time he reached the top of the first flight of stairs his heart was in his mouth. He bounded up the next flight, turned quickly down the passage towards the room he was looking for, and came face to face with the woman. Though there was not a soul about, neither paused an instant. They brushed by each other like two strangers, she as if going to the lavatory, he as if to his room. Only the look in her eyes, the drooping, sidewise glance, conveyed the message he knew was forthcoming: *"Elle est là!"* He walked swiftly to the door, removed the key which had been left outside, and pushed his way in.

Here he paused in his narration. His eyes were positively dancing. I knew he was waiting for me to say "Then what?" I struggled with myself not to reveal my true feelings. The words he was waiting for got stuck in my throat. All I could think of was the little girl sitting on the edge of the bed, half-undressed probably, and nibbling at a piece of pastry. *"Reste-là, p'tite, je reviens toute de suite,"* the woman had probably said as she closed the door behind her.

Finally, after what seemed like an eternity, I heard myself saying to him: *"Eh bien,* what then?"

"What then?" he exclaimed, his eyes aflame with a ghoulish glee. *"Je l'ai eue,* that's what!"

As he uttered these words I felt my hair stand on end. It was no longer Moricand I was facing but Satan himself.

The rains continued to descend, the leaks grew worse, the walls got wetter and wetter, the sow bugs increased and multiplied. The horizon was now completely shut out; the wind had become a howling fury. Back of the two studios stood three tall eucalyptus trees; under the lash of the gale they seemed to bend in two. In Moricand's shattered state they were three demons with a thousand arms beating a terrifying tattoo upon his brainpan. Wherever he looked, indeed, there was nothing but a wall of water, a forest of swaying, swirling, twisting tree trunks. And with it, what disturbed him more than anything, the whine and moan of the wind, the whistling, crackling, hissing sound which never abated. To anyone in his right senses it was grand, magnificent, absolutely intoxicating. One felt deliciously helpless, insignificant, even less than a rubber doll. To venture outdoors at the height of it was to be slapped down. There was something insane about it. All you could do was to wait it out. It must die of its own fury.

But Moricand could not wait it out. He was at the breaking point. He came down one afternoon—it was already dark—saying that he couldn't stand it another minute. "It's a howling inferno!" he cried. "Nowhere in the world can it possibly rain like this. *C'est fou!*"

At dinner, rehearsing his miseries, he suddenly burst into tears. He begged me—supplicated, rather—to do something to relieve him of his torment. He pleaded and entreated as if I were made of stone. It was sheer torture to listen to the man.

"What *can* I do? said I. "What is it you think I *should* do?"

"Take me to Monterey. Put me in a hospital. I *must* get out of this place."

"Very well," I said. "I'll do that. I'll move you just as soon as we can get off this hill."

What did that mean? he wanted to know. A feeble look of terror spread over his countenance.

I explained that not only was my car not working but that the road leading to the highway was blocked with boulders; the storm would have to abate before we could even think about moving.

This only increased his desperation. *"Think, think!"* he begged. "There must be some way to get out of here. Do you want me to go stark mad?"

The only thing left to do was to walk down the road to the highway next morning and leave a note in the mailbox for the mail man to deliver to Lilik. The mail was still getting through. All day long and into the night the highway crew kept clearing the road of debris. I knew that Lilik would get to us if it were humanly possible. As for the boulders that blocked the foot of the road, I would just pray that some Titan would push them aside.

So I got down, dispatched the message, making it life and death, and told Moricand to be in readiness. I had told Lilik to come the next morning, at six o'clock, or perhaps I said five-thirty. I figured that by that time the storm would have moderated and some of the boulders been cleared away.

That night, his last night, Moricand refused to go back to his cell. He decided to sit up all night in the armchair. We kept him at table as long as we could, plied him with drink, regaled him as best we could, and finally, towards morning, bade him goodnight. There was just the one room, and our bed was in the middle of it. We climbed in and tried to go to sleep. A tiny lamp flickered on the table beside him as he sat in the big armchair, bundled up in overcoat and muffler, his hat pulled down over his eyes. The fire went out, and though not a window was open, the room soon grew damp and chill. The wind was still whistling around the corners of the house, but it seemed to me that the rain was letting up.

Naturally, I couldn't sleep. I lay there as quiet as I could and listened to him mumbling to himself. Every now and then he groaned and broke out with a *"Mon Dieu, mon Dieu!* when will it end?"* Or—*"Quel supplice!"*

About 5:00 A.M. I climbed out of bed, lit the Aladdin lamps, put some coffee on the stove, and dressed. It was still dark, but the storm had broken. There was just a normal high wind which was sweeping away the rain.

When I asked him how he felt, he groaned. Never had he

known such a night. He was finished. He hoped he would have the strength to last till we reached the hospital.

As we were swallowing the hot coffee, he got a whiff of the bacon and eggs. That gave him a momentary lift. *"J'adore ça,"* he said, rubbing his hands. Then a sudden panic seized him. "How do we know he will come, Lilik?"

"He'll come, never fear," I said. "He would wade through Hell to rescue you."

"Oui, c'est un chic type. Un vrai ami."

By this time my wife had dressed, set the table, lit the stove, served the bacon and eggs.

"Everything will be fine," she said. "You'll see, Lilik will be here in a few minutes." She spoke to him as if he were a child. (Don't worry, dear, mamma's here, nothing can happen to you.)

Seized with a sense of the dramatic, I suddenly decided to light the lantern and go to the top of the road above us to signal Lilik. As I climbed the hill I heard his car snorting down below, probably at the bend near the Roosevelt's. I waved the lantern to and fro and, now thoroughly elated, gave a great shout. He must have seen the light, for immediately there came the honk-honk of his horn, and in a few moments the car came into sight, puffing and snorting like a wounded dragon.

"Christ!" I shouted, "What luck! You made it! *Grand!*" I gave him a warm hug.

"I had a bad time of it down below," he said. "I don't know how I ever cleared those rocks away. Luckily, I brought a crowbar with me. . . . How's Moricand? Is he awake yet?"

"Is he awake? Man, he's never been to sleep. Come on down and have a cup of coffee. Have you had breakfast?"

He hadn't. Not even a cup of coffee.

We walked in, and there was Moricand licking his chops. He seemed quite revived. As he greeted Lilik, tears came to his eyes. *"C'est la fin,"* he said. "But how good of you to come! You're a saint."

When it came time to go Moricand rose to his feet, tottered, staggered to the bed and collapsed.

"What's up?" cried Lilik. "You're not going to give out now, are you?"

Moricand looked up woefully. "I can't walk," he said. "Look!" And he pointed to the swelling between his legs.

"What's that?" we cried in unison.

"My testicles!" he exclaimed. "They've swollen up on me."

They had indeed. They were like two rocks.

"We'll carry you to the car," said Lilik.

"I'm too heavy," said Moricand.

"Nonsense!" said Lilik.

Moricand put his arms around our shoulders, and Lilik and I joined hands under his legs. He weighed a ton. Slowly, gently, we hoisted him up the garden steps and into the car. He groaned like a bull in agony.

"Easy, easy now. It will pass. Just hold your breath, grit your teeth. *Du courage, mon vieux!*"

As we cautiously picked our way down the winding hill, observing the havoc the storm had wrought, Moricand's eyes opened wider and wider. Finally we came to the last stretch, a rather steep descent. Huge boulders towered above menacingly. When we reached the highway I saw what Lilik had done. It didn't seem possible for human hands to have accomplished such a task.

Dawn had come, the rain had stopped altogether, and we were on our way. Every few yards we had to stop and clear the road of debris. This continued until we reached the sign which said: "Watch for falling rocks. Dangerous curves and falling rocks for the next 46 miles." But that was all behind us now.

My thoughts reverted to Moricand's promenade between the battlefronts. The two valises. And Iamblichus! By comparison, all that seemed unreal, a nightmare that he had dreamed up.

"How do your balls feel now?" I asked.

He felt them. Somewhat better, he thought.

"Good," said Lilik. "It's just nervousness."

I restrained a laugh. "Nervousness!" What a word to describe Moricand's anguish!

When we got to Monterey we stopped to fetch him a cup of coffee. The sun was out strong, the roof-tops glistened; life was pursuing its normal course again. Only a few more miles, we told him, and you'll be there. Meaning at the County Hospital in Salinas.

He felt his testicles again. The swelling had almost disappeared. "What did we tell you!"

"*Ouais!*" said Moricand. "*Mais, c'est drôle.* How do you explain it?"

"Nervousness," said Lilik.

"*Angoisse!*" said I.

We rolled up in front of the hospital. It didn't look as bad as I had imagined it would. From the outside, in fact, it seemed rather cheerful. Just the same, I was glad it wasn't my turn.

We went inside. It was still rather early. The usual routine: questions, explanations, papers to fill out. Then wait. No matter if you're dying, they always ask you to wait.

We waited a while, then inquired when the doctor would show up. I had thought we would get Moricand a bed immediately, then see the doctor. No, first you see the doctor, then a bed—if there is one vacant!

We decided to have a second breakfast. There was a glassed-in dining room which was connected with the hospital, or so it seemed to me. We had bacon and eggs again. And more coffee. The coffee was vile and weak, but Moricand said it tasted good. He lit a *gauloise bleue*—and smiled. He was probably thinking of the comfortable bed, the attention he would receive, the luxury of relaxing in the midst of ministering angels.

Finally it came time to visit the clinic. It was like all such places, cold, bare, glittering with instruments, smelling of disinfectants. You bring your poor, frail body and you hand it over to be inspected. You are one thing and your body is another. Lucky you if you get it back again.

He's standing there nude, naked as a herring. The doctor is tapping at him, just like a woodpecker. We've explained that it's the itch he's suffering from. No matter. Must see if there's anything else first—phthisis, gallstones, asthma, tonsilitis, cirrhosis of the liver, miner's elbow, dandruff. . . . The doctor's not a bad chap. Affable, courteous, willing to chatter. Speaks French too. Rather pleased on the whole to see a specimen like Moricand for a change.

Moricand too seems rather pleased. At last some real attention. Something indefinable about his expression gives me the impression that he hopes the doctor will find something seriously wrong with him, something more than the itch.

Without a stitch he looks lamentable. Like a broken-down nag. It's not merely that he's potbellied, full of sores and scabs, but that his skin has an unhealthy look, is spotted like tobacco leaf, has no oil, no elasticity, no glow. He looks like one of those derelicts one sees in the washroom of a Mills hotel, like a bum that has just crawled out of a flophouse on the Bowery. His flesh seems never to have been in contact with air and sun; it looks half-smoked.

The physical examination over, and nothing seriously wrong except that he's run-down, anemic, bilious, weak heart, erratic pulse, high blood pressure, spavined and double-jointed, it's now time to investigate the itch.

It's the doctor's opinion that he's suffering from an allergy, perhaps several allergies. Allergies are his specialty. Hence his certitude.

No one demurs, not even Moricand. He's heard of allergies but never attached any importance to them. Neither have I. Neither has Lilik. However, today it's allergies. Tomorrow it will be something else. Allergies then. Go to it!

While assorting and arranging his test tubes, syringes, needles, razor blades and what not, in preparation for the tests, the doctor plies Moricand with questions.

"You've had the drug habit, haven't you?"

Moricand nods.

"I can tell," says the doctor, pointing to Moricand's legs, arms, thighs, where traces of the needle still showed.

"What did you use?"

"Everything," said Moricand. "But that was some years ago."

"Opium too?"

At this Moricand seemed somewhat surprised. "How did you know?" he asked.

"I've treated thousands of cases," said the doctor. He fiddled with something behind Moricand's back. As he wheeled around, he said swiftly: "How did you break it, tell me that!"

"By my own will," said Moricand.

"What's that?" said the doctor. "Say it again!"

Moricand repeated: "By my own will. It was not easy. It almost killed me."

"If that's true," said the doctor, taking his hand, "you're the first man I've known to accomplish it."

Moricand blushed as a man might who was being given a medal for a deed of valor he had never performed.

Meanwhile the doctor had begun the game of ticktacktoe on Moricand's back. He started up near the left shoulder, worked clear across to the right shoulder, then down and across. Each time he finished a game he waited a few minutes. The first game was all in blue ink, the second in pink, the third in green, and so on through the spectrum. Nobody was winning. Since Moricand's back was only human size, and since it was completely covered with welts from neck to waist, there was nothing to do but call it a draw for the day. There were still thirty or forty more tests that could be given. One of them had to turn out positive. At least, that was how the doctor regarded it.

"And now what about a bed?" said Moricand, slipping into his shirt and trousers.

"A *bed?*" said the doctor, looking at him in astonishment.

"Yes," said Moricand. "A place to rest . . . to recuperate."

The doctor laughed as if it were a good joke.

"We don't have beds enough for our serious cases," he said. "There's nothing very wrong with you. Come back day after tomorrow and I'll give you some more tests." He wrote out a prescription for a sedative. "You'll be all right in no time."

I explained that we lived in Big Sur, that it wasn't easy to make frequent trips to Salinas.

"Why don't you put him up in town for a while?" said the doctor. "In a week or so I'll know what's what. There's nothing to worry about. He's been through much worse, I can tell you that. . . . Just a bit dilapidated. Hypersensitive."

Outside we decided to look for a bar. We all needed a drink bad.

"How does your back feel?" said Lilik, raising his hands as if to give him a clap.

Moricand winced. "It feels like a hot grill," he said.

We found a dingy bar and, while putting away a few drinks, discussed the opium habit. An illuminating subject, if one penetrates deeply enough.

In Monterey I engaged a room for him at the Hotel Serra. A room with a private bath. In comparison with the cell he had been living in this was luxury. We tested the bed to see if it was soft and springy enough, switched the lights on and off to see if they were good enough to read and write by, showed him how to manipulate the window blinds, assured him that he would get fresh towels and soap every day, and so on. He was already unpacking the small valise he had brought along. Already the dresser was arranged as he invariably arranged things wherever he might find himself. As he was getting out his manuscripts, his writing tablet, his ink and ruler, I suddenly realized that the table beside the bed would be too small to work on. We called the manager to find if he couldn't supply a bigger one. In a jiffy the bellhop arrived with a table just the right size.

Moricand seemed really overcome with joy. He looked around as if he were in Heaven. The bathroom especially put him in ecstasy. We had explained that he could take a bath as often as he wished—no extra charge, as in France. (This was the good side of America again. "A wonderful country!")

It only remained now to hand him some money and arrange with someone who had a car to drive him back and forth to the hospital. I didn't know, as I said *au revoir,* that it would be the last time I would see him.

He had grown ten years younger in the space of a few minutes. As we shook hands, as I promised to look him up in a few days, he said: "I think I'll go down in a little while to have a *porto.*"

Walking down the street, Lilik and I, we ran into the painter, Ellwood Graham. After a few words we learned that he was making trips to the County Hospital every day. It would be a pleasure he informed us, to drive Moricand back and forth.

We ducked back to the hotel immediately only to find that Moricand had already left, presumably to have his *porto.* We left a note explaining that he would have the use of a car and a private chauffeur.

The feeling of relief I experienced on arriving home was beyond words. It was high time we were rid of him, for my wife was already pregnant several months. Yet she had borne up under the ordeal better than I.

A few days passed but I simply could not bring myself to go to Monterey and look him up. Instead I wrote him a note, making some excuse or other. He wrote back immediately to say that he was feeling better, that the doctor hadn't discovered yet what was wrong with him, but that he was enjoying his most comfortable quarters. A postscript reminded me that the rent would be due in a few days, also that he would need some fresh linen soon.

We exchanged notes for about two weeks or so, during which time I did go to town but without looking him up. Then one day I received word that he had made up his mind to go to San Francisco; he thought he could find something to do there, and, if not, he would make efforts to return to Paris. He added that it was obvious I didn't wish to see him any more.

On receipt of this message I immediately packed the remainder of his belongings, had someone deliver them to him at the hotel, and sent him enough money to last him a couple of weeks at least. That he was putting this much distance between us gave me a still greater feeling of relief. And the fact that he had at last found enough gumption to do something on his own.

I then fumigated his cell, as Leon had recommended.

In writing him I had given him elaborate explanations and instructions. I told him where to look for modest French restaurants, bars, and so forth. I even went to the extent of telling him that if he could not make himself understood he was to write the address down and show it to the cab-driver, the policeman, or whoever it might be. I told him where to find the library, the avant-garde cinemas, the museums and art galleries.

I soon learned that he had found a suitable hotel, but at a much higher rate than I had named; he had also discovered a little bar where he could get his meals and where there were a few congenial French people. His money was going fast, he explained, because wherever he wanted to go he had to take a cab; he wouldn't trust himself to take streetcars and buses, his English was too poor.

To all this I gave a patient ear, thinking that he would soon adjust himself and settle down to a less expensive routine. The business about the cabs nettled me. Paris was a far bigger city than San Francisco and I had managed to find my way about in it with less money in my jeans and less knowledge of French than he had of English. But then I had no one to fall back on. *Ça fait une différence!*

He had, of course, reported to the Swiss Consul and had quickly learned that there was no question of finding employment, not with a visitor's visa. He could, to be sure, take steps to become an American citizen, but he was not interested in becoming an American citizen.

What *was* he going to do, I wondered? Would he request the Swiss Counsul to ship him back to Paris?

Perhaps he had asked the Swiss Consul to ship him home and perhaps they had told him that was *my* responsibility. At any rate, the impression I got was that he was simply drifting with the tide. As long as I could keep him in food, cigarettes, taxi fares, a comfortable room and bath, he was not going to get panicky. San Francisco suited him far better than Big Sur, even though he found it somewhat "provincial." At least there was solid pavement under his feet.

It was after he had been there over a month that the effort to maintain him in his own style became a strain. I had the feeling that the arrangement could continue indefinitely, so far as *he* was concerned. Finally I suggested that if he were seriously of a mind to return to Europe I would see what I could do to get him a passage back. Instead of being elated he replied in gloomy vein that if it came to a pinch, why yes, he would go back. As if he were doing me a great favor to even consider the thought!

It so happened that shortly after this exchange of views my good friend, Raoul Bertrand, came to visit us. He had met Moricand at our home several times and knew what I was up against. When I explained how matters now stood he volunteered to see if he could not secure passage for Moricand on a French freighter plying from San Francisco. A free passage, moreover.

I immediately apprised Moricand of the good news and drew an alluring picture of a long sea voyage through the Panama Canal, with stopovers in Mexico and Central America. I made it sound so enchanting that I began to wish I could change places with him.

What his reply was precisely, I no longer recall, only that he gave a grudging acquiescence. Meanwhile Bertrand had set to work. In less than a week he had found a freighter which offered Moricand passage. It would leave in thirty-six hours—just time enough to send Moricand a wire. In order to circumvent any misinterpretation of the message on the part of the telegraph company, I wrote the message out in English: a fifty-word telegram giving full details.

To my utter astonishment, I got a reply by mail after the boat had sailed, saying that his Highness was not to be rushed that way, that he should have had a few days' warning at least, that it was most inconsiderate of me to send him a message of such importance in a language he didn't understand, and so on and so forth. Extremely hoity-toity, to put it mildly. Besides, as he went on to explain in a postscript, he was not at all certain that he would relish a long sea voyage; he was not a good sailor, he would be bored to death, etc., etc. At the very end—would I please send him some more money!

I was thoroughly incensed. And I let him know it in no uncertain terms. Then I wrote a profuse letter of apology to Raoul Bertrand. Here he was, a French consul, not Swiss, putting himself to all this trouble, and that louse, Moricand, hadn't even the decency to be grateful for his efforts.

Bertrand, however, understood better than I the manner of man we were dealing with. He was not at all perturbed or dismayed. "We'll try again," he said. "You've got to get him off your hands!" He added: "Perhaps next time we'll get him a plane passage. He can hardly refuse that."

And by God, in about ten days he did come up with a plane passage. This time we gave Moricand ample notice.

Once again he agreed, grumblingly, to be sure. Like a rat that had been cornered. But when the time came to depart he was not on hand. He had changed his mind again. What excuse he gave I no longer remember.

By this time a number of my intimate friends had got wind of "the Moricand affair," as they called it. Everywhere I went people would ask—"What's happened to your friend? Did you get rid

of him yet? Has he committed suicide?" A few had the courage
to let me know in plain language that I was nothing but an idiot.
"Cut him loose, Henry, or you'll never get him off your hands!
He'll bleed you dry." That was the general tenor of the advice I
received.

One day Varda came to see me. He was now living in Sausalito
on a ferry boat which he had converted into a houseboat, dance
palace and studio. He was all agog about the Moricand business,
having received all the juicy details from a dozen different sources.
His attitude was one of high amusement and genuine concern.
How could he get in touch with Moricand? He referred to him
as some sort of parasitic monster for whom saints and simpletons
were easy prey.

Regarding me as an utterly helpless victim, he then proposed a
typical Varda solution. He said he knew a wealthy woman in San
Francisco, a Hungarian or Austrian countess, still attractive though
aging, who loved to "collect" bizarre figures such as Moricand.
Astrology, occultism—that was just her meat. She had a huge
mansion, money to burn, and thought nothing of having a guest
remain a year or two. If Moricand were as good a talker as I said
he was, he would be an attraction for her salon. Celebrities from
all over the world converged there, he said. It would be a real
haven for a man like Moricand.

"I'll tell you what I'll do," he went on. "As soon as I get back
to Sausalito I'll ask her to arrange a soiree. I'll see that Moricand
is invited. The man has only to open his mouth and she'll be
hooked."

"Are you sure she won't expect something more of him?" said I.
"An aging countess, and still attractive, as you say, may make
demands Moricand is no longer able to satisfy."

"Don't worry about *that!*" he cried, giving me a knowing look.
"She has only to wave her hand and she can have the pick of San
Francisco's finest young blades. Besides, she has a pair of the

most lecherous-looking lap dogs you ever laid eyes on. No, if she takes him, she'll use him for her salon."

I regarded Varda's proposal as a huge joke. Thought no more of it, indeed. Meantime another letter arrived from Moricand, a letter full of recriminations. Why was I in such haste to pack him off? What had he ever done to deserve such treatment? Was it his fault that he had fallen ill *chez moi*? He reminded me caustically that I was still responsible for his welfare, that I had signed papers to that effect, and that he had these papers in his possession. He even insinuated that if I didn't toe the mark he would inform the proper authorities of the scandal my books had created in France. (As if they didn't know!) He might even tell them worse things about me . . . that I was an anarchist, a traitor, a renegade, and what all.

I was ready to hit the ceiling. "That bastard!" I said. "He's actually beginning to threaten me."

Meanwhile Bertrand was making efforts to get him a second plane passage. And Lilik was getting ready to go to Berkeley on a business errand. He too was going to do something about this damned Moricand business. At least he would see him and try to talk some sense into him.

Then came a letter from Varda. He had arranged a soiree *chez* the Countess, had primed her for the jewel she was to get, found her sympathetic to the idea, and. . . . To make it short, Moricand had come, had taken one look at the Countess, and then had avoided her like sin for the rest of the evening. He had remained silent and glum the whole evening, except to unleash a cutting remark now and then about the vanity and stupidity of wealthy émigrées who exploited their salons to rustle up fresh bait to whet their jaded appetites.

"The bastard!" I said to myself. "Couldn't even take on a millionairess to help a fellow out!"

On the heels of this incident Bertrand came up with another plane passage, this one a good week off. Once again I informed

his Highness that a silver bird of the air was at his disposal. Would
he be so gracious as to give it a trial?

This time the response was clear and definite. All mystery was
ripped away.

I give the gist of his letter. . . . Yes, he would consent to accept
the passage which had been proffered him, but on one condition,
that I first put to his account in a Paris bank the equivalent of a
thousand dollars. It should be easy to understand the reason for
such a request. He had left Europe as a pauper and he had no
intention of returning as one. It was I who had induced him to
come to America, and I had promised to take care of him. It was
not his wish to return to Paris, but mine. I wanted to get rid of
him, renounce my sacred obligation. As for the money I had
spent thus far—he referred to it as if it were a bagatelle—he begged
to remind me that he had left with me as a gift an heirloom, his
one and only material possession, which was priceless. (He meant
the *pendule,* of course.)

I was outraged. I wrote back at once that if he didn't take the
plane this time, if he didn't get the hell out of the country and
leave me in peace, I would cut him off. I said I didn't give a shit
what became of him. He could jump off the Golden Gate Bridge,
for all I cared. In a postscript I informed him that Lilik would be
there to see him in a day or two, *with the pendule,* which he could
shove up his ass, or pawn and live on the proceeds for the rest
of his days.

Now the letters came thick and fast. He was in a panic. Cut
him off? Leave him destitute? Alone in a foreign land? A man
who was ill, who was getting old, who had no right to seek employment? No, I would never do that! Not the Miller he had
known of old, the Miller with a great, compassionate heart who
gave to one and all, who had taken pity on him, a miserable
wretch, and sworn to provide for him as long as he lived!

"Yes," I wrote back, "it is the same Miller. He is fed up. He
is disgusted. He wants nothing more to do with you." I called
him a worm, a leech, a dirty blackmailer.

He turned to my wife. Long, whining letters, full of self-pity. Surely *she* understood his plight! The good Miller had taken leave of his senses, he had made himself into stone. *Le pauvre,* he would regret it some day. And so on and so on.

I urged my wife to ignore his pleas. I doubt that she heeded me. She felt sorry for him. It was her belief that he would come to his senses at the last minute, take the plane, forget his foolish demand. "Foolish!" she called it.

I thought of Ramakrishna's words regarding the "bound" souls. "Those who are thus caught in the net of the world are the *Baddha,* or bound souls. No one can awaken them. They do not come to their senses, even after receiving blow upon blow of misery, sorrow and indescribable suffering."

I thought of many, many things during the hectic days which followed. Particularly of the beggar's life I had led, first at home, then abroad. I thought of the cold refusals I had received at the hands of intimate friends, of so-called "buddies," in fact. I thought of the meals which were dished up to me, when I hung on like a shipwrecked sailor. And the sermons that accompanied them. I thought of the times I had stood in front of restaurant windows, watching people eat—people who didn't need food, who had already eaten too much—and how I vainly hoped they would recognize the look in my eye, invite me in, beg me to share their repast, or offer me the remnants. I thought of the handouts I had received, the dimes that were flung at me in passing, or perhaps a handful of pennies, and how like a whipped cur, I had taken what was offered while cursing the bastards under my breath. No matter how many refusals I received, and they were countless, no matter how many insults and humiliations were flung at me, a crust of bread was always a crust of bread—and if I didn't always thank the giver graciously or humbly, I did thank my lucky star. I may have thought once upon a time that something more than a crust of bread was my due, that the most worthless wretch, at least in a civilized country, was entitled to a meal when he needed it. But it wasn't long before I learned to take a larger view of things. I not only learned how to say "Thank you, sir!" but how to stand on my hind legs and beg for it. It didn't embitter me hopelessly. In fact, I found it rather comical after a while. It's an experience we all need now and then, especially those of us who were born with silver spoons in our mouths.

But that bastard, Moricand! To twist things the way he did! To make it appear, if only to himself, that in promising to take care of him I was obligated to keep him in a hotel, dole out cash for drink, theatre, taxis. And, if that proved irksome, why just deposit a thousand dollars to his account in Paris. Because he, Moricand, refused to be a pauper again!

I'm on the corner of Broadway and 42nd Street again. A chilly night, and the rain beating in my face. Scanning the throng once again for a friendly face, for a fleeting look that will assure me I won't get a rebuff, won't get a gob of spit instead of a handout. Here's a likely one! "Hey, mister, *please,* can you spare enough for a cup of coffee?" He gives it without stopping, without even looking me in the face. A dime! A lovely, shining little offering. A whole dime! How ducky it would be if one could only catch a generous soul like that on the wing, grab his coattail, pull him gently around, and say with utter conviction and the innocence of a dove: *"Mister,* what can I do with this? I haven't eaten since yesterday morning. I'm cold and wet through. My wife's home waiting for me. She's hungry too. And ill. Couldn't you give me a dollar, or maybe two dollars? *Mister,* we need it bad, terribly bad."

No, it's not in the book, that kind of talk. One has to be grateful even for a Canadian dime—or a stale crust of bread. Grateful that when it comes *your* time to be hooked, you can say—and mean it with all your heart!—"Here, take this! Do what you like with it!" And so saying, empty your pockets. So saying, *you* walk home in the rain, *you* go without a meal!

Have I ever done it? Of course I have. Many's the time. And it felt marvelous to do it. Almost too marvelous. It's easy to empty your pockets when you see your other self standing there like a dog, begging, whimpering, cringing. It's easy to go without a meal when you know you can have one for the asking. Or that tomorrow's another day. Nothing to it. It's you, Prince Bountiful, as gets the better of the deal. No wonder we hang our heads in shame when we perform a simple act of charity.

I wonder sometimes why rich guys never understand this business, why they never take the opportunity to give themselves a cheap puffing up? Think of Henry Miller, the uncrowned emperor of California, coming out of the bank each morning with a pocket filled with quarters, handing them out like King Solomon to the poor blokes lined up the sidewalk, each and every one mumbling humbly, "Thank you, sir!" and raising his hat respectfully. What better tonic could you give yourself, if you had a soul as mean as that, before tackling the day's work?

As for that phony bastard, Moricand, in his palmy days he had been quite a giver too, from all I have heard. Nor had he ever refused to share what he had when he had little or nothing. But he had never gone out into the street and begged for it! When he begged it was on good stationery, in elegant script—grammar, syntax, punctuation always perfect. Never had he sat down to pen a begging letter in trousers that had holes in the seat, or even patches. The room may have been ice cold, his belly may have been empty, the butt in his mouth may have been rescued from the waste basket, but. . . . I think it's clear what I'm getting at.

Anyway, he didn't take the second plane either. And when he wrote, saying that he was putting a curse on me, I didn't doubt for a minute that he meant just what he said. To avoid a repetition, I promptly informed his Satanic majesty that any subsequent letters from him would be left unopened. And with that off my chest, I consigned him to his fate. Never again would he see my handwriting, nor the color of my money.

This didn't stop the flow of letters, to be sure. Letters continued to arrive, *toujours plus espaceés,* but they were never opened. They are now in the library at U.C.L.A. Still sealed.

I recall of a sudden the way he worded his break with Cendrars, his old friend of the Foreign Legion days. It was one of those evenings when he had been reviewing the good old days, the wonderful friends he had made—Cendrars, Cocteau, Radiguet, Kisling, Modigliani, Max Jacob, *et alii*—and how one by one they had disappeared, or else deserted him. All but Max. Max had been faithful to the end. But Cendrars, whom he spoke of so warmly, whom he still admired with all his heart—why had Cendrars also deserted him? Here is the way he put it:

"One day—you know how he is!—he got angry with me. And that was the end. I could never reach him again. I tried, but it was useless. The door was shut."

I never revealed to him what Cendrars had said to me one day, in the year 1938, when I made the horrible mistake of telling him that I had become acquainted with his old friend Moricand.

"Moricand?" he said. *"Ce n'est pas un ami. C'est un cadavre vivant."* And the door went shut with a bang.

Well, the *pendule.* I had given it to Lilik to deliver to Moricand. And Lilik had taken it into his head to find out just how valuable the damned thing was. So, before delivering it, he takes it to the very watchmaker whose address Moricand had given me in the event that it should need repair. Its value? According to this bird, who knew something about timepieces, one would be lucky to get fifty dollars for it. An antique dealer might offer a little more. Not much more, however.

"That's ridiculous," I said, when he recounted the incident.

"That's what I thought," said Lilik. "So I took it to an antique dealer, and then to a hock shop. Same story. No market for such junk. They all admired it, of course. Wonderful mechanism. But who wants it?"

"I thought you'd like to know," he added, "since the bugger always made such a fuss about it."

He then went on to tell me of his telephone conversation with Moricand. (Seems the latter was too wrought up to receive him.) It was a conversation that lasted almost a half hour. With Moricand doing all the talking.

"Too bad you weren't there," said Lilik. "He was in top form. I never knew anyone could be so furious, so venomous, and talk so brilliantly at the same time. The things he said about you . . . Jesus, it would burn you up! And the names he called you! You know, after the first few minutes I began to enjoy it. Now and then I helped him along, just to see how far he *would* go. Anyway, be on your guard! He's going to do everything in his power to make trouble for you. I really think he's out of his mind. *Cuckoo*. Absolutely. . . . The last thing I remember him saying was that I would read about you in the French papers. He was formulating a *plaidoyer*. Said he would give them, your admirers, the lowdown on their beloved Henry Miller, author of the *Tropics,* sage of the mountain top . . . *'Quel farceur!'* That was his parting shot."

"Didn't he say—*'Je l'aurai'*?"

"Yeah, that's right. He did too."

"I thought as much. *Le couillon!*"

The first intimation I had of Moricand's maneuvers was a letter from the Swiss Consulate in San Francisco. It was a polite, formal letter, informing me of Moricand's visit to their office, his desperate plight, and ended with a desire to have my view of the matter. I replied at some length, offering to send copies of Moricand's letters, and repeating what I had told Moricand, that I was through and that nothing would make me change my mind. To this I received a reply reminding me that, no matter what had taken place, I was, from an official standpoint, Moricand's sponsor. Would I mind sending the letters I had spoken of?

I sent photostat copies of the letters. Then I waited for the next move.

I could well imagine what must have ensued at this point. One couldn't repudiate what was written in one's own hand.

The next letter was to the effect that Moricand's was indeed a knotty case, that the poor fellow was obviously not all there. It went on to say that the Consulate would be only too glad to ship him back home had they funds for such a purpose. (They never do, of course.) Perhaps if he, the Vice-Consul, were to come down and talk it over with me, some suitable compromise might be arranged. Meanwhile they would look after Moricand as best they could.

Well, he came, and we had a long talk. Fortunately, my wife was there to corroborate my statements. Finally, after a snack, he brought forth a camera and took some snapshots of us and the surroundings. The place enchanted him. He asked if he could come again, as a friend.

"And that idiot couldn't stand it here!" he said, shaking his head. "Why, it's a Paradise."

"Paradise lost!" I countered.

"What will you do with him?" I ventured to ask, as he was leaving. He shrugged his shoulders.

"What *can* one do?" he said, "with a creature like that?"

Thanking me warmly for all I had done in behalf of a compatriot, expressing his regret for any annoyance he had caused me, he then said: "You must be a man of great patience."

I never had another word from him. Nor did I ever learn what happened to Moricand—until I received a copy of *Le Goéland*, the issue for July-August-September, 1954, announcing the news of his death. It was from the editor of *Le Goéland*, Théophile Briant— Moricand's last and only friend—that I recently received a few facts relating to the interval between our leave-taking in Monterey, hardly three months after his arrival in Big Sur, and his pitiful end.

It was in March 1948 when we parted. How he lasted until the fall of 1949, when he was deported by the immigration authorities, remains a mystery. Not even Briant could tell me much about this period. It was a black one, *évidemment*. Toward the end of September he appeared at Briant's home in Brittany, where he had been offered refuge. Here he lasted only six weks. As Briant tactfully put it in his letter, "I perceived all too quickly that a life in common could not be prolonged indefinitely." Thus, the 17th of November his faithful friend drove him to Paris—and installed him in the same old Hotel Modial. Here, though he held out for some time, things went rapidly from bad to worse. Finally, in utter despair, fate decreed that he should accept the last humiliation, that is, apply for admission to a Swiss retreat for the aged on the Avenue de St. Mandé, Paris. It was an institution founded by his own parents. Here he chose a small cell giving on the courtyard, where from his window he could see the plaque commemorating the inauguration of the establishment by his mother and his brother, Dr. Ivan Moricand.

"*Tous ses amis,*" writes Briant, "*sauf moi, l'avaient abandonné. Ses nombreux manuscrits étaient refoulés chez les éditeurs. Et bien entendu, des drames épais surgirent bientôt entre lui et les directrices de l'Asile. Je m'efforçai de le calmer, lui représentant que cette cellule, qu'il avait d'ailleurs merveilleusement aménagée, constituait son ultime havre de grâce.*"

The end came quite suddenly. According to Briant's obituary article in *Le Goéland,* on the morning of the day he died Moricand received a visit from a dear friend, a woman. This was towards noon. As they parted he informed her quite simply that she would never see him again. As he seemed to be in good health and good spirits, and since nothing in their conversation had warranted such a remark, she dismissed it as a *boutade.* That very afternoon, towards four o'clock, he had a heart attack. He went to the kitchen for aid, but despite his grave condition no one saw any reason for alarm. A doctor was called but he was busy. He would come later, when he was free. When he did arrive it was too late. There was nothing to do but rush poor Moricand, already breathing his last, to the hospital. He was unconscious when they delivered him to the Hospital St. Antoine. At ten-thirty that evening he died without regaining consciousness. August 31st, 1954.

In his last moments, writes Briant, he was "*seul comme un rat, nu comme le dernier des clochards.*"

EPILOGUE

Some years ago I came across these words of Milarepa, the Tibetan saint: "It was written; and it had to be. Behold to where it has led."

I often think of these words when the mail arrives. The mail! It is an event which happens three times a week along this coast. It means, to begin with, that the day is shot. You have hardly time to finish your lunch when you hear Jake, the mailman, honking his horn. You scramble up the cliff to the highway, dragging your mailbag, laundry, parcels, books, kerosene tin and anything you wish repaired, replaced or refilled. The mailman and his wife begin to unload from the truck. Everyone clamors for butter, eggs, cigarettes, bread, cake, milk, newspapers, all of which Jake brings together with the mail, express packages, trunks, mattresses, firewood, bags of coal, and other things. It takes a half hour or so to collect your things, during which time the gossip is disseminated free of charge.

Sometimes you have to wait an hour or two for Jake to arrive. Sometimes there is a washout on the road, or his truck breaks down.

On Mondays, Wednesdays and Fridays, rain or shine, you can think of nothing but the arrival of the mail truck.

When it leaves there comes the business of transporting your things back to the house, of sliding down a slippery bank with coal and wood, kerosene, laundry, mailbag, express packages, books, newspapers, food, and supplies from the druggist or the hardware store. This necessitates several trips. If you live on the mountain, instead of by the sea, each trip means an hour lost.

Finally you sit down, and as you sip another cup of coffee and sample a slice of store cake or a doughnut which will be too stale to eat the next day, you slowly open the mail. Soon the floor is

389

littered with envelopes, wrappers, cardboard, string, excelsior, etc. Oftimes I am the last one to read my own mail. By the time I get to it the most exciting communications have already been transmitted to me *viva voce*. I sift through the letters like a man looking for a lost glove in dead coals. A review of one of my books is thrust under my nose. Usually it's an unfavorable one. Some of the letters lie unopened; they are from the bores who persist in writing fat letters even though I never answer them. Someone is now reading the newspaper. There is a shout. "Listen to *this!*" And with one eye on a half-read letter, I listen to some unsavory piece of news dealing with the outside world. Now the packages have been opened and we begin to glance at the books, records, magazines and pamphlets which arrived. Sometimes there is something good in these and you find yourself riveted to the chair for an hour or so. Suddenly you look up and you see it is already five o'clock. You get panic-stricken. "Must get to work," you mumble to yourself. But then there is a knock at the door, and who should be standing there but three or four people whom you don't know, visitors who heard that you were living in this charming region and decided to call on you and see just how you live. You open the wine which some friendly soul from Minnesota or Oregon sent you and you pretend that you are not so busy after all. "Do stay and have dinner," you say, "it will soon be time to eat."

When the visitors have left, when you are thoroughly exhausted with food, wine and talk, you grope for the mail again. It is about time for bed, but you remember that there was one letter you had started to read and which you would like to finish. Then you discover in the pile a telegram which had been mislaid. It demands immediate answer, perhaps by cable, but the mailman has long since returned to town and there is no telephone, no car. You must wait until the mailman comes again—or get up early next morning, stand on the highway to signal a passing car, and beg the driver to stop in Monterey and send the message for you. (Whether he does as you ask or not you won't discover for several weeks.)

Next morning, just as you are sitting down to work, you glance quickly at the mail once again. You see that there are three or four letters which must be answered at once. You begin to answer them. Perhaps you have to dig into a trunk to get out a manuscript or a photo, to look up the reference in a book or pamphlet which is demanded. You have a filing system, of course, but it never works. Just as you are upturning everything in the place a neighbor knocks to ask if you could lend him a hand ... he wants to repair the roof or shift the water line, or put up a new stove. Three hours later you go back to your work table. The mail is still staring you in the face. You push it aside. The fading light warns you to hurry, hurry, hurry.

What can you work on in the hour or so that is left? You tackle this, then that. Nothing goes right. You are all too conscious of the speed with which the light is fading. Soon it will be time to chop wood, break coal, fill the kerosene lamps, hold the baby while it squawks. Perhaps there are no more clean diapers. Then it's a rush to the sulphur baths three miles down the road. Sometimes you get a hitch, sometimes not. To walk six miles with a bucketful of diapers is no joke. Especially if it's raining. Thoroughly done in and hoping to throw yourself on the couch and take a little snooze, what do you find on arriving but an old friend, someone who came a thousand miles or more to see you!

On the way home, despite the hard trudge, despite the rain, ideas had been streaming in on you. You thought you knew just how to go on from where you had left off a few hours ago. You tell yourself over and over to remember it—a word, a phrase, sometimes a whole paragraph. You must hold on to this little item or the thought will fall apart. (You never have pencil and paper with you, of course.) So you keep repeating some idiotic key words over and over as you plod wearily along. At the same time you wonder if there is enough coal and wood to last should the storm continue for several days or weeks. Did you close the win-

dow in the studio where your manuscript was lying? Don't forget
to drop so and so a line. . . .

Of course it is mail day again before you get round to answering
those important letters. Time presses. The mornings are always
short, what with one thing and another. There is no time to write
the letter you intended to write; it will have to be just a scratch,
a postcard perhaps. "More anon . . . in haste as always, your
friend, etc." Again Jake is honking the horn, and again you rush
up for a new batch of agony. Every Monday, Wednesday and
Friday, sure as fate itself.

One can work at night, of course. Certainly. I try that too.
When it is impossible to work any longer in the studio I drag my
papers to the house. I have hardly spread them out, it seems, when
it is time to set the table for dinner. I push the papers aside. We
eat. Then we clear the table, wash the dishes, spread the papers
out again. Strange, but I feel sleepy. I look at the clock. It is only
nine-thirty. In New York, Paris, or any big city, I would be wide
awake and wondering what movie to go to. But at Big Sur I have
only one thought—to hit the hay. I curse myself for being a slacker,
crawl into bed, and try to prepare myself, mentally, to jump out
of bed at the crack of dawn.

Sometimes I do get up with the dawn, by God. Then it's so
beautiful that I must first take a walk. I was never one to start
work first thing in the morning, and never on an empty stomach.

Well, the walk was wonderful. I have a thousand new ideas, all
of them brilliant, extraordinary. I am almost on the trot by the
time I near the house. So many ideas, I don't know what to tackle
first. Shall I go on with the Rimbaud opus or revise the Rattner
script? Or shall I tackle *The Rosy Crucifixion* this morning,
seeing as how the day began so auspiciously? No one is awake
yet. I tiptoe about, get the fire started, make breakfast, and between
times spend long minutes standing over the baby's crib. She looks
just like an angel when asleep. Soon she will be cooing and chirp-
ing and gurgling. I can't rush to work immediately after break-

fast; I want to see her being bathed and dressed, I want to hold her in my arms a while, talk to her in her bird and dog language. After that, just because the day has begun so well, I decide that I won't write after all . . . I'll paint. It's too lovely a day to waste time writing books which will only be condemned. No, I'll do something I really enjoy. I'll make a water color or two.

Now the six-foot table on which all my papers are carefully arranged has to be cleared. I make ready for the carnival, moistening the sheets, cleaning my palette, squeezing out bright new pigments which I have never used before. Then it's on, it's got me, the water-color mania. It may last a few days or a few weeks. Everything else is forgotten meanwhile. I am a painter again. *The only life!* Why in hell was I born a writer? Maybe I'm not a writer any more. But deep down I know that, after I have had my fling, I will go back to the typewriter. I will die sitting at the typewriter, in all probability. I know it. But now and then I allow myself the luxury of thinking that one day I will chuck it all. I will do nothing. *Just live.*

But what does that mean, to just live? To live without creating, to live only in the imagination . . . *is that living?* No, I know it isn't. I am not quite at this stage of renunciation. Too many urges still, too many desires, too great a need of communicating with the world. "But couldn't you slow up?" I ask myself. "Why not take it easy for a while?"

It is at such moments that I think of the unanswered letters, of the many who are clamoring for just a little word—of advice, of appreciation, of encouragement, of criticism, of this, of that. I think first of *their* problem, mind you. And then I think of the unfinished books. And then of the places I would still love to visit: China, India, Java, Burma, Tahiti, Peru, Persia, Afghanistan, Arabia, Tibet, Haiti, the Carolines. But will there be time for all that? I try to figure out how many years may be allotted me. I give it up. Maybe I will live to be a hundred. Maybe now, in my fifties, I am passing through a second youth. When I get to be seventy, perhaps then I will have the time to do all the things I want to do. . . . So it goes.

And then I hear Jake honking his horn! Mail day! It begins all over again. There's no use, I'm licked.

With all this caterwauling I haven't said a word about my friend Emil White who has been trying to lift me out of the rut these last two years. What would I have done without him? Ever since he came to Big Sur he has been giving unstintingly of his time and strength. The loads he carried up and down Partington Ridge, where I lived before, were enough to slay a donkey. Day after day he has gone to the forest, gathered wood for us, chopped it, dragged the coal sacks up the hill, fixed whatever was falling apart or leaking or tottering. And as if all that were not enough, on leaving he would take with him the letters I hadn't found time to answer and he would answer them for me. He has mailed out hundreds of books and water colors for me; he built me a studio out of thin air; he cooked my meals for me when my wife was away; he even bought a car so that he could drive to town and buy more cheaply for us, and then the car ran away with him and he almost lost two fingers of his good right hand. How can I begin to enumerate the thousand and one services he rendered me?

For a while I thought the problem was solved. Emil would be my secretary, chief butler, private bodyguard and big shoo-fly. He would take care of everything. And so he did for a while. It was perfect. Then, at my instigation, he took up painting. Soon he was painting in earnest. One day he came to me and said in all innocence: "I don't know what's wrong. I don't seem to have time for anything any more. When I first came here I had too much time on my hands."

I had to smile. I knew damned well what was wrong. The mail! You can't answer letters and do your own work too. I tried to explain it to him, but he wasn't convinced. He thought he could paint *and* take care of the correspondence. (And do the kribbery-boo in his spare time.) He never realized what a burden he had assumed. It seemed exciting, at first, to be corresponding with so many people all over the world. The letters of acknowledgment he received were stimulating and fascinating. Instead of diminishing, the correspondence increased. For a while he enjoyed it. Then slowly it dawned on him that he was getting enmeshed. And with this realization the desire to paint became stronger and stronger.

Well, the long and short of it is that I stopped turning my letters over to Emil to answer. He's become a painter, and a painter I want him to remain. The hell with the letters! Let them answer themselves!

And that's where we are this moment. Only now I have the bright idea that by writing this pamphlet* there will be no more letter writing. I will just send this.

We'll see. Something tells me that I'll be sending out these pamphlets *and* a letter or a postcard. That's what my wife thinks, anyway. She may be right. But the only way to find out is to go through with it.

A writer often has two great surprises in store for him: the first is the lack of proper response to his efforts; the second is the overwhelming nature of the response when it does come. One is just as bad as the other.

TO ANSWER EVERY LETTER THAT COMES TO HAND IS OBVIOUSLY IMPOSSIBLE.

I could hire a secretary, of course, but I have not the means for that, nor do I wish to be in the position of needing a secretary. *I am not in business.* I am making an earnest effort to free myself from a peculiar sort of bondage which I myself created.

This is an answer *en bloc,* an anticipatory acknowledgment of all the good wishes, the encouragement, the gifts, the advice, the criticism continually being showered upon me. I realize with grati-

---

* My original intention in composing this text.

tude that most people who write me are trying to aid me. Should they not be the first to understand my predicament, to realize that the only way to acknowledge their manifestations of faith and good will is by continuing to write books, not letters?

There are many, of course, who write to obtain valid information, and these I try to satisfy. There are others, men and women who have just embarked upon a literary career, whose questions I find difficult or impossible to answer. (And is it my business to answer such questions, just because I am a writer?) It is my belief that each one must find his own solution to the problems which beset him, and he must find it in his own way. No man can possibly tell another what or how to write, nor how to combat the hostile, paralyzing forces which threaten to annihilate him. I feel like replying sometimes: "Why don't you read my books again?"

"But won't you please glance at my manuscript? Can't you give me a word or two of advice, at least?"

No, I cannot. Even if I had the time and the energy for it, or the supposed wisdom, it would be useless. One has to believe wholeheartedly in what one is doing, realize that it is the best one can do at the moment—forego perfection now and always!—and accept the consequences which giving birth entails. One's best critic is oneself. Progress (a bad word), realization (Cézanne's bugaboo), mastery (the adept's goal), these are achieved, as every one knows, through continuous application, through toil and struggle, through reflection, meditation, self-analysis, above all through being scrupulously and relentlessly honest with oneself. To those who protest that they are not understood, not appreciated, not accepted—how many of us ever are?—all I can say is: "Clarify your position!"

We live in an age when art and the things of the spirit come last. The truth still holds, however, that through dedication and devotion one achieves another kind of victory. I mean the ability to *overcome* one's problems, not meet them head on.

Serve life and you will be sustained. That is a truth which reveals itself at every turn of the road.

I speak with inner conviction because I have been through the struggle. What I am trying to emphasize is that, whatever the nature of the problem, it can only be tackled creatively. There is no book of "openings," as in chess lore, to be studied. To find an opening one has to make a breach in the wall—and the wall is almost always in one's own mind. If you have the vision and the urge to undertake great tasks, then you will discover in yourself the virtues and the capabilities required for their accomplishment. When everything fails, pray! Perhaps only when you have come to the end of your resources will the light dawn. It is only when we admit our limitations that we find there are no limitations.

Here I must make a confession. Perhaps the true reason why the correspondence has become such a staggering problem is that I like nothing better than to write letters. It is almost a vice. I shall never forget how one day, upon receipt of an exceptionally big batch of letters, a friend of mine who had glanced through the mail, observed: "I see nothing here that demands answering." The remark flabbergasted me. To be sure, this friend was a person who detested writing letters; now and then he would dispatch a post-card, couching his message in a telegraphic style which lacked even the semblance of warmth. (When I send a postcard, on the other hand, I feel so apologetic that I usually follow it up with a long letter the next day.) The point, however, is that where my friend saw nothing to worry about, I saw at least three days' work.

No, it is not indifference which prompts my desire to curtail incoming mail. It is something more, something quite other. Let me say, to make my meaning clearer, that the effect of a single letter is often sufficient to unbalance me for the rest of the day. My impulse is to answer such a letter immediately. Often I think it imperative to telegraph an answer. (If I were a millionaire I would certainly burn up the wires.) There are occasions when I find it difficult to believe that the person who has written me can wait for my reply. It sounds like sublime egotism, does it not?

And yet. . . . Well, this is one of my failings, or delusions, if you like, this naive belief that the answer must be given *immediately*. But my nature is such that I am perpetually overflowing: my response is always disproportionate to the stimulus. To live more intensely, to participate more fully, to keep all channels of communication open—this seems to be my bent. . . . And then there is the remembrance of times past, when every effort I made to be heard proved to be nothing more than spitting against the wind.

It is the person you most want to hear from who never bothers to write. The complacency, if it's that, or the indifference, of such individuals is exasperating; it can drive one frantic sometimes. This sense of frustration can and does persist until the day one makes the discovery that he is *not* alone, *not* cut off, and that it is *not* important to receive an answer. Until the realization dawns that all that matters is to give, and to give without thought of return.

Some whom I once vainly expected answers from I later discovered were in the same predicament I now find myself in. How wonderful it would have been, had I known it then, to write and say: "Don't bother to make answer. I simply wanted you to know how indebted I feel to you for being alive and spreading creation." Today I occasionally receive such messages myself. Such is the way of love, which uses the language of faith and absolution.

Why, then, do I not stop thinking about those who put the pressure on me? Because of my own weakness, probably. Could there be this feeling of pressure if I knew for a certainty that I was giving my all? Always there is this residue of "unfinished business." Always this feeling that perhaps my aid *is* indispensable. How silly of me to appeal to my tormentors for pity or consideration! I should *not* be trying to protect myself. I should be so absorbed in whatever I may be engaged in that I would have no mind for anything else.

The answer which I am about to make is really an answer which I wish to make to myself. In my best moments I believe that my responsibility toward others begins and ends with the work of creation in which I am involved. It has taken me considerable time to reach such a decision. Like other men, better men than I, I have alternately been swayed by a sense of duty, a feeling of pity, a natural consideration for others, by a hundred and one different emotions. What precious hours I have squandered answering the thousands of pleas and inquiries addressed to me! I will do so no longer. From now on I intend to devote the best hours of the day, the best part of myself, to the best that is in me. That done, I intend to enjoy a few hours of leisure. Loaf in peace and tranquillity. Should I wish to paint—I often do when I am not in the mood to write—I will paint. But I will not answer letters! Nor will I read the books or write prefaces for the manuscripts which are hurled at me. I will do only what pleases me, what nourishes my spirit.

This is my answer.

If my words sound callous and unreasonable, ponder over them before you condemn me utterly. I have been giving thought to the problem a long, long time. I have sacrificed my work, my leisure, my obligations to friends and family in order to make answer where I thought answer was due. I no longer believe in making such sacrifices.

If, however, you can propose a better solution, I shall not spurn it. I do not look upon mine as the perfect answer. It is the best I can give at the moment. It is from the heart, if that means anything. As for the doubting Thomases, to them no adequate answer can ever be made.

It is always possible, of course, to penetrate the thickest coat of armor. To those who question my sincerity let me suggest that they turn their attention to a book now out of print but obtainable if one really makes a search for it: *The Maurizius Case*, by Jacob Wassermann.* Pages 357 to 370, wherein is recorded the visit of Etzel Andergast to his favorite author, state the case. Etzel is in

* The edition published by Horace Liveright, New York, 1929.

a dilemma, a tragic dilemma. But the author, Melchior Ghisels, is in an even greater dilemma. The situation, I may add, is not unique; there are many similiar ones to be found in the biographies of famous individuals. I cite this one because it seems classic. And because it is forgotten over and over again.

True, now and then there is a desperate soul who believes he must see you or die. A delusion, of course, but I sympathize with such individuals. I have been on the edge of suicide a number of times, and I know what the feeling is like. The best remedy, however, is not to look to another for solace but to lay hands on a gun, a knife, or a bottle of poison. The fear of death cuts sharper than words.

"God wants us to be happy," said Nijinsky. Likewise an author hopes that in giving himself to the world he will enrich and augment life, not deny it or denigrate it. If he believed in direct intervention, he would be a healer and not a writer. If he believed that he had the power to eliminate evil and sorrow, he would be a saint, not a spinner of words. Art *is* a healing process, as Nietzsche pointed out. But mainly for those who practice it. A man writes in order to know himself, and thus get rid of self eventually. That is the divine purpose of art.

A true artist throws the reader back upon himself, aids him to discover in himself the inexhaustible resources which are his. No one is saved or healed except through his own efforts. The only genuine cure is the faith cure.

Whoever uses the spirit that is in him creatively is an artist. To make living itself an art, that is the goal.

I said a moment ago that I enjoy writing letters, that it is a veritable passion with me. What grieves me is that I seldom find time to write those with whom I should enjoy regular communication. I mean my intimate friends, those who speak my own language. These letters I usually reserve till the last horn, till I am virtually worn out. Not to write these individuals more freely, more frequently, is in the nature of a deprivation, one result of which is that I find myself writing to them in my sleep. I could fill a page with the names of all those I would dearly love to keep in touch with.

Then there are writers with whom one would like to open communication. Reading a book, or a literary review, I suddenly find myself all afire. "Write him immediately!" I exclaim to myself. (If only to say Amen.) But I don't. I think of all the letters lying unanswered on my desk. The same old battle—between duty and desire. I limp along with the poor in spirit instead of romping with the gay old dogs. How I curse myself now and then!

Every so often I break out. Of a sudden I will take it into my head to write someone at the other end of the world—someone in Mozambique, Lahore, Cochin-China. I know in advance I shall never get a reply. No matter. It does the soul good. Obeying such impulses, I have written at odd moments to men like Keyserling, Céline, Giono, Francis Carco, Hermann Hesse, Jean Cocteau. Sometimes an answer *is* forthcoming, and then I am overwhelmed. Then it was a good day, a red-letter day. Then I thank Uncle Sam for the service he renders us: I bless the pilots in the stratosphere who deliver the goods, come wind, hail, snow, rain, sleet, frost, fog or rot.

And then there are times when such a stillness invades me that I am amazed to think I ever wanted to pen a letter to any one, even to God. "Wherever you are, you must be getting the message!" So powerful are the radiations emanating from within that I feel certain they reach to the most hidden recesses of the globe. Sometimes, as if in corroboration of this feeling, I receive a letter from a distant friend with whom I had silently communicated in these bright, quiet moments. We should have more such moments, all of us. Many more than we ordinarily do. We should get to know it for a fact, accept it as the norm, *live by it,* that it *is* possible to communicate instantly with whomever one wishes, at any time, no matter how remote (in any sense of the word) the person may be. When we are one with ourselves all is one. When we are completely alive we need no mail carriers, no telegraph or telephone lines. We do not even need wings. We are there, everywhere, without making a move.

I am certain that if I ever permanently attain such a state of being there will be no correspondence to plague me. A radiant being is like a sun which shines whether commanded to or not.

It is for me, then, to lift myself by the bootstraps, to remain in the heavens of my own being.

Curious, is it not, to see what a point I have reached in trying to solve my problem! How could I have foreseen, when beginning this lament, that I would arrive at such an admission? Was it not I who said: *"Tackle your problems creatively!"* What's good for the goose is good for the gander. Anyway, what began as a complaint, or appeal, ends as a prayer. Only get desperate enough, I said, and the light will dawn. Yes, the light is dawning for *me* now. More and more clearly I see that the solution lies wholly with *me.* It is I who have to change, I who must exhibit more faith and trust, more confidence in life itself.

It is good that I obeyed the impulse to voice my thoughts. Maybe it will do *you* good as well as me. For whatever itches me must itch you too. None of us is exempt. We are all one substance, one problem, one solution.

When first I beheld this wondrous region I thought to myself —"Here I will find peace. Here I shall find the strength to do the work I was made to do."

Back of the ridge which overshadows us is a wilderness in which scarcely anyone ever sets foot. It is a great forest and game reserve intended to be set apart forever. At night one feels the silence all about, a silence which begins far back of the ridge and which creeps in with the fog and the stars, with the warm valley winds, and which carries in its folds a mystery as deep as the earth's own. A magnetic, healing ambiance. The advent of city folk, with their cares and worries, is pure dissonance. Like the lepers of old, they come with their sores. Whoever settles here hopes that he will be the last invader. The very look of the land makes one long to keep it intact—the spiritual reserve of a few bright spirits.

Of late I have come to take a different view of it. Walking the hills at dawn, or at dusk, looking over the deep canyons or seaward toward the far horizon, absorbed in reveries, drowned in the awesome beauty of it all, I sometimes think how wonderful will be the day when all these mountain sides are filled with habitations, when the slopes are terraced with fields, when flowers burst forth everywhere, not only wild flowers but flowers planted by human hands for human delectation. I try to imagine what it may be like a hundred, five hundred, years hence. I picture villas dotting the slopes, and colossal stairways curving down to the sea where boats lie at anchor, their colorful sails unfurled and flapping listlessly in the breeze. I see ledges cut into the sharp flanks of the cliffs, to give purchase to chapels and monasteries suspended between heaven and earth, as in Greece. I see tables spread under brilliant awnings (as in the time of the Doges), and wine flowing into golden goblets, and over the glitter of gold and purple I hear laughter, laughter like pearling rapids, rising from thousands of jubilant throats. . . .

Yes, I can visualize multitudes living where now there are only a few scattered families. There is room here for thousands upon thousands to come. There would be no need for a Jake to deliver food and mail three times a week. There would be ways and means undreamed of today. It could happen, in fact, in a very few years from now. What we dream *is* the reality of tomorrow.

This place can be a paradise. It is now, for those who live it.

But *then* it will be another paradise, one in which all share, all participate. The *only* paradise, after all.

Peace and solitude! I have had a taste of it, even here in America. Ah, those first days on Partington Ridge! On rising I would go to the cabin door and, casting my eyes over the velvety, rolling hills, such a feeling of contentment, such a feeling of gratitude was mine that instinctively my hand went up in benediction. Blessings! Blessings on you, one and all! I blessed the trees, the birds, the dogs, the cats, I blessed the flowers, the pomegranates, the thorny cactus, I blessed men and women everywhere, no matter on which side of the fence they happened to be.

That is how I like to begin each day. A day well begun, I say. And that is why I choose to remain here, on the slopes of the Santa Lucia, where to give thanks to the Creator comes natural and easy. Out yonder they may curse, revile and torture one another, defile all the human instincts, make a shambles of creation (if it were in their power), but here, no, here it is unthinkable, here there is abiding peace, the peace of God, and the serene security created by a handful of good neighbors living at one with the creature world, with noble, ancient trees, scrub and sagebrush, wild lilac and lovely lupin, with poppies and buzzards, eagles and humming birds, gophers and rattlesnakes, and sea and sky unending.

Finis.

Big Sur, California
May, 1955–June, 1956.